MICKEY MANTLE

MICKEY MANTLE

AMERICA'S PRODIGAL SON

TONY CASTRO

BRASSEY'S, INC.
Washington, D.C.

Library of Congress Cataloging-in-Publication Data

Castro, Tony.
    Mickey Mantle : America's prodigal son / Tony Castro.—1st ed.
       p. cm.
    Includes bibliographical references and index.
    ISBN 1-57488-384-4 (cloth : alk. paper)
    1. Mantle, Mickey, 1931– 2. Baseball players—United States—
Biography. 3. New York Yankees (Baseball Team) I. Title.

GV865.M33 C38 2002
796.357'092—dc21
[B]

2002018417

ISBN 1-57488-531-6   (paper)

Printed in the United States of America on acid-free paper that meets
the American National Standards Institute Z39-48 Standard.

Brassey's, Inc.
22841 Quicksilver Drive
Dulles, Virginia 20166

First Edition

10 9 8 7 6 5 4 3 2 1

FOR MY OWN HEROES:
RENEE, TREY, and RYAN

CONTENTS

Prologue
ix

PART 1
FATHERS AND SONS
3

PART 2
HEROES AND REBELS
75

PART 3
THE KINGDOM AND THE POWER
155

PART 4
THE AUTUMN OF THE LEGEND
233

Epilogue
281

Author's Note
287

CONTENTS

Acknowledgments
294

Mickey Mantle's Hall of Fame Speech
298

Bob Costas's Eulogy
302

Mickey Mantle's Batting Statistics
306

Bibliography
335

Index
337

About the Author
344

PROLOGUE

I guess you could say I'm what this country's all about.
                                              —Mickey Mantle

If Mickey Mantle hadn't lived, broadcaster Mel Allen once said, he would have been invented. In a sense, then, Mickey Mantle, like most heroes, was a construction; he was not real. He was all that America wanted itself to be, and he was also all that America feared it could never be. The postwar America of the mid-twentieth century was like all societies with the need for heroes, not because they coincidentally made them up on their own but because heroes like Mantle express a deep psychological aspect of human existence. They can be seen as metaphors for the human search of self-knowledge. In his time, Mickey Mantle showed us the path to our own consciousness through the power and spectacle of his baseball heroics, particularly his prodigal home runs, often backlit by the cathedral-like solemnity of Yankee Stadium. In the atomic age of the 1950s, the tape-measure blasts of our national pastime took on the stature of peacetime symbols of America's newly established military dominance. After all, Hank Greenberg, the first Jewish slugger in the game, said that when he had hit his home runs from the mid-1930s into the 1940s, he had hit them against Hitler. In the 1950s, Mickey Mantle came to reflect the appearance and values of the dominant society in the world. He was the hero of America's romance with boldness, its celebration of power, a nation's Arthurian self-confidence in its strength during a time when we last thought that might did make right.

For most of history, religion has been the main vehicle for reproducing the dominant society's traits, using mythical figures to illustrate moral and societal principles that help form a common social conception of such things as death and gender roles. In the 1950s, as sport itself took on the role in our culture that religion had often played in the past, Mickey Mantle, as the contemporary cultural hero, contributed to American society's necessary business of reproducing itself and its values. Amid the threat of Russian satellites and the unsettling dawn of the computer age, Mantle helped affirm our belief in the power of mankind over technology's invasion of our world. Mickey Mantle gave America hope for such things as life beyond the nuclear threat, reprieve from the Cold War, and a sense that order ruled our lives.

Mickey Mantle was a figure through which an America profoundly affected by nuclear fear, by a dizzying plethora of atomic panaceas and proposals, and by endless speculation on the social and ethical implications of the new reality reconciled the conscious and unconscious aspects of the national psyche. People feared the bomb itself, yes, but such fears were probably overstated by authorities who wanted every new home to be built with fallout shelters. The bomb made midcentury Americans fear more acutely what they already had feared—that things that had been whole in their lives would now split, and that such splitting could not be controlled. The evolution, or maybe revolution, in technology, race relations, and the very fabric of national culture, of which Americans could whimsically reassure themselves every time they looked at a Norman Rockwell painting on the cover of *The Saturday Evening Post*—all of that was changing; the change affected a nation that naively had believed its world had been made safe when Hitler had been defeated. But as the poet Rolf Humphries noted, in the profession of anxiousness there is an element of fashion. In the 1950s, that fashion was also a last vestige of stability—pinstripes, the New York Yankees, and baseball. Thus, when Mantle hit a home run, he was not only slugging a tape-measure dinger in the real world but facing an aspect of the unconscious.

"When I was playing," Mantle said looking back from retirement, "I used to feel like everything was happening to some other guy named Mickey Mantle, like I was just me and this guy called Mickey Mantle was another person." As Mantle's close personal friend George Lois put it, "Mickey Mantle was the last American hero. He was a walking shrine to an age of innocence and a symbol of a time when all was right with the world."

Even had he not reflected the times, Mantle would have been walking Americana. He failed at what he set out to do, at what his father had groomed him for—to be the greatest player who ever played the game. Still, his career was storybook stuff, hewing more to our ideas of myth than any player since Babe Ruth. Mantle himself came to realize that Ruth and Joe DiMaggio represented a state of mind that never existed beyond the abstract. They were a mirage, just as he too would become an icon. A lesson to be reaffirmed, sportswriter Richard Hoffer once suggested about Mantle and perhaps heroes generally, is that we don't mind our heroes flawed, or even doomed. In America, failure is forgiven of the big swingers, in whom even foolishness is flamboyant; the world will always belong to those who swing from the heels.

"Ted Williams was a real hitter," Mantle himself once observed. "Me, I just got up there and swung for the roof ever' time and waited to see what would happen."

The unique relationship between America and baseball must be understood to appreciate fully Mantle's place in the equation. This was the age when baseball players were the princes of American sports, along with heavyweight boxers, Derby horses, and the odd galloping ghost of a running back from down south or the occasional lanky basketball player in short shorts. Baseball players were the souls of their cities—Stan the Man in St. Louis; The Kid in Boston; Pee Wee, the Duke, Jackie, and Furillo in Brooklyn; and of course, the incomparable Willie Mays for Giants fans. As 1950s historian Jacques Barzun was aptly to observe, "Whoever wants to know the heart and mind of America had better learn baseball."

Long before baseball Ruth and DiMaggio, long before baseball became an industry of multinational owners and millionaire players, Walt Whitman wrote, "Well, it's our game. That's the chief fact in connection with it: America's game. It has the snap, go, fling of the American atmosphere. It belongs as much to our institutions, fits into them as significantly as our Constitution's laws, is just as important in the sum total of our historic life." Baseball is, to be sure, an American cultural declaration of independence. It has come to express the nation's character—perhaps never more so than during the intense, anticommunist, post–World War II period, when a preoccupation with defining the national conscience might be expected, as well as with defining the national self in a tradition that is as culturally "middle of the road" as baseball. As American studies authority Gerald Early puts it, "I think there are only three things America will be known for 2,000 years from now when they study this civilization—the Constitution, jazz music, and baseball."

By the middle of the twentieth century, baseball as an unquestioned symbol and performance-ritual of the best qualities of something called "Americanism" was entrenched, even a truism. The fictional literary character Terence Mann perhaps states it succinctly in the Hollywood film *Field of Dreams*, when he says to protagonist Ray Kinsella, "The one constant through all the years, Ray, has been baseball. America has rolled by like an army of steamrollers. It's been erased like a blackboard, rebuilt, and erased again. But baseball has marked the time. This field, this game, is a part of our past, Ray. It reminds us of all that once was good and it could be again."

America in the 1950s was also not so much a stage as a set-piece for television, the new national phenomenon. It was a decade of design, a time when how things looked—and how we looked—mattered. From the painting-by-numbers fad to the public fascination with the First Lady's apparel, to the television sensation of Elvis Presley, to the sculptural refinement of the automobile, American life in the 1950s had a distinct style in material culture and in art history, at least at eye level. America in the twentieth century, to be sure, needed a Mickey Mantle to transform from a largely conventional baseball figure into a pop-culture deity of entertainment, which is what the game ultimately became in Mantle's time and thereafter. Mantle would be the cultural equivalent of Elvis, Marilyn, and James Dean. He was young, he was handsome, and he came to be seen on television in millions of homes in ways DiMaggio, for instance, never was. It should be no surprise that popular biography has reflected this conversion, or that the change parallels the way in which baseball has come to be viewed in the years since Mantle arrived on the American scene. In a sense, the image of all popular figures is a reflection of the public that follows them. But with a dead figure, that reflective process grows exponentially—like the compounding effect of a series of mirrors. As a cultural symbol whose life can now be made into anything with impunity, Mantle has become, in the words of Elvis biographer Greil Marcus, "an anarchy of possibilities"—a reflection of the public's mass fears and aspirations, and also a constant vehicle for discussing those sentiments. Thus Mantle, Elvis, and Marilyn alike have evolved into a collection of cultural deities—modern-day equivalents of the Greek gods, who were immortal but shared the characteristics of the human beings who worshipped them.

"We knew there was something poignant about Mickey Mantle before we knew what poignant meant," recalled broadcaster Bob Costas. "We didn't just root for him. We felt for him. Long before many of us ever cracked a serious book, we knew something about mythology as we watched Mickey Mantle run out a home run through the lengthening shadows of a late Sunday afternoon at Yankee Stadium."

Perhaps it is all too simple in the modern age of multimillionaire athletes to dismiss references to sports greats like Mantle as "heroes" in the context of our common humanity, as rare figures held in esteem for what the Greeks would call *arete*, or some special talent (rather than in the religious or spiritual context that hero theorists Joseph Campbell and Carl Jung proposed). But as great people pass on, our memories tend to mold them into the collective image of the archetypal hero, interpreting their lives in a more spiritual way as a reflection of society's need for men and women who are a touch above ordinary, able to live on the plane of basic right and wrong, good and evil, heaven and hell. Sports is an obvious arena from which to draw candidates for this category of immortality, elevating the super-athlete's accomplishments on the field to an almost religious pitch and unwittingly interpreting their lives as expressions of unconscious projections of our own dreams.

"The view of Mantle as a Homeric hero is correct, I think," Bryan M. Davis, a specialist on heroes in pop culture, says of Mantle as a heroic figure. "He reminds me much more of Achilles or Hector—heroes we revere for their ability to overcome the shortcomings of simply being human but finally having to succumb to those weaknesses—rather than an archetypal hero such as Moses or King Arthur. But the religion of baseball tends to deify its greats. Perhaps, in a thousand years, another civilization will look back and remember the hero Mantle, who slew the demon baseballs with a mere stick and led the people in ritual song every seventh inning."

Perhaps it is too much to say that, like Arthur, Mickey Mantle was one with his country, unless you believe that the grail Mantle set off to find— greatness in baseball—simply reflected the greatness America believed was its entitlement after World War II. In a sense, though, baseball has been a metaphor for American greatness. Indeed, baseball literature and films historically have been about what America could and should be—men seeking redemption on the ball field; baseball spoken of in religious terms, as if it had the power to heal; the nostalgia for lost idealism. In Mickey Mantle, more than any player, we also see that baseball is about not only heroes and rebels but also about fathers and sons. Baseball is about the loving father exposed and vulnerable and about the boy in the father made whole. Mantle is the eternal youth playing catch, forever trying to play with the father.

"The only thing I can do," Mantle was to ultimately conclude about his reason for being, "is play baseball. I have to play ball. It's the only thing I know."

PART ONE
FATHERS AND SONS

That Mickey Mantle was born at all is a minor miracle, or perhaps just good fortune—fate giving biology a helping hand. Who hasn't wondered at some time how different life might have been if one had been born to a different mother or another father? Years later, after the Hall of Fame career and the New York fast life, and long after he had become accustomed to and up to (or down to) the role of being "Mickey Mantle," Mickey Mantle occasionally would chuckle, with a hint of curiosity, at the thought that he might easily have been his aunt's child. For before his father, Elvin Clark Mantle, had his eye on the woman who would give birth to Mickey, he had had designs on the woman's younger sister, a neighbor in the mining town of Spavinaw in Mayes County, Oklahoma. Elvin, the first of four children, who from his crib days had been known as "Mutt," was in his mid-teens. Lovell Richardson, the woman who would one day be Mickey Mantle's mother, was a grown woman ten years older than Mutt and, at the time, married to her first husband, William Theodore Davis—a farm boy from nearby Craig County with whom she had run off at the age of seventeen. She bore two children by William Davis, Theodore and Anna Bea, before divorcing him. Later, she explained her marital breakup to Mickey by simply stating, "We had a bad misunderstanding." Lovell Richardson, a tall, slender woman with gray eyes and reddish-blond hair, returned to her parents' home, where she met Mutt one day when he came to court her sister. Months later, at the age of seventeen, Mutt Mantle married Lovell in a civil ceremony.

Mickey Mantle was born October 20, 1931, in an unpainted two-room house on a dirt road outside Spavinaw, Oklahoma, a town of a few hundred people about thirty-five miles southwest of Commerce in the flatland northeast corner of the state, which was also the hub of the Oklahoma mining district. Spavinaw, in the heart of Cherokee Indian country, was part of the legendary Dust Bowl, the Oklahoma plains, where red dirt blanketed everything when the wind blew. The Missouri state line is just ten miles east, and Kansas is five miles to the north. Decades later, on the day the last section of Route 66 reached the Kansas-Oklahoma state line, Cherokees would come down from their reservation to watch, squatting along the highway, wrapped in blankets, witnessing glumly the passing of an era.

The world in which Mickey Mantle was born and experienced his childhood is so closely linked in our minds with America's worst economic depression that it has become almost impossible to view it as anything other than cheerless. A period of drab and desperate existence, spiritually void and mired in hopelessness, the thirties for most people evoke the stolid and stunned faces of tenant farmers immortalized by James Agee and Walker Evans in *Let Us Now Praise Famous Men*. In the country as a whole, however, except for the hordes of forgotten poor, this era of economic debacle was marked by more major political, social, and intellectual developments than the nation had ever known. Baseball, already ingrained as the national pastime, was both a diversion and a summertime remedy. To raise funds to help the unemployed in the Depression, in September 1931 the three New York teams—the Yankees, Giants, and Dodgers—played a series of benefit games that raised more than a hundred thousand dollars. In a pregame fungo-hitting contest, Babe Ruth, normally a left-handed hitter, batted right and drove a ball 421 feet into the center-field stands.

The 1930s were hard times in the Oklahoma plains, characterized by the uprooted, impoverished existence of a Steinbeck novel. In Spavinaw, many of the Mantles' neighbors who were unable to make a living moved out to California, far away from what would become an ecological and human disaster in the southwestern Great Plains region. It would be caused by misuse of land and years of sustained drought. During the years when there was adequate rainfall, the land had produced bountiful crops. But as the droughts of the early 1930s deepened, the farmers kept plowing and planting, and nothing would grow. The ground cover that held the soil in place was gone. The plains winds whipped across the fields, raising billowing clouds of dust. The skies

4

could darken for days, and even the best-sealed homes could have thick layers of dust on furniture. In some places the dust would drift like snow, covering farmsteads.

At the same time, the Great Depression, the worst economic slump in U.S. history, was spreading to the entire industrialized world. The Depression began in late 1929 and lasted for about a decade. Many factors brought about the Depression; however, the main cause of the Great Depression was the combination of sharply unequal distribution of wealth throughout the 1920s and extensive stock market speculation during the latter part of that decade. The maldistribution of wealth in the 1920s existed on many levels. Money was distributed disparately between the rich and the middle class, between industry and agriculture within the country, and between the United States and Europe. This imbalance of wealth created an unstable economy. The excessive speculation in the late 1920s kept the stock market artificially high but eventually led to large market crashes. These market crashes, combined with the maldistribution of wealth, caused the American economy to capsize.

It was into this America, scandalously troubled economically but holding on to a moral purpose marked by unwavering optimism, that Mickey Mantle was born. As for every man, the intricacies of his nature can be traced back to where he came from and those who shaped him. For Mickey Mantle, it all started and ended with his father, a teenager when Mickey was born but ultimately the most influential person in his life. Mutt Mantle held the same dreams for his first son that other fathers have had for their children since the beginning of time. With Mutt, however, it is fair to say his dreams for Mickey were obsessive. "The feeling between Mutt Mantle and his son," Merlyn Mantle was to later recall, "was more than love. Mick was his work of art, just as much as if his father had created him out of clay. He spent every minute he could with him, coaching, teaching, shaping him, and pointing him toward the destiny he knew was out there. Baseball consumed Mickey. He talked, when he talked, of little else. It was the number one priority in his life and, in a way, always would be."

Mutt Mantle found the 1931 baseball season a fortuitous one. Months before Mickey was born, Mutt had decided that his son would be named after one of the princes of his beloved game. "If my child is a boy," Mutt told his friends, "he's going to be a baseball player. I'm naming him Mickey—after Mickey Cochrane." The catcher and sparkplug of the championship Philadelphia Athletics teams of 1929, 1930, and 1931, Mickey Cochrane had a .346

batting average for those three years. He later would lead the Detroit Tigers to two pennants and in 1935 to a World Series championship. In 1947, he and A's battery mate Lefty Grove would be elected to the Baseball Hall of Fame. But in 1931, in which he helped the Athletics win the American League title, Cochrane also caught Grove's historic thirty-one-win season. On October 10, ten days before Mickey was born, Mutt Mantle got the best of both worlds. His favorite player, who had hit .349 that season, made it to the World Series, but his favorite team, the St. Louis Cardinals, won the championship, defeating the A's in the seventh game of the series. On the day Mickey was born, Cochrane was still playing baseball, a member of an all-star squad on a barnstorming trip to Hawaii and Japan. On that day too, Frankie Frisch, the Cardinals' fiery leader, was named Most Valuable Player of the National League after hitting .313 and stealing a league-leading twenty-eight bases.

"Mama says dad showed me a baseball before I was twelve hours old and it almost broke his heart when I paid more attention to the bottle," Mickey would say years later. "Baseball, that's all he lived for. He used to say that it seemed to him like he just died in the winter, until the time when baseball came around again. Dad insisted on my being taught the positions on the baseball field before the ABCs. He was that crazy about baseball. . . . I was probably the only baby in history whose first lullaby was the radio broadcast of a ball game. One night, mama says, I woke up during the seventh-inning stretch. She pleaded with dad to please cut off that contraption and let me sleep. 'You got Mickey wrong, hon',' dad said. 'I don't blame him for screaming. He knew the situation called for a bunt instead of hitting away.'"

Mutt named his son Mickey Charles Mantle, after both Cochrane and his own father. Mutt apparently was unaware that Cochrane's given name was actually Gordon Stanley; "Mickey" was a nickname derived from "Black Mike," which Cochrane had been given at Boston University for his competitiveness on the football team. Mutt, though, was not one to be too concerned about the exactness of names. Mickey spelled his father's name "Elvin"—which was also the way Mickey's middle name was spelled. But Mutt Mantle's Oklahoma driver's license spelled his first name "Elvan," and it was spelled "Elven" on his headstone at the Grand Army of the Republic Cemetery between Miami and Commerce, where he was buried after his death in 1952. It was also spelled "Elven" on the birth certificate of Mickey's youngest brother, Larry. "I'm not sure how he spelled his name," daughter Barbara said years later. "The only way I ever saw him sign anything was 'E. C. Mantle.'"

From Mutt himself Mickey inherited something far more important than a name—an incredible, almost mythic physical strength that one day would produce his prodigious home-run power. Mutt Mantle was a lead and zinc miner who had played semiprofessional baseball, and his father Charles Mantle had played baseball on a mining company team. Mickey was later to look back on his father's baseball talents with a son's wishful memory, saying he believed Mutt could have been a fine major league baseball player if he had been given the chance. But it turned out to be the mines that were in Mutt Mantle's blood. Mutt worked in the lead and zinc mines of the area and had also been a tenant farmer both before Mickey was born and later, when Mickey was in his teens. For his entire life, Mickey was to lament the life that fate had imposed on his father. "I always wished my dad could be somebody other than a miner," a regretful Mickey would reminisce. "I knew it was killing him. He was underground eight hours a day. Every time he took a breath, the dust and dampness went into his lungs. Coughed up gobs of phlegm and never saw a doctor. What for? He'd only be told it was 'miner's disease.' He realized that if he didn't get cancer, he'd die of tuberculosis. Many did before the age of forty. 'So what the hell. Live while you can,' he'd say and light another cigarette. A confirmed chain-smoker, I hardly remember him without one stuck in the corner of his mouth."

Mickey Mantle's parents, Mutt and Lovell, had been raised in a town of dissimilar personalities and cultures, so it is no surprise that they too were a study in contrasts. Those two personalities were to polarize young Mickey's own self-image and his emotional development.

"My father was a quiet man, but he could freeze you with a look," Mickey later recalled. "He never told me he loved me. But he showed that he did by all the hours he spent with me, all the hopes he invested in me. He saw his role as pushing me, always keeping my mind on getting better. I worked hard at doing that because I wanted to please him. He would drape an arm around me and give me a hug. . . . I adored my dad and was just like him in many ways—I was shy and found it hard to show my emotions. I couldn't open up to people, and they mistook my shyness for rudeness." Sadly, the way he was molded by two unemotional parents would influence the way Mickey himself would model his relationships with his own sons. "He had been brought up a certain way," son Mickey Jr. would say of his father, "and if he couldn't deal with his feelings, he buried them. He paid a high cost for packing away the affection that was so close to his surface. For most of our lives, when we greeted each other after a separation of weeks or months, we would shake hands. It wasn't just him. Everybody in his family, my uncles, his cousins, kept the same distance."

For Mutt Mantle, that emotional detachment had been a method of self-survival. As a young man Mutt had been forced to grow up quickly, dropping out of school to take a job grading county roads. Not long after marrying Lovell and having Mickey, however, Mutt lost the grading job and thought seriously about taking his young family to California. Instead he became a tenant farmer, working eighty acres of land but seeing little return. Lovell, meanwhile, was busy raising her own two children as well as Mickey, and she was pregnant with the second of the five children she would have by Mutt. Lovell was a devoted wife to her second husband. What bound them together was that both came from long lines of Oklahoma people, five generations of Americans with English, Dutch and German bloodlines. At one point there was unfounded speculation, in part spurred by Mickey's pride in the American Indian heritage of his beloved Oklahoma, that his mother was part Native American.

What is undeniable is that Mutt fell in love with a woman not only significantly older but also more distant personally than even he was, and who had greater difficulty showing her emotions than he did. According to psychologists, men and women learn, in different ways, roles that early on can squelch the ability to express empathy and to connect. While all children start out as emotionally responsive, by age six boys have learned to suppress their emotions, according to research by University of Connecticut psychologist Buck Park. For young Mickey, the impact may have even been greater. Lovell, the daughter of a carpenter, was reticent even with her loved ones; Mickey would later say that his mother "didn't lavish affection on us either. . . . [W]hen mom wanted to show her love, she fixed a big meal." One of the few times that Lovell did show some emotion, she overdid it. Once a fight broke out when Mickey's twin brothers Ray and Roy were playing high school football; Lovell ended up on the field slapping the opposing players on their helmets with her purse. Still, it was not until later, at her eightieth birthday party in Oklahoma City, that she was to tell Mickey and the family why she had married Mutt: he had been tall, handsome, and a real gentleman under his rough exterior.

Merlyn Mantle's recollection of her mother-in-law, Mickey's mom, seemed to capture her essence best: "Lovell was not a warm or openly affectionate woman, but she was a tireless and protective mother. She had seven children, two by a first marriage, and I never saw anyone do as much laundry. She did it by hand, on a washboard in the back yard, and hung it on row after row of clotheslines to dry. They lived in the country and didn't yet have electricity."

As poor as they were at the time, however, Mickey always looked back with pride at how his parents persevered without reaching out for charity or even credit. "We were about the only family in Commerce that didn't buy groceries on credit," he remembered. "We only bought what we needed, and my dad paid cash. The grocer appreciated it so much that he let us kids pick out a free bag of candy."

The Mantles did not have much of a traditional spiritual life, which is surprising, considering that they lived in a community of God-fearing neighbors in the heart of the Bible Belt. Commerce had four churches. Mickey later said he had been in all of them at one time or another, "yet nobody in my family took religion seriously. I suppose it was my dad's influence. He used to say, 'Religion doesn't necessarily make you good. As long as your heart is in the right place and you don't hurt anyone, I think you'll go to heaven—if there is one.' Mom felt the same way. She backed him no matter what he believed."

If Lovell Mantle was not a God-fearing woman in a traditionally God-fearing community, she did have her own fears for her children—the biggest of which was a local area known as the "Alkali." This was a flat stretch of plain where the lead-mine shafts had been sunk and then left abandoned, and where tall piles of exhausted ore stood like miniature pyramids. The flat land of the Alkali was used for sandlot baseball games; a ball that got past the outfielders often rolled undisturbed for several hundred feet. Mickey would later joke that playing there as a boy in the endless outfield was what convinced him to be an infielder. Mickey, however, wasn't even supposed to be playing ball on the makeshift Alkali baseball field. His mother had strict rules forbidding him to play there. According to Mickey, his mother "would haul me home and really warm my britches" on the few occasions when she caught him disobeying here. The reason for Lovell's concern was the caved-in old mine shafts, which were closed off only by sagging fences that were regularly climbed over or cut through by curious youngsters. She had grown up with stories about children who had fallen into the cave-ins and died in the black holes, and she worried, like other mothers, that such a disaster might take one of her own.

Lovell Mantle, though, also had a dark side, something that wasn't talked about until years later. While there is no documentation to suggest that she was an abusive mother, Mickey later would reluctantly talk of whippings. Years later too, Mickey would see some of his mother's dark side in her treatment of little David Mantle, who would describe his grandmother as "always mean to me." David would recall, "She used to chase me around and hit me with a broomstick. Maybe it was because I was so hyper. One day I was sitting on a stool in her kitchen, and I did something a kid would do. Dad told me she just backhanded me and knocked me off the stool. After that, he never let her watch me any more because it really hurt him that she would give me that kind of swat. He said she used to whip him, too, something he didn't like to admit. She was still dad's mother, and I respected her, but I didn't have the love for her that I did for mom's folks."

That coldness that could sometimes border on cruelty was just one of many ways in which Lovell and Mutt were dissimilar. Whereas he was occasionally carefree, rugged, and athletic, if overly demanding of Mickey, she tended to be a loner, if not lonely, emotional on occasion, and subservient to her younger husband's wishes as to how Mickey would be raised. Yet Mutt, despite his unquestioned love for his oldest son, was far from possessing the emotional maturity ordinarily necessary for the dominant parent in a family. Mutt had not been even ten when his mother had died of pneumonia, just a week after giving birth to her fourth child, Emmett. Charles Mantle would struggle to raise his three oldest children, while an aunt and uncle raised the baby. As the oldest child, Mutt had taken charge of brother Eugene and sister Thelma, while Charles put in long hours as a butcher in Spavinaw. Mutt's own childhood was effectively sacrificed to help his father raise the family. Raising a family of one's own, however, presents an altogether different challenge, and it can be strongly argued that Mutt fell into a trap that has ensnared fathers throughout history. In raising Mickey the way he did, obsessed from the cradle with the idea of his son becoming a professional baseball player, Mutt imposed upon him the pressure not only of fulfilling his own dashed dreams but also of meeting an expectation of almost immortal achievement.

Year later, fans and friends were often touched to hear Mickey lament that he had not been the same kind of father to his own oldest son. "If my father had been his father," Mickey said on more than one occasion, "Mickey Jr. would have been a big leaguer." Mickey Jr. voiced some serious reservations. "I'm not so sure," he said. "More likely, if dad had cooped me up in the back yard for three or four hours every day, playing catch and pitching to me, I would have run away from home."

Merlyn Mantle, possibly the person closest to Mantle in his adult life, would be convinced that Mutt's overbearing fathering, unchecked by Lovell's detachment, left Mickey emotionally and psychologically traumatized and unable to turn even to his loved ones for help. In *A Hero All His Life*, she wrote:

> The early pressure on Mickey to play ball and his self-imposed drive to play it better than anyone, caused real emotional problems for him. A lot of the conflicts in him later had their roots in those years. Mick wet his bed until he was sixteen years old. I would hope that this would not be taken as demeaning him. But it is important, I think, in understanding what he went through, and how much he wanted to please his dad. This is what the pressure of wanting that approval did to him. He told me that he knew from the time he was five years old that he wanted to be a ballplayer, and how he could never face his father if he didn't make it to the major leagues. Interestingly, the bed-wetting stopped when the Yankees sent him to Independence, Missouri, for his first season in Class D. He had to solve the problems before any of his teammates found out. He could not abide anyone making fun of him. He stopped by asserting his own pure willpower, because the pressure didn't end then, or with the Yankees. It never ended. I know exactly how much he ached for his dad's approval. . . . His father had this wonderful but obsessive dream for Mickey, and only for Mickey. He was anointed from the cradle. When his dad would pitch to him for hours, out of a hundred pitches, Mick would be in terror of missing one and looking bad, and having his father frown or criticize.

Mantle would later talk about his bed-wetting one evening in 1970 on the *Dick Cavett Show*, on a night when songwriter Paul Simon was also a guest. It was Simon, in a nostalgic expression of longing for the innocence and simplicity of an earlier and happier time, who had written in the lyrics for a popular song of the 1960s, "Where have you gone, Joe DiMaggio? A nation turns its lonely eyes to you." In that talk show, Simon was dumbstruck by such a revelation by another of his heroes and expressed the shock of millions: "Mickey Mantle wet his bed?!" Sportswriter Phil Berger would observe of Mantle's relationship with his father, "Anything short of success would be an affront to Mutt, and the thought of disappointing his father weighed heavily on him. The wetting of his sheets was an early and vivid indication of the burden under which young Mickey toiled, and the pressure it exerted on him."

However, there was one childhood trauma that Mickey never spoke about publicly. Around the age of four or five years, his half-sister Anna Bea and some of her teenage friends sexually molested him. He was so humiliated and demeaned that he could never bring himself to tell anyone. Only much later, in the year before his death, would Mickey be able to confide to his wife Merlyn the sexual molestation he had suffered. Anna Bea would toy with him sexually, pulling down his pants and fondling his penis, often as her girlfriends watched and giggled, howling their laughter and derision when he would get a tiny erection. The molestation and the teasing continued for several years until Anna Bea moved out of the house, but the traumatic scarring would last a lifetime. Merlyn would suspect that it was the source of his unhealthy relationships with women—that it was why he never respected women, a reason for his affairs, his one-night stands, the crude and vulgar language he used around women when he drank.

Mutt would never know of the molestation. Like other abused children, Mickey felt shame and guilt. Beginning in childhood, he would go to great lengths not to disappoint his father. Mickey himself would later say of his childhood relationship with his father, "No boy, I think, ever loved his father more than I did. . . . I would do nearly anything to keep my father happy. . . . He never had to raise his hand to me to make me obey, for I needed only a sharp look and a word from him and the knowledge that I had displeased him to make me go and do better. . . . I knew from the time I was small that every small victory I won, and every solid hit I made or prize I was awarded, brought real joy to my father's heart."

Stories of the young Mickey being taught to switch-hit, and being pitched to for hours on end every afternoon, by his father and grandfather became as much a part of the Mantle lore as that of the young Arthur pulling Excalibur from the stone is central to the legend of Camelot. In 1934, when Mickey was three years old, Mutt took a job as a shoveler at the Eagle-Picher Zinc and Lead Company and moved his family from Spavinaw to Commerce, near Interstate 44, which connects Tulsa and Joplin, Missouri. Commerce was a small town of fewer than three thousand people; its main street was only seven blocks long. This was a town so small it was once called simply "North Miami," because it was only four miles north of Miami, Oklahoma, in Ottawa County. But in 1914, lead and zinc mines were booming, so business people thought "Commerce" would be a better fit. The same year the Mantles moved to Commerce, on April 6, 1934, the notorious outlaws known as Bonnie and Clyde got stuck in the mud on the road between Commerce and Miami. At gunpoint, they forced a trucker to pull them out. A passing motorist happened to notice a bullet hole in Bonnie and Clyde's windshield and called the police. In the ensuing shootout, the Commerce police chief was taken hostage, and the constable was killed.

Life was a lot calmer at 319 South Quincy Street, a four-room clapboard house that became home to the Mantles for the next ten years. Mutt by this time had become a ground boss in the Eagle-Picher lead and zinc mines, earning seventy-five dollars a week, extremely good pay in the 1940s in Oklahoma, or anywhere else in the country. Mutt, however, was supporting not only his growing five children and a wife but his father Charlie as well. The house on Quincy Street would become the one that Mickey would most associate with his youth. It was some hundred yards off the highway on a gravel road leading down from the family mailbox. Often Mickey would wait at the mailbox for his father to come home from the mines, and they would walk together down the road to their house talking about baseball. From the time Mickey had been in his crib, Mutt had made sure his son had a baseball cap nearby. Lovell Mantle had used material from some of her husband's old baseball pants and shirts to fashion miniature uniforms for her son. Here, on Quincy Street on the edge of town, sometimes in uniform and sometimes without, young Mickey began honing his swing, using a tin shed for a backstop.

"You take this bat," Mickey remembered his father telling him, "and you try to hit the balls we throw to you. We won't throw them hard, so don't worry about getting hit. Anyway, these tennis balls won't hurt you."

Mickey took the bat and swung it enthusiastically, right-handed. Mickey was a natural right-hander.

"Now there's one other thing I want to tell you," Mutt explained to his son. "When I throw the ball, you go ahead and swing the way you're doing it now. But when Grandpa Charlie throws the ball, I want you to turn around and swing the other way. Understand?" Mutt pitched left-handed. Charlie Mantle pitched right-handed. In conventional baseball wisdom, right-handed hitters generally have greater success against lefthanders and left-handed hitters greater success against right-handed pitchers. A right-handed pitcher's curve ball will break away from a right-handed hitter and therefore be harder to hit, and vice versa. Mutt calculated that switch-hitters—hitters who could hit both right-handed and left-handed—were a valuable commodity in professional baseball. In 1938, about the time Mickey's switch-hitting lessons began, there were only eleven switch-hitters on the rosters of major league teams. (In 1951, there would be only ten major league switch-hitters, counting

Cleveland Indians pitcher Early Wynn. But by 1971, in the generation of players influenced by Mantle, major league rosters would have forty-one switch-
hitters.) So in the front yard of 319 Quincy Street, at the age when other
children were playing cowboys and Indians, Mickey Mantle began learning the
art that would one day make him the greatest switch-hitter in the history of
the game.

"Mickey didn't like it at all in the beginning," Lovell Mantle recalled
years later, "but I know now that he is glad he listened to his father."

Indeed, at first Mickey found it extremely difficult to switch-hit, especially
to hit left-handed. But the practice continued, day after day, starting around
four o'clock in the afternoon, as soon as Mutt returned home from his day
at the mines, and continuing until nightfall. It was not unusual during the
summer, when there was no school, for Mickey to put in as many as five hours
a day taking batting practice, with his father and grandfather pitching. "Once
I learned to hit a ball with a bat," said Mickey, looking back, "I needed none
of my father's urging to play the game. Knowing that it pleased my father to see
me do well at the game only made it twice as much fun to me."

Soon Mutt and Charlie began throwing harder and tossing the incredible curves that can be thrown with a tennis ball. However, when Mickey
turned six, real baseballs replaced the tennis balls. To sharpen Mickey's interest in the game, Mutt and Charley devised a set of Quincy Street ground
rules. A line drive was a single. A ball hit off the side of the house became a
double. A ball off the roof was ruled a triple. A ball hit over the house or into
the adjoining lot was a home run. Mickey, who often listened to radio broadcasts of St. Louis Cardinals games with his father, imagined himself to be a
slugger with the Cardinals' legendary Gashouse Gang.

This was Mickey's childhood, in which his two closest friends and playmates were his father and grandfather. Mickey's first real friend his own
age was LeRoy Bennett, who lived up the street on Quincy. His other close
childhood pal was Nick Ferguson, who lived on Vine Street, about eight
blocks away. But each afternoon, as the time neared for Mutt to return home,
Mickey's mother could often be heard yelling out "Mickey Charles!" Neighbors even used to joke, "When Mutt comes home from the mines, Mickey has
to stop playing and start practicing."

Mickey himself would look back on the long ritual of hitting drills with
fond memories: "The practice paid off. By the time I was in the second grade,
I was hitting them pretty good from the right side. But dad also wanted me to

bat lefty, which I hated. When it got dark and supper was ready, dad would turn me around, from righty to lefty. 'Your belly can wait,' he'd say. Then he'd start pitching again. He believed that any kid could develop into a switch hitter if you taught him early enough."

In the middle of the Depression, baseball was the only way Mutt saw for Mickey to escape the cycle that had gripped Mutt, as it had most young men from similar backgrounds in northeast Oklahoma: a nearly poverty-stricken existence and a lifetime chained to either the mines or farms of the area. Unlike a generation later, this was a time in America when the only two sports through which youngsters could seriously dream of rising out of meager circumstances were baseball and boxing. Mutt's second brother, Eugene, had shown some signs of pugilistic promise and was nicknamed "Tunney," after world heavyweight champion Gene Tunney. Eugene once put out a man's eye, though not with his fists but with a shovel. At a dance in Spavinaw a fight had broken out in which Mutt, Eugene, and other Mantle family members found themselves outnumbered. In defending himself, Eugene apparently picked up a shovel and struck one of his assailants. The Mantle men would always boast of never having lost a fight, including that one. Baseball, however, was the real passion for all the Mantle men. Many of them spent their weekends playing on semipro teams in Mayes County. Even after Mutt moved to Commerce, he returned to Spavinaw every weekend to play with the local team.

Baseball was also a bond between Mickey's father and mother. Over the years, Lovell Mantle developed a love of her own for the game. Mantle friend Nick Ferguson remembered visiting and seeing Mickey's mother doing her housework while listening to radio broadcasts of St. Louis Cardinals games. With Mutt away at work during the day, Lovell would jot down notes about the games on a makeshift scorecard that she would later use to recount the games for Mutt, the family, and friends over dinner. "She'd tell you how this happened and that happened—she had it right in front of her," recalled Ferguson, "and she made it sound exciting, too. And everybody had to know what went on. They'd keep asking for more and more, and she'd just keep telling them like she had actually been at the game herself."

Just how knowledgeable Lovell Mantle was about baseball, however, is debatable. Mantle was to later describe his mother as having been a fan, though hardly with the baseball knowledge and insight of his father. Nick Ferguson, on the other hand, has been quoted as claiming that Lovell Mantle—

and not Mutt—had been the parent with the true "inside" perspective on the game, especially in what she would reportedly tell Mickey about his own play. "She'd never raise her voice," Ferguson said in one interview. "You'd barely hear her. But she'd sort of whisper to Mickey about what he had done in games she saw. She'd say, 'You know, in that situation, if you bunted, you woulda done this or that. If you backed a little bit at second, you'd have more room to take a ball. Or on this hitter or that hitter, you should maybe move over a little more.' She knew the game, and she could always get him to think about what he was doing."

Mantle himself remembers that his mother was most demonstrative as a basketball fan, when he was playing on the Commerce High basketball team. "Mom used to rant and rave at those games," he recalled. "If she objected to a referee's decision, you could hear her voice travel across the gym: 'Where are your glasses, you bum!' Believe me, if the referee called anything against Commerce, she'd cuss him out like a sailor. It unnerved my father. He'd cover his head with his hands and sit a few rows behind her to get away from the shouting."

Although his name became associated with Commerce and he became known as the "Commerce Comet," Mickey himself later became characteristically unsentimental about his adopted hometown. He would go so far as to tell friends in his later years that as a youth he had always felt like an outsider there. There were things in Mickey's childhood, things he would never reveal until many years later, that made for an unhappy childhood, and there was a level of dysfunction in the family that planted the seeds for addictive behaviors in most of the family. Alcoholism ran through much of Lovell Mantle's side; her brothers were all alcoholics. It was a problem that also later afflicted Lovell's two children by her first husband. Mickey's half-sister Anna Bea married young, left home, worked as a barmaid, and died in her twenties. "Hers," said Merlyn Mantle, "was a short, sad life." Theodore, Mickey's half-brother, was also an alcoholic, though with a heart of gold. When he was discharged from the army, Theodore used most of his discharge pay to help Mickey buy Merlyn's wedding ring.

Mickey later would describe his father as "a light drinker who bought a half-pint on Saturday and sipped it for days. He would have whipped my fanny if he caught me taking a drink. . . . Every night when he came home from working eight hours at the Eagle-Picher Zinc and Lead [mine], he'd head for the icebox and take a swig of whiskey. Dad would get drunk once in a while, like when he went to a barn dance and he might have five or six drinks. Hell, for me five or six drinks wouldn't have been a full cocktail party!" Mickey's pal Nick Ferguson, however, suggests that Mutt's drinking may have been more than what Mantle has indicated in his autobiographies and interviews. "I'm sure he didn't chase around with women," Ferguson recalled, "but Mutt drank, and he used to take Mick and us kids into the bars with him when we weren't even old enough to drink." One addiction is known for certain about Mutt Mantle—he was a chain-smoker. Mickey excused it as something all the miners did, miners who "didn't see how nicotine could do any more damage to their lungs than the dust they inhaled every day." As a Yankee, Mickey would later endorse Camel cigarettes. Every week he was provided with a free carton of Camels, which he mailed home to his father, who would exchange the carton at a Commerce store for his favorite brand, Lucky Strike. With Mickey the hottest name in baseball, the Commerce grocer would often boast to his customers, "See these Camels? They came straight from Mickey."

Even when Mickey was an adult, Commerce did not hold the fondest of memories for him. In 1956, during the Christmas after his greatest season, when he won baseball's Triple Crown, Mickey and Merlyn were visiting family when Mickey decided to call on some old pals at Mendenhall's bar on Main Street. The only problem was that he was supposed to be babysitting Mickey Jr., who was then three; he took the boy along to Mendenhall's with him. A fight broke out when Mickey tried defending the bartender against a drunk. Sitting on a bar watching his father roll around on the floor, Mickey Jr. picked up his father's beer and took his first swig, just as his grandfather, Giles Johnson, came in the door looking for them. The grandfather scooped Mickey Jr. off the bar into his arms and, on his way out, kicked his famous son-in-law in the side of the head, warning him, "Don't ever let me catch you with this kid in here again."

In later life, Mickey looked back on Commerce with many reasons for mixed feelings about his life there. Former Commerce postmaster Bill Brumley would recall that when the Civic Pride Committee tried to start a Mantle museum in Commerce in the 1980s, Mantle's lawyer had threatened a lawsuit. Some townspeople harbored hard feelings against Mantle even after his death because he had often slighted Commerce; among them was Mayor Jack Young, a seventy-four-year-old local native.

"Mickey Mantle didn't even show up when they dedicated Mickey Mantle Boulevard," he said. "People got down on him for stuff like that."

However, there were others, especially among the younger generation in Commerce, for whom Mantle remained a source of local pride and admiration. To this day, Mickey is the biggest thing that ever happened to Commerce, Oklahoma. In 1993, two local men, Brian Brassfield and Todd McClain, buddies since Little League, bought Mantle's boyhood home. Over the next few years they used their savings to begin restoration of the dilapidated house in hopes of turning it into a Mickey Mantle museum. Said Brassfield, "We've even talked about the tin barn and letting kids bat against it, just like he did." They envisioned life-sized bronze statues of a young Mantle and his father, posed as hitter and pitcher.

If he could, Mickey might tell them about another day, when he was ten and playing as an undersized catcher with twelve-year-olds on the Douthat team in the Peewee Division of the Gabby Street League. Overmatched against an outstanding right-handed pitcher, Mickey had struck out three times batting left-handed. Discouraged, Mickey decided on his own to try batting against the overpowering pitcher from his natural, right-hand side. However, as soon as Mickey took his stance in the right-handed batter's box, a deep, booming voice stopped the game.

"Go on home!" Mutt Mantle shouted from the far edge of the baseball field. "Go on home! And don't you ever put on that baseball uniform until you switch-hit like I taught you." Feeling punished and humiliated, Mickey hurried home. That night, after dinner, Mickey apologized to his father and promised not to do that again.

"He never drove me to play baseball, for no one ever had to do that," Mickey would later write in *The Education of a Baseball Player,* his 1967 autobiography. "But he worked hard to help me improve and he gave me good advice to follow and played with me when he had the chance. It wasn't the thought of riches or fame that drove me. I didn't think about those things. I had no desire to leave home or to get very far from Commerce and the towns around us. What did keep me driving hard, from the time that I was ten, to hit the ball better and farther was first of all my own love for the game and then my love for my father. I knew from the time I was small that every small victory I won, and every solid hit I made or prize I was awarded, brought real joy to my father's heart."

Mickey Mantle most often dreamed of his boyhood in Commerce, Oklahoma, and inevitably the dream would start out the same. Mantle would relive taking batting practice after school outside the house on Quincy Street, hitting tennis balls off the roof from the right side against his father and then from the left side against Grandpa Charlie. The dream was one that Mantle could have enjoyed for eternity. Sometimes he would wake up in the dead of night, and the dream would linger in a half-sleep twilight, blurring with the memories of his childhood. But occasionally, the dream would go on and cause him to stir and turn in his sleep, unable to fight off the dream image of Grandpa Charlie struggling for breath after throwing a pitch, of himself admiring the tennis ball he had just hit off the roof and then seeing his grandfather collapsed on the ground. Crying, Mickey would rush with his father to Grandpa Charlie's side. Mickey would suddenly look down to his grandfather's face and, to his horror, would see his own image staring back at him.

At some point in our lives, often at an early age, we all come to know that someday we will die. Usually, however, death casts only a faint shadow, like that of a high cloud on an otherwise sunny day. In 1944, at the age of thirteen, Mickey found that cloud suddenly enveloping him in its shadow. That year Mickey came face to face for the first time with what he later would come to call "the Mantle curse." "Grandpa suddenly became old and feeble, almost overnight," Mickey recalled. "My father would help him out of bed and support his wobbly legs that used to stride along South Quincy Street with so much vigor. . . . Dad was worried sick over Grandpa's condition. He began looking for a place in the country, as far away from the mining areas as Grandpa could get." Actually, the mines, though not good for anyone's health, had little to do with Charles Mantle's illness; Mickey's grandfather was suffering from Hodgkin's disease. Shortly after Mickey's first year of baseball, in an attempt to get Charlie into a better climate, the Mantles moved to a farm outside Commerce. Mutt swapped the house on Quincy Street for a horse, a tractor, some cows, and 160 acres of land that the family could farm, sharing the crops with the landowner, a Dr. Wormington.

At the time, Hodgkin's disease was virtually terminal. It had been named after Thomas Hodgkin of London, who first described it in 1832. It is a cancerous disorder that strikes the lymphatic system, which plays a key role in the body's immune defenses. Because the lymphatic system consists of channels that course through the body like blood vessels, the cancer has a ready route to any organ or tissue. The most common symptom of Hodgkin's disease is a painless swelling in the lymph nodes in the neck, underarms, or groin. Other symptoms may include fevers, night sweats, tiredness, weight loss, or itching skin. By Mickey's recollection, his grandfather had all of these symptoms. Modern medicine would eventually develop radiation and chemotherapy treatments to fight the disease, usually with an 80 percent success rate in putting the disease in remission for ten years and longer. In the 1990s, hockey Hall of Famer Mario Lemieux would survive Hodgkin's disease. Major league reliever Scott Radinksy would miss the 1994 season at the age of twenty-six with Hodgkin's disease but return the following season and continue with his career. But as can be the case even now if the disease goes untreated or is diagnosed too late, it ravaged Charles Mantle's body quickly. He died shortly after the family moved to the farm.

"I never forgot that moment, standing beside the casket with my little twin brothers, Ray and Roy, the three of us looking down on him, and my father whispering, 'Say goodbye to Grandpa.'"

"I was just a kid then," Mickey would recall. "I didn't understand death and sickness very well. Even now I don't remember the order of events from that time in my life. It just seemed that all my relatives were dying around me. First, my Uncle Tunney, the tough one, then my Uncle Emmett. Within a few years—before I was thirteen—they had died of the same disease. I knew Uncle Emmett had it because the doctor had to cut the lymph nodes out of his ravaged body for nearly a year. To no avail. . . .

"That [molded] my belief that I would die young. I lost my grandfather, my father and two uncles, all to Hodgkin's disease. None of them lived beyond the age of forty-one. I took it for granted that this would be my fate; it took all the Mantle men."

The so-called Mantle curse would become part of the lore surrounding Mickey. By Mantle's own admission, talk of it became trite and melodramatic. "I hope to make it to 40," Mantle said while in his twenties. "Sure, I kid about it, but I think about it, too." Howard Cosell would even go so far as to call Mantle "the doomed Yankees slugger, playing out his career in the valley of death." Understandably, Mantle tired of it. He could not, however, put it out of his mind altogether; its impact on his psyche was indelible. What man, after call, can be subjectively secure with the concept of his own mortality? At a very early age, Mantle had lost something that cannot be regained. Each succeeding death of a male Mantle relative was one step closer to the abyss. Death seemed to haunt every crucial moment of his childhood and adolescence.

The year 1941 is regarded as one of the most memorable in baseball history. In the middle of May, New York Yankee star Joe DiMaggio settled for a first-inning single in a game that the Yankees lost to the Chicago White Sox, 13–1. The Yankees had lost five games in a row, eight of their last ten, and were in fourth place, five and a half games behind the league-leading Cleveland Indians. At the time, the hit did not seem memorable. DiMaggio was barely hitting .300 and had greatly disappointed the crowds that had seen him hit .352 the year before and .381 in 1939. But DiMaggio also got a hit in the next game, and the next, and the next. Still, no one paid much attention to his hitting streak until it reached twenty-nine games in mid-June. DiMaggio continued getting at least one hit in each game for another twenty-seven games until the streak ended in Cleveland on July 17. By then, however, the Yankees were in first place, en route to an American League pennant and World Series championship, and America was singing songs about and praises of the great DiMaggio. The fifty-six-game hitting streak ultimately became one of the legendary achievements of the game and a record that would outlast almost every other baseball milestone. That same season, Boston Red Sox hitter Ted Williams set a record that would not be surpassed in the twentieth century. Williams, who would come to be regarded as perhaps the greatest hitter ever, hit .406 in 1941, the last player to hit better than .400 in a season.

America needed DiMaggio's fifty-six-game hitting streak and Ted Williams's .406 season as an escape from the real world; just as it needed Orson Welles's *Citizen Kane* and *The Maltese Falcon*, both released in 1941; just as it needed Frank Sinatra on radio, on records, in nightclubs. Outside the baseball stadiums and the movie theaters and off the airwaves, the real world in 1941 was full of calamity, uncertainty, and tragedy. In Europe, Nazi Germany had launched its aggression against the world. On June 22, 1941, Adolf Hitler commenced a massive attack against the Soviet Union. In August, President Franklin D. Roosevelt effectively committed the United States to the fray, meeting with British prime minister Winston Churchill at sea to draft the Atlantic Charter, which aligned America with Britain, thereby worsening relations with Japan. On December 7, Japan's surprise attack of Pearl Harbor would plunge the United States into the war. Four days later, in a speech to the Reichstag, Hitler declared that Germany was at war with the United States.

In 1941, Mickey was ten years old and still being shaped in the mold of Mickey Cochrane. He was an undersized catcher and a fascinating sight. "Soaking wet," his mother later remembered, "he didn't weigh more than eighty or ninety pounds. When he squatted down behind the batter wearing that [chest] protector that was too big for him, you couldn't see his feet. About all you could see of him—except for his arms—were those two little eyes sticking out of the protector like a scared turtle looking out of its shell." As silly as he looked, Mickey helped Douthat to its Peewee Division championship. The next year Mickey began playing for the Junior Cardinal League team from nearby Picher. Mickey was still only eleven, and the league had to waive a rule that required all players to be at least twelve years of age. In his second season with Picher, Mickey was switched from catcher to second base. It was a move that upset Mutt, who was still determined that his son be a catcher like his hero Mickey Cochrane. Even Mutt, however, had to concede that Mickey's speed lent itself more to the infield.

At the time Mickey's only friends were other boys who also played baseball. LeRoy Bennett and Nick Ferguson were both Mickey's age and lived within a few blocks of the Mantles. LeRoy and Nick's own interest had been spurred by hanging out with Mickey after school and then sometimes staying around at the Mantle house on South Quincy Street to watch Mickey take

switch-hitting batting practice from his father and grandfather. "I don't recol-
lect that I was any better at the game than Nick and LeRoy," Mickey would
later say. "Both my playmates were just as good as I was at the bat. . . . The
difference was—and the difference between me and many other boys who
played ball with just as much skill—that I had a father to encourage and
push me."

Mickey was later to say that one of the things that made him endure the
daily grind of afternoon hitting sessions was having his friends LeRoy and
Nick around to break up the intensity of his practice sessions. LeRoy and Nick
joined Mickey in the Gabby Street League team in nearby Douthat. Each
afternoon the threesome would hike three miles to the practice field at
Douthat. This took the place of Little League, which was not around at the
time. On Saturdays and Sundays, the Douthat team would play against from
teams from nearby mining towns. Those games often were the only weekend
social events in the area, attracting hundreds of people for lazy afternoon pic-
nics and baseball.

Soon, with the onset of Grandpa Charlie's illness, the Mantles were
learning to love their new life out in the country. Mutt cleared out a place
in the pasture for their own ball field, with cow dung for bases; all the Mantles
played there. "We were more like caretakers," Mickey remembered. "There was
a great big lawn and one of our duties was to mow the grass. I played a lot of
ball out there, all kinds of games, with my twin brothers and sister and
youngest brother Butch." Mickey's twin brothers, Roy and Ray, were old
enough to start playing; they spent springs and summers chasing down Mickey's long drives in the pasture. By this time, Mickey was known around Commerce as a youngster who had a passion for baseball and little else. Mickey
would always be seen wearing an old baseball cap, which he later recalled was
"one of my deepest vanities. . . . I would have worn that cap to bed, I believe,
if my mother had let me, and I often put it on first thing in the morning."
Mickey also loved his outdoors life on the farm. He milked the cows, and he
had a horse named Tony, which he rode to school and tied to a hitching post.
As he would later recall: "Early spring we planted oats, wheat and a field of
corn and milked the cows, bringing the filled buckets to our house where mom
separated the milk from the cream. A milk truck would stop by and she sold
him whatever we didn't need. This way my parents could afford a few extra
groceries. . . . It was fun farming, particularly because it made it a lot easier to
hunt and fish. I rode a horse to school, about ten miles away. He sure was an

understanding horse. He didn't like school either. He loved to run away with me on his back and start grazing around some fishing hole."

"He was no angel," one of his teachers told a newspaper reporter who later visited Commerce. "But he was a good, clean boy, alert, quick and willing to learn. Sometimes he'd skip school and we'd have to go find him and bring him back."

These were innocent times for Mickey. On some Saturdays he would join his friends at a matinee to see a western, then head over to the Black Cat Café to order his favorite, the twenty-five-cent blue-plate special—a hamburger, a bowl of chili, and a soda pop. Nothing, however, could match the time Mutt took Mickey to a minor league game between Joplin and Springfield (a team that included the young Stan Musial, who would soon become Mickey's first baseball idol). Mantle was to recall that "every now and then, when he had saved up enough money and he could round up his companions, my father and one or two of his brothers would schedule a pilgrimage to St. Louis to watch the Cardinals in a Saturday night game and a Sunday doubleheader. To me, this was like a journey to the Big Rock Candy Mountain. It meant an early bath on Saturday, then getting into a clean T-shirt, clean blue jeans, and my beloved baseball cap."

However, farm life can be a precarious occupation, as the Dust Bowl period of the 1930s had shown. There is little defense for a farmer against the calamities of nature. One summer it rained and kept raining so long and hard that Mutt couldn't get out in the field to bring in the crop. The torrential rain overran the banks of the nearby Neosho River and flooded the farm and surrounding land. The Mantles lost the crop and the farm too. They were forced to move to a down-and-out community called Whitebird on the edge of Commerce. For Mutt Mantle, this may have been the lowest point in his life; he would have to return to the mines. There were seven Mantles living in a beaten-down old house in which Mickey shared a bedroom with his parents and his little sister Barbara. The house had no kitchen or indoor plumbing, and only later was a small kitchen added. For the family to bathe, Lovell Mantle had to heat water on a wood-burning stove and pour it into a number-three zinc tub that she also used to do laundry. The house was in such bad shape that Mickey yearned to live in the old rusted barn next to the house on South Quincy Street. Years later, during the off-season, Mickey took teammate Billy Martin to see the abandoned little shack. Martin shook his head at disbelief that anyone, much less his friend, could have lived there.

In later years, friends believed Mantle had developed his incredible speed out of necessity. When the family lived in Whitebird, Mickey would take a school bus to an old pump house in nearby Cardin, a mile away from his home. It would be dark, and young Mickey would take off running home along the gravel road. "He was so scared," recalled longtime friend Marshall Smith, that "he would run as fast as he could because he was afraid somebody was going to grab him." Smith also believed Mantle's reflexes and quickness were sharpened by chasing rabbits in open fields. "Nobody told him to do it," said Smith. "It was no scheme. He just didn't know any better."

When Mickey started high school in 1946, he pleaded with his father to allow him to play football in his sophomore year. Although a football fan himself, Mutt was reluctant at first. He had seen and heard of knee and shoulder injuries ruining promising baseball careers. All of Mickey's friends, however, were going out for football, and Mutt finally relented—a decision he was to regret. With his incredible speed, Mickey played halfback and appeared ready to earn a starting position in the Commerce High School lineup. But in an early-season practice, a teammate accidentally kicked Mickey in the left shin; Mickey shook off the bruise and finished the practice. After the workout, the pain worsened. Mickey had a restless night trying to sleep and got up in the morning to find the ankle swollen to twice its normal size and a frightening blue. Mutt Mantle rushed his son to a local hospital, where a doctor diagnosed an infection but suggested that Mickey be taken to a hospital in nearby Picher, which was equipped with X rays and other diagnostic equipment. At the Picher hospital, doctors diagnosed something far more serious than a simple infection. Mickey, they said, had a serious disease called osteomyelitis. A disease that produces chronic inflammation of the bone, osteomyelitis can be arrested temporarily but can never be completely cured. In Mantle's case, it was never clear whether the injury to the leg caused the onset of osteomyelitis or whether bacteria or fungus was responsible. Only two out of ten thousand people ever contract the disease, and Mantle happened to be one of the unlucky ones.

When Mickey learned the gravity of his illness, his immediate thought was that he might never play sports again. Mantle's recollection: "When it finally dawned on me that possibly I would be forced to forget about baseball, football and any other sports, I thought I'd go crazy." Mutt had the same fear, but he reacted quickly. He drove his son to Oklahoma City, where the latest medical facilities were available. For two solid weeks, Mickey remained at

Crippled Children's Hospital in Oklahoma City. Every day, every three hours, he received penicillin injections. Between the shots, his ankle underwent heat treatments. At first the disease refused to respond to treatment, and the attending doctors mentioned the possibility of amputation.

Worse, Mickey feared that he might die. His weight, which had been a little more than 130 pounds when he was injured, dropped dramatically. Nick Ferguson would recall seeing Mickey at the hospital and thinking that he may not have weighed even a hundred pounds. Alone at night in his hospital bed, he suffered hallucinations and sweating spells, partly from the fever, which at one point got as high as 104 degrees, and partly from anxiety. In one night-mare, Mickey dreamed that he had awakened to find his leg already ampu-tated. In another dream, he saw himself hitting a home run only to find that he was unable to run with a leg swollen to the size of a tree trunk.

Mantle's hospital stay to treat the osteomyelitis was made more miserable by the fact that it was his first time away from home. Mickey also harbored a youngster's normal fear of hospitals, worsened by the recollection that his only other time in a hospital had been to visit Grandpa Charlie when he was dying. To ease her son's fears, Lovell Mantle would stay with him during the day, and Mutt would be with him in the evenings.

"[Mickey] was really sad. He was depressed," recalled Ferguson, one of Mantle's regular visitors during his extended hospital stay. "He was always used to having his brothers and sister around. The people he saw most of the time [at the hospital] were doctors and nurses, and he wasn't getting any bet-ter, and he didn't know what was happening to him. He was scared, and he didn't know what was going on." Ferguson also remembers, however, that soon Mickey began putting on weight almost as dramatically as he had lost it shortly after the injury. According to Ferguson, Mickey wondered if the doc-tors hadn't given him a steroid medication; his body was quickly up to 160 pounds.

Adds Mickey's cousin Max Mantle, whose father, Tunney Mantle, was to die of Hodgkin's disease a year later in 1947, at the age of thirty-four: "They moved [Mickey] to Oklahoma City, and it was there that they told him he was going to have to have his leg off. I don't know what his dad said, but his mom was the one who said no. His mom said there was no way in hell they were going to do that. She's the one who did that. She's a tough woman, yes, she is. Said, 'Ain't a-gonna take that leg off.' And then, after that, with all that penicillin, he had these boils all over him, had boils on his arms and legs and even his eyes. And they disappeared."

A few years earlier, Mantle in fact might have lost his leg. Osteomyelitis occurs when bacteria invade bone, grow, and cause damage and destruction. The blow to Mickey's leg had apparently punctured the leg all the way to the bone and exposed it to bacteria. Without penicillin—which, although discovered in 1928, was not readily available in the United States until the 1940s—the outlook for saving Mantle's leg would not have been promising. Most likely he would have eventually developed gangrene and required surgery.

"The leg was abscessed, swollen to almost grotesque size and turning purple," Mantle was to recall. "I had a fever of 104. But mom yanked me out of there when a doctor at the first hospital said they might have to amputate. At the next hospital they treated me with a new wonder drug, penicillin, and though I was in bed for weeks and lost thirty pounds, I recovered."

Finally the swelling subsided, and the pain eased. The osteomyelitis had been arrested. Late in September 1946, not yet fifteen years old, Mickey was sent home on crutches. He was under doctor's orders not to exert himself.

The strongest believer that Mickey would get well was the man whose dreams were wrapped up in his son. Mutt Mantle could hardly bear to watch Mickey hobble around the house on crutches. Fortunately, the 1946 baseball season was at its height. Mutt managed to scrape together enough spare money to surprise Mickey with a dream trip to St. Louis, three hundred miles away, where Mutt's beloved Cardinals were in the World Series against the Boston Red Sox.

For the longest time, the family car was an old, beat-up LaSalle, which Mutt also used to transport livestock. Sometimes he would buy a calf at a sale and remove the back seat from the car in order to get the calf in. Over the years, the LaSalle also served Mutt, Mickey, and some of Mutt's friends on their annual baseball pilgrimages to St. Louis to take in a weekend of games. In the mornings in St. Louis they would always eat breakfast at the Fairgrounds Hotel, where many of the players also ate and could be seen coming and going. Even if Mickey hadn't been shy about approaching them for autographs, he wouldn't have been allowed to; Mutt disapproved of the people who intruded into the players' privacy with autograph requests and made it clear to Mickey that he was to respect their rights.

In 1946 Mickey attended his first two World Series games, watching the Red Sox win the opener, 3–2, but cheering on the Cardinals to a 3–0 win the following day. Back home, Mickey followed the series on radio. The Cardinals won the World Series in seven games, the seventh going into baseball lore for the winning run, which Enos Slaughter scored all the way from first base on a single. Mickey later would say that Slaughter's run inspired him to stop feeling sorry for himself and made him determined to overcome osteomyelitis and run with the same reckless abandon himself. "Burn the crutches," Mickey would say that he told his parents. "I'm going to play ball."

Mickey began by returning to the Commerce High Tigers football team and, despite his injury, playing well enough at halfback to be named to the all-district team. "In my opinion," Mickey's high school coach, John Lingo, later recalled, "baseball was Mickey's second-best sport. He was the best high school football player I ever saw."

After the season, he played on the high school varsity basketball team, then in the spring he pitched and played shortstop on the baseball team. In one game Mickey struck out fourteen hitters; in another, he slugged home runs from both sides of the plate.

It was in football, however, that Mantle captured the attention of college recruiters. In his senior year Mantle was invited to a recruiting visit to the University of Oklahoma, where the legendary football coach Bud Wilkinson was in the process of building his national championship teams. Mantle never met Wilkinson during his visit but was instead given a tour of the campus by the Sooners' star quarterback, Darrell Royal. "I knew who he was, but you know, he could never remember my name," Mantle said, looking back years later. "Probably didn't even think about it, but about 1958, I was living in Dallas, Texas, and the Texas Longhorns were playing over at Fort Worth, playing TCU [Texas Christian University], and I went to the game and they gave me a pass to go down on the field. It was right after the World Series, and I met Darrell Royal [by then the coach of the Longhorns] and he goes, 'Hey, nice meeting you. I always wanted to meet you.' I said, 'Darrell, I met you a long time ago, don't you remember that?' I said, 'You carried me around Oklahoma University in your car one day and showed me all the dormitories and tried to talk me into coming to OU to play football.' And he says, 'In 1949?' I said, 'Yeah.' He says, 'Hell, you weren't even Mickey Mantle then.'"

3

In the spring of 1949, Cleveland Indians scout Hugh Alexander heard from a friend about an outstanding teenage baseball player in Commerce, Oklahoma. Meticulous about checking out tips, Alexander noted the name on a piece of paper. He had become a baseball scout at age twenty in 1937, and the first player he had signed was pitcher Allie Reynolds, who would win 182 games over thirteen seasons with the Indians and the Yankees. Later known as Uncle Hughie, Alexander had become one of baseball's best-known scouts and had gone on to sign dozens of future major leaguers in a career that spanned six decades and countless miles on the back roads of America. A few weeks after getting the tip on Mantle, he drove from his home in Oklahoma City to Commerce and went directly to the local high school. When Alexander inquired about the promising prospect named Mickey Mantle, the school's principal, Bentley Baker, did something curiously out of character for a small-town educator. He lied. He told Alexander that the school did not have a baseball team and that the young man he was interested in had been hurt playing football and had developed arthritis in his legs. "It's hard enough to make the majors if you're healthy and when I got back to my car I took the piece of paper and threw it away," Alexander recalled. "I can still see it blowing across the parking lot."

The signing of Mickey Mantle would always be recounted, even by Mantle himself, as having a touch of homespun heroic adventure. On the night of his graduation, the principal excused Mickey from commencement exercises so that he could play baseball in front of a New York Yankee scout, who signed him immediately after the game. According to Mickey, it was scout Tom Greenwade who "got me excused from the commencement exercises." But the signing of Mickey Mantle was far more complex and involved than even Mantle fully realized at the time, although later he came to understand that not all had been as the Yankees and Greenwade made it out to be. Signing Mickey, in fact, would be a steal, not only in the incredibly unfair deal the Yankees made with the Mantles but also in that the Yankees appear to have violated baseball's rules against dealing with youngsters still in high school. Hugh Alexander would later suggest, and the facts certainly would support the charge, that the Yankees effectively monopolized what should have been a healthy bidding competition for Mickey—with the help of his high school principal who, for reasons he took to his grave, scared off Greenwade's competitors. The shrewd and resourceful Greenwade, a former Internal Revenue Service tax collector, obviously ingratiated himself with Mickey's principal as much as he did with his father.

This was before the creation in 1965 of the professional baseball draft, which would effectively tie an amateur player to a single major league team. Until then, a hot young prospect out of high school was a free agent, who could negotiate and sign with the highest bidder. Young players who signed contracts with big signing bonuses were called "bonus babies," and Mickey would quickly come to know some in his first years with the Yankees. Bill "Moose" Skowron, who roomed with Mickey briefly in 1950, was a bonus baby; having less talent than Mantle, he had been signed by the Yankees for twenty-five thousand dollars but didn't make the major league team until 1954. Yankee infielder Bobby Brown had signed for a fifty-two-thousand-dollar bonus. Yankee third baseman Andy Carey received a sixty-thousand-dollar signing bonus in 1951. In 1950, Greenwade himself signed Elston Howard for a fifteen-thousand-dollar bonus. The free-agent situation of the time for promising young talent amounted to a system not altogether different from that which would eventually inflate baseball salaries to astronomical levels.

Then as now, the owners of America's major league baseball teams had a vested interest in keeping salaries down while at the same time signing the best players in the country. Historically, one of the few rules that have governed the professional recruiting process for American players has been a restriction against contact with a player before his high school graduation. Prospects could not even be approached by professional scouts until after they were out of high school, and teams could lose all negotiating rights to a player for even making premature contact with him. Yet Greenwade and the Yankees were apparently in touch with Mantle as early as his junior year. According to Mantle, Greenwade talked with Mickey about playing for the Yankees after the first game the scout saw him play in 1948—telling Mickey and his father that he was talking only "unofficially," because Mantle was still in high school. "Don't sign with anyone else," Mickey recalled Greenwade saying, "and the day you graduate I'll be back." Mutt, according to Mickey, wanted to know if Greenwade meant he would return with a contract offer. Greenwade smiled reassuringly. The carrot had been left dangling. "No question," Mutt told Mickey, "we oughta wait on Greenwade."

Lee MacPhail, the Yankees' Midwest farm-system director and the general manager of the Yankees' Triple-A team in Kansas City, later confirmed that Greenwade personally brought Mickey and his father to an invitation-only tryout camp in Branson, Kansas, when Mickey was still a seventeen-year-old senior. "For a high school boy," said MacPhail, "he had excellent power from both sides, great speed and a great arm."

In the late 1940s, Greenwade was still trying to impress the Yankee front office brass with his own performance. He had joined the Yankees in 1945, recruited by then President Larry MacPhail, with whom he had worked in the Dodgers organization before World War II. Greenwade had made his reputation with the St. Louis Browns and the Brooklyn Dodgers. Like MacPhail, he was a protégé of the Dodgers' Branch Rickey, and he had been one of the Brooklyn scouts instrumental in the Dodgers' signing and grooming of Jackie Robinson, who eventually broke baseball's color barrier in 1947. Rickey was close-mouthed about what his true plans were with Robinson until that fateful season, but Greenwade boasted on occasion that Rickey had confided in him as to his intentions. Greenwade's claim, however, apparently was untrue, though he was in fact involved in the Dodgers' signing of catcher Roy Campanella out of the Negro Leagues.

With the Yankees, Greenwade jumped to a fabled but fading organization, for whom the seasons of the mid and late 1940s were unkind, except for the 1947 World Series championship. His friend, the tempestuous Larry MacPhail, departed the Yankees after the 1947 World Series, leaving a trail of bad feelings. Leo Durocher, whom MacPhail fired as the manager of the Dodgers after he had led them to their first pennant in twenty-one years, once said of MacPhail, "There is a thin line between genius and insanity, and in Larry's case it was sometimes so thin you could see him drifting back and forth." With the Yankees, MacPhail had upset the organization's chemistry both on and off the field. He once allegedly arranged a deal with Boston Red Sox owner Tom Yawkey to trade Joe DiMaggio for Ted Williams, a trade that supposedly fell through when Yawkey sobered up and asked for Yogi Berra as well. In 1946, MacPhail had three managers quit on him—Yankee legend Joe McCarthy, former Hall of Fame catcher Bill Dickey, and Johnny Neun. MacPhail had also been personally involved in the questionable fifty-two-thousand-dollar signing bonus paid to Bobby Brown, a bad-fielding medical student whose only accomplishment in baseball would be one day to become president of the American League. In 1948, with Larry MacPhail gone and the skeptical George Weiss now comfortably ensconced as general manager, Greenwade found himself accountable to a new front office.

Greenwade scoured America's heartland looking for a prize prospect who would validate his life as a scout and the Yankees' decision to hire him. Mantle, of course, would be that prospect; signing him would forever cement Greenwade's place with the Yankees and in baseball. He would remain with the organization for forty years, retiring in 1985, a year before his death. Throughout his life, Greenwade would deny violating the high school tampering rule. Although he admitted to being worried that other scouts would move in on Mickey, he claimed to have waited patiently until the Sunday after Mickey's graduation from high school before offering him a contract. That contract was ironed out in fifteen minutes of negotiations between himself and Mutt. Mickey was signed for a total of $1,500—four hundred for playing the remainder of the season with the Independence, Missouri, team of the Kansas-Oklahoma–Missouri League, and a $1,100 bonus. Altogether, Mickey signed for a tenth of the money Elston Howard would receive from the Yankees a year later. "That amount *is* a pittance even by the standards of that day," says Kevin Kerrane, author of the classic *Dollar Sign on the Muscle: The World of Baseball Scouting.* "It's amazing when you think that he was signed for so little."

It is all the more incredible when you consider that around the time Mantle was signing for $1,500, another young phenom—Jim Baumer, a promising power-hitting shortstop who was half a year older than Mickey—was signing in Broken Bow, Oklahoma, with the Chicago White Sox for a fifty-thousand-dollar bonus. Baumer would go directly to the majors, then become a journeyman minor leaguer for the entire 1950s before playing briefly with the Cincinnati Reds in 1960. Eventually Baumer himself would become a scout, whose signings included Hall of Famer Robin Yount. In an interview with Kerrane, Baumer once boasted of how on his high school graduation night his parents' living room had been filled with scouts, including Greenwade—who seemed confident he had Mickey Mantle safely in his pocket.

Mantle was to insist throughout his lifetime that Greenwade signed him on May 16, 1949, the night of his graduation, in Greenwade's 1949 Chrysler, having arranged with Principal Baker for Mickey to be excused from his commencement exercises to play a game with the area's prized travel team, the Whiz Kids of Baxter Springs, Kansas. After the game, Mantle recalled, Greenwade approached his father to tell him things didn't look promising for his son, because of his small size and his erratic play at shortstop—but that he was willing to gamble on a contract for a modest signing bonus. But like the Commerce High School principal, Greenwade was lying. "When I first saw him," Greenwade would eventually admit of Mantle, "I knew he was going to be one of the all-time greats." On still another occasion Greenwade would say, "The first time I saw Mantle I knew how Paul Krichell felt when he first saw Lou Gehrig. He knew that as a scout he'd never have another moment like it."

That day, however, Mutt Mantle did not dare call Greenwade on his lie. Mutt was anxious to get his son a professional baseball contract and too inexperienced to do justice to Mickey's interests in negotiations. When Mickey was sixteen, Mutt had gone so far as to take him to St. Louis to get him a tryout with the Browns, who had shown no interest. Mutt was disappointed, failing to understand that Mickey was still too young to impress the scouts. Mickey was also just starting to pack on muscle and weight. In his senior year in high school, other scouts began showing an interest, but possibly they were more mindful than Greenwade of the major league high school tampering rule. Runt Marr, a Cardinal scout who was well known in the area, visited the Mantle home one day to express interest in Mickey and asked that he not sign with anyone else until St. Louis could make an offer. Mantle said that he gave up hope that the Cardinals would make an offer after days passed without hearing from their representative. The Mantles, however, apparently didn't fully understand that major league teams were prohibited from even *contacting* Mickey until he had graduated, let alone making a signing offer.

Mutt's impatience about getting his son signed to a professional contract is troubling—unless one understands that Mutt Mantle had been molded by the Great Depression. Although he was filled with optimism about Mickey's potential, a cold wind sometimes blew through the back of his mind—the conviction that the world could collapse. Even as Mutt managed to overcome obstacles, the '30s of his young adulthood whistled thinly through his memory. Those bleak years had given him a particular sense of life and its pitfalls. Not too surprisingly, the Mantles used almost all of Mickey's signing bonus to pay off the mortgage on the family home. If Mutt's extreme anxiety to get Mickey playing professional baseball as soon as possible that summer is understandable, his decision to have Mickey sign so soon after becoming eligible even to talk to the pros appears to have been ill advised at best. At the time, Mickey was one of the area's most talented amateur athletes. The University of Oklahoma tried to recruit him for its football program. Bill Mosely, who quarterbacked Mickey's high school football team at Commerce and graduated with him, received a football scholarship and went on to play at Pittsburgh State Teachers College in Kansas.

Undoubtedly, Mutt could have used the college football offers as negotiating leverage with the Yankees. As Al Campanis, the late Dodger baseball executive and himself a former scout, would later say of Mantle's signing, "[Baseball's] rule against signing someone before he graduates from high school doesn't mean that on the day you graduate you have to sign a contract. That just marks the start of the race. Mantle was just coming into his own then. The only reasons I can see for him signing so quick would be if there'd been a big bonus—and there wasn't—or if there'd been a contract that put him on the major league team roster—and there wasn't that either. Mantle could've played [amateur] ball that summer and built up his value the more he was seen and scouted. There's no telling what he could've signed for."

Instead, the Mantles jumped at the first offer and even then mismanaged the negotiation, according to what Greenwade told a reporter at the time. "I asked Mutt what they wanted to sign," Greenwade said he told Mickey's father.

"Well, you'll have to give him as much as he'd make around here all summer, working in the mine and playing ball on Sunday," said Mutt, effectively missing an opportunity to ask for top dollar. "His pay in the mine is eighty-seven and a half cents an hour, and he can get fifteen dollars on a Sunday playing [semipro] ball."

"We wrote down how much he could make working with his father up in the mines in Picher and how much he'd be making playing semipro weekends in Spavinaw on the same team as his father," Greenwade told the *New York Herald Tribune*'s Harold Rosenthal a decade later. "Then we added up how much he'd make in three months in the minors and subtracted and subtracted from the first figure. It came to $1,150. That's what I could get for him to sign."

In another life, Greenwade, with that flat, ridge-runner accent that made him sound so convincing, might also have been a used-car salesman; he kept manipulating the numbers. Finally, he threw out to Mutt a monthly salary of $140 that Mickey would earn playing for Independence, Kansas, a Yankee farm club, the rest of that summer, almost three months. "That's around four hundred dollars," he told Mutt. "Suppose we make up the difference and give you $1,100? That's about $1,500, right?"

The result would be one of the biggest signing coups ever made by a professional sports team and, unfortunately for the Mantles, a horrendous negotiating blunder that would cost the family tens of thousands of dollars. But this was to be only the first of numerous business deals during his career and after retirement in which Mickey would wind up on the short end of the stick.

"It was not until the signing was announced in the paper and I read Tom Greenwade's prediction that I would probably set records with the Yankees, equaling Ruth's and DiMaggio's, that I began to wonder if my father and I had been outslicked," Mickey said years later. "Greenwade, by *his* account, had just been going through Oklahoma on his way to look over a *real* prospect, when he stopped to talk to us. I never did find out who that *real* prospect was." In his autobiography, *The Mick,* Mantle acknowledged that it had all been a negotiating ploy by Greenwade. "When I read the announcement about my signing," wrote Mickey, "it quoted Greenwade as saying I would probably set records with the Yankees. Stuff like that. He did tell me later that I was the best prospect he had ever seen."

For Tom Greenwade, signing Mickey Mantle was a well-designed plan that had been in the works for the better part of two years. He had first laid eyes on Mantle in 1948, when he went to scout a Whiz Kids third baseman named Billy Johnson in a game in Alba, Missouri. A baseball scout needs to be a consummate poker player, rarely letting on his true feelings about a prospect. It was to Greenwade's advantage to downplay Mickey's potential as a future professional player to Mutt Mantle, who in turn used this as motivational fodder for his son. Mickey, consequently, came to believe what Greenwade had said to his father—that he had not been overly impressed by his first look at what would ultimately become his prize signing. Mickey was still slight of build; he was known as "Little Mickey" to some of his teammates.

Mantle, however, had hit two home runs the first day Greenwade saw him, one from each side of the plate.

Moreover, Mickey's prodigious power was already in evidence. The Whiz Kids' home field in Baxter Springs—which manager and coach Barney Barnett had personally built, including a $3,500 set of lights for night games—was bordered in right and center field by the Spring River, which was some four hundred feet from home plate in dead center field and some five hundred away in right field. As a sixteen-year-old in 1948, Mantle was routinely hitting balls almost those distances. In one game in late summer, with 250 to three hundred people looking on, Mickey hit three home runs—two right-handed and one left-handed—into the Spring River. In the frenzy that erupted in the crowd, someone in the bleachers behind home plate passed a hat around to reward their slugger. After the game, Mickey was presented with fifty-three dollars in small change—which soon became a minor headache for the Mantles. Someone reported the incident to the Oklahoma State Athletic Commission, which regulated high school sports. That commission determined that since Mickey had accepted the money, he had lost his amateur status and could not compete in high school sports at Commerce High in his senior year. Mutt challenged the ruling, going to Oklahoma City personally to make the appeal. The ruling was reversed, and Mickey's amateur status was reinstated, on the condition that he return the money. Mantle would later say he returned the fifty-three dollars, which he had already spent, by working at odd jobs. It is uncertain, however, whether that actually happened, since that fall Mickey was busy playing football after school. According to at least one version, Mickey repaid Barnett with a fifty-three-dollar check, which was never cashed.

Mickey's power at that age, along with his speed, gives further credibility to the story that Greenwade, in fact, had been so impressed when he first saw Mantle that he wanted to sign him on the spot before learning he was a sixteen-year-old high school student. Greenwade's own admission of having reacted to first seeing Mantle the way the scout who signed Gehrig undoubtedly had suggests that Greenwade must have been torn, at the least, at having found his prize jewel at a time when big signing bonuses were becoming part of the business of the sport.

Learning that Mickey was only sixteen must have also impressed Greenwade, who had more than a passing knowledge of Barney Barnett and his Whiz Kids team. The Whiz Kids were a highly competitive semipro team with the best players from Kansas, Oklahoma, and Missouri. The team played in the Ban Johnson League, which operated in the tri-state area and had produced several major leaguers. At sixteen years of age, Mickey was its youngest player and an obvious phenomenon. His team was composed mostly of eighteen-year-olds; the other Ban Johnson League teams were made up of players eighteen to twenty-one years of age, and on them players younger than eighteen were a rarity. "On the Whiz Kids, Mickey was ahead of his years," said Ivan Shouse, Mantle's childhood friend. "Everyone knew it. He was a boy playing with men, and he was better than all of them."

By Mantle's own account, the Whiz Kids experience was a turning point in his development as a ballplayer. "I think the first real baseball uniform—and I'm sure it is—the most proud I ever was when I went to Baxter Springs in Kansas, and I played on the Baxter Springs Whiz Kids," Mantle said in his emotional 1974 Hall of Fame induction speech. "[They] gave me a uniform and it had a BW on the cap there and it said Whiz Kids on the back. I really thought I was somethin' when I got that uniform. It was the first one my mom hadn't made for me. It was really something."

On the Whiz Kids Mickey joined two longtime friends, Nick Ferguson and LeRoy Bennett, who because they were older than Mantle had been on the team since 1946. Mickey had attended some of their games while recovering from osteomyelitis. Photographs of that year's team, in which Mickey posed with his friends, show him looking small and almost frail. By 1948, however, Mickey had bulked up from his hospital weight of 110 pounds to 150 pounds, and he would gain another fifteen pounds by the spring of 1949. While Mickey would later become even more muscular working in the mines during the 1949–50 and 1950–51 off-seasons, by 1948 he had built up his upper-body strength by digging graves and carrying tombstones for a friend of Barnett's, Harry Wells, who owned a cemetery business in Baxter Springs. Wells was also a friend of the Whiz Kids team, and on occasion he drove Mickey and some of his teammates to Cardinals games in St. Louis, three hundred miles away.

Another factor that made the Whiz Kids special was its manager and head coach, Barnett. Mutt had known him for a number of years. Barnett was a ground boss in the lead and zinc mines, and as a baseball coach he had a reputation for having connections with several major league scouts. Barnett also had been one of the coaches who developed Sherman Lollar, who would become a major league catcher with the Chicago White Sox in the 1950s.

When Mickey joined the Whiz Kids in 1948, Barnett immediately converted him into a shortstop and patiently stuck with him at that position despite defensive shortcomings that Mickey would never overcome. Still, Barnett was one of the first coaches to see Mickey as a major league prospect and to encourage him. "Mickey," Barnett said to him early on, "the big leagues seem like a million miles from here and out of reach. But if you work real hard, they're not out of reach for you."

By 1948 Mickey had come a long way, considering that less than two years earlier he had been on the verge of having a leg amputated. The spring after his battle with osteomyelitis, Mickey had returned to baseball, playing second base for a youth team from Miami, Oklahoma, in the Ban Johnson League with the Whiz Kids. That season Mantle had had strong games against the Whiz Kids, although in their final game he had had the dubious distinction of lining into a rally-killing triple play. Nevertheless, Barnett had been impressed and recruited Mickey for his team for the 1948 season. Barnett was so taken with Mantle that the following spring he arranged a tryout for him at Joplin, Missouri. There Mantle caught the eye of Johnny Sturm, the manager at Joplin and a former Yankee first baseman. Sturm mentioned Mickey to Greenwade, who was coming to the realization that others were also recognizing Mantle's potential. Mickey was still a few months away from graduation, so the challenge for Greenwade and the Yankees became how to keep Mantle from becoming interested in any other teams—or better still, to keep those other teams away from him.

Greenwade was able to do that by promising the Mantles a contract on the night Mickey graduated from high school. No one else did that. No one else was willing to risk the consequences of being caught breaking the rules. In Mutt Mantle, a father with a burning desire to see his son become a professional baseball player, the Yankees had a willing accomplice.

A decade after signing Mantle, Greenwade told the *New York Herald Tribune*, "The Cardinals' scout in the area, Runt Marr, had heard of the kid, and I was a little surprised when he didn't show up that [graduation] night. It was a pretty busy time, and the Yankees wanted me to go over to Broken Bow to look at another kid who was after big money, Jim Baumer. He looked a lot better than Mantle but he was asking for big money, and that meant you had to keep him on the big club if you signed him.

"So I told Mickey's father, Mutt, that I'd be back and made him promise that no matter what anyone else offered not to sign until I got back and I could try to match it. I got back Sunday night and no one had come after Mickey, Runt Marr or anyone else."

Greenwade's lengthiest account of how he signed Mickey came in a letter to Taylor Spink, the legendary sportswriter of *The Sporting News*. Even that account betrayed established facts surrounding his relationship with the Mantles. In some instances, Greenwade was completely untruthful, such as in claiming not to have known the Mantles until Mickey's graduation day, or in claiming not to have known that Mickey was a switch-hitter until the game he played instead of attending his own graduation.

"On Friday I drove to Commerce," Greenwade said, "and this is the first time the Mantles ever knew there was such a person as Tom Greenwade. I found out the graduation exercises had been postponed till that night for some reason. Since I had no desire to violate the [high school] tampering rule, I was careful not to mention contract or pro ball either, but had understood Mickey to play in Coffeyville that night and I wanted to see him play and I didn't mention that I had seen him play before. Well, they talked things over with the coach and superintendent and decided to pass on the exercises since Mickey already had his diploma and go to Coffeyville instead. Of course, I was there. Mickey looked better at bat, hitting left-handed. I still don't know he switches since the only pitching I have seen him against is right-handed. After the game, Mr. Mantle tells me that Mickey will play Sunday in Baxter Springs. I told him I would be at his house Sunday morning and go to the game with them. I was there about 11 A.M. I was scared to death for fear some scout had been there Saturday. I asked Mr. Mantle if anyone had been there. He said 'no.' I was relieved. We all went to Baxter Springs, and for the first time I see Mickey hit right handed. Mickey racked the pitcher for four 'clothes-lines,' and I started looking around for scouts, but none were there. When the last out was made, Mr. Mantle, Mickey, and I got in my car behind the grandstand and in fifteen minutes the contract was signed."

Greenwade's account to Spink is laughable in the way he attempted to rewrite the history of his wooing of the Mantles and of Mickey itself. He would tell several versions and never settle on one, which is odd, considering he was a scout known for his fastidious neatness and had once been a federal income-tax collector.

The life of the baseball scout was not then, and is not now, a game for gentlemen. According to Kerrane, in those days all was fair in fighting other scouts for the signature of a promising prospect. The passing of money under the table was not unheard of, especially when it came to keeping competing scouts away from a prized player. Occasionally, says Kerrane, there were suspicions and allegations of scouts and their teams circumventing the rules on bonus babies. A player signed to a high bonus, such as Jim Baumer, was required under baseball's rules to be placed on the major league team itself (as opposed to one of its farm clubs) for a period of time, a requirement that would create havoc with the team's roster. To get around this, some teams were suspected of paying part of the bonus to a new signee under the table in cash, thereby leaving their rosters unaffected.

Often these were matters left completely in the hands of the scouts, as the late catcher-manager Birdie Tebbets told Kerrane in an interview: "They drove all over hell to find ballplayers, and they made final decisions on their own about how valuable the players were, and they competed to sign them. They weren't just legmen. They built ball clubs. And they never had a pension or a share in the things that other baseball people were given. I've been in every seat in baseball, and I'd have to say that the old time scouts were the most important people I ever came into contact with."

For Tom Greenwade, Mickey Mantle would become the showpiece in a the parade of 1950s and 1960s Yankee stars and mainstays that he signed, Hank Bauer, a friend and roommate of Mantle, as well as Ralph Terry and Bobby Murcer.

As for Mickey's signing, what really happened, and what has become myth? An examination of documents, records, histories, and interviews reveals that maybe Mantle's memory was as faulty as Greenwade's recollections were selective.

On the evening of Friday, May 16, 1949, Mickey's high school class was scheduled to graduate in exercises that were in conflict with a night game of the Baxter Springs Whiz Kids in Coffeyville. Tom Greenwade apparently interceded with the high school's principal, whom he had gotten to know over the past year. He asked Baker if Mantle could be excused, but the principal evidently passed the decision to the district's superintendent. Mutt Mantle then approached Mickey's high school coach, John Lingo, and together they broached the question with the superintendent, Albert Stewart, who sympathized and agreed to excuse Mickey. That afternoon, Stewart personally presented Mickey with his diploma and wished him well in the game that night. Later that afternoon, Greenwade drove Mickey, Mutt, and Lingo to Coffeyville. There Greenwade and Mutt left Mickey and Lingo and drove off to discuss Mickey's future with the Yankees. They returned in the second inning, in time to see Mickey get the first of his three hits in four at-bats, batting right-handed against a left-handed pitcher.

After the game, however, Greenwade played the coy suitor, lying to Mutt by telling him he had doubts about Mickey's potential as a future big leaguer. There seems to have been a reason. Greenwade was also pursuing Jim Baumer in Broken Bow, and he suspected that he could sign one of the two but not both. Baumer's father had already told Greenwade and other scouts that he wanted a big signing bonus for his son. The figure of twenty-five thousand dollars had been mentioned to scouts, Greenwade included; Yankee general manager George Weiss later told friends that he had authorized Greenwade to offer that much—the same bonus Bill Skowron would receive. Weiss, a brilliant businessman who had been with the Yankees since 1932, had been the architect of the organization's farm system, which he had shrewdly built by signing Depression-era players cheaply and often making incredible profits when he sold some of them to other teams. After one of those deals, then Yankee general manager Ed Barrow asked Weiss, "George, doesn't your conscience bother you?"

Weiss was trying to rebuild his sagging Yankees by whatever means it took, including signing bonuses to promising players. The 1947 Yankees had won the pennant and the World Series, but the 1948 Yankees had faded to third place. The 1949 Yankees had started the season inauspiciously after losing Joe DiMaggio in the spring to an unexpected second operation to remove bone spurs from his right heel. The Yankees had entered the bonus-baby market, and Greenwade was aware that he had a blank check to sign a prospect like Mantle. Greenwade appears to have been baffled that, unlike Baumer's father, Mutt had not even so much as hinted at what kind of signing deal he wanted for Mickey.

Mutt, in fact, seemed to be more concerned with where his son would be assigned after turning professional. He was insistent that Mickey play somewhere close to home that summer, preferably at the Yankees' Class D team at Independence, Kansas, seventy-five miles from Commerce. So on Friday night after the game that Mickey missed his graduation for, Greenwade seems to have informed Mutt that he was still weighing the decision on his son and would return, if possible, on Sunday for another of the Whiz Kids' games in Baxter Springs. Nevertheless, Greenwade got Mutt to promise that he would give him the chance to match any offers. Greenwade, though, knew what no other scout in the area knew—that Mantle wasn't the damaged prospect with bum legs that Hugh Alexander and other scouts were being told he was by his own high school principal. Why Bentley Baker was telling these scouts that story may never be known, but obviously the only beneficiaries of the lie were Greenwade and the Yankees.

On Sunday, Greenwade indeed returned to watch Mickey, determined to sign him. He had failed to sign Baumer, who signed elsewhere for twice what the Yankees could offer, but he now had all that money to use, if necessary, to sign Mantle. He didn't need it, for Mutt virtually gave Mickey away. The irony that Baumer, who was courted by fourteen of the sixteen major league teams, eventually proved to be a big league bust was not lost on Baumer himself, who would later tell Kevin Kerrane, "The night I graduated was the same night Mickey Mantle graduated. And Greenwade, who ended up signing Mantle, was at *my* graduation. I was supposed to be hot property, but hardly anybody knew about Mickey, so Greenwade told him to wait, that he'd get to Commerce to see him in a few days."

Ultimately, the signing of Mickey Mantle would became part of Americana, a heroic fable, suitable for a *Saturday Evening Post* cover by Norman Rockwell. As author David Halberstam would later put it, "The myth of Tom Greenwade, the greatest scout of his age, blended with Mantle's myth to create a classic illustration of the American Dream: for every American of talent, no matter how poor or simple his or her background, there is always a Tom Greenwade out there searching to discover that person and help him or her find a rightful place among the stars."

4

Intense public interest in a person, a pastime, or an idea is one of the most familiar and important characteristics of American life. For weeks, for months, sometimes for years, one person or thing is a topic of conversation, a seedbed of jokes, an object of passionate curiosity or of some other emotion that pre-occupies the public mind. When this happens, it becomes what can only be called a national phenomenon. Over the years, these national pastimes have been of every variety and kind, native and foreign. Sometimes it has been a new word game, such as Scrabble or crossword puzzles; sometimes a new singer or actor, a new cartoon, a new television show; or a new kind of eccentric. Any complete list for the twentieth century would have to include flagpole sitters, child stars, boy wonders, quiz kids, pilots, Channel swimmers, the kings and queens of Europe, and an occasional great scientist or thinker. In the spring of 1951, it was a nineteen-year-old baseball player. Before he had ever had an official at-bat in a major league baseball game, Mickey Mantle found himself in the limelight.

In 1951, Mickey Mantle became the talk of the Yankees spring training camp, a camp he wasn't even supposed to attend. The annual ritual of spring training for major league teams has historically been a workout camp for vet-erans and players returning from the previous year's team, and for promising players from the team's minor league organization. Usually these minor league players are from the team's best farm teams, the Class AAA and AA clubs, which are, respectively, one and two levels below the majors. Rarely does a player from one of the lower levels of a team's system get invited to spring training with the major league club, especially back in baseball's so-called glory years, when the minors were a widespread labyrinth of talent pooled throughout the American backwoods. Whereas a major league team today will have only six or seven minor league affiliates, in 1950 teams often had three times that many. In 1950, the Yankees had eighteen minor league teams.

Mantle had set the stage for his 1951 spring training display a year earlier, when he reported to his first spring camp in St. Petersburg, Florida, along with dozens of other minor leaguers from the Yankee organization. Mickey, still eighteen, had spent half a season in 1949 with the Independence, Kansas, Class D team after signing with the Yankees out of high school. In that 1950 spring training, Mickey had spent most of the time with other minor leaguers, away from the attention of Yankee manager Casey Stengel. Without the benefit of the pre–spring training instructional camp for rookies, which would begin the following year, Stengel heard of promising youngsters only from other coaches. In the sprints, Mantle had timed the fastest in the entire camp. It was Mickey's switch-hitting, however, that brought attention to the freckle-faced kid, who was a virtual unknown. In an intrasquad game on the fourth day of camp, Mantle slugged home runs from both sides of the plate—shots farther than anyone could remember balls being hit before in spring training. The first time most of the rookies in camp even saw Stengel was after Mantle's second blast, when the impressed, aging manager ran out on the field, waving a fungo bat as he chased after Mickey circling first base, asking other coaches, "What'sis name? Mantle?"

That year, Mantle's second season as a pro, Mickey finished spring training with the Yankees' Class AAA Kansas City team, the top minor league club in New York's system, before being sent to play at Class C Joplin, which was the next to the bottom rung. Mickey was a sensation. He led the Western Association in four offensive categories, winning the league batting title with a .383 average and also leading the league with 199 hits, 141 runs, and 326 total bases. At the end of Joplin's season, the Yankees called Mickey up to join the major league team for a series against the Browns in St. Louis, traveling with the team as a nonroster player on their final two-week road trip.

On a Sunday, September 17, 1950, Mickey arrived in Sportsman's Park in St. Louis, carrying a straw suitcase with only two pairs of pants, and terrified at the thought of being in the same dugout with Joe DiMaggio and the defending world champion Yankees. The first day he remained in the Yankee clubhouse, too scared to go on the field with the rest of the team, until two of the players, Jerry Coleman and Bobby Brown, coaxed him into joining them. After the workout, Mickey stopped outside the carpeted clubhouse to remove his spikes, until he noticed that all the other players didn't think twice about it.

"I remember Mantle joining us in St. Louis, and that was the first time I ever saw him," Yankee pitcher Whitey Ford was to recall. Whitey himself had been brought up from the minors to the Yankees in the second half of that season. "I didn't meet him. He was so shy, he didn't talk to anybody but [lefty rookie pitcher Bob] Wiesler for the two weeks he was with us. But I remember him and Moose [Skowron, another September call-up] taking batting practice with us before the games, and they put on a great show of power hitting."

Mickey saw no action in those final two weeks of the season and returned to Commerce that fall unconvinced that he was a major leaguer. Mutt Mantle, however, was understandably proud of his son, who would become visibly embarrassed, turn away, and shuffle his feet self-consciously every time his father bragged to friends that Mickey was a New York Yankee who knew Di-Maggio personally. By this time, Mutt was a ground boss in the mines, where Mickey himself again went to work in the off-season. Mickey spent the winter of 1950–51 working as a "screen ape," which is what they called miners who used sixteen-pound sledgehammers to shatter rocks that were too large to pass through the screen filters. The work proved beneficial for Mickey. Pounding away with a sledgehammer in the mines that off-season made him even stronger, further developing his muscular arms.

In 1951, the Yankees moved their spring training camp from St. Petersburg to Phoenix, Arizona. Yankee co-owner Del Webb, a resident of Phoenix, had personally arranged the swap of spring training sites with New York Giants owner Horace Stoneham so that he could showcase his world championship team to his influential friends on the West Coast. Casey Stengel, in his third year as manager of the team, had persuaded Webb to establish a special three-week instructional camp preceding spring training for rookies, bonus players, and promising minor leaguers. In 1950, the Yankee farm teams had produced sixty all-star minor leaguers, including Mantle; of these, forty were invited to the 1951 instructional camp. Mantle was not among them. Yankee general manager George Weiss feared that rushing a young prospect like Mickey could harm his development and so didn't want Mantle at the camp. Unknown to Mickey, however, his cause was being championed by two influential men in the Yankee organization. Stengel had caught glimpses of Mantle the previous spring, then again in the batting cage during his brief stint with the Yankees in September, and a third time in an instructional camp the Yankees held for promising prospects in the late fall of 1950. The Yankee skipper wanted to see more of him. Tom Greenwade, the Yankee scout who had signed Mantle, also campaigned aggressively with Yankee minor league director Lee MacPhail, insisting that Mickey be invited to the camp. Between Stengel and Greenwade, the case for Mantle's attendance was made to sound convincing. Even so, when the instructional camp opened, Mickey wasn't there. Stengel was irate.

Back in Commerce, Mickey had received a letter from MacPhail shortly after New Year's Day, instructing him to report to their instructional camp. Mickey was excited at the prospect of leaving the mines for spring training but waited for additional instructions and a plane or bus ticket. In mid-February, with the instructional camp already under way, Mickey still had not shown up in Phoenix. The Yankees tried contacting him but had a difficult time trying to reach Mickey, because the Mantles did not have a telephone in their home. Finally, a reporter and photographer with the Miami [Oklahoma] *Daily News Record* showed up in Commerce to find out why Mickey wasn't in camp.

"They didn't send no ticket or nothing," Mickey told them.

"Yeah? Well, we got a call from Lee MacPhail, saying to get ahold of you because he doesn't have your home telephone number or any idea in the world where you work."

Mantle headed straight for the Blue Goose Number One mine to call MacPhail. "Where are you?" MacPhail demanded. "Why aren't you here in Phoenix?"

"I'm broke," Mickey told him. "I don't have any money for transportation."

Meanwhile, a story was going out nationwide on the Associated Press wire service that began: "Mickey Mantle, heading for Yankee stardom, has not yet reported to the team's spring training camp because 'I haven't gotten my ticket yet.'"

The next day, Greenwade arrived in Commerce to deliver personally a ticket and expense money to his prize recruit. A day later Mickey was on his way to join the Yankees. In Phoenix, Weiss explained to Stengel and other Yankee management brass that he had forgotten to send Mantle the expense money. Weiss, however, was an extremely meticulous man; Stengel and others suspected that he had never intended to send it.

It did not take Mantle long to impress. Speed has always been an intangible quality in sports. Even in sports where speed is not usually considered the most important of attributes, raw, natural swiftness afoot can be impressive. Stengel and his coaches at the instructional camp were immediately awestruck by Mantle's speed. In the early footraces, Mickey outran other players by such margins that Stengel at first thought he was cheating, taking head starts. Stengel and the coaches had Mantle running sprints against everyone at the camp, including some of the roster players—who were there as "instructors," so as to not violate the restriction against major leaguers coming to camp before March 1. Mantle outran everyone. He was clocked running from home plate to first base; his times were 3.1 seconds from the right-handed hitter's side of the plate and 3.0 seconds from the left-hander's side. No one in the major leagues was that fast.

Stengel began calling Mickey "Mantles." No one is sure why. Some have suggested it was simply "Stengelese," the special use and misuse of the language for which Stengel came to be known as much as for his championship Yankee teams. Others believe Stengel may have considered that he had two Mantles, because of the youngster's switch-hitting talent, which by itself was a rarity. At the time of Mantle's arrival, the American League featured just one regular switch-hitter, Dave Philley of the Athletics. Moreover, switch-hitting was seen as a device employed by hitters who were lacking other weapons. Of the switch-hitters who had preceded Mantle—among them Frankie Frisch, Red Schoendeinst, and Max Carey were the best—nearly all had been disdainful of the long ball. In 1951, the career leader in home runs by a switch-hitter was Rip Collins, with 135. The idea of tape-measure power from both sides of the plate was enough to get anyone's attention.

As a switch-hitter, slugging home runs from both sides of the plate, Mantle quickly began to impress the other Yankees as well. Aside from his running faster than any player Stengel had ever seen, his hitting talent and potential were prodigious. Only his defensive skills underwhelmed. Mickey had a tremendous arm, but he was no major league shortstop. The Yankee had left him at the position he had played in high school, but at Joplin in his first full minor league season he had committed fifty-five errors, unusually high for a shortstop. Nevertheless, Stengel had plans for Mickey. The thinking among MacPhail and others had been that Mantle might ultimately be converted into an outfielder. Once an outfielder himself, Stengel wanted to shift Mantle. Within days of Mantle's arrival at the instructional camp, Stengel made Mickey his own project, personally trying to teach him the new position and then retaining Tommy Henrich, a retired Yankee right fielder, to coach his young protégé. Stengel could barely contain himself; in a burst of enthusiasm, he invited the sportswriters at the camp to come watch.

"Mantles," Stengel told the writers, "is a shortstop and he ain't much of a shortstop, either. But he sure can switch-hit hard, and run as fast as anybody I ever saw. I've seen some pretty good runners and ol' Case was a pretty fair runner himself. You fellers be out here tomorrow and you might see this Mantle at a place that could surprise you." Although they dismissed Stengel's comments as more Stengelese, sportswriters came by early the next morning and caught Mantle taking outfield practice under Henrich's tutelage.

The Yankees were determined to turn Mickey into a major leaguer, and Mickey was soon to learn that there was little room for sentiment. Yankee coach Frank Crosetti worked with all the infielders, and the first thing he noticed about Mickey was his glove.

"Where'd ya get this piece of . . . ?" the former Yankee great asked.

Mickey didn't hear exactly what Crosetti said about the glove, and perhaps didn't want to hear. Neither could he bring himself to tell him just how special the glove was. It was a Marty Marion autograph model, designed for infielders and endorsed by the shortstop of the great St. Louis Cardinals teams Mantle and his father had rooted for. The glove had been a Christmas present that his father had given him when he was sixteen and that Mickey had used throughout high school and his two seasons in the minors. "I knew exactly what it cost, for I had yearned after it for a long time," Mickey would recall of that special Christmas gift. "It was $22, about one-third of my father's weekly salary. And I knew, as all poor boys do, exactly what that amount of money meant in a family like ours. Of course, I doted on the glove with an unholy passion, loving even the smell of it, and I caressed and cared for it through the winter as if it had been a holy relic. But most of all, my heart was bursting with the realization of what a sacrifice like this said about my father's love for me and about his pride in my ability."

Crosetti never knew the story and might not have cared. The next morning he presented Mantle with an expensive professional-model glove that Mickey suspected Crosetti had bought with his own money. Mickey put away the glove his father had given him, one of the first of many steps he would take over the next few years in attempts to break his unusually close bond with Mutt, both as father and coach. Of course, plans to convert Mickey into an outfielder were already in the works. Although Mickey didn't realize it at first, the glove Crosetti bought him was a slightly bigger model designed especially for outfielders. Crosetti may also have been sending Mantle a subtle message—perhaps it was time for Mickey to understand that his father had not known all there was to know about playing the game. That same day, Mickey used that glove in an intrasquad game that followed his outfield practice session with Henrich. He played center field, where he made one put-out and committed no mistakes. It was at the plate, however, that Mickey made the writers take notice. He lined a triple to center field in his first at-bat, then drove a home run over the right field fence in his second time up.

"In Mickey Mantle," many of the sportswriters began reporting in their spring training updates, "the Yankees are grooming the successor to Joe DiMaggio."

When Mickey arrived in the Yankee camp in 1951, an uncanny sense of destiny was already at work. The man with the acumen to pick up what was happening was not Stengel or anyone else in the Yankee's upper echelons. Rather, it was a man who for more than half a century worked in virtual anonymity with the Yankees—anonymity except among the Yankee players and the Yankee family. He was Pete Sheehy, the clubhouse attendant, a short, wispy man who later was to be memorialized when the home locker room at Yankee Stadium was named the "Pete Sheehy Clubhouse."

Sheehy recognized an obvious continuity in the Yankees line of succession: Lou Gehrig had assumed the superstar role after Babe Ruth; DiMaggio's debut had come at the end of Gehrig's career; and now Mantle appeared headed to join the Yankees in DiMaggio's last season. Sheehy was known as one of the few people who could joke around with the somber, stoic DiMaggio, who was like an ice-god emotionally. The story goes that DiMaggio once asked Sheehy to check out a red mark on his backside.

"Hey, Pete, take a look at this," Joe said. "Is there a bruise there?"

"Sure there is, Joe," Sheehy replied in a matter-of-fact tone. "It's from all those people kissing your ass."

Among Sheehy's duties was assigning new players' uniforms and, in particular, assigning them uniform numbers that were not already worn by players or retired to honor players like Ruth, Gehrig, and other Yankee legends. It is little known that when DiMaggio joined the team in 1936, Sheehy issued him number eighteen, which had been worn by a tempestuous pitcher named Johnny Allen before he was traded to the Cleveland Indians. Later, sensing that DiMaggio would be the historical successor to the legacy of Ruth and Gehrig, Sheehy changed his uniform to number five. Ruth, of course, had worn number three, and Gehrig had been number four. Perhaps Sheehy's per-spective had been sharpened with anticipation or intuition, but when Mickey arrived at the Yankee instructional camp, Sheehy issued him the only num-ber that made historical sense—six. Mickey would wear this through his fabu-lous spring training and into the first few months of the season before history would take a different twist. "Around this club," Sheehy would say, "you always had the feeling that great things would happen. It started with Ruth and kept going on."

No one contributed more to the puffing of Mantle as the next great Yan-kee than Stengel, whose expectations of Mickey were no lower than those Mutt Mantle had of his son. In one of the early *New York Times* reports from the Yankee instructional camp in 1951, sportswriter James P. Dawson wrote, "Mickey Mantle, rookie from Commerce, Oklahoma, will be the subject of an extensive experiment in the Yankee training campaign. No less an author-ity than Manager Casey Stengel revealed this information today. . . . Stengel said he would work the twenty-year-old [Mickey actually wouldn't turn twenty until the next October] Mantle in center field, and immediately speculation arose over whether the Yanks regarded the rookie as the eventually successor to the great Joe DiMaggio."

"When I came up, Casey told the writers that I was going to be the next Babe Ruth, Lou Gehrig and Joe DiMaggio all rolled up in one," Mantle would later say. "Casey kept bragging on me and the newspapers kept writing it and, of course, I wasn't what Casey said I was. I don't mind admitting that there was incredible pressure on me because of what Casey was saying, and the fans were expecting so much, which I wasn't able to deliver."

Stengel, of course, should have known better than to have placed that kind of burden on a youngster, especially an obviously unsophisticated nineteen-year-old straight out of Class C Joplin. Stengel, however, had an agenda all his own, for which the enormously talented young Mickey Mantle was an answered prayer. Stengel was already sixty-two and childless. His life was his baseball career, which until he started working for the Yankees had been well traveled. He had played in three World Series with the New York Giants and had kicked around with the Dodgers, Pirates, Phillies, and the Braves. Casey had also earned the reputation for being a clown, both as a player and as a coach. Once in a game with Montgomery, Alabama, in the Southern League, Stengel lowered himself in an outfield manhole when no one was looking. As a fly ball sailed in his direction, he magically appeared out of the ground to shag it. His career as a major league manager with Brooklyn and Boston was also filled with clownish antics (and mediocrity) until, to the surprise of many, he landed the Joe DiMaggio–led Yankees in 1949.

That year, and again in 1950, the Yankees won the World Series. In time, Stengel gained the reputation as being what *Sports Illustrated* would call "the most remarkable man in baseball, this old campaigner, this paradoxical personality. . . . There is nobody remotely like him in the game. A superb baseball tactician, a master strategist, his manipulation of his players is based on sound, solid reasoning, the percentages, and his precise knowledge of every man in the league, his strength and weaknesses." But in 1951 Stengel faced the challenge of proving he could win with teams that he had developed and not just with the talent that he had inherited. He also faced the challenge of winning with an aging team. None of Stengel's starting pitchers—Vic Raschi, Eddie Lopat, Allie Reynolds, or Tommy Byrne—was younger than thirty-one. His top reliever, Joe Page, broke down that year in training camp and never pitched for the Yankees again. Henrich, the Yankees' "Old Reliable," had startled the baseball world with the admission that he was three years older than previously thought. He had called it quits before the season. DiMaggio had been plagued with injuries, and the 1951 season would be his last.

The Yankees of the era of manager Joe McCarthy would soon be history. In their place would be a team built around Mantle, Yogi Berra, Whitey Ford, and others who would come to represent the new Stengel era. Once during that spring training, Stengel had looked around at all his promising young players and complained,. "I wish I didn't have so many green peas, but I can't win with my old men. We have to rebuild."

Stengel would never openly admit that he had rushed Mantle. In fact, he could with good cause convince himself that Mickey needed him as much as he needed Mantle. Stengel was aware that Mickey's talent, especially his ability to hit from both sides of the plate, had been developed and honed by Mutt Mantle's dedication to his son; he even joked to some of his coaches that spring that maybe he should add Mickey's father to the Yankee coaching staff. But Stengel knew that Mantle, if he were to ever realize his potential at the major league level, now needed the nurturing and tutelage that only someone like himself could provide.

On a grander scale, Stengel also needed Mantle to help him fulfill what he believed to be his own destiny. A baseball man his entire life, Stengel sensed that he was on the verge of etching his name into a special place in baseball history. When he was named manager of the Yankees in 1949, it had not been without serious second-guessing throughout baseball, especially in New York. The doubt was justified. Stengel had managed the Brooklyn Dodgers and the Boston Braves without much success and a fair amount of second-division mediocrity. The back-to-back pennants and World Championships had gone a long way toward silencing the skeptics, but there were still some who argued that Stengel was little more than a pretentious baseball clown who had had the good fortune of stepping into a manager's dream job. DiMaggio, though at the end of his career, was still DiMaggio. Henrich, Charlie Keller, and DiMaggio formed one of baseball's most acclaimed outfields for the Yankees before and after World War II. The Yankees had an outstanding pitching rotation, anchored by Allie Reynolds and Vic Raschi. Veteran Phil Rizzuto was arguably the best defensive shortstop in the league, and Yogi Berra had emerged as a valuable catcher who could both handle the Yankee pitchers and pose a dangerous offensive threat at the plate. Even with DiMaggio declaring that 1951 would be his final year, Stengel felt confident that with some retooling and tweaking, the Yankees could be contenders for the next few years.

Stengel made no secret that he had patterned his life in baseball, especially his teaching and managing, after that of the great John McGraw. The two most prominent names among baseball managers at this time were McGraw, for whom Stengel had played while with the Giants, and Joe McCarthy, whose managing stints included the great Yankee teams of the 1930s. In fact, the idea of Yankee skippers being "father" to the players, as Stengel at times was prone to try to be, had originated with McCarthy. After McCarthy's resignation in 1946, Joe DiMaggio had lamented, "He was like a father to most of us." McGraw had won four straight pennants, and McCarthy had gone one better by winning four straight pennants and four straight World Series. But it was John McGraw who was Stengel's hero. In 1921, when Stengel joined the Giants, with whom McGraw was in his twentieth season as manager, only the newly emergent Babe Ruth was a more dominant figure in baseball than McGraw. The Giants manager was arrogant, combative, temperamental, and extremely successful. He imposed his personality on the team and obviously on Stengel, who was to boast, "I learned more from McGraw than anybody."

One thing he learned in watching McGraw was that aside from winning championships, very little compares with molding and developing young baseball players, especially when they become some of the best players in the game. John McGraw had always taken great pride in his role in developing Hall of Famer Mel Ott, who as a sixteen-year-old had come to McGraw through one of his baseball friends. McGraw refused to send young Ott to the minor leagues, for fear that some manager down there would change or ruin the youngster's unorthodox swing, which would ultimately become Mel Ott's trademark. Ott had a distinctive batting style, in which he lifted his front foot high off the ground in a kind of exaggerated stride that no batting coach would ever teach. McGraw kept Ott close to him on the bench for the first two seasons, nurturing him and increasing his knowledge of the game before unleashing him. Ott became the National League's home run king of his day, and his success has been heavily credited to McGraw's influence.

Cleveland Indians manager Al Lopez would say admiringly of Stengel, "He took chances with kids, and he won with them. McGraw was that way. He'd stick with a young guy and nurse him along. McGraw and Stengel were both very good with young kids. Casey would sit and talk to them by the hour. He never had any children of his own, so he had a lot to give them. Come to think of it, McGraw had no children of his own either. Just thirty years' worth of baseball teams."

In young Mantle, Stengel saw his own Mel Ott. In Mickey, he felt he had the next great ball player, maybe even the greatest who would ever play the game—and he would be taught by Stengel. "Can you imagine," he would ask a friend, "what McGraw would say if he saw this kid?" Undoubtedly, he would have said the same thing other veteran baseball men were saying. "This is the kind of kid a scout dreams of," said Bill Essick, the Yankee scout who had signed DiMaggio. "You come up with one like this in your lifetime, you're lucky. I had that moment when I got DiMaggio."

Mickey Mantle's 1951 spring training was something out of a fairy tale; it appeared that the torch of Yankee greatness was being passed to him. If he was bothered by anything, it was not by Stengel's expectations or the spotlight of the news media but by the crowds that came to the Yankee spring training games.

On March 10, the Yankees officially opened their 1951 exhibition season against the Cleveland Indians in Tucson. In the clubhouse before his first exhibition game, Mickey was so nervous and frightened that he could barely raise his arms high enough to have caught a ball. DiMaggio rested that day;

Mickey played center field and got two singles off veteran right-hander Early Wynn, as well as a double. The Yankees lost 6–5, but Mantle quickly established himself in the lineup as the team's most consistent hitter off both right- and left-handers, whether they threw curves, sliders, fastballs, or change-ups. In a way, for Mickey, it harked back to batting practice with Mutt and Grandpa Charlie on South Quincy Street. Yankee teammates watched in awe. "I've always had to be sold on these rookies," said veteran first baseman Johnny Hopp, "and at first I thought Mickey was just ahead of the rest in the intrasquad games. But he's still going. He doesn't look like an accident any more."

Mantle was utterly amazing that 1951 spring training season. He hit .402 in the Yankees' exhibition games, and reporters talked of him as the most exciting young player since Jackie Robinson. In his first few spring training games in Arizona, Mickey hit around .400 before the Yankees moved to California for a series of eleven games. Against the Pittsburgh Pirates, Mantle hit home runs from each side of the plate. Branch Rickey, the man who had signed Robinson for the Dodgers, was the general manager of the Pirates in 1951. Rickey could hardly contain himself watching Mickey and, normally conservative with money, did something highly uncharacteristic. He tore a blank check from his checkbook, signed his name, and handed it to Yankee co-owner Dan Topping, who happened to be sitting next to him. "Fill in the figures you want for that boy," said Rickey, "and it's a deal." Topping smiled politely but left the check untouched.

Journalist Dick Schaap would recall that "Mantle was so incredibly good on the field that even the men who praised him wondered, at times, whether they were maintaining their sanity." Jack Orr, who was then covering the Yankees for the *New York Compass*, reflected the general attitude among sportswriters in a column written toward the end of spring training: "Some of us were kicking it around in a compartment on the Yankee train speeding through Texas. We worked over a couple of subjects, but, as always, we got back to the same old one. It was bed time when somebody said: 'Cripes, we've been going for three hours and we've talked about nothing but Mickey Mantle.'" Pitching coach Jim Turner said he never saw anybody who could excite another ballplayer the way Mantle had already done. "When he gets up to hit," he said, "the guys get off the bench and elbow each other out of the way to get a better look. And take a look at the other bench sometimes. I saw

[Pittsburgh Pirates slugger] Ralph Kiner's eyes pop when he first got a look at the kid. [Cleveland Indian] Luke Easter was studying him the other day, and so was [fellow Indian player] Larry Doby. . . . Here's one sure tip-off on how great he is. Watch DiMag when Mantle's hitting. He never takes his eyes off the kid."

Publicly, DiMaggio made all the politically correct comments about the rookie who was being groomed to replace him. "He's a big-league hitter right now. Who does he remind me of? Well, there just haven't been many kids like him. Maybe he has something to learn about catching a fly ball, but that's all. He can do everything else." In San Francisco, Joe's hometown, where the Yankees played an exhibition that spring, DiMaggio was asked if he resented Mantle's moving in on his center field position. "Hell, no," said DiMaggio. "Why should I resent him? If he's good enough to take my job in center, I can always move over to right or left. I haven't helped him much—Henrich takes care of that—but if there is anything I can do to help him, I'm only too willing. Remember what I said back in Phoenix about those Yankee kids and how great they were? Well, the more I see of the ones we have now, the more convinced I am the Yankees won't even miss me."

The California trip was also the Yankees' first West Coast appearance ever, and they were an instant hit. Their two dominant personalities, Stengel and DiMaggio, were Californians. Stengel lived in Glendale and had preceded his tenure with the Yankees by managing the Oakland Oaks to a Pacific Coast League championship in 1948. DiMaggio, a native of San Francisco, had played four years for his hometown Seals before the Yankees bought him in 1936. San Francisco was also home to a slew of the Yankees' infielders: Frank Crosetti, Tony Lazzari, Jerry Coleman, Gil McDougald, and Jackie Jensen. McDougald was another rookie getting Stengel's attention in spring training. Jensen was a twenty-three-year-old who had signed as a forty-thousand-dollar bonus baby after starring in the 1949 Rose Bowl for the University of California. That spring, in addition to moving Mantle to the outfield, Stengel had decided to make Jensen a pitcher. Jensen had previously been tabbed as heir to DiMaggio, although without the buildup and expectations placed on Mickey. But after hitting .171 in forty-five games in 1950, Jensen had raised doubts that he could hit major league pitching. Still, Stengel liked the way the California kid threw and figured he could convert him into a promising pitcher. Those plans, however, were short-lived; Jensen was hit hard in his first spring training start. A few days later, however, Jensen exploded in an offensive outburst that included two home runs. Stengel decided to give him another chance as an outfielder.

Stengel made no secret of favoring the California-bred players during that West Coast swing. "I didn't start," Mantle recalled later. "I was from Oklahoma." But Mantle was playing regularly and hitting well. At Gilmore Stadium, in Hollywood, Mantle drove balls out of the park from both sides of the plate. In a game at Wrigley Field in Los Angeles, Mickey hit a home run against a red brick building next to the right center field bleachers, a feat that had been accomplished only by Babe Ruth and a handful of other players. Mantle ended the California trip with a phenomenal game against the University of Southern California on March 26. At Bovard Field on the USC campus, Mickey slugged two home runs, a triple, and a single. One of those home runs left the ballpark at the 439-foot sign, cleared a football field behind it, and landed an estimated 650 feet from home plate. Everyone was awestruck, and no one could recall having seen a baseball ever hit that far. "It was like a golf ball going into orbit," said legendary USC coach Rod Dedeaux. "It was hit so far it was like it wasn't real. It was a superhuman feat." At the end of the game, USC students who were Mickey's age or older mobbed him, begging for his autograph, almost tipping over the Yankee bus.

"Mickey," said fellow rookie Gil McDougald, "had a spring training like a god."

Johnny Hopp, who would later be one of Mantle's roommates in New York, had the locker next to Mickey that spring and took to calling him "The Champ" because of his incredible streak of power hitting. "You're going to make a million dollars out of this game, the Lord behold," Hopp said to Mickey after one spring game. Mantle simply laughed. He was still unconvinced that he was doing anything special on the field.

Mickey, however, was not without his skeptics. One of them was Stan Isaacs, Orr's fellow staff writer on the *New York Compass;* he was also critical of all the media hoopla being made over Mantle. He wrote, "Since the start of spring training, the typewriter keys out of the training camps have been pounding out one name to the people back home. No matter what paper you read, or what day, you'll get Mickey Mantle, more Mickey Mantle and still more Mickey Mantle. Never in the history of baseball has the game known the wonder to equal this Yankee rookie. Every day there's some other glorious phrase as the baseball writers outdo themselves in attempts to describe the antics of this wonder: 'He's faster than Cobb. . . . he hits with power from both sides of the plate the way Frankie Frisch used to. . . . he takes all the publicity in stride, an unspoiled kid. . . . sure to go down as one of the real greats of baseball. . . . another Mel Ott.'"

Mantle's defensive work in the outfield had improved remarkably under Henrich's tutoring, although the occasional lapse remained. One of Mickey's most embarrassing moments in the outfield came the first time he wore flip-down sunglasses. He still wasn't sure how to flip them down when Ray Boone of the Cleveland Indians slugged a deep fly in an exhibition game. Giving chase, Mickey tugged at the glasses, then tugged again and lost sight of the ball, which hit him squarely between the eyes. Fortunately, Mickey was un-hurt except for his pride. Meanwhile, Stengel kept being second-guessed as to why he had moved Mickey to a completely new position. "Well," the manager told a gathering of Yankee-beat writers in a rambling take on Mantle, "as far as his hitting, he's a big-league outfielder right now. He can run the bases and his speed kinda keeps you on edge. His speed is so big that maybe he can use it in the outfield. And his arm is so strong that he won't have to think out there. All he'll have to do is throw the ball in. He made a lot of errors, I understand, at shortstop, and it might take him a couple of years to make it there. He'd have too many things to learn and if he wasn't playing, I couldn't keep him up there, but would have to send him down to the minors. . . . All I know is that he has me terribly confused, and he's getting me more so every day. I know he's not a big league outfielder yet. He should have more minor league ball under his belt. That's the only logical thing. But this kid isn't log-ical. He's a big league hitter *now*."

When the Yankees returned to Phoenix from their West Coast trip, Mickey surprised everyone with his improved fielding. In a game against the Chicago White Sox, Mantle made a brilliant play, a running catch off a low line drive, following it with a perfect throw to home plate that kept the runner at third base from scoring. "How do you like that?" said an admiring Stengel. "He caught it and threw it the right way, and he's only been taught that play for a week and a half. He's going to be tremendous." The Yankees were rarely impulsive about promoting minor leaguers, much less kids from the low minors. But Casey was now wondering whether this time the old rules applied. "This kid ain't logical," Stengel was telling his coaches. "He's too good. It's very confusing." Stengel was speaking openly about wanting Mantle to stay with the team, knowing full well he was bucking the team's owners and upper management. "The kid's got to play in New York this year," Stengel insisted. "He'll help me."

Yankee general manager George Weiss, however, was just as insistent that Mickey needed another year of seasoning; he wanted to send him to the Yankees' Class AAA team in Kansas City. Mickey himself did not meet George Weiss or owners Del Webb and Dan Topping until April 15, in the smoking lounge of the train the Yankees were taking to Washington, D.C., for the season's opening game against the Senators. Although Mantle was still with the major league team, along with rookies Gil McDougald and Tom Morgan, he was concerned that he would be shipped to the Yankees' minor league team in Kansas City or worse, the Yanks' Class A team in Binghamton, New York. Mickey wanted to play under Harry Craft at Beaumont in the Class AA Texas League. Craft had been his manager in Independence in his first year out of high school and again the next season in Joplin; he had established a special relationship with Mickey, who looked upon his manager as a surrogate father. Mickey carried a strong memory of his father Mutt driving him to Independence and together meeting Craft in his hotel room. Mickey recalled his father passing his son's obedience and loyalty to his new manager, and he imbued the incident with the solemnity of a religious ritual.

"From now on," Mickey remembered his father telling him in Craft's presence, "Mr. Craft is your boss. I want you to do just as he tells you and pay attention to what he says, just as if I were saying it myself. And I want you to play this game just the way you would play it if I were here to watch you. And to act in every way just as if I were right handy."

To Mickey, Harry Craft was the only man who could come close to the pedestal on which he had placed his father. "He was the man, next to my father, whom I wanted to be like," Mickey said. "He taught me many things about baseball but he taught me many more things about being a man. . . . I looked up to him, enjoyed being in his company, and found myself imitating his manner of dress and public deportment occasionally, the way boys will when they find someone they admire."

Childhood friend Nick Ferguson, who by Mickey's 1951 spring training had moved to the West Coast, spent several days with Mantle in Phoenix during that exhibition season. "I don't think [Mickey] was confident at all that he was going to be with the Yankees when the season started," Ferguson recalled. "I remember calling him up then and pretending that I was the general manager from Beaumont and that he had to come and report to Beaumont, and he just said, 'Yessir, yessir.'"

The train the Yankees were taking to Washington was still typical of baseball travel in the early 1950s. Baseball and train rides are part of the fabric of the American culture. For teams, the train trips from city to city were extensions of the clubhouse. Players passed the time on long train rides with card games and baseball banter. The main dining car, with its Art Deco lights and etched-glass dividers, made an immediate impression on Mickey, who was still getting used to walking normally through a speeding train as he followed Casey from car to car toward the bullet-shaped smoking lounge. He practically forced himself to ask, "Casey, can you tell me something? Am I going to play at Beaumont this year?"

Stengel winked. "I think you'll stay with us. When we get back there, just be quiet, and I'll do the talking."

In the smoking lounge, Stengel told Weiss that Mantle was ready to play with the Yankees. Weiss shook his head. He thought Mickey was too young.

"I don't care if he's in diapers," Stengel insisted. "If he's good enough to play for us on a regular basis, I want to keep him."

Webb and Topping both agreed with their manager.

"George," began Webb, "they've been writing so much stuff about Mickey, I feel we have to keep him."

"The thing is, George," said Topping, "we're not opening in New York. We're opening in Washington. After two or three games under his belt, I think he'll be all right."

Mickey swallowed hard, trying to hide his excitement. He was going to be a Yankee. The contract talk that followed was like an afterthought; for Mickey that, at the time, didn't seem to matter. Stengel himself negotiated Mickey's contract with Weiss, a contract that was of course structured in the Yankee's best interests. Under Mickey's rookie contract, he would get $7,500 for the season—which was $2,500 above the minimum but still a bargain for the player being touted as the successor to Ruth and DiMaggio. However, the Yankees' apparent generosity had a catch—if Mickey floundered and was sent to the minors, the Yankees would only be on the hook for the minimum.

Mickey returned to his train seat in a fog. He had just signed his first big league contract. He had achieved his dream of making it to the majors. He had achieved his father's dream. He thought about his father, about Mutt's sacrifices, not only on the long afternoons when he and Grandpa Charlie pitched batting practice to him, but about how his father doted on him—down to saving a piece of his cupcake every day and bringing it home to Mickey in his lunch bucket after work. He looked out at the rain that was falling as the train sped toward Washington, D.C., and tears welled in his eyes.

When he heard the news the next day in Commerce, Oklahoma, an exuberantly proud Mutt Mantle accepted congratulations from some of his fellow miners. "Mickey did it, Mickey's a major league ball player," Mutt kept repeating. There was pride, and there was relief. Mickey's dream—and Mutt's, too—now seemed so close that they could hardly fail to grasp it.

In 1950, nine months before Mickey Mantle's sensational spring training camp, North Korean military forces crossed the thirty-eighth parallel, dividing North and South Korea, an invasion that precipitated the entry of the United States into the Korean War. The United States began drafting young men to strengthen both its peacetime army and to provide forces for the American presence in Korea. While the draft was not as extensive as it had been during World War II, its impact was felt across the country, even in baseball. Yankee pitcher Whitey Ford was drafted immediately after the 1950 World Series and was lost to the team for two seasons. Infielder Billy Martin had also been drafted, although he had been discharged after six months when he claimed family financial hardship—after which the army changed its mind, recalling Martin to duty. In December of that year, Mickey himself was called by the Ottawa County draft board in Oklahoma to undergo his preinduction physical examination. However, his local draft board ruled that he was physically unfit for military service because of the chronic osteomyelitis in his left leg. His official classification for the draft was 4-F, which during World War II had been a subject of mild shame and curiosity among Americans. Seemingly perfectly fit young men were expected by society to put in their required military duty—"military obligation" it came to be called—and a sense of social bewilderment surrounded those who were not in the service.

America in the mid-twentieth century was intensely patriotic, fueled by what became known as "McCarthyism"—the paranoia created by Senator Joseph McCarthy's charges that the country was being infiltrated by communists. Already, a group of writers and actors in Hollywood had been blacklisted by the film industry after being targeted in a congressional "un-American activities" inquisition that attempted to ferret out communists in Tinseltown. According to critics like Victor Navasky, the House Un-American Activities Committee helped create a climate in which fewer films with "social themes" were made. Paranoia suspicions of "un-American activities" reached such a peak that in a 1951 speech President Harry S Truman would say, "This malicious propaganda has gone so far that on the Fourth of July, over in Madison, Wisconsin, people were afraid to say they believed in the Declaration of Independence. A hundred and twelve people were asked to sign a petition that contained nothing except quotations from the Declaration of Independence and the Bill of Rights. One hundred and eleven of these people refused to sign that paper—many of them because they were afraid that it was some kind of subversive document and that they would lose their jobs or be called Communists. Can you imagine finding 112 people in the capital of Wisconsin that didn't know what the Declaration of Independence and Bill of Rights provided? I can't imagine it."

In this climate, military service had become a sad litmus test for what McCarthy biographer Richard H. Rovere would call a "militant patriotism" that had swept the country. In its January 1, 1951, issue, *Time* magazine had celebrated the American soldier as its "Man of the Year" for 1950. *Time* praised the G.I. for his valiant defense against communism—a political force that was trying to "turn the worldwide forces set free by U.S. progress back into the old channels of slavery."

With Mickey emerging from the Yankees' spring training as the new American baseball hero, questions inevitably were asked as to why this nineteen-year-old athletic wonder had not yet done his military duty. Mantle had first become aware of the intense public interest in his draft status in the fall of 1950, upon returning home from his September stint with the Yankees and a fall instructional camp in Phoenix. As in all wars, the toll of casualties and deaths was heaviest on working-class families. In Mickey's hometown, that burden was shouldered by the sons of miners, many of them lifelong friends of the Mantles. Mickey had no illusions about his own military obligation. Like most teenage boys of that time, he had spoken about it with his friends with the same enthusiasm as other small-town young men seeking to see the outside world. Mutt Mantle, on the other hand, worried about the impact going into the military would have upon Mickey's career and hoped that his son might have a chance to make the big leagues before doing his military duty. Better still, knowing Mickey's medical history, Mutt had wondered whether he might not be exempted from military service altogether. However, it was not something he wanted to make an issue of. No one at the time dared boast that his or her son was classified 4-F, a military reject. One of the few people Mutt Mantle had spoken to about Mickey was Joe Payton, a linotype operator at the Miami (Oklahoma) *Daily News Record,* who also happened to be a member of the Ottawa County draft board. Payton had hinted to Mutt that Mickey would likely be rejected for service because of the osteomyelitis and suggested that he have copies of all his medical and hospital records ready the day he was called for his preinduction physical examination.

Mutt, however, kept this from Mickey until late one afternoon that November, when he said to his son, "By the way, Mickey, you got a postcard from Joe Payton today. He wants you to drop around for an examination in a couple of weeks."

Mickey showed up for his examination with a set of X rays of his left leg and a copy of his medical history. The records bore out that Mantle had been hospitalized for extensive treatment of osteomyelitis in 1946 and again for a flare-up in 1947. The grandfatherly doctor who examined him was convinced. Osteomyelitis happened to be one of the medical conditions that the government had made automatic grounds for exclusion from all branches of the military. Even if the disease had been arrested, it could recur at any time. If that were to happen while in the service, the government would be liable for a lifetime disability pension—conceivably hundreds of thousands of dollars in pension payments and medical bills. A month later, the draft board notified Mickey that he had been classified 4-F and was exempt from military service.

During the following spring of 1951, however, Mickey Mantle found that he was no longer simply the unassuming youngster from Commerce, Oklahoma. The news coverage of the Yankees' spring training in Phoenix and the team's exhibition season had focused heavily on the young Yankee phenom, whose arrival, in the eyes of some fans, had led the heroic DiMaggio to announce that he would retire at the end of the season. Of course, DiMaggio's retirement and Mantle's arrival were coincidental. DiMaggio's announcement on March 2 that he would not be back the following year had long been anticipated, in the wake of his mounting injuries and his slow, painful recoveries. At the end of Mantle's triumphant showing on the Yankees' exhibition swing to the West Coast, Mickey returned to the team's spring training facility in Phoenix to find a letter from his father and learn that his draft board wanted him to take another physical examination.

"My dad wrote . . . that a lot of people were asking why I wasn't soldiering in Korea," Mantle recalled. "To be candid, the war was the furthest thing from my mind. Certainly I knew about the mounting casualties, the talk going around that General [Douglas] MacArthur was planning an all-out fight against Communism, even thinking of dropping an atomic bomb on China. Well, I could understand how some people felt, especially those who resented seeing young, apparently healthy guys hitting baseballs while their own sons and husbands were being killed in battle."

Mickey stayed with the Yankees through the last leg of the exhibition season, which included games in Texas, where his family and girlfriend Merlyn Johnson showed up to see him. Mantle hit his sixth home run of the spring that day, along with a double and a single. In Kansas City, Mutt met him and drove him back to take his physical examination. The countless drives like this one that they had made together over the years to Mickey's games or to St. Louis for Cardinals games, were vital elements in Mantle's relationship with his father. They were filled with conversation about baseball and with instruction that Mutt was always giving Mickey. This had continued even when Mickey became a professional. Steve Kraly, one of Mantle's minor league roommates, remembered seeing Mutt at most of Mickey's games with the Joplin Miners in 1950. Mutt, according to Kraly, was one of Mickey's toughest critics, even when he was tearing up the league's pitching and hitting around .400 for most of that season. On this drive, Mutt offered Mickey advice, criticism, and encouragement for his upcoming season. When Mickey arrived in Miami, Oklahoma, he learned that his local draft board, concerned about the public perception of favoritism for a local hero, had turned the case over to the state induction center in Tulsa. Mickey and Mutt got back in the car and continued their drive.

In his biography of Casey Stengel, author Robert W. Creamer claims that the Yankee organization, seeking to quell growing criticism about Mickey's 4-F status, went so far as to ask the Oklahoma draft board to reexamine Mantle's case. Indeed, no one was more aware of the potential public backlash over Mickey's draft status than the Yankee brass, especially general manager George Weiss, who soon enough would develop a protective attitude toward Mantle. Weiss had an aristocratic gentility about him, and he saw Mickey as a naïve, vulnerable country boy completely out of place in the big city. Weiss would later help bail Mantle out of business deals with hustlers who had taken advantage of him. He would also unsuccessfully attempt to discourage Mickey's friendship with Billy Martin, believing Martin to be a negative influence over the young star. It had been Weiss, too, who had felt strongly that the Yankee's nineteen-year-old phenom needed another year in the minors and opposed his staying with the Yankees that season. Even if Mantle had to do two years of military service, Weiss figured, in 1953 Mickey would be twenty-one years old and better able emotionally to deal with the pressures of New York and the majors. So with the public clamor over the draft building, it was Weiss who apparently attempted to defuse the controversy by personally contacting the country's Selective Service System and asking that Mantle be given another physical examination. According to Ottawa County draft board member Joe Payton, the decision to reexamine Mickey's case was made by Lewis Hershey, director of the Selective Service System, and by Mantle's own draft board in Miami, Oklahoma, which had come under a flood of criticism.

Hershey and the Selective Service had been completely unprepared for the Korean War and the subsequent manpower requirements of the military. The country's armed forces needed an additional half a million men, and it was the job of the Selective Service to conscript these from among the eligible young men in America. Hershey was the central figure in the American military draft for the three decades spanning the U.S. involvement in World War II, Korea, and Vietnam. Soon after the start of the Korean War, Hershey had come under criticism around the country, and especially with some congressional leaders, over the operation of the country's military draft. Hershey wanted to relax standards that were disqualifying an unusually large number of men on the basis of physical and mental conditions—"We are missing some of the fighters by these tests." At the time, the rejection rate was over 35 percent of the 1,555,198 men examined between July 1950 and June 1951. Clearly, Mantle had plenty of company. Appearing before a congressional committee at one point, Hershey raised eyebrows when he claimed that the high number of rejections meant that the Selective Service might soon have to begin drafting youngsters as soon as they turned eighteen, as well as drafting World War II veterans and implementing a special draft for physicians.

Mantle and other young men had become pawns in a power game being played by the ambitious Selective Service director, a game in which he could call upon the country's sense of overzealous patriotism. In his biography of

Hershey, Texas Tech University history professor George Q. Flynn concludes that "the Selective Service System had provided more men than the army could use during the initial Korean buildup." Moreover, Hershey, a professional soldier as well as a bureaucrat and politician, had the American public on his side. A Gallup poll at the time reported that almost three-fourths of the public supported his call for a stronger draft system. However, Hershey could not completely sell his manpower-crisis theory to President Truman and the Congress. After the early demand for soldiers, the army began cutting back on calls for draftees and recruits. Nevertheless, Hershey continued his campaign against what he considered overly rigorous selection. The Mantle case was a classic example. Already rejected once, at Hershey's instigation he was being called back for another physical examination, and he would be called back again twice more. It was clear that although he publicly supported the independence of local draft boards, Hershey was actively involved in their decisions. It reached the point the American Legion accused Hershey of exerting undue political pressure to override a local board decision. Hershey himself was hardly unbiased on the issue of seemingly fit young men being exempted from military duty for medical reasons. One of his sons, Capt. Gilbert Hershey, had received a severe stomach wound in combat in Korea and almost died.

In 1951, at the height of American patriotism and with the war raging in Korea, to question the politics of the Selective Service System would have been almost as foolish as to question the role of baseball as America's pastime. The two were linked. Already the impact of the war was being felt by major league teams, especially those with draft-eligible players. In the home stretch of the 1950 National League pennant race, the Philadelphia Phillies lost number-two pitcher Curt Simmons when his Pennsylvania National Guard unit was mobilized. Simmons had already won seventeen games when he was activated, and his loss almost cost the Phillies "Whiz Kids" the pennant. Although furloughed to attend the World Series, Simmons wasn't activated; he watched as the Yankees won their second straight championship in four games.

However, fears that the Korean War would affect baseball the way World War II had proved unfounded. No large-scale call-up ever took place, and teams lost only one or two players each. Baseball's biggest loss may have been Boston Red Sox outfielder Ted Williams, a World War II veteran aviator, whose Marine Corps Reserve unit was called up. Williams completed thirty-eight combat missions in Korea, missing most of the 1952 season and half of 1953 before being discharged. Without Williams, the Red Sox plunged to sixth place in 1952. The Yankees were without Whitey Ford in 1952 and 1953, and without second baseman Billy Martin in 1954. In the National League, two of the biggest losses to the Korean War were Willie Mays of the New York Giants and right-hander Don Newcombe of the Dodgers, for 1952 and 1953.

Ironically, the only public criticism from the baseball world of the Selective Service System and its seemingly selective targeting of young baseball stars came from one of the game's leading spokesmen and veterans—Ted Williams. When Dodger left-hander Johnny Podres was drafted not long after pitching Brooklyn to its 1955 World Series championship over the Yankees, Williams blasted the "gutless" draft board, politicians, and media for allowing Podres to be shanghaied. "Podres is paying the penalty for being a star," he told reporters. "If Podres had lost those World Series games, he probably would still be with the Dodgers. But when Podres became a hero in the World Series, some politician said, 'Why isn't a big strong kid like that in the Army?' The draft boards didn't have the guts to oppose the politicians, and the sportswriters are equally to blame because they didn't take up for him."

Williams had resented being called back to active duty for the Korean War, although he was publicly gracious about doing his patriotic duty. He felt that the only reason he and Jerry Coleman of the Yankees had been called up in 1952 was for their publicity value. Another time, in a controversial interview that helped eventually sour his relationship with the Boston sportswriters, Williams criticized Presidents Truman and Eisenhower, along with Republican senator Robert A. Taft, as "phony politicians." Said Williams, "If the [Marines] had called back everyone in the same category as me, I'd have no beef, but they didn't. They picked on me because I was well known. . . . I used to respect Senator Taft. I thought he was a wonderful man. But he was just a gutless politician. A friend of mine was recalled for Korea. He knew Taft. He asked him to help him get deferred. Do you know what Senator Taft told my friend? He said, 'I can't touch you. You're pretty well known where you live. If you were just another guy [then I would be] able to help you.' Now do you know why I think politicians are gutless?"

Of course, the drafting of major league baseball players to the military during wartime was misleading. With the exception of Ted Williams and a few others, most players never saw combat. Instead, during the Korean War most of the professional ballplayers drafted wound up playing baseball on military teams, both stateside and overseas. The 1951 Fort Myers, Virginia, team boasted pitchers Johnny Antonelli of the Braves and Bob Purkey of the Giants.

The 1953 all-army champions at Fort Belvoir, Virginia, included shortstop Dick Groat of the Pirates and pitcher Tom Poholsky of the Cardinals. According to *Total Baseball,* only one former big leaguer lost his life in combat in the Korean War: Bob Neighbors, an air force major, was lost in a mission over North Korea in August 1952. He had played in seven games for the St. Louis Browns in 1939.

All of this suggests that the public furor over Mantle serving his country and performing his military obligation may have been illusory. Mickey, in all likelihood, would have wound up playing on one of the service teams, as his friend Billy Martin did during one of his stints in the army (in 1954, Martin was player-manager of his post team at Fort Carson, Colorado). But a realistic portrayal of what most drafted ballplayers were doing to serve their country was not what the American public was getting from the super-patriot propaganda of the early 1950s. Unfortunately for Mantle in 1951, as the anointed successor to Ruth and DiMaggio, with the spring training exploits to prove it, he had become virtually a walking expression of the American culture's irrationality, as he would be throughout his career and even beyond. He was loved for what America thought he should be—a personification of the country's own aspirations; he was vilified for his human vulnerability that kept him from realizing those expectations. For Mickey, though he did not realize it, this was yet one more in a set of personal crises, crises touching on a common philosophical issue—the fluidity of human life bumping up against man-made categories, ideologies as masks that a vacillating public adopts to manipulate or delude.

Mantle would drive the point home in his own way: "Millions of people didn't seem concerned one way or another about the fate of a kid ballplayer not yet old enough to vote. Still I had gotten an incredible amount of publicity, and the crank mail really poured into Washington."

In Tulsa, with the start of his rookie season only days away, Mantle underwent his physical examination; three days later he learned that he had been rejected again. A few writers covering the Yankees sought out the advice of a private physician to explain why osteomyelitis was so debilitating that it could cause rejection for military duty. "[Osteomyelitis] never goes away," the writers were told. "It just lies there dormant. The Army would never take a chance on something like that." Mantle, meanwhile, was already on a plane to New York to rejoin the Yankees.

In 1953 Mantle would again fail a draft physical examination, this time being ruled unfit for service not only because of the osteomyelitis of the left leg but also because of the ligament damage he had suffered in his right leg in the 1951 World Series.

"Mantle began to receive vituperative hate mail and as the debate raged around him, the shy, uncommunicative boy shrunk deeper and deeper into his shell of silence," Yankee historian Peter Golenbock wrote in *Dynasty, The New York Yankees, 1949–1964.* "In private Mantle would ask, 'Would they rather have a son in the Army or a son with osteomyelitis?' Cries of 'draft dodger,' 'coward,' and 'commie' were often shouted at him from the stands when he batted." In Chicago, fans threw firecrackers at Mantle, leading Stengel to threaten to pull the Yankees from the field. The criticism of Mickey's draft-exempt status would not subside, even with news that he had failed his second physical examination. In fact, it seemed that the hate mail and public taunts increased the more the legitimacy of his draft exemption was mentioned, throughout the rest of the decade.

Yankee infielder Jerry Coleman, who missed most of the 1952 and 1953 seasons because of military service, recalled that the abuse Mantle endured would have been intolerable for most others. "When I came back from Korea," he later said, "I heard people in the stands yelling at him, calling him a 4-F coward, awful things. Mantle would have paid his way to go to Korea. And yet people shouted those things, things that went right to a man's masculinity. If they had said those things to me, I think I would have killed somebody. But he never said a word. Mickey never complained about anything. But it had to bother him. It had to make him wonder: What kind of people would say those things? I've often wondered if it affected the way he acted toward people outside baseball."

According to a report filed with the Federal Bureau of Investigation, at one point Mantle received a threatening letter from someone who apparently had lost a son in the military and believed Mickey was a draft dodger. Sent to Mantle at Cleveland's Municipal Stadium, the letter read, "I had a son that was drafted with a bad leg & bad eyes. He got killed but a rotten draft dodger that could run like you gets turned down. I have a gun with microscopic [telescopic] lenses and I'm going to get you thru both of your knees and it's going to happen soon." Mantle and the Yankees took the threat to federal authorities, who traced the letter back to Tonawanda, New York, but the investigation stalled when the bureau failed to come up with any suspects. In its report, the FBI special agent on the case wrote, "Mantle stated that he does not have any suspects as to the sender of the letter and, as far as he can recall, he does not have any acquaintances in Tonawanda, New York. He stated that this is the first threatening letter that he has ever received and he is quite concerned about it. Mantle stated that he has been thinking about the letter and about getting shot by some crank and, in his opinion, if he were to get shot it would be in Yankee Stadium, as some person could stand on the rooftop on one of the buildings surrounding Yankee Stadium and take a shot at him. Mantle stated that he does receive a lot of fan mail, both laudatory and critical, but this is the first really bad or disturbing letter which he has ever received." Mantle had yet to build up the thick skin he would need over the coming years.

Flying into New York for the spring exhibition finale against the Brooklyn Dodgers, Mickey came face to face with the animosity that had begun to build up over his draft status in even the first few weeks of his major league career. He opened a newspaper and there in the sports page, it hit him: "So Mantle has osteomyelitis," a columnist had written. "What's the big deal? He doesn't have to *kick* anybody in Korea."

"I can't knock the system," Mantle would later say. "It's democracy and I wouldn't [criticize] anything that happened to me in those years, even though my goal and my dad's dream of me playing in the majors was on the line. I thought they'd judged me fair and square when the Tulsa [draft] board ruled that anyone having osteomyelitis would be automatically disqualified for military service. But on that plane coming into New York for the preseason Yankee-Dodger windup, I discovered that the controversy wasn't over."

Bewildered by the controversy swirling around him, Mantle found himself at war with the phantoms and prejudice of misguided national pride. Just as everything in popular culture throbs with impermanence, so too the public consciousness that once had worshipped Ruth and DiMaggio now looked at Mantle as the heretical embodiment of a flawed heroism it could not understand or accept, and that would, in Mickey and others to come, gnaw away at and eventually transform the way America looked at itself.

Mickey Mantle, on his father Mutt's lap in 1933. *The Mickey Mantle Museum, Cooperstown, N.Y., and Mr. Tom Catal and Mr. Andrew Vilacky*

Mick speaks on the telephone under the watchful eye of his mother Lovell in 1952. Mickey's 1951 World Series share was the down payment on a house for his parents, complete with their own telephone. *The Mickey Mantle Museum, Cooperstown, N.Y., and Mr. Tom Catal and Mr. Andrew Vilacky*

Mickey's high school photograph. Mantle would actually miss his own graduation to compete in a game under the eye of a Yankee's scout, and signed his first contract that same weekend after 15 minutes of negotiation. *The Mickey Mantle Museum, Cooperstown, N.Y., and Mr. Tom Catal and Mr. Andrew Vilacky*

Mickey chats with his father and teammate Cliff Mapes outside an Oklahoma mine. *The Mickey Mantle Museum, Cooperstown, N.Y., and Mr. Tom Catal and Mr. Andrew Vilacky*

Mick (right) sits with Nick Ferguson (left) and coach Barney Barnett (center) of the Whiz Kids in 1948. It was while Mantle was with the Whiz Kids that Yankee scout Tom Greenwade first laid eyes on him. *The Mickey Mantle Museum, Cooperstown, N.Y., and Mr. Tom Catal and Mr. Andrew Vilacky*

Mickey, Merlyn, and Mutt at an exhibition game in Dallas in 1951. *The Mickey Mantle Museum, Cooperstown, N.Y., and Mr. Tom Catal and Mr. Andrew Vilacky*

Mickey poses for the picture which would be used for his subsequently famous 1951 Bowman rookie card. *The Mickey Mantle Museum, Cooperstown, N.Y., and Mr. Tom Catal and Mr. Andrew Vilacky*

Mickey crosses the plate after connecting on a home run at Ebbets Field prior to the 1951 regular season. Note number 7 congratulating Mickey on the feat. Mantle wore number 6 when he first started with the Yankees, switching to number 7 only after he returned from his demotion to the minors. *The Mickey Mantle Museum, Cooperstown, N.Y., and Mr. Tom Catal and Mr. Andrew Vilacky*

PART TWO

HEROES AND REBELS

6

When he arrived in New York as a nineteen-year-old kid, Mickey Mantle was the embodiment of what baseball in springtime can evoke, a symbol of innocence and hope. For the America that existed then—and the America that nostalgia subsequently established in the national consciousness—Mickey was the eternal glory of youth. He was a country boy, innocent of the temptations of an urban jungle that was already becoming a predominant feature of American life. To be sure, that was the New Yorker's perspective, because in the eyes of his fellow Oklahomans, Mantle's arrival in New York was that of a hero venturing forth from the world of common into a region of glamour, splendor, and fabulous forces. Mantle's ability as a baseball player was as innate as his essential goodness. Yet he had long been warned by his watchful father that he couldn't rely solely on his gift alone, or he would fail.

Mickey himself would later say that when he arrived in New York his view of the world wasn't much wider than the strike zone. "My childhood was part of what made me popular with the fans in New York and elsewhere," he said. "I was a classic country bumpkin, who came to the big city carrying a cardboard suitcase and with a wardrobe of two pairs of slacks and a pastel-colored sports coat."

Just how shy *was* Mickey? That spring, the Yankees completed their preseason with a weekend exhibition series against the Brooklyn Dodgers at Ebbets Field. In the final game of the exhibition season Mantle had four hits, finishing the spring with a .402 average, nine home runs, and thirty-one runs batted in (RBIs). The Yankees total attendance for the spring, 278,880, was a new record. After the Saturday game at Ebbets Field, April 14, Casey Stengel insisted that the entire team attend Whitey Ford's wedding reception. Ford, on furlough from the army, had been married that Saturday afternoon, and a bus carrying the Yankees showed up at the reception at Donahue's bar in Astoria, in Queens. Every player went to the reception except Mickey, who remained on the bus the entire time, feeling too shy and out of place even to make an appearance. Later that evening, Whitey and his bride Joan accompanied the players back to the bus, where the Yankee left-hander was introduced to Mickey for the first time.

"I remember my impression of him the first time I met him," Whitey later said. "I thought, 'What a hayseed.'"

Yogi Berra had a similar recollection. "I remember he was a big, scared kid who we already knew could hit the ball out of sight. You know something else I remember? Even when he was a kid, we already knew he was a helluva guy."

On opening day at Yankee Stadium, Mickey was flabbergasted at the sight of the towering triple-deck stands, which were already filling up. He had been to Yankee Stadium before, when he joined the team for the final two weeks of the previous season. Mickey had been ineligible for the Series roster, but at general manager George Weiss's invitation he had attended the first two games of the Yankees' 1950 World Series against the Philadelphia Phillies. He had been joined in New York by his mother and father, the twins Roy and Ray, and his girlfriend Merlyn in what Mickey was to remember as "a visit to paradise." But on opening day of the 1951 season, Mickey stared around the stadium for the first time from the playing field. As he studied the famous façade above the upper deck, Yogi Berra came up behind him and playfully snarled, "Hey, what kind of an opening day crowd is this? There's no people here." Mickey had quickly come to realize that the Yankee catcher didn't say things so much as growl them out. He stared at Yogi, then understood he was joking. Jim Turner, one of the coaches, came up to them. "How many people watched you play at Joplin last year?" he asked Mickey.

"I'd say about 55,000 all season," he answered.

"Well, take a good look," said Turner. "We got about 45,000 here today for one game—almost as many people as saw you in Joplin all year."

Mantle gulped. "No!" he muttered.

"Yes," said Turner, trying to put Mickey at ease. "And most of them came to see what you look like."

After getting his draft physical, Mantle had flown from Oklahoma to New York, just in time for the exhibition game with the Dodgers in Ebbets Field on the Saturday before the season opener. Stengel had penciled him into the lineup in right field and, for good measure, walked him out there to show him the unusual concrete barrier, in front of which Stengel himself had played in 1914, when Ebbets Field first opened. The cement bevel near the ground could make a ball rebound oddly; Stengel also wanted him to be aware that a ball hit off of the scoreboard above the wall could drop straight down.

"Now when I played out here . . ." Stengel said, stopping abruptly at the sight of Mantle looking at him with astonishment.

"*You* played out here?" Mickey asked.

Stengel returned to the dugout in stitches. "Boy never saw concrete before," he told the sportswriters waiting for him. "I told him not to worry about it, that I never had no trouble with it, and I played that wall for six years. He don't believe what I'm telling him. I guess he thinks that I was born at the age of sixty-two and started managing immediately."

Mantle played Ebbets Field's tricky right field flawlessly that afternoon, but his bat had again raised expectations. He homered over the scoreboard Stengel had warned him about, then added three other hits that finished his incredible spring exhibition season with a .402 batting average. He went on to Washington with the Yankees for their season opener, signing his first big-league contract on the train to the nation's capital. When the opening series against the Senators was rained out, the Yankees returned to New York, where the opener against the Red Sox would also be Mantle's major league debut. After Mickey's sensational spring, Stengel was indeed beginning to look like another McGraw. The opening day lineup he posted in the dugout had Mantle playing right field and batting third, behind left fielder Jackie Jensen and shortstop Phil Rizzuto, and ahead of DiMaggio, who was batting in the cleanup slot. Berra was batting fifth, first baseman Johnny Mize sixth, followed by third baseman Billy Johnson, second baseman Jerry Coleman, and starting pitcher Vic Raschi.

An hour and a half before the game, sportswriter Red Smith saw Mantle looking nervously into the stands from the top step of the Yankees' dugout. From the bench, Smith would recall, Stengel could see Mickey only from the chest down, but he noticed that the sole of one of his cleats had torn loose. The Yankee skipper got up to talk to Mickey and then returned shaking his head. "He don't care much about the big leagues, does he?" Stengel said. "He's gonna play in them shoes."

"Who is he?" asked a visitor in the dugout who hadn't seen Mantle that spring.

"Why, he's that kid of mine," said Stengel.

"That's Mantle?"

"Yeah. I asked him didn't he have any better shoes, and he said he had a new pair but they're a little too big."

The visitor chuckled along with Stengel. "He's waiting for an important occasion to wear the new ones."

As he waited to take the field at Yankee Stadium for the first time in his career, Mickey couldn't keep his eyes off Ted Williams in the Boston dugout. DiMaggio had been Mantle's hero growing up, but Williams was still in his prime, and would continue to be throughout the 1950s. Military service had taken away a couple of seasons in the 1940s. Williams was also coming off an ill-fated 1950 season, in which he had broken his left elbow in the All-Star game and played only eighty-nine games. At age thirty-two, Williams was already being acknowledged among his peers as the game's consummate hitter. That reputation was what Williams lived for. As a rookie in 1939, when Mickey was not yet eight years old, Williams had laid out what he wanted his epitaph to be. "All I want out of life," he had said, "is that when I walk down the street folks will say, 'There goes the greatest hitter who ever lived.'" Bernard Malamud would appropriate the line and change it ever so slightly— "Sometimes when I walk down the street I bet people will say there goes Roy Hobbs, the best there ever was in the game"—for the mythical slugger in *The Natural,* published in 1952. The 1951 season would mark the tenth anniversary of the year Williams had become the last major leaguer to hit .400. Williams had already won Triple Crowns in 1942 and 1947; he would go on to hit 521 home runs and a career .344 average.

The first time Mantle had seen Williams play in person had been in September of 1950, when he had been brought up for two weeks after the end of his season at Joplin. "I saw Ted hit two home runs off Vic Raschi," recalled Mickey, "and I became convinced he was the greatest hitter I'd ever seen." Mantle had another reason that opening day for not being able to take his eyes off Williams. Three players had been in the spotlight that spring: DiMaggio, who was playing what would be his last season; Mantle for his magnificent exhibition season; and Williams for his controversial refusal to play in exhibitions. During spring training just a few weeks earlier, Williams had set off yet another of the many disputes in his career by publicly criticizing the spirit of the Boston Red Sox fans while praising that of the Yankees. Now, at Yankee Stadium, Williams was the object of stares and admiration from fans and players alike.

There was a telling incident just before the game began. Williams came over to the Yankee dugout to greet DiMaggio; Mickey was standing by his side, awed and nervous. Instead of introducing the rookie, DiMaggio said nothing, leaving it to Williams to acquaint himself: "You must be Mick." Unlike Mantle when he later became a veteran, DiMaggio wasn't one to grant favors to rookies, especially one who was being hailed as his successor.

As Mantle watched Williams and DiMaggio talk, a couple of other sportswriters nearby were talking to Bill Dickey, the former Yankee catcher and manager who was now one of Stengel's coaches. They all turned to look at Mantle and one of the writers said, "Gosh, I envy him. Nineteen years old and starting out as a Yankee!"

"He's green," said Dickey, "but he's got to be great. All that power, a switch-hitter and he runs like a striped ape. If he drags a bunt past the pitcher, he's on base. I think he's the fastest man I ever saw with the Yankees. But he's green in the outfield. He was at shortstop last year."

"Gosh, Bill," said the writer, "do you realize you were in the big leagues before he was born?"

"He was born in 1932," said Dickey, "and that was the year I played my first World Series."

Half an hour later, after the traditional opening-day speeches at home plate, Whitey Ford walked out to the mound wearing his army uniform and threw the first pitch.

The Red Sox's Dom DiMaggio opened the game with a single to right field, which Mickey fielded cleanly and returned to second base. At the plate, Mantle broke his bat on the first major league pitch he saw and almost ran out the infield grounder. He popped up in his second at-bat. He came to the plate for the third time in the sixth inning with the Yankees leading 2–0, with nobody out and runners at first and third. Waiting on deck, DiMaggio called Mantle aside and for one of the few times in the only season in which their paths were to cross, spoke to him. Mantle nodded, stepped to the plate, and got his first major league hit. Batting right-handed, Mickey hit a fastball off lefty Bill Wright past the outstretched glove of shortstop Johnny Pesky into left field, driving in the runner from third base. Mantle scored later in the inning, as the Yankees went on to win, 5–0. The next day, Mickey drove in two runs in another Yankee victory. He had three hits in five at-bats a few games later—and was suddenly off to a .320 start.

Mantle's transition to life in New York outside of Yankee Stadium was another matter. Mickey was overwhelmed by New York, especially living alone as he did those first few weeks at the Concourse Plaza Hotel in the Bronx, just a few blocks from Yankee Stadium. Mantle spent most nights reading the sports pages from the various New York newspapers and staring at the walls thinking about the next day's game. Sometimes he would walk down to a diner where, unrecognized by anyone, he would sip on a cup of coffee or eat a hamburger while listening to die-hard Yankee fans talk about their team. Every once in a while he would walk outside the Concourse and watch the local stickballers playing on 162nd Street and Sheridan Avenue.

One of those stickball players, Stephen Swid, recalled that time years later. "The Concourse Plaza was *the* hotel in the Bronx during the '40s and '50s. Visiting teams and Yankee ball players who weren't married would stay at the hotel. Every once in a while one of the players would come down and join in one of our games. Now back then, you'd measure a guy by how many sewers he could hit the ball. Each sewer [manhole cover] was ninety feet apart. I was a two-and-a-half-sewer guy, not bad at all. A really big hitter would be a three-sewer guy. One day Mickey Mantle came down. We gave him a bat and pitched in. He swung and missed, swung, and missed again. A few more swings, a few more misses. Finally he connected. Boom. It was the deepest shot any of us ever saw, more than four sewers. That was it—the news spread all over the neighborhood and then throughout the Bronx: Mickey Mantle was a four sewer man!"

However, in those first weeks of his rookie season in New York, Mantle also became easy prey for con men and scam artists. From one hustler Mantle bought what he thought was two hundred dollars' worth of sweaters for thirty dollars, only to learn that they were made of a cheap, highly flammable material. But possibly the worst deal Mickey got himself into was with a Broadway opportunist named Alan Savitt, who in the early weeks of the season convinced Mantle that he needed him as his agent. Savitt promised Mantle he could get him fifty thousand dollars a year in endorsements and personal appearances, which they would split fifty-fifty. Mickey had no experience with agents. His father, after all, had naively undersold his own son's talents to Tom Greenwade and the Yankees without so much as waiting to see what other clubs offered. Mickey was also too shy to broach the topic with his teammates. The best friend Mantle had in those early weeks was teammate Hank Bauer, who in Mickey's first days in New York had taken him out shopping and bought him two suits with his own money. Bauer and several other Yankee players were represented by Frank Scott, who had been the team's traveling secretary through the late 1940s. Bauer soon learned about Mickey's deal and enlisted both Scott and the Yankee front office in trying to extricate Mickey from the deal with Savitt. Bauer and Scott even developed a clever plan for Scott to seek out Mickey as a client. For a country rookie, however, Mickey could be unusually stubborn.

"I've got bad news for you," Mantle told Scott when he approached Mickey about representing him. "This fellow wants to be my agent, and he's giving me a contract that guarantees me $50,000 a year."

Although skeptical, Scott said he couldn't offer any guarantees but would only take 10 percent, which was a more typical agent's fee. Scott also advised Mickey to have the Yankees' lawyers read over the contract. Mickey, however, was naïve enough to believe he had somehow latched onto a better deal than anyone else had. When Scott again ran into Mantle a few days later, Mickey informed him he had signed the contract.

"Did you take it to the Yankee lawyers?" Scott asked.

"Nope," said Mickey, confidently. "I didn't have to. This fellow had a lawyer for me."

Mickey had been conned, and this wasn't the end of it. Although he had become engaged to Merlyn back in Commerce, in New York he had started dating a beautiful showgirl named Holly Brooke. She began showing Mickey the New York nightlife that he wouldn't see with Bauer and his other Yankee teammates. "I guess I developed my first taste for the high life then," Mantle would later recall, "meeting Holly's friends, getting stuck with the check at too many fancy restaurants, discovering scotch at too many dull cocktail parties."

Unknown to Mickey, Holly became friendly with Savitt, who soon concocted a scheme to make money off both of them. One day that spring, Savitt met with Mantle to inform him of a new twist in their deal. "Mick," he began, "I just sold Holly 25 per cent of my 50 percent interest in your earnings." For a $1,500 loan, Mickey's agent had given Holly Brooke a quarter of his interest in Mickey's endorsement and personal-appearance contract. The young show-girl would never see a cent off the deal, but it would become a costly personal matter to Mickey down the way.

Soon Mickey learned the awful truth. There was no fifty-thousand-dollar guarantee in the contract, and the budding Yankee star had locked himself into a horribly exploitative deal. It took George Weiss and Arthur Friedlund, Yankee owner Dan Topping's personal lawyer, to extricate Mickey finally from the contract with Savitt.

Mantle's first road trip with the Yankees that season provides insight into just how big the jump was from Class C ball to the majors. The first day on the road trip Mickey hoarded his money and ate hamburgers and French fries for all three meals. That evening on the train, the team's traveling secretary surprised Mickey when he came through the cars handing players their ten dollars a day meal money. Mantle was ecstatic. "This is great!" Mickey exclaimed. "I oughta be able to save five dollars a day!"

Mantle hit his first regular-season home run off right-hander Randy Gumpert on May 1 in Chicago, a 450-foot drive into the White Sox bullpen, beyond right field. A fan who recovered the ball later exchanged it for a dozen baseballs autographed by Mickey. Four days later, the Yankees were in St. Louis to play the Browns in Sportsman's Park. In the stands that day were Mickey's mother, his girlfriend Merlyn, and her mother. Mantle hit another home run. A reporter approached Merlyn after the game and asked her what she thought of Mickey's homer. "I expected it," she said. "He promised me he'd do it."

As he had in spring training, Mantle impressed everyone with his speed. In a game against Detroit, Mickey was sacrificed from first base to second on a bunt. But when the first baseman turned after the force out to check on Mickey at second base, he found that Mickey was already streaking to third base. Mickey slid in safely ahead of the throw, and in the dugout Stengel jumped up from the bench, boasting to all around, "He went from first to third on a bunt!" Against Cleveland, Mantle lined a hit into left center field; Indians center fielder Larry Doby quickly gathered it in, but when he looked up to throw the ball to second base, he was shocked to see Mantle sliding into the bag. Mickey had never slowed down as he circled first and turned a routine single into a double.

"You ain't seen nothing yet," Stengel told the writers traveling with the team. "The kid doesn't run—he flies. He's positively the fastest man on the bases I've ever seen."

His speed also helped Mantle make a quantum leap in his play in the outfield. Even when he was late getting a jump, Mickey was able simply to run down fly balls. He could cover incredible amounts of territory for a right fielder, an especially prized ability in the cavernous expanse of the Yankee Stadium outfield. With DiMaggio slowed by age and injuries, Stengel would eventually pull Mantle aside and quietly ask that he take balls that might ordinarily be fielded by the center fielder. "You can run faster than any other outfielder in the business," Stengel told Mantle, "but one never would know that from watching you out there. Put on a show. Run hard for the ball. Haul off. Throw a foot high into the air when you heave the ball. Don't be afraid to throw."

As much as Stengel may have taken pride in Mantle's improved defensive play, the real credit belonged to Yankee outfielder turned outfield coach Tommy Henrich. That spring Henrich had spent long days with Mantle teaching him how to catch the ball and get rid of it all in one motion. Mantle was especially attentive to Henrich for two reasons. First, Mickey was the first to acknowledge that he knew little about playing the outfield, particularly the techniques Henrich was teaching him. The other was that it had nothing to do with hitting and therefore changed nothing that his father might have taught him. Over the years Mantle would earn a reputation as a poor learner, especially from Stengel, but it was almost always hitting lessons that Mickey completely tuned out. How well Mantle had learned his lessons from Henrich became clear early that rookie season, against Chicago. Jim Busby of the White Sox was at third base tagging up on a fly ball to Mickey in right field. Mantle caught the ball at the same instant that he planted his right foot, the way Henrich had taught him. In almost the same motion, Mantle fired a strike to the plate; Busby was forced to stop halfway home and retreat to third. The Yankees in the dugout came to their feet, and Henrich walked over to Stengel. "That's the best throw I've ever seen anyone make," Henrich said. "I don't think I have anything else to teach him. He's got it down pretty good."

It all continued to go well for Mantle for several weeks. He was striking out more often than Stengel liked, but he was leading or near the top of the team's statistics in several categories. No one was more surprised than Mickey himself. But then the wheels came off. Yankee pitcher Allie Reynolds, a fellow Oklahoman who often spent time that season trying to instruct Mickey on the ways of the big leagues, later took blame for inadvertently putting a jinx on Mantle that led to his rookie slide.

In the dugout one day, Mantle casually said to Reynolds, "Do you know that I'm leading the league in average, RBIs and home runs?"

Reynolds knew that Mantle was saying this to him more in amazement than as a boast, so he tried to tease him. "Did you ever stop to think what that can mean to you economically?" he asked Mantle.

"After that he lost twenty-five points off his batting average," Reynolds later recalled. "I created the pressure."

Mantle sank into a slump at the plate that worsened as he began to press. For most rookies, this is a normal period of adjustment to better, smarter pitching than what they had faced in the minors. Mickey, however, stubbornly refused to change his approach to hitting after pitchers discovered that he was a sucker for high fastballs just above the letters. Mantle didn't have the discipline not to chase those pitches, or the patience to drive outside pitches to the opposite field. Walt Masterson of the Washington Senators and Satchel Paige of the St. Louis Browns may have been the first pitchers to find Mickey's weakness, and they begin his downward spiral. "Man, he was striking out like crazy," recalled Yogi Berra. Soon word of how to pitch to Mantle got around the league. What concerned Stengel most wasn't the slump but that Mickey wasn't even putting the ball in play consistently. Mantle's skid reached a low point in a doubleheader in Boston, where he struck out three times in the first game and twice more in the second game, returning to the dugout in tears and throwing his bat in a fit of anger.

"Put someone in there who can hit the ball," he cried to Stengel. "I can't."

Stengel tried being patient and even fatherly, protecting Mickey from the press, especially dismissing the negative stories that pointed out how often he was striking out.

"Never mind that crap," he said to Mantle after the appearance of one critical story. "All you need is a couple of hits. It's only a slump. Everybody has 'em."

Stengel tried playing Mantle only against right-handers, believing he was a better hitter left-handed. But Mantle began having troubles that way too, and his batting average sank to .260 by mid-July. Stengel then tried batting Mickey in the lead-off spot, thinking he could capitalize on his great speed to get on base. Mantle, however, continued to strike out, chasing the high fastballs that were his weakness. In Cleveland in mid-July, Bob Lemon struck him out three times. In the dugout, Mickey smashed two of his bats against a wall. At other times, he smashed his fists against walls after striking out. Stengel threatened to fine him, but Mantle's outbursts continued unchecked. At one point, Paige was seen laughing on the mound at Mickey's frustration. At his wit's end, Mantle tried to lay down a two-strike bunt with a runner in scoring position in the bottom of the ninth inning, but he fouled the bunt attempt for an out to end the game. Stengel was furious. "Nice going, son," he said to Mickey in front of his locker. "You sure fooled us. Next time I want you to bunt, I'll give you the sign."

For a while that spring, Stengel had given Mantle the same liberty he gave to some of his veterans—allowing them to swing away with a count of two balls and no strikes. Mantle was now chasing such bad pitches on 2–0 counts that Stengel withdrew the veterans' privilege from his rookie and began giving him the take sign on those counts. When he saw that Mickey's confidence eroded further, Reynolds pulled him aside and tried to explain the manager's decision.

"If you can stand up there and swing at good pitches, hitting them isn't the point," he told Mantle. "You're going to miss some because you swing so hard, and you go for the long ball. But you have to swing at good pitches, and if the count is 2–0 and you swing at a pitch over your head, the pitcher has an advantage [in being able to throw unhittable pitches when he'd ordinarily have to throw strikes to avoid a walk], and Casey has to take the advantage away from him."

The veteran who might have been expected to take Mantle under his wing during this critical period in his career was Joe DiMaggio, who had experienced the highs and lows of slumps as well as the unforgiving cruelty of fans. DiMaggio, however, was experiencing one of the most difficult years of his career. He had shoulder and neck injuries that sidelined him in April, then suffered a muscle pull that kept him out of the lineup again in early June. DiMaggio was also in the throes of mounting personal troubles. An attempted reconciliation with his first wife Dorothy was not going well, and in mid-July his ailing mother slipped into a coma and died. To top that off, the relationship between DiMaggio and Stengel, which had never been good, deteriorated as the Yankee Clipper's season worsened. It would reach the low point in a game in which DiMaggio misplayed a fly ball and was pulled off of the field, in front of thousands of fans at Yankee Stadium, at the start of the next inning after he had already taken his position. DiMaggio stopped talking to Stengel or anyone else on the team.

Reynolds, known as "Superchief" because of his one-quarter Creek Indian ancestry, tried to fill the leadership void on the team off of the field, just as he was doing on the field. That season he became the first American League pitcher to throw two no-hitters in one season, and he would be awarded the prized Hickok Belt by the National Sportswriters Association for being named the Professional Athlete of the Year of 1951.

"You know, problems of life are not hard," Reynolds was to recall to author Peter Golenbock of that time in Mantle's career. "They are pretty simple. It's accepting them that is the tough part. Mickey fought himself very hard. . . . He was a nice kid. A country boy. He had a tough road to hoe though, coming from a C league. And I was complaining about coming from an A league. He had another thing working against him—Mickey didn't have the advantage of a formal education. His father was a miner, and nothing had really been easy in their life. That's one reason it was so hard for him to go from the C league at $200 a month to the major leagues. He was making more money than he ever dreamed of and he had leisure time. How to use your leisure time is the biggest problem of a ball player."

Some might argue, however, that the biggest problem facing an athlete is controlling emotions. Mantle's temper, as was becoming evident that rookie season, was every bit as big and raw at his talent. If Mutt Mantle is to be faulted for anything in the way he raised Mickey, perhaps it is in not having reined in his son's temperament. Mantle's legendary temper and childish attitude would become a source of embarrassment; unforgivable displays of boorish behavior continued throughout his career and for almost all of his personal life. There are no stories or accounts of Mutt's ever having disciplined Mickey when he had thrown temper tantrums as a young ballplayer. Mickey himself claimed that his outbursts did not become a problem until he joined the Yankees, possibly as releases of pent-up pressures from the great expectations placed upon him. In those early Yankee years, Casey Stengel never firmly disciplined his young star when he kicked water coolers, flung bats, or took out his anger on fans.

Mantle once told about an isolated incident involving a Yankee fan he knew only as Mrs. Blackburn, who owned season tickets in a box next to the Yankee dugout. In that rookie season, the woman used to dote on Mickey, often giving him candy and chewing gum as he waited on the on-deck circle. But she grew increasingly disappointed with Mantle's cursing and obscenity-laced tirades after striking out and slowly withdrew her encouragement. There came a day when she finally had her fill of Mickey's foul mouth as he returned to the dugout after striking out yet another time.

"Stop that talk," she screamed at Mickey, who was momentarily dumbstruck but whose anger was not about to subside.

"Shut your goddamn mouth!" Mantle shot back.

Mickey thought she would never speak to him again, but she did a few games later when she called him over to her.

"Any more outbursts like that," Mrs. Blackburn told him icily, "and I'm going to make a personal protest to Mr. Topping."

In mid-July, however, Mantle's slump and temper were the least of the Stengel's problems. His chilly relationship with DiMaggio had become a public relations nightmare for the Yankees, who had had to issue an official clarification of the apparent slight of the Yankee Clipper in benching him in the middle of an inning. The sportswriters who had always been skeptical of Stengel as a manager now rallied in support of DiMaggio and again questioned Stengel's handling of the team, as well as the direction of George Weiss. *New York Times* beat writer John Drebinger was especially critical of Stengel, writing in midseason, "Probably for the first time since taking over the Yankee management, Casey isn't finding the shifting of his talent easy. For no matter how he maneuvers things, weak spots continue to pop up, while his alternating hitters do not seem to fit so well defensively as in other years." Clearly, it had not been a good year for Stengel in personnel decisions. As the manager of the American League All-Star team, he had come under criticism in his selection of pitchers, especially after his squad lost to the National League All-Stars. A day after Stengel had chosen Bob Lemon of the Cleveland Indians over teammate Bob Feller, Feller pitched the third no-hitter of his career. Stengel had also picked the Yankees' Ed Lopat over Reynolds for the All-Star team; two days after the game, Reynolds threw the first of his two no-hitters that season.

Understandably, Mantle's failure to establish himself immediately as the next Yankee star only frustrated Stengel further. Along with Weiss, he was being second-guessed by some of the writers, as well as some among the Yankees' brass, for having invested so much of the team's hope on a nineteen-year-old rookie straight out of Class C baseball. For his part, Stengel was desperately trying to communicate with the nineteen-year-old prodigy, but he was getting the impression that Mantle was bored, skeptical, and unimpressed with much of what he had to tell him. Mantle himself was equally at a loss as to how to deal with his manager, except to sense that all Stengel was concerned about was how well he performed. "You couldn't fool Casey because he'd pulled every stunt that was ever thought up," Mantle would say years later. "He didn't mind it too much either, so long as you didn't start to lose it on the ball field. That's where it all came out, on the field. You could run around like some of the guys, or you could travel with the club looking like DiMaggio in those beautiful blue suits and Countess Mara ties. Either way you did it, if you played like DiMaggio, you'd keep Casey off your back."

Unfortunately for Mantle, in 1951 he was playing like DiMaggio was at the end of his career, although arguably better. By the middle of July, although his average had dropped to .260, Mantle had driven in forty-five runs. The forty-five would equate to over ninety runs in a 154-game schedule. By midseason, Mantle had fourteen more RBIs than New York Giants' rookie rival Willie Mays, as well as sixteen more hits and fourteen more runs scored. Mays's only edge was his batting average, which was thirteen points higher than Mantle's at that point. Rookies with forty-five RBIs by the All-Star break are, if not in the midseason classic itself, hardly on their way back to the minor leagues. Gil McDougald would go on to win Rookie of the Year honors with sixty-three RBIs in 1951, two fewer than Mantle had for the season (Mantle played in thirty-five fewer games). Even Mantle's strikeouts, which raised concern for Stengel and the Yankees, are not that alarming, considering Mickey's run production. By midseason he had struck out fifty-two times in less than 250 at-bats, which would equate to 104 for the full season. The following season, Mantle would strike out 111 times; he would strike out over a hundred times in eight seasons over his career.

For all the connections that have traditionally been made between Mantle and Stengel, a much stronger argument can be made that Stengel was anything but the ideal manager for Mantle, especially during his rookie year. Stengel had hoped that Mickey would be the monument he would leave to baseball, but the Yankees' colorful manager did not have the temperament necessary to nurture and develop young talent. Stengel often preferred to fill out his roster with veterans to support the core that George Weiss assembled. In the 1950s, a series of promising rookies came up through the Yankee ranks. but under Stengel none developed into major stars, with the exception of Mantle and Whitey Ford. For all the great Yankee teams of that era, the only Hall of Famers developed by Stengel were Ford and Mantle. Even then, Ford's greatest seasons came under Ralph Houk, and Mantle never wavered in crediting his own father for making him the player he became. Throughout his career with the Yankees, Stengel proved that he was outstanding at getting the most out of journeymen players who had already been developed but that he lacked patience with those who were young or inexperienced. His platoon system of using right-handed hitters when a lefty pitched and vice versa was designed as a short-term solution; it never allowed right-handed hitters to develop themselves batting against right-handed pitchers. or left-handed hitters to improve themselves against lefties. Players caught up in Stengel's platoon system resented him for it and for what it ultimately did to their careers. Among them was Gene Woodling, an outfielder and a left-handed .300 hitter five times in a career that spanned fifteen seasons. He was among eight players who appeared in every victorious Yankee World Series from 1949 to 1953. However, Woodling was never secure in a full-time outfield position and was often platooned by Stengel. "I liked Stengel, but I did a lot of fussing with him," said Woodling long after his playing days. "And I didn't care for the platoon system. I always felt that I could hit any pitcher."

With Mantle in 1951, Stengel was prepared to deal with his temperamental phenom when he succeeded but found that he had little use for a struggling rookie whose slump threatened his own success. It appears that a disproportionate amount of the blame for the Yankees' sluggishness was being placed on Mantle. By mid-July, the Yankees had fallen to third place, behind the Red Sox and the White Sox and only a game ahead of the fourth-place Indians. Mantle, however, was not alone in his struggles. Bauer, for instance, was mired in a zero-for-seventeen batting slump. Jerry Coleman had fallen off from the previous year's form. DiMaggio was having the worst season of his career.

Meanwhile, Stengel found himself under increasing scrutiny from the writers covering the team.

During this summer slide, Raschi had failed in three straight starts to win his thirteenth game of the season. Yankee pitching, which had been largely responsible for carrying the team to championships in 1949 and 1950, had faltered throughout the first half of the season. Stengel could not allow an opportunity for a third straight pennant to get away from him, and he and Weiss began toying with their options. Stengel felt that the Yankees could overtake the Red Sox and hold off anyone else in the pennant race by improving their pitching. So desperate for pitching were the Yankees that on July 12 they gave the Dodgers two minor league pitching prospects plus cash in exchange for left-hander Art Schallock, a minor league sensation who, at not quite five feet nine inches, was considered by many scouts too small to succeed in the big leagues. That same afternoon, Reynolds and Feller engaged in one of the great pitching duels of the decade. Reynolds no-hit the Indians, while Feller carried a no-hitter against the Yankees into the sixth inning, when Mantle doubled for the first hit of the game. The Yankees won the game 1–0 on Gene Woodling's solo home run in the seventh. In the next day's *Times*, Drebinger wrote ominously, "When Schallock reports one player on the New York team will have to be sent to Kansas City."

The Yankees' pitching broke down over the next two days, giving up nineteen runs to the Indians, with Mantle going one for five in the first game, and being benched in favor of Jackie Jensen in the second game. The Yankees' decision on who would be sent down to make room for Schallock had already been made. With the team struggling and criticism mounting, Stengel needed a scapegoat. He had developed a pattern in how he took out his frustrations; as Leonard Koppett wrote in *The Man in the Dugout: Baseball's Top Managers and How They Got That Way*, "He was hardest on the best talents, like Mickey Mantle, driven by what he saw as unrealized potential even beyond Mantle's accomplishments, yet quite tolerant toward those with lesser ability."

On July 15, three days after Allie Reynolds pitched a no-hitter against Cleveland, Mantle was called aside by the clubhouse man at Briggs Stadium in Detroit, who told him Stengel wanted to see him. Mickey knew what was coming and walked into the manager's office to find Casey with tears in his eyes. "This is gonna hurt me more than you," he began.

"No, skip, it's my fault." Mickey struggled to hold back his own tears.

"Aww . . . it ain't nobody's fault. You're nineteen, that's all. Mickey, you're getting a little nervous and tight at the plate, swinging at too many bad pitches. You're going to develop into a big-league star one of these years. But maybe a change of scenery might do you a lot of good. I want you to get your confidence back, so I'm shipping you down to Kansas City."

Mantle was crushed. Stengel later said that it was one of the most difficult things he ever had to do in his life.

"It's not the end of the world, Mickey," the Yankee manager said. "In a couple of weeks you'll start hitting and then we'll bring you right back up again. I promise."

Understandably, Mantle took Stengel's assurance of bringing him back to the Yankees as what he later described as "no more than a crude effort to take the curse off of the sentence he had just passed."

"Casey probably assumed that, as I had been ready to go to Beaumont in Double-A ball, it would be no serious jolt to find myself in Kansas City, which was Triple-A then," Mickey said years later. "But he might as well have told me he was shipping me back to Independence. I had been a Yankee, and now I was nothing. I was always one of those guys who took all the bad luck doubly hard, who saw disaster when there was just everyday trouble, and who took every slump as if it were a downhill slide to oblivion."

In the *New York Times* the following day, Drebinger called Mantle's demotion "startling." "For in order to keep within the player limit, the Yanks had to lop off somebody and the fellow who drew the unlucky straw was Mickey Mantle, the highly touted youngster the Bombers had confidently expected to win the rookie-of-the-year accolade."

7

Casey Stengel had no inkling of the emotional tailspin Mantle's demotion created. As the DiMaggio fiasco had shown, the Yankee manager's uncanny intuitive sense about baseball did not extend to superstars, who often required special handling. At times, Stengel may have been a player's manager, but he was not a star's manager. He admired the stars he had seen in the game—Ott, Gehrig, Williams, even DiMaggio. But he was not emotionally equipped to pamper and cater to the sensitive egos of the game's premier players. If Stengel could treat the legendary DiMaggio the way he did in the three years he managed him, there was no reason to believe he could or would be any more understanding of what Mantle was going through his rookie season. Unfortunately for Mantle, Stengel was not Leo Durocher, the manager of the New York Giants, whose stormy personality did not prevent him from developing a nurturing, close bond with his own temperamental rookie, Willie Mays. On one occasion, after Mays went one for twenty-five in his first six games with the Giants that year, the rookie collapsed in tears by his locker. Durocher put his arm around the young center fielder and gave him a pep talk. Then he moved him down to eighth in the batting order, and Mays took off. He wound up National League Rookie of the Year, batting .274, with twenty home runs and sixty-eight RBIs, and the Giants went to the World Series.

A Durocher-type pep talk is what Mantle desperately needed during his summer slump, which was not the worst slump on the Yankees, and no worse than some of the bad stretches Mays went through that same season. Stengel, however, did not have that kind of relationship with Mantle, nor would he ever. If he had, he would have recognized that underneath Mantle's nineteen-year-old man-child frame was an insecure youth not that different from Mays. Both were high-strung perfectionists, given to tears, foul language, and temper tantrums when things went poorly for them. Mays was also prone to fainting spells and mysterious bouts of nervous exhaustion, for which he was twice hospitalized during his career.

Anxiety and panic attacks are not usually associated with heroes, especially baseball heroes—courage, coolness, cockiness, even arrogance, yes. But nerves are also part of the game. Most great players perhaps have better reins on their fears or hide their insecurities and nervousness with the stoicism of a professional athlete. Underneath, however, their tears and tantrums offer a glimpse of a virtue that most men of their time held in bitter disdain: authentic human emotion. In Mays and Mantle, especially in their rookie seasons, one witnessed fear and hope colliding—the hero's fear, his frustration, his confusion, and his elation as he pursued his dream.

When he was sent down to the minors, Mantle's world came down utterly crashing around him. "It is a depressing thing being sent down to the minors, and I felt low," he later recalled. "I thought I had missed my big chance. I figured they had looked at me and didn't want me. I felt like running off and hiding some place where there was no baseball. Perhaps it wouldn't have been as hard to take if there had been no ballyhoo. But now the big bubble had burst, and I felt I was the laughingstock of the league. The same newspapers that billed me as a superstar in April were now saying I was through."

It was a period of failure that would haunt Mickey the rest of his life. He would later look back on it with remorse and self-deprecation. "When I was twenty years old," he said after he retired, "I was a better ballplayer than [in my prime]. I could hit better, run faster, and throw better. Yet they farmed me out to the minor leagues. I was too young to take all the pressures of major league ball. When a boy of twenty can handle it, you've got yourself a real special ballplayer—a Williams, a Musial, or a Cobb."

Merlyn Mantle, in *A Hero All His Life*, would later describe Mickey as having suffered from extreme insecurity all his life. She believed Mickey had emotional problems stemming from his unresolved relationship with his father—Mutt's exceptionally high expectations and Mickey's fears of failing to meet them. Merlyn would later say that an entire book could be written about Mantle's relationship with his father. Mantle, however, did not want to deal with it, either as a young man or later in life. In 1989, screenwriter Angelo

Pizzo, who wrote the highly regarded basketball film *Hoosiers*, met with Mantle to discuss a possible motion picture based on Mickey's life. "When I started probing below the surface of his life," said Pizzo, "he got uncomfortable and angry, especially about his father." Much mutual love existed between father and son, but it was never shown. Even when Mickey returned home after being away during his 1949 and 1950 minor league seasons, Mutt always greeted him not with a hug but a handshake. Merlyn felt that the early pressure on Mantle to play baseball, along with his own drive to be the best, contributed to the bed-wetting problem he had, even through high school. Mantle apparently corrected the problem himself, through sheer willpower, after signing his professional contract and going to play his first minor league season at Independence, Kansas. Mantle also had unresolved emotions from the sexual abuse his older half-sister and her friends had inflicted upon him as a young boy. Mantle never forgot the image of his half-sister and her friends laughing at him; being made fun of was one of the few things he could not tolerate. Mantle couldn't deal with humiliation, either personally, off the field, or professionally, on the field.

The demotion to the minor leagues after his half-season with the Yankees was a public humiliation for Mantle of a scope that perhaps only a professional athlete can appreciate. After Mantle's death, DiMaggio, summing up his career among the Yankee greats, praised Mickey, as any former player of his stature would have been expected to do—but then he went out of his way to note that, of course, Mantle had had to be sent to the minors in 1951. DiMaggio, Ruth, Gehrig—none of the Yankee greats and few of the legends of baseball—had been humbled in such a way. For Mantle, riding off to join the Kansas City Blues in Minneapolis, it might have been better to have started the 1951 season in the minors. Stengel and George Weiss apparently were not aware just how far Mantle's self-confidence sank. If they had been, they might have sent him down to the Yankees' Class AA team in Beaumont, where Mantle might have felt more comfortable playing for Harry Craft, who had coached him his previous year in the minors.

The Yankees, however, thought they were doing their best by sending Mantle to learn patience at the plate from Kansas City manager George Selkirk, a former Yankee who in 1935 had replaced Babe Ruth in right field and had even been given Ruth's famous number three on his uniform. While he could not come close to Ruth's home run output—he hit twenty-one at his best in 1939—he batted better than .300 in five of his first six seasons. A patient hitter, Selkirk had the distinction of having drawn two walks in an inning four different times, and he had walked 103 times in 1939. In 1935, Selkirk had been the first to suggest that a cinder path six feet wide be installed in the outfield so a player would know when he was nearing the wall—the modern-day warning track. The Yankees also thought that Selkirk, someone who had played with Ruth, Gehrig, and DiMaggio, might impart some badly needed wisdom to these greats' presumed heir. In addition, Stengel had a fondness for Kansas City and thought Mantle would be better off there than at an outpost in Texas. Stengel had been born and raised in Kansas City, and he had quit high school in 1910 just short of graduating to play baseball professionally with the Kansas City Blues.

When Mantle finally joined the Blues, it was with the same mixed reception that welcomes any major leaguer coming down to "slum." The minors, from where only one of fourteen ever makes it to the major leagues, are a world of underpaid, overworked players and coaches who do not look kindly on squandered talent and overblown press clippings. Mantle later described the Blues as a group of "malcontents" whose pitchers "carried pints of whiskey in their back pockets." For Mantle, there was also the torment of jealousy from teammates, who knew that Mickey was down in the minors with the understanding that he would get special treatment designed to get him back to the majors. Mantle, in fact, was immediately inserted into the lineup as a promising hot prospect. On his first at-bat he surprised everyone by beating out a drag bunt down the first base line. He needed that hit for his self-confidence and as a positive upon which to build. Mantle desperately needed a pat on the back or just a word of encouragement. Instead, when he returned to the dugout at the end of the inning, Selkirk, as Mickey later recalled, began berating him. "What's the matter with you?" he yelled at Mantle. "They didn't send you here to bunt. You're here to get some hits and get your confidence back."

"That finished me," said Mantle. "I felt like hell when I went out to my position, I could feel the tears of self-pity stinging my eyes. 'What did a guy have to do?' I asked myself."

From then on, Mickey could do little right. American Association pitching made him look even worse than the American League pitchers had. After the bunt single, he went hitless in his next nineteen at-bats before the team returned to Kansas City. Mantle was practically friendless on the team and among the fans. He spent most of his free time by himself, often poring over the Yankee box scores. He had learned from the newspapers that his replacement on the Yankee roster, Art Schallock, had bombed in his first start and would not be the solution to the Yankees' pitching problems. Harry Wells, the undertaker for whom Mickey had dug graves back in Commerce, visited Mantle during his minor league stay and was stunned to find a stack of hate mail from fans in a corner of his hotel room. Much of it, Wells said, was about Mantle's draft status. The Korean War was in full swing, and the "draft dodger" issue had followed him to Kansas City. The real war for Mantle, however, was no longer against opposing pitchers. It was instead against his own fear and foreboding. The real slump wasn't on the baseball diamond—it was in his own head. Years later, a therapist working with Mantle and Merlyn had concluded that "Mickey is totally controlled by fear. He is filled with fear about everything."

At the height of his slump, each time Mantle came to bat he was overcome by sudden surges of overwhelming fear that came without warning and without any obvious reason. It was more intense than the feeling of being "stressed out" that most people experience. Baseball slumps, according to Kevin Elko, adjunct professor to the Sports Medicine Fellows at the University of Pittsburgh School of Medicine, are largely fueled by panic. "The panic," said Elko, a consultant to several professional sports teams, "has become a condition. More than any other variable, panic is the malady." Selkirk and some of the other Blues coaches had begun to suspect that Mantle's problem was a case of nerves—that maybe Mantle just didn't have it. It may, however, have been something far more serious—a panic disorder. Later in his life, Mantle would exhibit similar symptoms that were perhaps too quickly attributed to his drinking.

These panic or anxiety attacks became more frequent as Mantle traveled around the country for trading-card shows. The most publicized of these attacks occurred aboard an airplane on a flight back to Dallas. Mantle began to hyperventilate and was at first feared to be having a heart attack. Emergency paramedics met the plane at Dallas's Love Field. Mantle was checked out and diagnosed as having had a panic attack. In 1993, Mantle admitted that "depression was a regular part of my life. At times, I thought about killing myself." In 1951, at age nineteen, Mantle fit the profile for panic disorder, which usually appears during the teens or early adulthood. While the exact causes are unclear, doctors say there does seem to be a connection with major life transitions, which are potentially stressful. In Mantle's case, having his dream—and his father's—of becoming a major league baseball player turn into a nightmare certainly qualified as a major life transition. Baseball, specifically being a major leaguer, was how Mantle measured himself and his self-worth. "When Mick retired," Merlyn later observed, "a big chunk of his self-esteem went out the window. I question whether he ever had much to begin with."

Now, with his career in a frightening free fall, Mantle decided to quit. He called his father, found him at the Eagle-Picher mines, and told him it was over. He couldn't hit even minor league pitching and wanted to come home. The slump was no surprise to Mutt. He had been keeping up with Mickey in the newspapers, as had a good portion of the people in the Commerce area who either knew the Mantles or had an interest in baseball. What Mutt had not expected was the desperation in his son's voice. He had never heard this kind of panic and anxiety in Mickey and quickly concluded he needed to see his son. He left almost immediately on the five-hour drive from Commerce to Kansas City, where he found Mantle at the Aladdin Hotel.

"I was living there, and boy, was I glad to see him," Mantle recalled. "I wanted him to pat me on the back and cheer me up and tell me how badly the Yankees had treated me and all that sort of stuff. I guess I was like a little boy, and I wanted him to comfort me."

"How are things going?" Mutt asked Mickey.

"Awful. The Yankees sent me down to learn not to strike out, but now I can't even hit."

"That so?"

"I'm not good enough to play in the major leagues," Mickey said. "And I'm not good enough to play here. I'll never make it. I think I'll quit and go home with you."

"I guess I wanted him to say, 'Oh, don't be silly, you're just in a little slump, you'll be all right, you're great,'" Mantle later said. "But he just looked at me for a second and then in a quiet voice that cut me in two he said, 'Well, Mick, if that's all the guts you have, I think you better quit. You might as well come home right now.'"

Mickey wanted to tell him that he had *tried*, but he knew better than to argue with his father when he was in this mood.

"Mickey, you can't have it easy all your life. Baseball is no different than any other job. Things get tough once in a while, and you must learn how to take it—the sooner the better. It takes guts, not moaning, to make it. And if that's all the guts you have, I agree with you. You don't belong in baseball. Come on back to Commerce and grub out a living in the mines for the rest of your life."

Then Mutt said words that tore into Mantle's heart: "I thought I raised a man, not a coward!"

Mickey later said in an interview that Mutt's lecture that night "had been the greatest thing my father ever did for me. All the encouragement he had given me when I was small, all the sacrifices he made so I could play ball when other boys were working in the mines, all the painstaking instruction he had provided—all of these would have been thrown away if he had not been there that night to put the iron into my spine when it was needed most. I never felt as ashamed as I did then, to hear my father sound disappointed in me, ashamed of me.

"I have wondered sometimes exactly what it was. I know that I wanted my father to comfort me. He didn't. He didn't give me any advice. He didn't show me how to swing the bat any different. He didn't give me any inspiring speeches. I think that what happened was that he had so much plain ordinary courage that it spilled over, and I could feel it. All he did was show me that I was acting scared, and that you can't live scared."

The fear that ruled and motivated him as both a boy and a man, as both a player and a husband, had begun as a mixture of fear and respect for his father. Many youngsters are pushed to succeed in endeavors that are as meaningful to the parents as to the children, if not more so. But Mutt's influence over Mickey—Mutt's ability to motivate his son though Mickey's fear of disappointing him—would extend far beyond Mickey's childhood, as well as beyond baseball. Mickey's marriage to Merlyn later that year would be an act possibly more out of love of (and fear of disappointing) Mutt as out of love for Merlyn. In later years Mickey would measure himself, as a husband and father, against the example of his own father and, of course, come up short in the comparison—because anything short of perfection would have failed his father.

That evening, with his father watching from the grandstands, Mantle broke out of his extended slump with two prodigious home runs. Mickey became as hot as he had been in spring training. Over the next forty-one games, Mickey hit .361 with eleven home runs, fifty RBIs, three triples, and nine doubles. Mantle suddenly was the darling, if not of Broadway, then at least of Kansas City. The Blues rode Mickey's success into an American Association championship chase that effectively ended the day he was recalled back to the Yankees. Years later, Calvin Trillin would write an essay lamenting his own disenchantment with baseball and dating it back to when the Yankees took Mantle back from his beloved Blues. "I hate the Yankees," he wrote. "They called Mickey Mantle up from Kansas City right in the middle of a hot pennant race with the Indianapolis Indians." If Mickey did this for the intelligentsia of Kansas City, imagine what he must have done for the fans in the cheap seats.

Something more may have contributed to Mantle's turnaround. Around the same time, he was visited by his New York girlfriend, Holly Brooke, and they began a long-distance romance that she later insisted was serious. "I was calling him 'Mickey Mouse,' a pet name only his mother had used before," she recalled. "More than once, Mickey would ask me how I felt about marrying him, owning him 100 per cent . . . permanently. But he always answered his own question. 'No, I guess not,' he'd say. 'You'd never be happy in a little town like Commerce.' And he was right on that. Other towns were different though. For instance, I remember flying to Columbus [Ohio] to see him and buck up his spirits. I'd planned to stay one night but wound up staying three days. That was in 1951 when the big blow fell and the Yankees shipped him off to their Kansas City farm club. When he heard the news, Mickey broke down and bawled like a baby. He often called me from there and other minor league towns, asking me to fly out and spend a few days with him because he was so lonesome." Brooke also wound up with one of the few existing photos of Mantle in a Kansas City uniform; he inscribed it, "To Holly, with all my love and thoughts."

In mid-August, Stengel and the Yankees decided to bring Mantle back to the majors, only to learn that they would have to stand in line. The Selective Service had called Mantle back for yet another physical examination. He underwent the physical by army doctors at Fort Sill, Oklahoma, on August 23, and was once again classified 4-F because of the osteomyelitis. The next day the Yankees recalled Mantle.

When Mantle returned to New York, one of the first people he went to see was Pete Sheehy to get his uniform. Sheehy was no less superstitious than any other veteran baseball man, which is to say that he was as superstitious as they come. He had issued Mantle uniform number six in the spring, and he now wondered if maybe that hadn't been a mistake. It had been Mickey's uniform number when he was sent down, and now Sheehy didn't want to take any chances. This time he issued Mantle number seven. Mickey wasn't so superstitious. He had liked number six because it was also Stan Musial's number, but now he was just glad to be back with the Yankees. The change of uniform numbers would prove fortuitous, for in baseball Mantle would forever after be associated with number seven. "To be honest," he later said, "I didn't put any stock in whether I was wearing number six or number seven. But after I had number seven on for a while, no one was gonna take it off my back."

Mantle also didn't want to make the mistakes he made earlier in the year, like living alone, so he passed up the Concourse Plaza Hotel. Mickey's incident earlier with the agent who tried to take advantage of him also convinced Hank Bauer and some of Mantle's other teammates that the team's prize rookie needed watching over. When their agent, Frank Scott, moved out of New York later that summer, Bauer and Johnny Hopp invited Mantle to join them in his former apartment in Manhattan. The apartment was above the Stage Delicatessen on Seventh Avenue at 53rd Street in the White Light District, and the delicatessen was often Mickey's security retreat from the intimidation of the big city. Max and Hymie Asnas, who owned the delicatessen, befriended Mickey and often made him special meals that were not on their menu. "Like all shy people," said Mantle, "I had a hard time going into new restaurants, not knowing whether to grab a table or wait to be shown, afraid to order something different for fear of making a jerk of myself, unable sometimes to tell the waiter from the busboy. But in the Stage Delicatessen I might have been in my home town."

Upon his return to the Yankees that summer, Mantle's budding friendship with the team's second baseman began blossoming. If Casey Stengel saw in Mantle the son he never had, Billy Martin saw in him the little brother of his dreams. Mickey was the adoring kid brother who would go along with anything Billy proposed and would never dare to talk back. For starters, there was Martin's unique friendship with DiMaggio, of which Mickey could only be admiring and envious. Few Yankee players could boast of anything but a passing acquaintance with DiMaggio, who often could sit in the clubhouse for hours without speaking to anyone. Martin, however, had managed to endear himself to DiMaggio; his clubhouse pranks and joking manner amused the stoic Yankee Clipper.

Teammates were often stunned to watch Billy enter the clubhouse behind DiMaggio, imitating his distinctive walk all the way to their lockers, which were next to one another. Billy would then continue to mirror comically everything DiMaggio did—ordering coffee, taking off his pants, hanging up his shirt and coat. It would approach a Marx Brothers routine, with even DiMaggio having to laugh. "You fresh little bastard," DiMaggio would say. No one could explain why DiMaggio took to Martin, except perhaps that both were Italian. In the past DiMaggio had opened up a part of himself to players from Italian backgrounds. With Martin, he often spent hours in the clubhouse after games, nursing a beer and talking baseball. They eventually became after-game dinner companions. Martin's candid, unpretentious manner put the formal DiMaggio at ease.

"I think the reason they became friends," said Phil Rizzuto, "was because Billy would do anything DiMaggio wanted, any time. You had to want to do anything Joe wanted to do and, you know, that's hard to do. But Billy was the type who wasn't bothered by that, and Billy loved Joe. He idolized him."

But another reason why the Martin-DiMaggio friendship clicked may have been that Billy always treated Joe not like a star but like any other teammate. "Billy would say to me, 'He's just like anyone else,'" Whitey Ford later recalled. "'All you have to do is open up when you're around him.' I'd tell him, 'I can't do that.'"

Mantle had similar recollections about and reactions to the DiMaggio-Martin relationship in that 1951 season. "Joe DiMaggio was my hero," said Mantle, "but Billy used to play jokes on him and hang around with him. Billy wasn't afraid of Joe, maybe because they both came from San Francisco. Besides, Billy was a fresh kid, and he even pulled some stunts on Joe. There was one in particular I'll never forget. Billy had one of those pens with disappearing ink. Well, Joe would always come to the ballpark in a shirt and tie and these expensive suits. Anyway, I just couldn't believe that Billy would do this, but he goes up to Joe and asks him for an autograph for a friend. And as he hands him the pen, he shoots ink all over Joe's nice-looking suit. Joe started getting angry, telling Billy, 'Damn it, how could you do that?' Well, Billy got a laugh and quickly explained that the ink would disappear. Billy could get away doing things like that with Joe and then going out to eat with him. I used to watch and ask Billy what Joe was like. And he'd say, 'Shit, he's just like anyone else. All you have to do is open up when you're around him.' And I'd say, 'Shit, I couldn't do that.'"

Billy took to Mickey as he had to no other player and helped smooth over Mantle's rookie year, especially after his return from Kansas City. On the road, the two became roommates. Back in New York, the pair behaved like the city's most eligible bachelors, despite the fact that Billy had a wife at home. Mickey and Billy also were keeping postgame company with teammates Hank Bauer and Charlie Silvera, and their nightlife was a far cry from the small town lights of Commerce. One of their regular spots was the Harwyn Club on the East Side, where on any given night Mantle and his pals would be rubbing elbows with Grace Kelly when she was being courted by Prince Rainier; with Rocky Marciano celebrating the latest of his boxing championship defenses; and with singer Teresa Brewer, who, according to Martin, had a crush on Mickey. Mickey and Brewer later sang a duet; photos of the two circulated in the newspapers and were even made into pins that ultimately became collectors' items. But if life on the town could be high, through pranks and hijinks it could also sink to lows. Once, at the same Harwyn Club, Mickey and Billy slipped a whoopie cushion under the seat of a contractor friend; their side of the club erupted in laughter.

"That place—I was like a kid in a candy store," said Jack Setzer, a friend of Martin's who had grown up with Billy in West Berkeley, California. "I met Joe DiMaggio, Leo Durocher, Charlie Dressen, some umpires—I don't know who—and I met Sid Caesar, Jo Stafford and her husband, Paul Whiting, Imogene Coca, Carl Reiner—the whole 'Show of Shows' cast. . . . And then the other nights on my trip. . . . I'm having dinner with Yogi Berra and Mickey Mantle and Billy . . . the first five or six nights, Mickey's with a different gal every night and each one's better looking than the last. Gorgeous gals. I couldn't believe what I'd seen."

Anyone looking inside the Yankees' clubhouse or in their dugout might not have believed the sight of Mickey and Billy as two merry pranksters, beginning late in the 1951 season and continuing for several years. They bought water pistols and squirted each other with them in the clubhouse. They sneaked Polaroid camera shots of one another on the toilet. They wrestled on the trains on road trips. For Mantle, baseball had never been such fun.

A day after his return to the Yankees, Mantle slugged a home run off Mike Garcia that helped New York beat the Indians, 7–3. A week later, against the Browns in St. Louis, with his family looking on, Mickey hit another home run and drove in four runs. In the thirty-seven games after his return to the majors, Mantle hit .283 and drove in twenty runs to help the Yankees win their third straight American League pennant. He was not in the lineup for a doubleheader on September 28, the day Allie Reynolds pitched his second no-hitter of the season and the Yankees clinched the pennant against the Red Sox, and he hadn't expected to start in the World Series. But on the day that Bobby Thomson hit his dramatic home run off the Dodgers' Ralph Branca to win the National League pennant for the Giants, Mantle grabbed the evening papers at a newsstand and got a surprise. The sports page carried the Yankees' starting lineup for the first game of the series at Yankee Stadium. Leading off and playing right field for the Yankees would be the rookie Mickey Mantle.

8

In that roller-coaster rookie year, Mickey Mantle never fully realized that he had unwittingly become the target for the frustration of the Yankee he himself most idolized. From when he had first followed baseball as a child, Joe DiMaggio had been Mantle's hero. While the Cardinals had been his father's favorite team, young Mickey had followed the Yankees and, like millions of his generation, worshipped DiMaggio. In 1941, Mickey and his father had spent most of the summer evenings glued to the radio to learn whether DiMaggio's historic hitting streak had continued. Some nights Mantle would fall asleep with DiMaggio still hitless, only to wake up in the morning to learn that his hero had come through late in the game. (On July 17, however, Mickey had stayed up late enough to learn that Cleveland left-hander Joe Smith had ended DiMaggio's streak at fifty-six.) DiMaggio had even been one of the reasons Mantle hoped throughout his last year of high school that Yankee scout Tom Greenwade would offer him a contract. Even then, however, Mantle never dreamed that he would one day be playing in the outfield alongside DiMaggio, let alone that he would be hailed as the successor to DiMaggio and Ruth. Mantle, after all, had been a shortstop through high school and even his first two years in the minors. More importantly, Mickey and Mutt had sat down on more than one occasion over the years to plot out his progression, based upon how players usually moved up through the minors. Mutt had figured that it would be 1953, when Mickey would be twenty-one, before he would make the majors—1952 at the earliest. They were as aware as anyone who kept up with baseball in the late 1940s that DiMaggio's career was near its end, especially as the injuries continued to mount. Neither Mutt nor Mickey—nor anyone else, for that matter—figured that DiMaggio would still be playing in 1953, just as they couldn't imagine Mickey making the Yankees' roster as a nineteen-year-old in 1951.

There was no way for Mantle to understand the resentment that DiMaggio felt toward him, and he mistook the Yankee Clipper's iciness as part of his legendary aloofness. Some of it, of course, was just DiMaggio being himself. But there was also a real bitterness toward Casey Stengel and whomever was tapped by Stengel as his successor. For the abominable treatment of DiMaggio in his final season, responsibility can be placed only in Stengel's lap. Stengel never explained his behavior at the time, and he was never challenged about it during his lifetime. From spring training in 1950 on, Stengel had made no attempt to disguise his hope that one of the younger outfielders might soon be able to replace the oft-injured center-field legend. An American hero and icon, DiMaggio found himself receiving an unheroic, iconoclastic shove out the door.

For his part, Stengel delighted in pitting the young rookie against the old pro. That spring training, as he was trying to convert Mantle into an outfielder, Stengel had gone up to him after one of his workouts with Tommy Henrich.

"Kid," Stengel said to Mantle, "you wanna play in the major leagues?"

"Yes, sir," Mickey replied.

"Well, do yourself a favor. You see that fella out in center field there?"

"You mean, DiMaggio?"

"Yeah," said Casey. "You go out and have him teach you how to play that position. Because you'll never be a shortstop."

"Yes, sir."

Stengel may have simply been trying to goad the silent, aging Yankee Clipper by sending his young heir apparent to ask for tips. Mantle, however, never approached DiMaggio; Mickey was simply too shy. He remained in awe of DiMaggio even after he joined the Yankees for two weeks at the end of his minor league season in 1950.

"Now, to sit right close to the great man as he stretched his tired legs by his locker and called for a can of beer was something like having a seat near the President of the United States," he would recall. "I had no ambition to talk to him or even have him notice me, as long as I could gaze my fill at him when he was not looking."

DiMaggio began his final season struggling to come to terms not only with his mortality as a hero but, more importantly, mortality itself. His mother Rosalie DiMaggio died that summer at age seventy-two of cancer, from which she had suffered for several years. In little more than a year's time he had lost both his father and his mother, just as it was becoming unmistakable that he was losing his skills and gifts on the field. How far DiMaggio's talents had slipped was summed up in a World Series scouting report prepared by the Brooklyn Dodgers and leaked to *Life* magazine. "His reflexes are very slow," said the report, "and he can't pull a good fastball at all. He cannot stop quickly and throw hard, and you can take the extra base on him. He can't run, and he won't bunt."

Thus the DiMaggio Mickey saw during his rookie season was barely a ghost of the DiMaggio he had grown up hearing and reading about in Commerce. DiMaggio played in only 116 of the Yankees' 154 games that year. His batting average was a humiliating .263, four points lower than Mickey's. He hit only twelve home runs and drove in seventy-one runs. DiMaggio's season was made even worse by Stengel's apparent insensitivity. Once, after a first-inning rout of the Yankees, Stengel immediately pulled several of his veterans. In a move that could have been handled better, the Yankee skipper substituted Jackie Jensen for DiMaggio by dispatching Jensen out to center field where DiMaggio was already standing. Visibly unhappy, DiMaggio had even more reason for a strained relationship with Stengel. That day *New York Times* sportswriter John Drebinger wrote, "This has been DiMaggio's mood for a long time. In fact, he rarely talks to his teammates or manager, let alone anyone remotely associated with the press. On a recent train ride following a night game in Philadelphia, DiMaggio, in the Yanks' special diner, sat by himself at a table set for four. It's a queer set-up, but almost everyone traveling with the Bombers is leaving the Clipper severely alone."

"I hardly knew the man," Mickey himself would recall years later. "He was a loner, always restrained, often secretive. If you weren't family or a very close friend, you didn't dare probe into his personal life. He'd shut you off in a minute. Shy as I was, I never went to him seeking advice. Too scared. It was a simple hello and goodbye. Press me further and I'll also admit that DiMaggio never said to me, 'Come on, kid, let's have a beer and talk.'"

When he didn't have other things to do, however, Mantle had his eyes glued on the man he was too shy to talk to. He especially kept a close eye on DiMaggio during batting practice, watching his trademark wide stance, long stride, and classic, smooth swing. Above all, DiMaggio was the consummate professional, never giving any indication in public that he was often in excruciating pain from bone spurs on a bad heel. Mantle and all the other Yankees, as well as the rest of the sports world, would read the daily newspaper stories about DiMaggio's aching heel. Mantle's earliest recollection of DiMaggio was of the day the Yankee star arrived in camp that spring. Mickey was involved in a game of pepper, hitting and fielding short but sharply hit ground balls. As DiMaggio walked behind him, Mickey missed a ground ball, which nicked Joe's ankle and skidded away. "He swiveled his head in my direction," said Mickey, "staring bullets. I felt sure I'd be gone that night."

Unfortunately for Mantle, DiMaggio in the final year of his career was only going through the motions and no longer cared to exert the kind of influence over the clubhouse that he once had. However aloof, DiMaggio also could be the consummate team player when he chose to be. His dedication to the game was unquestioned, and he expected the same in his teammates. In the late 1940s, as the senior member of the team, DiMaggio had established himself as the clubhouse conscience of the Yankees. His presence demanded an all-out effort by his teammates. When presence was not enough, DiMaggio didn't hesitate to berate someone. Once, coming into the Yankee clubhouse exhausted from a doubleheader and limping from the incessant pain in his heel, he found Yogi Berra joking around; DiMaggio wasn't amused, because the Yankees' promising young catcher had begged off the second game. Resentful, DiMaggio blew up.

"You're twenty-three years old," he said to Berra, "and you can't catch a doubleheader? My ass!" Berra quickly came around.

There were other awkward moments involving the Yankee Clipper. Berra, who also played the outfield, later remembered that DiMaggio had one rule for the players on either side of him in the outfield: "If you call for it, it's yours. If you don't say anything, it's mine."

"One day," Berra would recall, "I said, 'I got it,' and he just stopped. The ball was nowhere near me." The ball dropped between them. "He just gave me the look. He didn't even have to say a word. As a kid coming from the hills of St. Louis, I watched everything he did. He was such a great ballplayer. He never made a mistake on the field. I never saw him dive for a ball. You'd see him head for second and you'd wonder where he's going, but he always made it. He never, ever walked off the field. You've got to admire a guy like that. He's got to be like Babe Ruth. They are the two greatest."

Yet DiMaggio could be extremely protective of what he felt was his territory. Perhaps nothing upset him more about how Mantle was being groomed to supplant him than seeing pictures in the papers that spring of his longtime friend and nightclub owner Toots Shor with his arm around Mickey, his newest pal. DiMaggio didn't know who to resent more—Mantle, for taking his place as the toast of the town in Toots Shor's bar, or Shor, whom DiMaggio suspected of having committed the ultimate betrayal of talking to the press. That spring, *Look* published a story on DiMaggio's personal life, including the woes of his breakup with his first wife Dorothy, along with anonymous quotes that Joe knew must have come from Toots Shor. DiMaggio would remember, and he would never forgive. Years later, when Toots was old and had lost his bar, Mantle, Whitey, Yogi, and others sent him money. DiMaggio, however, refused. When he was recovering from a stroke, Toots showed up in the Yankee clubhouse to see his old pals at an Old Timers' Day game at the Stadium. He got a big reception from all the players except DiMaggio. When he saw Toots struggle, using canes to walk across the clubhouse floor toward his corner, Joe turned and hurried away into the trainer's room.

Mantle did not see this side of the ever-stoic DiMaggio. But if DiMaggio didn't show his resentment, his fans did. In the middle and late 1950s, booing at Yankee Stadium would become deafening whenever Mantle came to the plate. It began with a smattering of catcalls and boos that rookie year, which prompted Hank Bauer to tell Mickey, "In New York, most of the fans here are DiMaggio fans, so you're surely gonna get booed for being the guy who's gonna take his place. It's just a New York thing."

Mickey himself later said, "I don't care who you are, you hear those boos. . . . I well understood that my being made into a rival of Joe DiMaggio turned plenty of fans against me. But I was not ready for the dirty names or the screaming profanity or the tireless abuse [of the New York fans]."

Worse, Mantle's own actions around DiMaggio did little to endear him to the Yankee great. Once Stengel called to Mickey on the bench to pinch-hit. Mantle quickly tore off his team jacket and flung it behind him as he hurried to the bat rack. Hearing a muffled yell from the bench, he looked around. The jacket had landed in DiMaggio's face and was covering his head like a hood.

"He's a rockhead," DiMaggio told his newspaper pal Lou Effrat.

From DiMaggio's point of view, he was simply giving the young phenom much the same treatment he had been given by Ruth when he had been a rookie himself with the Yankees. "Joe met Ruth well after the Bambino's playing career, and their relationship was formal," said DiMaggio biographer Richard Ben Cramer. "Joe remembered well how Ruth dismissed him as a rookie and said he hadn't proved yet that he could play in the big leagues. In Gehrig's case, Joe and he were teammates for more than two years before Lou took sick and left the lineup, but both Gehrig and Joe were silent souls who came to the clubhouse dressed, did their business, and left without a word beyond simple greetings. . . . Joe was certainly responsible for the chill between him and Mantle in Mickey's rookie year. In 1951, when Mantle arrived, he was so shy he couldn't say a word to DiMaggio unless the big guy spoke to him first."

In the time he was away at Kansas City that year, Mantle missed some of the dramatics between DiMaggio and Stengel. At one point, frustrated with DiMaggio's offensive struggles, Stengel dropped him from his usual cleanup spot in the lineup and moved Gil McDougald into it. McDougald had a tremendous day, going four for four and driving home every runner in scoring position during his at-bats. The move, though, was short-lived, much to Stengel's chagrin—between games, the front office overruled him. In the second game of that day's doubleheader, McDougald was dropped to the eighth place in the lineup, and DiMaggio was back batting cleanup. On September 16, DiMaggio was dropped back to the fifth spot, this time in favor of Yogi Berra, in a crucial game against the league-leading Indians, whom the Yankees trailed by a game. It was a rare chance for Mantle to see at close range a glimpse of the old DiMaggio. With the Yankees trying to add to a 3–1 lead against Bob Feller, Mantle opened the fifth inning with a drag-bunt single. Two outs later, Mantle was at second base when Cleveland decided to add one more insult to DiMaggio's farewell year. The Indians intentionally walked Berra to pitch to DiMaggio, who dispatched a two-strike fastball to the deepest part of Yankee Stadium for a game-clinching triple that scored Mantle and Berra. The Yankees moved into a tie for the league lead, then went ahead of the Indians the next day on DiMaggio's game-winning run in the bottom of the ninth inning. On September 28, DiMaggio climaxed the last regular season game of his career with a three-run home run that sewed up the Yankees' pennant-clinching doubleheader sweep of the Red Sox.

For Mantle, the world had completely turned around in less than six weeks. His strong comeback against American League pitching in the home stretch of the pennant race had reaffirmed the Yankees' faith in him, and he was already looking ahead to the next year with anticipation. Mutt had been pleased with the courage his son had shown in Kansas City and then with the Yankees after he had been recalled—so much that he arranged to take time off at the mine to watch Mickey play in the "subway series" against the Giants. Mickey couldn't wait to show the New York he now knew to his father, or at least the New York he knew Mutt would approve of. Mutt was driving up from Commerce with only two of his friends, which was going to make the Series a little easier for Mickey; he didn't know what he would have done had the entire Mantle family decided to come to New York and brought Merlyn with them, as they had to St. Louis earlier in the season. All summer long Mickey had been torn between his love for Merlyn, waiting for him in Commerce, and his newfound feelings for Holly. Mickey was engaged to Merlyn, but he was sleeping with Holly. Holly had helped him adjust to life in the big city, solving part of the problem that had doomed Mantle early in the season. Mickey was indebted to her and uncertain of what to do next. He wanted his father to meet her, and he was hoping that Mutt would understand that he needed her in his life.

When it came to dealing with his father, however, Mantle would forever remain the child, always trying to please, rarely asserting himself, and never standing up to him even on anything important with which Mutt might have disagreed. Mickey's relationship with Holly was perhaps the best example, a potentially life-altering decision that Mantle would leave completely in his father's hands. The moment Mickey introduced Holly to him, he sensed that his father didn't approve.

"Mickey, you do the right thing and marry your own kind," Mutt said to Mickey after pulling his son aside.

Mantle tried to explain his relationship.

"Merlyn's a sweet girl," Mutt said, cutting him off, "and she's in love with you."

"Yeah, I know."

"The point is, she's good for you," said Mutt. "She's what you need to keep your head straight."

"I know."

"Well, then after the Series, you ought get on home and marry her."

Once again, Mantle's father had decided his future, and Mickey had neither the courage nor the ability to protest.

In the World Series, the Yankees faced the New York Giants, who were fresh off an incredible pennant-winning comeback. Trailing the Dodgers by thirteen and a half games in the middle of August, the Giants won thirty-seven of their last forty-four games and finished in a tie with Brooklyn. Then in a three-game playoff, the Giants again came from behind to win at the Polo Grounds, on Bobby Thomson's famous ninth-inning home run off Ralph Branca. Mantle and his father watched the game with most of the Yankee players, who all expected they would be playing the Dodgers in the World Series. "We were all sitting behind third base that day," recalled Hank Bauer, "and until Thomson hit the homer, we thought we were going to play the Dodgers, but we were rooting for the Giants because the Polo Grounds was bigger than Ebbets Field. We'd make more money if the Giants won."

On deck when Thomson hit his home run had been Willie Mays. Like Mantle, he would be playing in his first World Series, in what would be the last of DiMaggio's ten fall classics. It was the only time the career paths of all three New York baseball legends converged—though none of them had much to do with the outcome of the 1951 World Series.

DiMaggio, his knees, back, and shoulder often hurting, had become a defensive liability. Shortstop Phil Rizzuto and second baseman Jerry Coleman had to go unusually deep into left and right-center field to take cutoff throws from the increasingly weak-armed Yankee legend. DiMaggio also had misjudged more fly balls than ever before in his career. Before the World Series began, Stengel took Mantle aside and instructed him to be especially aggressive from his right-field position. "Take everything you can get over in center," Stengel told Mickey. "The Dago's heel is hurting pretty bad."

Riding their momentum, the Giants won game one of the Series, 5–1. Left-hander Dave Koslo, the Giants' number-four starter, pitched a seven-hitter, Monte Irvin stole home in the second inning, and Alvin Dark hit a three-run homer in the sixth inning. Mantle was hitless but walked twice against Koslo.

Determined to get a World Series hit, Mantle led off the third inning of the second game with a drag-bunt single and scored his first Series run on Gil McDougald's bloop single to right field. For Mickey, the scene at Yankee Stadium that afternoon was something out of a dream. He was playing in the World Series, in the Yankee outfield next to DiMaggio, with his father watching from the stands. When Willie Mays led off in the top of the sixth inning,

Mantle shaded over a couple of steps toward centerfield. Looking over at DiMaggio, it was still hard to imagine the great Joltin' Joe was even a step slower than in his prime. He still moved gracefully under fly balls and made every catch appear easy and effortless. A moment later Mays connected and drove a fly ball into short right-center field.

There had been a time when a fly ball like this one would have been routine for DiMaggio, who was notorious for selfishly guarding his territory in center. One time in 1949, then-rookie Hank Bauer had eased over into right center to take a fly ball, much as Mickey had now been instructed to do. DiMaggio had stared at the young outfielder between innings in the Yankee dugout until Bauer asked him if he had done anything wrong. "No, you didn't do anything wrong," replied DiMaggio, "but you're the first son of a bitch who ever invaded my territory."

Mantle sensed that Mays's short fly ball was exactly the kind of play Stengel had asked him to make. "I knew there was no way DiMaggio could get to it," Mantle would recall, "so I hauled ass. Just as I arrived, I heard Joe say, 'I got it.' I looked over, and he was camped under the ball." Mickey would later tell friends that as he saw DiMaggio, he thought, "Oh, shit! I'm gonna hit DiMaggio. I'll put him in the hospital. They'll never let me play again! That's when I slammed on the brakes. My spikes caught on the rubber cover of a drain hole buried in the outfield grass. Pop. There was a sound like a tire blowing out, and my right knee collapsed. I fell to the ground and stayed there, motionless. A bone was sticking out the side of my leg, [and] the pain squeezed like a vice around my right knee."

Mickey was convinced from the cracking sound he had heard that he had broken his leg and figured his career was suddenly over. He lay on the outfield grass with his eyes closed; people thought he had passed out from the pain— or had had a heart attack. For a moment, Mickey wanted to be a child again and pretend that this hadn't happened, that he would be jumping to his feet any second. Most of all Mickey felt like crying, but he couldn't with a stadium full of fans looking at him—and his boyhood hero standing over him.

DiMaggio thought for a split second that Mickey might have been shot.

"I was afraid he was dead," DiMaggio later recalled. "I shouted, 'Mick! Mick! And he never moved a muscle or batted an eye. Then I waved to our bench to send out a stretcher. . . . After what seemed like a couple of minutes but probably wasn't that long, Mantle suddenly opened his eyes and burst out crying. He bawled like a baby. I don't know whether he thought maybe he had missed the ball or that he was seriously injured. I leaned over and told him, 'Don't move. They're bringing a stretcher.'"

Mantle was to later say, "I guess that was about as close as Joe and I had come to a conversation. I don't know what impressed me more, the injury or the sight of an aging DiMaggio still able to make a difficult catch look easy."

Richard Ben Cramer would write, "In later years, among friends, the Mick was neither so stoic nor impressed by the Clipper. The way Mantle figured, DiMaggio wouldn't call that ball until he was damn sure he could make it look easy. Joe had to look good, . . . but Mickey would never play another game without pain."

Mutt, who had been seated not far behind the Yankee dugout, moved toward the field when he realized the seriousness of the injury. He made his way to the dugout and was there to see Mickey being carried off on the stretcher. In the trainer's room Yankee trainer Gus Mauch put splints on both sides of the leg and wrapped it up to protect the knee. The team made arrangements for Mantle to go to Lenox Hill Hospital the next day, but that night the knee began to swell to almost twice its normal size. Mickey took the bandages off to sleep and rewrapped the knee the next morning before heading off to the hospital with Mutt.

Mantle was disappointed that his first World Series had ended so abruptly, but that abruptness would be matched by the suddenness with which his personal life would soon take another turn. On the steps of Lenox Hill Hospital, the life he had known since childhood would begin coming to an end.

"[My father] got out of the cab first, outside the hospital, and then I got out," Mantle remembered years later. "I was on crutches and I couldn't put any weight on the leg that was hurt, so as I got out of the cab I grabbed my father's shoulder to steady myself. He crumpled to the sidewalk. I couldn't understand it. He was a very strong man, and I didn't think anything at all about putting my weight on him that way. He was always so strong."

Both Mickey and Mutt were rushed into the hospital, where Mantle underwent surgery to repair two torn ligaments in his right knee. At the same time, doctors at the hospital ran a series of tests on Mutt. Father and son were put in the same room, where they watched the remainder of the World Series on television. The Giants regained the lead in game three with a 6–2 victory. They scored five unearned runs in the fifth inning, including a three-run home run by Whitey Lockman. The game also included a controversial play at second base, in which Eddie Stanky, trying to steal second base, kicked the ball out of Phil Rizzuto's hand and into the outfield and then took third base.

"Then we got a bad break when the fourth game was rained out," said Wes Westrum, the Giants catcher, who later managed the Mets. "Sal Maglie had been all ready to pitch Sunday, but Monday he didn't have a thing. Joe DiMaggio hit his last home run off him. We tried to keep the ball away from him, but Maglie didn't. And with the rainout, the Yankees were able to come back with Allie Reynolds on Monday instead of Johnny Sain."

The Yankees won game four, 6–2, as Allie Reynolds held the Giants to two runs and DiMaggio hit a fifth-inning, two-run home run—the last home run, as Westrum noted, of his career. DiMaggio drove in three runs in game five, as did Rizzuto, and Gil McDougald hit a grand slam, in a 13–1 victory. In game six, at Yankee Stadium, Hank Bauer rid himself of a career-long World Series slump that had kept him to five hits in thirty-two at-bats, with a two-out, three-run triple off Koslo in the sixth inning. "He had me struck out with a knuckleball that I took," Bauer said, "but the umpire called it a ball for 3 and 2, then I hit the next pitch over Monte Irvin's head in left field. He didn't know that when the wind was blowing in, it really was blowing out because it would hit the stands in right field and swirl around."

Bauer's triple broke open a 1–1 tie and sent the Yanks to a 4–3 victory, sealed when Bauer made a sensational series-ending catch of a line drive by Sal Yvars with the tying run in scoring position. "Nobody could tell me where to play Yvars because he hardly ever played," Bauer recalled. "I anchored myself on that drain pipe that Mickey tore up his knee on and when Yvars hit that liner, I saw it, then I didn't see it, then I dove for it and it stuck in the webbing of my glove."

Mantle cheered on the Yankees to their third straight world championship, but the celebration for Mickey would be short-lived.

Years later, Mantle would say that he suspected his father had been ill— that he had noticed some weight loss when Mutt had visited him in Kansas City that summer to confront him about "being a man." If so, Mickey apparently did not act on it, nor did anyone else close to Mutt. Mantle may have been in denial of anything that threatened the most formidable figure in his life. But if Mantle did truly fear that there was something seriously wrong with Mutt's health, his reluctance to urge or insist that he see a doctor would only underscore the inability of this major league ballplayer, on the verge of stardom, and seemingly a world away from Commerce, Oklahoma, to assert himself with his father.

A few days after Mantle's surgery, the doctor who had examined his father came to see Mickey, who was alone, resting in his hospital bed. Mutt had cancer. It was Hodgkin's disease, the dreaded Mantle curse—the same form of cancer that had killed his grandfather Charlie and his uncles. The doctor advised taking Mutt home and allowing him to return to work, for as long as he could. The diagnosis offered little of the hope that the suddenly shocked Mantle desperately sought.

"I'm sorry, Mick," the doctor said with finality. "I'm afraid there's not much that can be done. Your father is dying."

In the winter after his rookie season, Mickey began to realize that he would never again have the same kind of speed that he had had prior to his injury in the second game of the 1951 World Series. The injury was the worst he had ever endured. He would have osteomyelitis for the rest of his life, in an arrested stage, but since the hospital stay when he had almost lost his left leg, the rehabilitation required had been minor. He had begun running at full speed almost as soon as he could walk again. Mickey quickly learned that the injury to his right knee would take considerably longer to heal. For six weeks, until late November, he wore a full-length brace that locked at the knee. After that, he was given a modified brace that allowed the leg to bend at the knee. The team physician, Dr. Sidney Gaynor, devised a weighted boot for Mickey to use in a series of exercises designed to strengthen his knee. Mickey, however, lacked the patience and dedication required for the physical rehabilitation it would take to make the knee as close to normal again as possible.

"I lazed around, feeling sorry for myself instead of doing the exercises prescribed by Dr. Gaynor," Mickey was to later say. "I thought the muscles would automatically come back, good as ever. I was twenty years old, and I thought I was a superman."

There was also another reason for Mantle's intoxicated headiness that winter. He was getting married.

The relationship between Mickey and Merlyn would be a curious one from beginning to end. In Mantle's books and in some of the magazine articles of the 1950s, their relationship was portrayed as young love between hometown sweethearts that was severely tested in the big city. The description, however, does not tell the full story—which, as with all relationships and marriages, was far more complex and convoluted than the small-town fairytale cover story. Love was certainly a large part of it. Mickey's letters to Merlyn, especially during his minor league season and his rookie year, are filled with endearments and expressions of love. At various other times through his life, Mantle also talked or wrote about his love and devotion for his wife, though usually in the context of her as the mother of his sons. Thus, another major aspect of their relationship was duty—duty to Merlyn, especially later in their lives, but perhaps, more importantly, duty to his father.

When Mickey and Mutt returned to Commerce after the World Series in the fall of 1951, a sense of portending doom clouded any celebration. Mantle had completed his first major league season. The Yankees had won the World Series, giving Mickey's income for his rookie year a boost. With his World Series share, Mantle made a down payment on a new home for his mother and father. The new house at 317 South River Street had seven rooms and a telephone, a party line. "Two rings meant us," said Mickey.

In Mantle's world, however, nothing could undo the devastation of learning that his father was dying. As the dutiful son, he wanted to make his father's last months as pleasant and as comfortable as possible. In this context especially, whatever Mutt wanted—Mickey's father's dying wishes—became sacred. Mantle had never questioned his father's decisions or his demands, and he would not begin to do so now, as he tried to make Mutt's last months as comfortable as possible. On more than one occasion, Mutt reiterated his desire that Mickey marry Merlyn. Mantle later remembered having a conversation with his father in their living room. Mutt refused to talk about his health and turned the conversation to the Yankees and to Merlyn. Mutt apparently feared that Mickey's career would be sidetracked if he were to play in New York while remaining single. "After you make the majors," Mutt said, "I'd like to see you marry Merlyn, and I'd like to have a little freckle-faced, red-headed grandson." Mutt would repeat this wish yet again in New York after meeting Mickey's girlfriend Holly Brooke, and he brought up the matter yet again when they were back in Commerce.

Mickey first saw Merlyn Johnson at a high school football game at neighboring Picher High School. It did not begin as love at first sight, although that night he returned home and said to his mother, "I met the cutest little thing in Picher tonight. She twirls one of the batons for the Picher band. She's got freckles, reddish hair and is no taller than that." Mantle's friend Ivan Schouse was dating Merlyn's sister Pat, and both were majorettes at Picher High. A few days later Ivan arranged a triple date in which Mickey was paired off with yet another majorette, Lavanda Whipkey, and Merlyn went out with another of Mickey's friends, Preston Christman. Mickey was disappointed. Fortunately for Mickey, things soon worked out in his favor. When Lavanda was unable to go on a date they had tentatively planned, Mickey asked Preston Christman if he would mind if he asked Merlyn out on a date. Christman told him to go ahead. Even then, however, Mickey still had to ask Ivan Schouse, this time, to arrange a double date. The story goes that when Schouse called Merlyn to ask if she would go out with Mickey, her response was, "Who's Mickey Mantle?" Mickey quickly made a firmer impression on Merlyn. After the third date, he asked Merlyn to go steady. She agreed, and from then on in the Commerce-Picher area she was known as Mickey's girlfriend.

"I developed an instant crush on Mickey Mantle," Merlyn would recall, "and by our second or third date, I was in love with him and always would be."

Merlyn's mother was among those amazed at their relationship. She knew how quiet her daughter was, and she was also aware of how shy Mickey appeared to be. "I don't know how Merlyn and Mickey ever got acquainted," she would say later. "Neither of them ever says a word."

Merlyn was the daughter of a highly respected family in Picher. Her father, like her grandfather, had been a deacon in the Baptist church. He was now a member of the local school board. Merlyn's grandfather had founded the Johnson Lumber Company, which annually sponsored a team in the area's summer baseball leagues. Her father Giles had worked in the local mines until he suffered a head injury in an accident. A subsequent operation to remove a blood clot had left him with epilepsy, and he had been forced to take an office job in the family lumberyard. Merlyn herself grew up in a loving family which encouraged her to excel in her studies as well as in her singing. She once entertained the troops at nearby Camp Crowder during World War II and another time won a music contest in which she sang an aria in Italian. During her senior year in high school, Merlyn won a scholarship to Miami (Oklahoma) Junior College. Merlyn was dazzled by the movies and Hollywood, secretly harboring a fantasy that one day she might find herself in the world of celebrities and recording stars. Once she fell in love with Mickey, however, Merlyn gave up her dreams of college or a career. Mickey became her focus, and she ultimately became one of those women who live in both the glory and shadow of their famous husbands. By her own admission, being Mrs. Mickey Mantle "was all I had really wanted since the second or third time I had seen him."

Merlyn was as addicted to Mickey as she later became to alcohol. She would write in *A Hero All His Life* that she "loved Mickey Mantle so much that I wanted to crawl inside him and underneath his skin. I wanted to control everything he did." Few who grew up knowing Merlyn would ever have suspected her to be capable of harboring not only such strong emotions but also emotions that, by her own account, would become unhealthy and contribute to destroying their love.

Mickey and Merlyn were married on December 23, 1951, in a small ceremony at the home of Merlyn's parents in Picher. Mickey had just turned twenty that October. Merlyn was nineteen. Mickey's best man was Turk Miller, his father's closest friend. Only the immediate families attended, and Merlyn's mother's cousin played the wedding march on the Johnson family piano. "The wedding was happy and tearful at the same time," Merlyn would recall. "His father looked on, and we both knew this ceremony was partly for him. Next to me, the groom's father was the happiest person in the room. Mick was somewhere in the top five. He would have done anything for his parents, and his lingering sadness was the fact that he was not able to do it sooner." The honeymoon, however, turned out to be a small disaster. First, the new Mantles took along Mickey's friend Bill Mosely and his girlfriend on what they thought was going to be a fabulous, all-expenses-paid weekend in the bridal suite of a luxurious hotel in Hot Springs, Arkansas. In his typically unsuspecting manner, Mickey had believed a man who had claimed to be from the Hot Springs Chamber of Commerce. Of course, there was no free honeymoon, and Mickey and Bill barely had enough money on them to pay for one night at a motel. Back home, the newlyweds moved into a small motel on Main Street in Commerce. Mutt would stop by to check on them each night because he was afraid that the motel's open-draft heaters might malfunction and release a deadly natural-gas leak.

Merlyn, however, quickly realized that her new husband was an extremely distracted newlywed. She found herself competing with the two most important things of Mantle's life: his love for his father, and his career. Mutt's health continued to deteriorate that winter, and he was forced to retire from his job at the mine. Shortly after New Year's Day in 1952, Merlyn and Mickey drove Mutt over snow-covered and ice-slick roads to the Mayo Clinic in Rochester,

Minnesota. There, Mutt underwent exploratory surgery, from which the doctors learned that the disease was so advanced that he had only months to
live. "They gave him treatments that eased his pain, but there was nothing
anybody could do to cure him," Mantle was to recall. "When I saw the despair
settle deeply in his eyes, I began to doubt God. . . . All I knew was a bottom-
less sorrow, and I couldn't express it to anyone."

Least of all, it seemed, could he express it to Merlyn. She was to complain bitterly years later of feeling locked out by Mickey from his suffering
and pain over his father's illness. Mantle would never adequately explain the
reason for shutting his wife out of the despair he felt over seeing his father
wither away. He would be equally reclusive over their years together about his
injuries and the prescribed rehabilitation programs that he invariably failed
to follow. That winter, the days leading to spring training passed without
Mantle investing any time or effort in rehabilitating his knee, even after
DiMaggio formally announced his retirement and Mickey learned that Stengel planned to move him over to center field. Unfortunately for Mickey, this
would become a ritual marking much of his career. An untimely injury—and
they would be numerous—would curtail a promising season, sending Mantle
into an abyss of self-pity and a period of half-hearted rehabilitation. "I hated
getting hurt," Mickey would say in one conversation. "That's why I hated
going to doctors. I didn't want to see them because I didn't want to know what
they would tell me."

Dr. Gaynor years later explained that Mickey's tendency to injury was
the result of his muscles' being too strong for his bones, a condition that led
to an unusual number of torn ligaments and cartilages during his career. Publicly Mickey would subsequently downplay his injuries. "They keep talking
about me getting hurt," he said. "I still played eighteen years. I played in more
games than anyone else in Yankee history."

Stengel and the Yankees were surprised and disappointed to see Mickey
report for spring training in 1952 limping and unable to run. Plans to put
Mantle in center field were put on hold indefinitely. In spring training, Stengel would try Hank Bauer, Jackie Jensen, Bob Cerv, and Gene Woodling in
center field, but they were not what he had envisioned for his team in the
post-DiMaggio era. When Mantle finally did get into a spring training game,
it was as a pinch-hitter. He reached bases on a fielder's choice, and Stengel
immediately sent in a pinch-runner. His worst nightmare was to see Mickey
reinjure his weakened knee and perhaps miss the entire season.

Mickey opened the regular season in right field. He was rehabilitating the knee by playing, and by the end of April he was running at top speed. Even then, Stengel didn't want to press Mantle into center-field duty. Center field in Yankee Stadium's original configuration was a cavernous canyon that could easily overwhelm an unprepared outfielder. The dimensions at Yankee Stadium, dwarfing those of ballparks half a century later, could be intimidating to both hitters and outfielders: 457 feet to deep left center, 461 feet to dead center, 407 feet to deep right center. It was a tribute to DiMaggio that he developed a reputation for making difficult catches seem easy. However, center field in Yankee Stadium was a position that demanded speed, or at least healthy legs. With Mickey in right because of his ailing knee, center field was played in rotation by a committee of Jensen, Cerv, and Woodling. In early May, George Weiss made a multiplayer deal in which the always-promising Jensen and two other players were traded to the Washington Senators for Irv Noren, who was slated to become the Yankees' fourth center fielder of the young season.

Meanwhile, Merlyn moved to New York to join Mickey and found herself in culture shock. Home in New York that first year of marriage was a small, uncongenial room, without a stove or refrigerator, at the Concourse Plaza Hotel, where Mickey had lived for part of his rookie season. Even using a telephone could intimidate her. In Oklahoma, Merlyn had used crank telephones her entire life, cranking a handle a couple of times until the operator came on the line to connect the number. Merlyn had never used a rotary phone until she moved to New York. Merlyn got to know some of the Yankee wives through get-togethers they would have whenever the team went out on the road. But Merlyn was made uncomfortable by the competitiveness and rivalry of some of the wives, just as she felt shy and uncertain about how to dress and wear makeup in the big city. For Merlyn, life in New York finally took a positive direction when she and Mickey began hanging out with Billy Martin and his first wife, Lois. Eventually, the two couples decided to share a two-bedroom apartment in the Concourse Plaza.

Mickey happened to be at the apartment alone with Merlyn on May 6, 1952, when the Yankees were in a home stand, when he got the phone call he dreaded would come. Stengel was on the line.

"Mickey," Stengel began—signaling to Mantle the solemnity of the call, because Stengel rarely called him by his Christian name—"I'm at the Stadium. Your mother called here looking for you. It's your father, son. He's passed."

"He knew they couldn't cure him," Mantle would later recount. "But he went out to Denver so that the little kids in our family—I'm the oldest and my sister and my three little brothers were just little kids at the time—wouldn't see him wasting away, getting thinner and thinner and sicker and sicker. So he went out to Denver, and he died there. He never complained, he never acted scared, and he died like a man. I realized then that he was dying when he came to see me in Kansas City, though he never gave any sign to me. He didn't die scared, and he didn't live scared."

Mutt Mantle, according to family and friends, had insisted on going to Denver alone, leaving Lovell in Commerce with their four youngsters still at home. Mickey would later say that his father had told his family he was going to Denver to check out a center that he thought might be able to help him. "My father," Mickey would say throughout his lifetime, "was the most courageous man I've ever known."

Mantle was inconsolable and filled with guilt over the fact that his father had died alone. Mantle was later to write in his autobiography, "He needed me and I wasn't there. I couldn't make it up to him. He died alone. I cried, 'What kind of God is there anyway, to let him die like that!'"

For no apparent reason, Mickey took out his frustration on Merlyn. "Everything about that day is still vivid to me," she would later recall. "Mickey pounded his fist against the wall. And then he asked me to leave the room. I was stunned."

Merlyn walked to the door and asked, "When are we going home?"

"I guess I'll leave tomorrow," Mickey said.

"I'd like to go with you," Merlyn told him.

But Mickey shook his head. "No, you don't need to go. I'll be back in a day or two."

"I had to let that sink in. He didn't want me there. I was not going to be at the funeral services for my father-in-law. I didn't understand then and I don't understand now. I was in tears, so hurt I couldn't even ask why. I can only guess that Mick wanted to grieve alone. In his mind the funeral was only for his family, and that did not include me, not yet. . . . I can only guess that Mickey wanted to grieve alone."

Mantle alone attended his father's funeral in Commerce. Mutt Mantle was thirty-nine years old. He was buried in the cemetery between Commerce and Miami in which his father and two brothers were also buried. Mickey did not have the maturity to deal with his father's death. So much had been left unsaid between them for so many years that no amount of tears or sorrow could now span the chasm of unresolved emotions and feelings between father and son. Death and the moment of death would now figure prominently in Mickey's life. In dire moments, Mickey would come to reflect on his life, reconsider his experiences, and try to puzzle them out anew. In the years ahead, he would take the hard view. If Mickey, in his bitter rumination, was not precisely an alter ego for Mutt, he was the different self the father had nurtured, modeled after the personal experiences and private defeats of Mutt's own early life. Ultimately, the black knowledge of this looming end affected everything Mickey did. Yet, as he said his final farewell, Mantle found himself torn by guilt and filled with recriminations over his failure to express in life what now seemed almost meaningless in death. "I stood before my father's grave, remembering a thousand things from the past," Mantle would recall. "So many chances then to let him know how much I love him—and I never said it, not once."

It would be years before Merlyn was to comprehend the issues that were preying on Mickey then and made her an unwitting victim of his frustration. In fact, Mantle would go to his own grave unable to come to terms fully with his father. He would never be able to untangle their complex relationship that had begun and ended as a one-way dialogue—Mutt speaking, asking, demanding; Mickey, with the obedience of a child, never speaking his own mind. For Mickey, to challenge his father or second-guess what he had taught him, especially after his death, was unthinkable. Their relationship was not a topic that any of the writers who ever worked with him on his books could raise with Mantle; he would regard it as intruding too far. The closest Mantle came to reexamining his relationship with his father may have been in *The Mick*, in discussing teammate Bobby Brown and his relationship with *his* father. Brown, who went on to become a cardiologist and later still the president of the American League, retired in 1954 while still capable of playing several more seasons. "Of those I've played with," Mickey wrote, "I think his situation came closest to mine, in the sense that his father always wanted him to play baseball, was always on him to do better, working tirelessly to prepare him for the majors. The same devotion as my dad's, 'Goddamn, how could you have swung at that pitch?' Once Bobby had a lousy night at the stadium. His father drove him home. They were driving across the George Washington Bridge and Bobby's moaning, 'Oh, I feel awful. I was terrible.' When they came to the middle of the bridge, his father pulled over and stopped. He said,

'Why don't you jump?' It shows what can happen when you get totally wrapped up in dreams about somebody else's future. They become your own. And that's the kind of background Bobby had, same as mine, insofar as father-son relationships go."

Losing Mutt weighed heavily on Mantle throughout that season. Between games, especially when the Yankees were on the road and Merlyn wasn't around, Mantle would dwell on him. Unfortunately for Mickey, his happiest memories of his father and himself—his being taught to switch-hit as a child, the long drives to watch the Cardinals in St. Louis, signing his professional contract with Tom Greenwade—were dwarfed by the dark thoughts of his father's illness and his suffering alone. "All that season he was in pain," Mantle said in an interview years later. "He was so sick he couldn't sleep in bed at night, and he used to sit up in a chair. But he wouldn't let my mother tell me he was dying. He just said he had a backache. He figured I was having a hard enough time [with] the Yankees."

When Mantle returned to the Yankees after his father's funeral, it was to playing time as sporadic as it had been just before Mutt's death. He was only a shadow of the player he promised to be the previous year. Mutt's illness and death had preoccupied him. Like the other Yankees, Mantle was also at the mercy of Stengel's managerial inspirations. In one game against Cleveland in which the Yankees were trailing by seven runs, Stengel inserted Mickey at third base, which he had not played since his early teenage days. Out of position at third base against the Indians, Mantle made two errors in half a game; it would be the only game Mantle ever played at third base. Stengel would also insert him for part of a game at second base; over the next three seasons he would use Mickey at shortstop in seven games. Mickey then rode the bench for several days until May 20, when, without telling him, Stengel made out a lineup that had Mantle batting third and playing center field. Finally, the Yankees had their successor to DiMaggio.

Getting Mantle ready to play, however, became an extensive daily project. Once at the stadium, Mickey would go to the trainer's room for several rolls of tape and bandages and begin the ritual of carefully wrapping his legs from the ankles all the way to mid-thigh, so that his legs resembled a mummy's. Cleveland Indians pitcher Early Wynn later recalled watching Mantle dress in the American League clubhouse before an All-Star game and coming away stunned at the courage he saw on display. "I watched him bandage that knee— that whole leg—and I saw what he had to go through every day to play,"

Wynn said. "He was taped from shin to thigh. And now I'll never be able to say enough in praise. Seeing those legs, his power becomes unbelievable."

The bandaged, injured legs would be Mantle's cross to bear on the field, and there would be enough glimpses of his amazing speed to make fans and fellow players wonder what he might have done with healthy "wheels." After returning from his Korean War stint as a jet pilot, Ted Williams would sometimes tell how he had once nearly died landing a flaming fighter plane that was about to explode, and hurrying out of the cockpit. In that story the image of Mantle's speed was his measure of quickness. "I got outa there," he would say, "and I must have been running as fast as Mantle."

10

In 1952, Mickey finished third in the Most Valuable Player balloting after competing his second season with a .311 batting average, twenty-three home runs, eighty-seven RBIs, and helping lead the Yankees to their fourth straight pennant. That season, Mickey also batted against the only pitcher who would have the distinction of facing both Mantle and Babe Ruth. In his rookie year in 1934 with the Red Sox, right-hander Al Benton pitched to Ruth, and he pitched to Mantle in his final season, which he played with the Philadelphia Athletics. Neither Ruth nor Mantle hit a home run off him. Mickey, though, would top off his second season with one of the best World Series of his career—hitting .345 and deciding the seventh game with a tie-breaking home run as well as driving in an insurance run in a 4–2 victory over Brooklyn.

Mantle's timely hitting in the 1952 World Series, especially the home run off Joe Black in the deciding game, impressed the National League–champion Dodgers. However, what particularly impressed Jackie Robinson about Mickey was a defensive play Mantle made on a line drive the Dodger second baseman hit into right center field. Mickey fielded the ball on the third hop, as Robinson made a big turn around first base and checked to see what the inexperienced young center fielder was doing. Manager Casey Stengel had warned Mickey that Robinson would be watching for his throw. If Mickey tried to throw behind him to pick him off at first base—something the Dodgers scouting report noted that he had been doing—the ever-aggressive Robinson would almost certainly break to second base. As soon as he fielded the ball, Mickey looked toward first baseman Johnny Mize and began his throwing motion in that direction, and Robinson immediately began running to second base. Mickey, however, faked the throw to first base and then rifled the ball to Billy Martin, covering second base. A surprised Jackie Robinson was thrown out sliding into second by more than ten feet.

"I'll never forget the sight," Mantle recalled. "Jackie getting up, dusting himself off, and giving me a little tip of the hat, his eyes saying, 'I'll get you next time.'"

So dominant was Mantle's presence in that fall classic that after the final game, a heartbroken Robinson nevertheless went into the Yankee clubhouse to congratulate Mickey personally. "You're a helluva ballplayer," he told Mantle.

"Man, what a classy guy," Mickey said years later. "I never could have done that, not in a million years. I'm a really bad loser."

"Mantle beat us," Robinson told reporters after the game. "He was the difference between the two clubs. They didn't miss Joe DiMaggio. It was Mickey Mantle who killed us."

Baseball was only five years removed from the 1947 season, in which Jackie Robinson had integrated baseball. In the next half-century, baseball would undergo a dramatic demographic revolution, and it all began when Robinson and the Dodgers on April 15, 1947, broke the "color barrier"—the national pastime's segregationist policy that had mirrored American society's politics of exclusion.

Mantle would remember that just a few years earlier there had been civil rights picket lines outside Yankee Stadium with signs and chanting: "Don't go past the gate! Don't go past the gate! The Yanks dis-crim-i-nate!"

In the summer of 1947, the summer before his senior year in high school, Mickey had seen Robinson play in person. Mickey, pal Nick Ferguson, and a couple of Mutt's friends had driven all night with Mutt in the family's old LaSalle to St. Louis to watch the Cardinals play the Dodgers. They arrived at eight o'clock in the morning at Sportsman's Park, where they saw an unforgettable sight. Thousands of blacks had lined up around the park, waiting for tickets to the bleachers, which was the only place blacks were permitted. It was a completely new experience for Mickey, and not necessarily one in which he felt altogether comfortable. Race relations and integration were not everyday topics in Commerce, for the simple reason that, as Ferguson put it, "There were never any black people in our area."

The Yankees themselves would not have a black player for another three years. In 1955, after a sensational 1954 season in the minors, Elston Howard would join the Yankees and immediately face the same discrimination that other black major league players encountered when their teams trained or played in the South. St. Petersburg, Florida, was no different. During spring training, the Yankees were housed at the Soreno, one of the city's fancy old hotels. Howard, however, was forced to room with a family in one of the city's black neighborhoods. The exhibition season, with the Yankees traveling to play other teams training in Florida, presented the same set of discriminatory problems that confronted other blacks. Not only was Howard not permitted to stay with the team at its traveling hotel, but he was not allowed into the restaurants along the way from city to city. Someone, usually the team's traveling secretary, would bring food out for Howard to eat on the team bus.

Mantle's friendship with Howard would flourish during their years together, and Howard would be among the players who would look to Mickey for the inspiration and leadership that an earlier generation of Yankees had found in DiMaggio. "When Mickey's playing well," Howard would say, "his actions kind of spill over on everybody. Just to know he is in the lineup ready to swing with somebody on base, gives a ball club like ours a lift it needs. He is the kind of player who is so good himself, it makes everybody want to follow his example."

Years later, upon the publication of Jim Bouton's *Ball Four*, Mantle would be more offended by Bouton's portrayal of Elston Howard as a baseball Uncle Tom than by what he had written of Mickey—which, of course, had made for the juicier reading. Bouton wrote of his former catcher, "The best way I can explain Howard is to recall the day Jimmy Cannon, the elderly columnist, Howard, his wife Arlene and I got involved in an argument about civil rights. Arlene on one side, Cannon and Howard on the other. Arlene and I were the militants." Bouton would come to regret that portrayal and would write in a later edition of his book, "Today, I see Elston Howard, not as the less-than-militant fellow portrayed in the book, but as a black man who survived growing up in the '40s and worked his way to the top of what was once a white man's game. I think of Elston behind the plate in his catcher's gear hunching his big body forward and squatting low to give me a target at the knees. He's a teammate to me now, not a token." Bouton, though, apparently still failed to understand that one of the qualities he originally criticized in Howard, his diplomacy, was an elementary part of his selection as the first black Yankee. The Yankees, in their own way, were looking for qualities in Howard not that dissimilar from what Branch Rickey found in Jackie Robinson.

It is accurate to suggest that baseball changed Mickey's view on race, much as the country underwent a change in the two decades after Robinson broke the game's color barrier. Not only was the age of all-white major league baseball over, but so was the era in which the white American dominated sports. In the eyes of many, including Mantle, Willie Mays would become the dominant baseball player of his time. In future years, when Joe DiMaggio would be introduced in public as "America's greatest living baseball player," many blacks and others who had seen Mays play would chuckle to themselves—they knew better. Bob Gibson of the Cardinals was arguably the dominant pitcher of the 1960s, certainly at least sharing that distinction with Sandy Koufax. Hank Aaron would break Babe Ruth's career home-run record. Reggie Jackson would come to be called "Mr. October." To be sure, playing with and against black players would have an impact on Mantle, as would his own sense of right and wrong. Mickey Jr. would recall one Christmas Eve in the mid-1960s in which he and his father pulled into a gasoline station in Dallas to discover a middle-aged black man stranded with a flat and no spare tire. Mantle noticed that the back seat in the man's battered old car was filled with Christmas presents. The man just wanted to get home to put the gifts under his family's Christmas tree, but the white service station attendant ignored him completely. Losing his patience, Mantle finally called the attendant over and counted out three hundred dollar bills on the counter. "Put two new tires on this man's car," Mickey barked to the attendant. "Do it now, right now, dammit, so he can get home and give his kids their Christmas presents."

Reflecting in an interview after his retirement on his early years with the Yankees, Mantle would credit Jackie Robinson for raising his consciousness on race, equality, and civil rights. "I don't know if until the series in '52, if there'd ever been another player I played against who praised me the way Jackie did then," he said. "On top of winning the series, there he was in our clubhouse, not just congratulating me but saying, 'You're gonna be a great player, kid. You're gonna be a great player, kid.' That meant a lot, especially after the year I'd been through, with my father dying that May and all. I can't tell you how thrilled he would've been to hear Jackie Robinson say that about his son."

In the months after Mutt's death, Mantle had begun reaching out for someone—if not a father figure then someone who, like Mutt, could offer validation and approval. Marshall Smith, one of Mantle's friends from Oklahoma, later said that in a sense, "Mickey was looking for someone to take his father's place, not as a father but as someone who could be there like a rudder in his life. Mutt never got the chance to see Mickey's great success. He never got the chance to tell Mickey that he succeeded beyond his wildest dreams. And Mickey, I think, needed that."

Ultimately, the person he reached out to for that support was Billy Martin. Martin established himself as Mantle's closest friend during the 1952 season. Martin had broken his ankle during spring training and spent the first part of the season rehabilitating alongside Mantle, but by mid-May they both were in the starting lineup. Not only were the two best friends and roommates on the road, but Martin became Mantle's personal coach, giving him advice, tips, and pointers—even flashing him signs during games.

"We didn't talk too much baseball away from the field," Mantle recalled. "The only time we did was if I messed up. Then the first thing he'd do before we got to having too much to drink was to say, 'You know, Mick, I got to tell you something. On that ball you caught in right center, the one you threw over my head? From now on you better be sure you hit the cutoff man.' Hell, he'd tell me stuff like that any time. It was like he was my big brother. . . . See, I was never known for being very smart as a baseball player. Like people ask me if I'd ever want to manage? Well, there's no way I could manage. I didn't know when to bunt or steal or hit and run or squeeze or take a pitcher out. I was just—I could run and throw and hit. That was it. But I didn't know the game. He did. He taught me a lot about baseball, yeah. He'd even tell me when to steal sometimes, like if Casey didn't give the signal to steal second. I hardly ever got thrown out. . . . If it was like the eighth or ninth inning and we were one run behind or tied or something, I'd look in to the bench and Billy'd give me the go-ahead. He'd tell me to go ahead and steal and I would."

It was a relationship that would infuriate Stengel, who would never be able to communicate with Mantle in the way he so desperately wanted to. Stengel was bitter and unforgiving about one player, "almost irrationally so" in the words of Stengel biographer Robert W. Creamer. That player was Mickey Mantle, who from 1952 through 1954 did not live up to Stengel's expectations.

"He's gotta change a lot," Casey said after the disappointing 1954 season, when the Indians ended the Yankees' five-year hold on the American League pennant. "He's gotta change his attitude and stop sulking and doing things he's told not to do. He'll have to grow up and become the great player he should be when he reports next spring."

Stengel had·difficulty accepting Mantle's injuries, beginning with the 1951 World Series injury that slowed him at the start of the 1952 season. Every time Stengel turned around, it seemed to him, Mickey had incurred a new leg injury—ligaments, cartilage, muscles—that hampered his ability to play, kept him out of games, or slowed him down so that people only occasionally got glimpses of the player he really was. In the 1953 season, Mickey missed more than thirty games, and his average slipped from the .311 of his 1952 season to under .300. After the 1953 season, Mickey underwent two operations on his knee but failed to follow the strict rehabilitation program designed to strengthen it. Instead, Mantle spent much of the winter hunting, fishing, and fooling around with Billy Martin. When he reported to camp the spring of 1954, Mickey's immobility kept Stengel from pressing him into an intensive instructional program designed to address some of his weaknesses. It was not until the final days of spring training that Mickey was able to run. However, even then he had to wear a bulky metal-and-leather brace that made it difficult for him to bat left-handed. Stengel, frustrated and unhappy with Mickey, chose to platoon him with Irv Noren. Seeing that Mantle was unable to play in most of the exhibition games, the Yankee manager made little attempt to hide his disgust.

"If he did what he was told after the first operation," said Stengel, "he would be able to play now. This kid—you can't ever teach him nothing in the spring because he's always hurt. You want to work with him batting left-handed and you can't. You want to do something for him and he don't let you. What's the good of telling him what to do? No matter what you tell him, he'll do what he wants. He's got it here and here." Casey touched his arm and his body, then, tapping the side of his head: "But he ain't got it here."

In his biography of Stengel, however, Creamer reports that it was "doubtful that [Stengel could] have had much luck teaching Mantle. Once when Mickey was having trouble with his bunting, Stengel arranged for Frank Crosetti, the coach, who had been a skillful bunter, to work with Mantle each day before practice. Crosetti showed up for the sessions but Mantle didn't. After three fruitless days the lessons were abandoned."

Another Stengel project for Mickey was to get him to reduce his strikeouts. During his years playing under Stengel, Mickey led the league in strikeouts five times, which thoroughly infuriated the manager. Stengel often pleaded with Mantle to cut down on his swing, arguing that with his strength he would still be able to drive balls out of the park with a shorter swing. Stengel also tried to get Mickey to swing down on the ball instead of uppercutting, explaining to his young star that with his speed he would be able to turn a lot of ground balls into infield hits, while still maintaining his power. Mickey, of course, listened dutifully, but he did not bother to change a thing in his swing. This was the swing his father had developed, and Mickey's devotion to Mutt Mantle continued even after his death. He would not openly defy the authority figure that Stengel represented; instead, his defiance would be manifested in silent refusal to accept change.

Stengel was beside himself with frustration. He considered himself the consummate baseball teacher and Mantle the ultimate baseball prodigy. But he felt himself a total failure at communicating with him. "What's the good of telling him what to do," Stengel often complained. "No matter what you tell him, he does what he wants."

Years later, Mickey would admit of his relationship with Stengel: "I never learned anything."

"Stengel was never able to teach Mantle because he was never able to reach him," wrote Creamer. "It was a genuine father-son relationship, but it was an angry father and a stubborn son." Mickey vented his own anger and frustration by throwing bats and kicking water coolers. Few players had ever pushed Stengel's buttons the way Mantle did. Once, after seeing Mickey slam a bat in the dugout after striking out, Stengel grabbed a bat and handed it to him. "Here," he told Mantle, "why don't you bang yourself on the head with this?" Billy Martin said he witnessed an incident in which Stengel became physically abusive with Mantle. "Once I saw the old man grab Mickey by the back of the neck and shake him hard when he did something the old man didn't like," Martin recalled. "He said, 'Don't let me see you do that again, you little bastard!' Can you imagine him doing that to Mickey?"

Seemingly lost on Stengel were the successes of 1952 and 1953. In 1952, the Yankees won their fourth straight world title; Stengel had matched Joe McCarthy's record of four consecutive World Series crowns. It was a series that looked as if the Dodgers might finally break through for a championship. They took a three-games-to-two lead back with them to Ebbets Field, and they no longer had to contend with DiMaggio, who was now in retirement. In the bottom of the sixth inning of game six, the Dodgers' Duke Snider ripped a Vic Raschi pitch over the right-field wall, breaking up a scoreless pitching duel between Raschi and Dodger starter Billy Loes. But in the top of the seventh, Yogi Berra led off with a homer over the same wall Snider had just cleared.

Later that inning, Raschi gave the Yankees a 2–1 lead with an RBI single off Loes's knee. In the eighth, Mantle provided what would be the decisive run when he hit his first World Series home run. Snider hit his second home run of the game in the bottom of the eighth inning before twenty-game winner Allie Reynolds relieved Raschi, held the lead, and assured the Yankees of a seventh game the next day. The deciding game was started by the Yankees' Eddie Lopat, who had struggled with shoulder problems after winning twenty-one games in 1951, and the Dodgers' Joe Black, a rookie who had compiled a 15–4 record in fifty-six appearances, the first fifty-four coming in relief. Mantle was now in a groove, hitting a solo home run and a run-scoring single to help the Yankees carry a 4–2 lead into the bottom of the seventh. Raschi came in to pitch for the second day in a row and loaded the bases with one out, then gave way to left-hander Bob Kuzava to face the left-handed-hitting Snider. Kuzava got Snider to pop out to third baseman Gil McDougald, but Jackie Robinson was next. With a 3–2 count, Robinson lifted a seemingly harmless popup near the mound. But Kuzava froze, and first baseman Joe Collins—the man in position to make the play—lost sight of the ball. The Dodgers base runners, meanwhile, were circling the bases; two had crossed the plate and another was rounding third when second baseman Billy Martin sprinted in to make a knee-high catch. Kuzava held off the Dodgers in the eighth and ninth, but the game-saving heroics had been provided by Martin, who had also been the hero of game two, with a three-run home run and an RBI single. Mantle also performed well, going ten for twenty-nine for a .345 average and outsmarting Robinson with his throw to second base in that crucial seventh game.

In 1953, it appeared as if Mantle might finally have that season he had hinted at being capable of in his rookie season. As in his rookie year, he had a phenomenal spring, hitting .412 and capping the exhibition season with a monstrous home run over the hundred-foot-high double-deck grandstand in the distant right field of Forbes Field in Pittsburgh. Yankee lefty Eddie Lopat later recalled sitting in the dugout talking to Allie Reynolds when the Pirates' pitcher threw Mantle a slow curve ball. "I'd like to see him throw that again," Lopat mumbled. When the pitcher tried fooling Mantle with the same pitch, Mickey planted it where only Babe Ruth and an obscure minor leaguer named Ted Beard had hit baseballs. But the promise soon faded, betrayed in large part by midseason injuries. After spraining his left knee, Mantle began favoring his right knee, which he had torn up in the 1951 World Series. The right knee eventually buckled with torn ligaments, but he continued to play, with a heavy brace to support the knee. Mantle's statistics fell off from his sophomore season—a .295 average with twenty-one home runs and ninety-three RBIs. Just as surely as the sportswriters had built up Mantle and the Mantle myth, they could also reduce both to ridicule and rubble. As author David Halberstam would note about Mantle and the press, "His anger, his ability to look right through men he dealt with every day, men whose reporting had in general helped build the myth of Mantle as the greatest ballplayer of his era, could be shattering. Once when Maury Allen, the beat writer on the *Post,* was standing near the batting cage and Mantle was taking batting practice, Mantle turned to him and said, 'You piss me off just standing there.' That became something of a motto in the Allen household when one member of the Allen family was irritated with another."

The Mantle myth, however, wasn't without foundation—Mickey's play on the field gave it substance. On April 17, 1953, Mantle turned heads when he hit what was then considered to be the longest home run ever hit in the majors. Batting against Senators' southpaw Chuck Stobbs with the wind behind him in Washington's old Griffith Stadium, Mantle drove a ball over the fifty-five-foot-high wall behind the left-field bleachers. The ball left the field at the 391-foot mark, ricocheted off a sixty-foot-high beer sign on the stadium's football scoreboard some 460 feet from home plate, and continued traveling until it landed in a neighbor's yard, where ten-year-old Donald Dunaway found it. Yankee publicity director Red Patterson immediately sensed the importance of what Mantle had done.

By the end of the game, the tape-measure home run had been invented. Patterson quickly regaled writers covering the game with the story of how he had bolted from the press box to track down the baseball and measured the distance at an incredible 565 feet. The sports pages the next day and for days after recounted the feat, and the myth of the Mantle's prodigious power was quickly established. However, it is unclear how much of Patterson's account was factual and how much was hyperbole. Years later Mantle would say that Patterson had told him he had never left the park but had been given the ball by the youngster who found it, and then had made a guess at the distance the ball had traveled. The exact distance, however, is irrelevant. Mantle hit the ball so hard that the Senators' left fielder didn't even move, and Mickey's teammates in the dugout shook their heads in disbelief. Nobody in the major or the Negro leagues had ever hit a ball over the bleachers in Griffith Stadium, and other than Mickey Mantle, nobody ever would again. Not long after that, the home run ball and Mantle's bat were placed on display at the National Baseball Hall of Fame in Cooperstown, New York. As for the wind that was blowing that day at Griffith Stadium, Senators owner Clark Griffith said it had made little difference. "I don't care about that," he said. "That consarned wind has been blowing for 100 years, and nobody else ever hit one out of this ballpark like that."

In the 1953 World Series, the Yankees faced the Dodger team that would come to be immortalized as the "Boys of Summer." That Dodger team had won the National League pennant by thirteen games over the Milwaukee Braves, led by the league's Most Valuable Player, catcher Roy Campanella, who had hit forty-one homers and drove in 142 runs. The Dodgers also boasted the league's Rookie of the Year in second baseman Jim Gilliam. Center fielder Duke Snider had slugged forty-two homers and driven in 126 runs, and first baseman Gil Hodges smacked thirty-one homers and knocked in 122 runs. Right fielder Carl Furillo had won the National League batting championship with a .344 average, and Jackie Robinson hit .329. The Yankees would nevertheless win the series in six games, marking the seventh time in as many tries that the Dodgers lost the World Series.

Billy Martin was again the Yankee hero, hitting .500, smacking twelve hits, and driving in eight runs. Martin got the Yankees going in an explosive game one with a three-run triple in the first inning and two more hits in the Yankees' 9–5 win. Yogi Berra and Joe Collins hit homers for the Yankees; Gilliam, Hodges, and George Shuba homered for the Dodgers. Martin came through again in game two, hitting a game-tying solo home run in the seventh. An inning later, Mantle followed with a two-run shot to help Eddie Lopat win, 4–2. Carl Erskine, the Dodgers' twenty-game winner, won game three for Brooklyn, setting a Series record with fourteen strikeouts—including Mantle four times. Campanella showed his MVP form, hitting a tie-breaking home run in the eighth inning that gave the Dodgers a 3–2 victory. In game four, Snider drove in four runs with two doubles and a home run, while Gilliam cracked three doubles, helping Billy Loes to a 7–3 victory. But those wins were the last two of the Dodgers' superb season. Martin again hit a two-run homer in the Yankees' 11–7 triumph in game five. Gene Woodling led off game five with a home run. Mantle then delivered a grand-slam home run in the third inning, giving the Yankees a 6–1 lead. Martin added a two-run homer in the seventh. The Yankees won game six in dramatic fashion. The Dodgers' Carl

Furillo tied the game with a two-run home run in the top of the ninth inning. In the bottom of the inning, Martin resurrected all the ghosts haunting the Dodgers by driving in Hank Bauer for the winning run with a single. Mantle had advanced Bauer to second by legging out an infield single, setting up Martin's game-winning hit. The World Series win was the fifteenth in sixteen tries by the Yankees, and their fifth straight. It placed Stengel in a unique position among managers—which may have spoiled him.

Understandably, after such a run, the 1954 season was an especially disappointing one for Stengel. Ultimately, he came to blame part of the Yankees' failure to win their sixth straight pennant on Mantle. It did not seem to matter to the crusty Yankee manager that his team won 103 games that season, more than it had in any of the five previous years. Stengel found it difficult to credit Cleveland manager Al Lopez and the Indians for winning an incredible 111 games, an American League record. For the proud Stengel, losing to the Indians meant having to eat his words. In the spring of 1954, Stengel had simply but emphatically declared, "If the Yankees don't win the pennant, the owners should discharge me." Recuperating slowly from yet another knee injury, Mantle started the season slowly, although he did finish with a year that most managers would have gladly accepted from one of their star players. Mickey drove in 102 runs, hit twenty-seven home runs, and batted an even .300. Stengel, however, could only see the shortcomings: Mickey's high number of strikeouts, his sullenness at times, and his lack of heart in occasionally not running out ground balls as hard as he should. "You try to tell him something and he acts like you tell him nothing," Stengel complained. "After all, all it means is a player running ninety feet. And if he can't hustle for ninety feet at the salaries they're paid these days, something's got to be wrong."

Stengel might have had a point. While it would be unfair to suggest that Mickey was a lazy ball player, it would not be too much to say that Mantle tended to indulge sloppy habits that were particularly detrimental when it came to rehabilitating his injuries. Even so, his failure to rehab the way he should have was not so much the result of bad work habits as it was of the off-field life he had begun living in the company of Billy Martin. By the end of the 1953 season, Mickey was already established as a heavy drinker; the off-season, especially after the just-separated Martin arrived in Commerce as the Mantle's houseguest, was simply an encore. "When Billy was with me," Mickey said of that off-season, "I fell into the routine of getting out of the house by saying we were going fishing. Instead we would go into Joplin, have a few drinks, and before I knew it, I was drunk. I wouldn't even think about going home."

"All I saw of them that winter was their backs going out the door," recalled Merlyn Mantle later. "If they did all the hunting and fishing they claimed they were doing, the fish and quail population of Oklahoma took a fearful beating."

It was not as if Mickey himself wasn't aware of Martin's destructive influence. "One day," Merlyn wrote in *A Hero All His Life*, "he admitted to me, 'You know, if my dad were alive, he would take one look at Billy and tell him to get back in his frigging car and go back to California.' Mutt would have known from looking at him that Billy Martin was not good for Mick."

However, on the whole, Mantle friends like Marshall Smith believe that Mickey needed Martin, in part because Martin was one of the few people Mickey would listen to. "I think Billy Martin helped Mickey more than he hurt him," said Smith. "People were always saying Billy hurt Mickey, but that never came from Mickey. And that'll never come from me. Billy had a lot of class. When I say class, Mickey never learned how to present himself in public. Billy could absolutely drag you into loving him. Mickey couldn't. Billy used to chew out Mickey all the time about not giving autographs. One thing about Billy, he'd tell you what the hell he thought."

It can be argued that Stengel's frustration with Mickey was irrational. Clearly, Mantle would become the greatest player to develop under Stengel, but Stengel wanted to develop the greatest player of all time. Stengel's 1951 predictions of Mantle's being the next Ruth and DiMaggio were unlike any claim ever made of a Yankee rookie, or of anyone else. In Stengel's mind, the 1956 Triple Crown season would not be enough, nor would the Hall of Fame career and five hundred–plus home runs. The great expectations that Stengel placed on Mickey—and the equally great disappointment that was inevitable—was perhaps best summed up by sportswriter Milton Gross, who wrote: "Mantle was to be the monument the old gent wanted to leave behind. Casey wanted his own name written in the record books as manager, but he also wanted a creation that was completely his own on the field every day, doing things no other ballplayer ever did, rewriting all the records."

The public, and even the sportswriters covering the Yankees at the time, did not see this private, petty side of Stengel. In another age, the age of the athletes of the 1990s and afterward, for example, it is doubtful Stengel could have gotten away as long as he did with the way he privately treated Mantle and other players. Years later, Phil Rizzuto looked back and confessed that he "did not enjoy" playing for Stengel particularly. "He had two tempers," said Rizzuto. "One for the public and the writers, and one for the players under him. The players were frequently dressed down in the dugout and clubhouse. He could charm the shoes off you, if he wanted to, but he could also be rough. And after the first couple of seasons, he began to believe he had as much 'magic' as the newspapers said he did."

Under Stengel, Mantle ultimately suffered the fate of the adopted son of an undeserving father who would have gladly accepted all the credit for the greatness but wanted none of the despair that comes with failure. Stengel had wanted a combination of Ruth and Cobb and nothing less, although neither Ruth nor Cobb had had to play with the ghosts and expectations that cast such long shadows over Mantle. Stengel's anger toward Mickey subsided with the years, but the tragedy of their relationship may have been that Stengel failed to appreciate or even publicly acknowledge Mantle's own exceptional career. Years later, when Stengel was asked to pick his all-time all-star team, he had DiMaggio on it, Yogi Berra, and even Phil Rizzuto. Mickey Mantle's name was conspicuously missing.

11

Years later Mickey Mantle would boast that his first two years of marriage "were unspoiled and perfect," perhaps forgetting his occasional infidelities and the way he had treated Merlyn when his father had died. Also, he could be both sentimental and careless when it came to one of the most important dates in a marriage. He would often brag proudly that he and Merlyn continued to celebrate their wedding anniversary even after years of being separated. But in his autobiographical chapter of *A Hero All His Life*, Mantle got the year of his wedding wrong. Still, with the help of his ghostwriters, Mickey sometimes wrote about the early days of his marriage with a Hemingway-esque reminiscence: "There were other good years, but those two were the last ones before the drinking started. We were both young and unsure and awed by New York."

During this period and for years to come, Merlyn would blame Billy Martin for Mickey's womanizing and excessive drinking. Mickey sensed Merlyn's disapproval of his friend and perhaps knew deep down that Billy was a bad influence on him. George Weiss and the Yankee executives certainly felt that way and ultimately decided to trade Martin largely for that reason. But Merlyn saw that Billy's influence over Mickey extended beyond baseball and into the off-season, particularly into their lives in Commerce. Billy's intrusion became especially noticeable in the winter of 1953. Martin's wife Lois left their tempestuous marriage and took their young daughter with them; Billy headed out from California to Commerce in his brand-new Cadillac to be the Mantle's winter-long houseguest. The Cadillac had been given to Billy as the Most

Valuable Player in the Yankees' World Series triumph over the Dodgers, and he arrived wearing a fur coat and bearing gifts from a postseason trip to Japan.

Billy became an off-season resident of Commerce, staying at Mickey's mother's home during Mickey and Merlyn's spats, when he felt out of place. Mickey even went so far as to help get Billy a job where he worked, with Harold Youngman's construction company. The beneficiary in this was primarily Youngman, who for three hundred dollars a week apiece had two of the most prominent names in baseball at his disposal. Part of Youngman's business was building public roads and highways; what better way to sweeten his bids than by bringing in Mickey and Billy for photos, autographs, dinners, and anything else it took to win influence?

Conversely, it could be argued that the loser in the deal was Mantle—or perhaps more accurately, the Mantles. For if any point in time in Mantle's life could be singled out as the beginning of his self-destruction, it would have to be the off-seasons of the early years of his career following the death of his father. Mickey never allowed himself time to mourn his father's death adequately. In the weeks and months after Mutt's death, Mantle faced the enormous challenge of assuming his central role in the Yankees' plans as well as his new responsibility as the sole source of support for an extended household.

"Up to dad's death, baseball had been a game," Mantle said, looking back on that period of his life. "Now it was a profession. I had to make good for mama, for my twin brothers, Ray and Roy, for my sister Barbara, my kid brother Larry and my wife, Merlyn. I had to make it, and I felt that I would. Dad had raised me to be a ballplayer."

Mantle's sentiments were right, but his actions over the next few years failed to live up to the ideals. As he and Martin became closer, Mickey increasingly modeled his personal life on Billy's. The drinking and nightlife that the two enjoyed during the off-season by themselves, and then during the season with Whitey Ford, became legendary. The most famous of these evenings during the early 1950s may have been the celebration after winning the 1953 pennant. After the team party, Martin, Mantle, and Ford went with Hank Bauer, Gil McDougald, Andy Carey, and Gus Triandos to the Latin Quarter nightclub for dinner, drinks, and a show. The seven ran up a bill of $250, which Martin offered to pay in cash. Mickey thought they should split it up. Then Ford, the perennial prankster of the threesome, suggested they play a joke on Yankee owner Dan Topping. "He's got a million bucks," said Ford as he signed Topping's name to the bill. Unbeknownst to the players, however, Topping was at the Latin Quarter himself that evening, out of sight at another table. When the waiter turned around and brought the bill to Topping, he was hardly amused. The next morning the general manager called the players into his office, where he threatened to file criminal forgery charges. Weiss settled for fining them five hundred dollars apiece, and Topping added another five hundred—fines that were forgiven and returned a few days later after the Yankees defeated the Dodgers in the World Series. The incident helped convince Weiss that Martin was a negative influence on the team's budding superstar. Martin, Mantle, and Ford all sensed Weiss's disapproval of their after-hours lifestyle in general and of Martin in particular, but they didn't change anything. On road trips they missed the team's curfew so often, sometimes not returning to the team hotel until daybreak the next morning, that Stengel began telling writers, "I got these players who got the bad watches, that they can't tell midnight from noon."

More devastating to Mantle personally and to his family was the influence that Martin had on the way Mickey treated Merlyn and his young family. Even after seeing Billy's first marriage fall apart, Mantle failed to understand that Martin's behavior might have been a major contributing factor to the breakup of his own marriage. "Billy was a better ballplayer than he was a husband, that's for sure," Mantle would later say. "He was a competitor at everything he did, including his marriages, and that's probably asking for trouble."

The baseball-imposed separations in those first years of Mickey and Merlyn's marriage were extensive. In 1953, pregnant with Mickey Jr., Merlyn remained in Oklahoma during spring training and into the beginning of the season. Mickey Jr. was born April 12 in Joplin, Missouri. The way Mickey learned of the birth was fitting. As he stepped up to the plate in an exhibition game against the Brooklyn Dodgers in Ebbets Field, the public-address announcer said, "Ladies and gentlemen, now hitting, number seven, Mickey Mantle. Mickey doesn't know it yet, but he just became the father of an eight-pound-twelve-ounce baby boy."

Although he would be known as "Mickey Jr." the rest of his life, Mickey's first-born son was technically not a "Jr." He was named Mickey Elvin, after his father and grandfather. Little Mickey was more than a month old before Mickey was given time off to go home to meet his son. Mickey might not have been given time off even then had he not developed over much of his body a rash that became inflamed whenever he perspired. When the team doctor instructed him not to play for a few days, Stengel gave him the time to go home and see his baby and his wife. The rash quickly cleared up, and Mickey just as quickly became bored staying at home with his young family. When a photograph of Mantle out at a fishing hole appeared in the newspapers a few days later, he got a call from Stengel ordering him to be on the next plane.

In typical fashion, Merlyn accepted having to undergo childbirth and later child rearing by herself. "When you sign up to be a baseball wife," she said, "you forfeit your right to bitch about not having your husband at the hospital when you go into labor. That's part of the game—a phrase every baseball wife needs to keep handy."

Merlyn and Mickey were apart again until late in June, when she flew up to New York with the baby and her sister Pat. He rented a house for them in New Jersey that was far more accommodating for Merlyn than the small apartment at the Concourse Hotel. By then, Mickey was the head of two households. Mickey had the responsibility for two mortgages in Commerce, and now the rent on the house in New Jersey. Mickey and Merlyn had used his seven-thousand-dollar World Series share in the winter of 1952 to buy their own house across the street from the home he had bought for his mother and father after his rookie season. Merlyn had barely begun settling into her own home when she found herself relocating to New Jersey, all the while facing the challenges of motherhood. Being a young mother was made even more complicated by little Mickey's health problems. He had been diagnosed with asthma, and with Mantle sometimes on the road, Merlyn often had to handle the baby's asthma attacks by herself. Little Mickey was also allergic to milk, which added to the complexity of feeding him and keeping him healthy.

By Mantle's own admission, the emotional trauma he inflicted upon Merlyn, especially in their early years together, was nothing less than mental cruelty. The winter after the 1954 season was especially dreadful. Mickey spent most of his free time either hunting or in bars with his friends, usually returning home drunk to start fights with his wife. One night Mantle returned home drunk and found the front door locked. He suffered a severe gash in his hand breaking a window to get into his house; the cut required thirty stitches to close. He learned that Merlyn had moved out to her parents' home. After being released from the hospital, he arrived at the Johnson house, still drunk, and demanded the keys to his Lincoln. Mickey unloaded all of Merlyn's clothes from the car and threw them all over the front lawn. Despite his father-in-law's pleas, Mantle then got into the car and proceeded to drive it into a telephone pole, ripping the driver's door off the hinges and plowing the Lincoln into a ditch. Unfortunately, Merlyn never sought professional advice. Instead, she then did what counselors of abused spouses suggest that they not do in such circumstances: the next day she forgave Mickey and returned home, in what would become a ritual. She would forgive Mickey for his mental cruelty, his abuse, his infidelities, and the way he treated people. Mutt had been the last person able to control and restrain Mickey. With him gone, no one could, least of all Merlyn.

Perhaps what made life with Mickey livable for Merlyn was life without him during the season. The 1955 season was an example. Merlyn was pregnant again and lived in Oklahoma, apart from Mickey, most of the season. The 1955 campaign would be a prelude to Mantle's Triple Crown season; he won the first of his four home-run championships, with thirty-seven home runs. He drove in ninety-nine runs, batted .306, and recorded a .611 slugging percentage. On May 13, Mickey had the only three-homer game in his career and first switch-hit homer game—one righty and two lefty—going four for four and driving in all five runs to beat the Tigers at Yankee Stadium. That summer he hit the first of his only two home runs in an All-Star Game, a three-run shot off the Phillies' Robin Roberts. That September, Mantle appeared to be headed toward becoming the first Yankee since DiMaggio in 1937 to hit forty home runs—when he came up with another leg injury. On September 16, Mantle tore a muscle in the back of his right thigh while trying to bunt. The Yankees, however, were still able to edge out the Indians and the White Sox for their sixth pennant in seven years.

In the World Series, the Yankees met a Dodgers team that had started the season with a 22–2 record and cruised to the National League pennant, finishing thirteen and a half games over the second-place Milwaukee Braves. However, the Dodgers had never won a World Series, and for the first two games looked like they wouldn't now. Still nursing the injury to his thigh, Mantle did not play in either of the first two games. Dodgers ace Don Newcombe, a twenty-game winner in 1955, was beaten up in the opener, giving up two home runs to Joe Collins and a third to Yankee rookie Elston Howard, as Brooklyn lost, 6–5. In game two, thirty-five-year-old left-hander Tommy Byrne pitched the Yankees to a 4–2 triumph. But then Johnny Podres, who had struggled to a 9–10 record for Brooklyn, scattered seven hits and beat the Yankees 8–3 at Ebbets Field. One of those hits was a second-inning home run by Mantle, whose leg injury allowed him to play in only two other Series

games, one of those as a pinch-hitter. Mickey tried to play only because Hank
Bauer pulled a muscle in game two. The Dodgers then took the next two
games as well. Roy Campanella, Gil Hodges, and Duke Snider all homered
in an 8–5 game-four win. Snider hit another home run in game five, leading
the Dodgers to a 5–3 triumph and the Series lead. Back at Yankee Stadium,
Whitey Ford evened the Series with a four-hitter, a 5–1 win.

Game seven, at Yankee Stadium, matching Byrne against Podres on the
mound, was scoreless until the fourth inning, when Campanella doubled and
scored on a single by Hodges. The Dodgers gave Podres another run in the
sixth inning and then made the defensive change that may have decided the
game. In the bottom of the sixth, the Dodgers moved Jim Gilliam from left
field to second base; reserve Sandy Amoros replaced Gilliam in left. Billy Martin drew a walk to lead off the Yankee sixth, and Gil McDougald followed with
a bunt single. Yogi Berra sliced a fly ball just inside the left-field foul line. The
left-handed Amoros, who had played shaded toward center with a left-handed
power hitter at the plate, appeared to have little chance of getting to the ball.
However, the fleet Amoros raced toward the line and stole a certain extra-base
hit from Berra. Both runners were off with the crack of the bat, and would
have scored, tying the game; Amoros, however, after making the catch, relayed
to Peewee Reese, who threw to Hodges, doubling McDougald at first. Podres
battled out of another jam in the eighth, getting Mantle to pop up as a pinch-
hitter, and held on to give Brooklyn its first World Series championship. (Two
years later the Dodgers would leave Brooklyn for Los Angeles.)

After the Series Mantle could not wait to get home, and when he got
there could not wait to leave. No matter how much love Mickey vowed for
Merlyn, there was an equally prominent part of Mickey that resented her. He
never explained why, at least not publicly. Merlyn might have represented
the duty and the demands that his father had always imposed upon him. From
his earliest childhood, Mantle had had his life scripted by his father: the long
hours each day learning how to switch-hit, the year-to-year planning of his
baseball career, passing up a football scholarship to the University of Oklahoma for baseball. Sons routinely live out their fathers' dreams until the day
that their own dreams take over. Usually that passage comes without the
father's realizing that his son has moved on with his own life. Occasionally,
that passage is turbulent and traumatic—a son's act of independence is perceived by the father as rebellion. For Mickey, that passage never came. His
father determined that he would marry Merlyn—the same kind of patriar-

chal whim that had decided his son would become a switch-hitter. It was what Mutt wanted, and what Mutt thought was right for Mickey. Mutt had chosen the course for Mickey's life, but it would be Mickey who would have to live it. The only instance of physical abuse that Merlyn has ever talked about involved an incident on Christmas Eve of 1955, in Commerce, when she was only a couple of days from giving birth to their second son, David. One of the Mantles' many houseguests that day had apparently walked off with Mickey's house key. Mantle had gone off drinking with his friends while Merlyn had taken little Mickey to her parents' home. When Merlyn returned home, she found Mickey and his drunken pals unable to get into the house. Mantle was furious and blamed his wife for locking him out. Abruptly he pushed his wife aside. Merlyn almost fell. Later she would half-jokingly say that had she fallen, she would have given birth on the spot. It was the first time Mickey had embarrassed Merlyn in front of other people, but again she was quick to forgive him. On Christmas morning, Mickey gave her a $2,500 mink stole. Among Mickey's drunken entourage on Christmas Eve were his twin brothers Roy and Ray, who were visibly upset by their older brother's treatment of their sister-in-law. They returned home and told their mother about the incident, and on Christmas Day Lovell Mantle lit into her famous son.

Away from Commerce, Mickey's abusive treatment of Merlyn became a matter of embarrassment to both her friends and Mickey's. In New York, Mickey once pulled a chair out from under his wife as she was about to sit down at a restaurant where they were having dinner with teammate Clete Boyer and his wife. Mantle would try to excuse the incident as one of his drunken pranks, but Merlyn eventually concluded that there was something sadistic in her husband's treatment of her. In the incident with the Boyers, Clete had tried to smooth things over with Merlyn, who ran out of the restaurant crying and started to drive away. With Boyer in the front seat of the car, still trying to calm her down, Merlyn saw Mickey in her headlights; she floorboarded the accelerator and tried to run him down. Mickey was unhurt, and both he and Merlyn stopped drinking for a couple of weeks. In another embarrassing incident, Mickey humiliated Merlyn in front of Toni Webb at a Las Vegas dinner that the widow of the late Yankee owner was hosting for a few of the Yankee players. As he listened to his wife express her gratitude to Mrs. Webb, Mantle soaked his napkin in a water glass and then threw it in Merlyn's face. The other guests pretended not to see the incident, but Merlyn was humiliated and crushed.

New York had indeed changed Mickey, and it had also had its impact on Merlyn. The common denominator in all the incidents, in all the partying, and in all the womanizing, was booze.

"When I came up with the Yankees in 1951, at age nineteen, I'd hardly ever had a drink," Mantle would later tell *Sports Illustrated*. "My father wouldn't have stood for me getting drunk. But the following spring, when dad died of Hodgkin's disease at age thirty-nine, I was devastated, and that's when I started drinking. I guess alcohol helped me escape the pain of losing him.

"The Yankees traveled to away games by train in those days, and Casey . . . had a two drink limit on trips, although he didn't really enforce it. On the road, Billy Martin and I were wild men. We drank up a storm and didn't go to bed until we were ready to fall into bed. The drinking escalated after the '53 season when Billy came to live with me and my wife, Merlyn, in Commerce. Billy and I were bad for each other. We were always on the go—rushing out the door, telling Merlyn we were going fishing but, instead, heading straight for a bar."

To some degree in those early years, possibly because of the tolerance of youth, Mantle was able to get away with the drinking and the late hours. After drinking heavily throughout much of the off-season, Mantle would arrive in spring training and quit, cold turkey. This abstinence would continue through the exhibition season and into the first few weeks of the regular season. Then the partying would begin anew. Sometimes there would be breaks in the all-boys partying, as when DiMaggio brought Marilyn Monroe to New York to show off his new bride to his former teammates.

Mantle and several of the Yankee players joined DiMaggio and Monroe for dinner at Joe's invitation. "Mickey said they had all been impressed with Marilyn because she had shown so much interest in their lives," Greer Johnson, Mantle's companion in the last ten years of his life, was to recall. "She wanted to know about their families and their home lives. She was sincerely interested, and it surprised them because she wasn't at all the self-centered person she could have been. It was a thrill for Mickey to meet her and to have dinner with [Marilyn and Joe]." However, most afternoon and night games would be followed by drunken binges for Martin, Ford, and Mantle.

In New York, Mantle's favorite watering hole became Toots Shor's restaurant on 52nd Street, where DiMaggio had hung out after games. After home games, especially if he had hit a home run, Mantle would hop a cab from

Yankee Stadium and head to Toots Shor's to celebrate with Martin, Ford, and Shor well into the night, while Merlyn waited for him at home.

"He was just a kid then, a little naïve," Shor said, remembering those times. "Just a good old country boy. I loved to kid him. He just wanted to have fun."

Mantle himself recalled those nights at Toots Shor's: "All the bright lights, all the famous people I would meet there, it was something. Billy seemed to know everybody. Toots always was a good friend, just taking care of us and seeing that we got home in time for the next day's game."

Perhaps Stengel, who had been a legendary drinker in his own time, saw something of himself in Mantle's partying. Usually the Yankee manager looked the other way. Once, however, after Mantle arrived at the ballpark hung over just half an hour before the game, Stengel ordered him into the starting lineup. When Mickey responded by slugging a home run and driving in four runs, Stengel smiled with a mixture of awe and admiration and said to a sportswriter, "He's got it in his body to be the greatest ever."

Not everyone turned a blind eye to Mickey's drinking. Weiss did not approve of what he was seeing in his team's young star and started keeping tabs on Mantle and Martin. The Yankee general manager hired private investigators and began compiling a dossier—not so much on Mickey but on Billy—and building a case strong enough to override any protests from Stengel, Martin's longtime protector. Weiss also had to convince Yankee owners Topping and Webb that Martin had become a cancer threatening the future of the ball club. Along the way, Weiss was aided in his project by what would be, for him, a fortuitous turn of events. In June 1956, arguably Mickey's career year, the Federal Bureau of Investigation contacted the Yankees with a request to interview Mantle. According to FBI files obtained through the Freedom of Information Act, federal officials had received information from unnamed sources that Mantle was being "blackmailed for $15,000 after being found in a compromising position with a married woman."

The incident only further convinced Weiss and the Yankee owners that Mantle's personal life was out of control, even though there had in fact been no violation of federal law on Mickey's part. "Mr. Mantle subsequently denied ever having been caught in a compromising situation," a memo in Mantle's FBI file states. "Mr. Mantle readily admitted that he had 'shacked up' with many girls in New York City, but stated that he had never been caught."

"That sounds like him," said Phil Pepe, a former sportswriter for the *New York Daily News* who covered many of Mantle's escapades with the Yankees and later cowrote a book with him. "Not that I have firsthand knowledge of it, but I had my suspicions when I traveled with him. He had friends, he had ladies who he was friendly with, and he would be the first to admit that his marriage was always rocky and shaky."

Through the early and middle fifties, Mantle tried his best to keep his womanizing secret from Merlyn. Sometimes Mickey went to herculean, if not absurd, lengths to keep his affairs from his wife, as when he and Merlyn flew to Cuba with Harold and Stella Youngman in their twin-engine Beechcraft one winter. At an airport in Montgomery, Alabama, where they had stopped to refuel, Harold tugged at Mantle and pointed to a newsstand in the terminal. "Hey, Mickey," said his friend, "is that your picture?"

Mantle's photograph was on the cover of *Confidential* magazine, a celebrity gossip rag bought by 4.5 million readers each week, along with a picture and story of Holly Brooke, the showgirl Mickey dated in the 1951 season and with whom he had continued to stay in touch even after she left New York for Hollywood and a promising acting career. Mantle immediately bought all the copies of *Confidential* that were on display at the newsstand and threw them in the trash. Trying to keep Merlyn from seeing the magazine, Mickey and Youngman then proceeded to sprint out of the plane at every airport on that trip to buy up all the copies and dump them all out of sight. Mantle's efforts, however, were to no avail. When they returned home from the trip, Mickey and Merlyn found a stack of the magazines sitting in their front yard. Merlyn eventually learned about Mickey's relationship with Holly and even about her "owning" 50 percent of Mickey's contract for life. "There was a side of him," said Merlyn, "that would always be drawn to that kind of woman."

Mickey reads a letter from his father during his often-lonely rookie season. *The Mickey Mantle Museum, Cooperstown, N.Y., and Mr. Tom Catal and Mr. Andrew Vilacky*

Mickey with New York showgirl Holly Brooke in 1951. Mantle and Brooke dated until Mickey's father pushed him back to Merlyn. Mickey would later say of his times with Brooke, "I guess I developed my first taste for the high life then." *The Mickey Mantle Museum, Cooperstown, N.Y., and Mr. Tom Catal and Mr. Andrew Vilacky*

The Yankee slugger inscribed his picture . . . "To Holly, with all my love and thoughts," Mickey Mantle.

One of the few photos of Mickey in a Kansas City uniform, inscribed to his then-girlfriend Holly Brooke. *The Mickey Mantle Museum, Cooperstown, N.Y., and Mr. Tom Catal and Mr. Andrew Vilacky*

Three of the greatest ballplayers of all time pose together during the 1951 season—Joe DiMaggio, Mickey Mantle, and Ted Williams. *The Mickey Mantle Museum, Cooperstown, N.Y., and Mr. Tom Catal and Mr. Andrew Vilacky*

Joe DiMaggio puts his arm around Mickey in 1951, the only year they played together. *The Mickey Mantle Museum, Cooperstown, N.Y., and Mr. Tom Catal and Mr. Andrew Vilacky*

Mickey with Kansas City Blues Manager George Selkirk. Mantle played his way back to the parent club for good in late August. *The Mickey Mantle Museum, Cooperstown, N.Y., and Mr. Tom Catal and Mr. Andrew Vilacky*

Mutt sits with his son in Yankee Stadium in 1951. *The Mickey Mantle Museum, Cooperstown, N.Y., and Mr. Tom Catal and Mr. Andrew Vilacky*

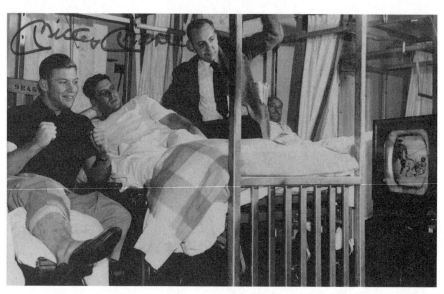

Mickey and his father Mutt watch the end of the 1951 World Series together from the hospital—Mick for an injured knee, and Mutt for what would turn out to be Hodgkin's disease. *The Mickey Mantle Museum, Cooperstown, N.Y., and Mr. Tom Catal and Mr. Andrew Vilacky*

PART 3

THE KINGDOM
AND THE POWER

12

All of living is a process of coming of age, of reconciling the essence of the inner self with one's outer being, with the world, and with the changing expectations for that self in the world. For Mickey Mantle, the year 1956 would mark the time of his life when promise and potential would be fulfilled in a season that, in its own way, only raised expectations even higher. He had turned twenty-four the previous October. Orson Welles was twenty-five when he made his film debut in the classic masterpiece *Citizen Kane*. In later years, Welles would lament the expectations that had been placed upon him after *Citizen Kane* and the weight of slowly coming to the realization, year by year, that he had reached the top of the world at the age of twenty-five. In 1956, Mickey Mantle was twenty-four and about to achieve a similarly bittersweet pinnacle.

There were no signs in early 1956 to suggest that this would be the year that Mantle would emerge as the Yankee superstar who finally superseded the memories of the great DiMaggio. In fact, early in spring training, Mantle pulled the hamstring that had troubled him throughout the homestretch of the 1955 season and had limited him to only three appearances, one as a pinch-hitter, in the World Series loss to the Dodgers. Ordinarily, Casey Stengel might have been consumed with frustration that his young star was once again hurt, but that spring he had to contend with a rash of injuries to his team. Gil McDougald, whom Stengel had penciled in as his starting shortstop that season, strained a tendon in his left knee in a parking lot accident. Elston Howard broke a finger, outfielder Bob Cerv was sidelined by a pulled stomach muscle, and promising young rookie Norm Siebern fractured his left kneecap crashing into an outfield wall.

In Mantle, Stengel had a symbolic means of motivating his injured players to quick recoveries or, if at all possible, to play despite the pain. Mantle's ritual of bandaging his legs from his thighs to his ankles, even when healthy, was an inspiration to his teammates. Virtually all of Mantle's teammates over the years spoke of Mickey's courage in enduring the pain of all his injuries. Opposing players felt the same way, and some recognized what Mantle was accomplishing despite such odds. Nellie Fox, a White Sox second baseman who played against Mantle for most of their careers, once said, "On two legs, Mickey Mantle would have been the greatest ball player who ever lived." In many games, Mantle probably should not have been in the lineup—and might not have been, had the ever-clever Stengel not managed to play psychological games with him. Knowing Mantle was hurting, Stengel would sometimes approach his ailing star in the clubhouse. "Well," Stengel would say, "I guess I better keep you out today." Mantle, who hated for anyone to dwell on his injuries, would irritably tell Stengel, "Goddamn it, Case, put me in." Stengel, of course, had already made out his lineup card, with Mantle's name on it.

The 1955 season had been a sobering experience for Mantle, and not just because the Yankees lost the World Series to the Dodgers. Mantle had been the offensive catalyst for the Yankees, leading the club in most categories. He had outhit Yogi Berra by thirty-four percentage points, had hit ten more home runs than Yogi, and driven in only nine fewer runs than the Yankee catcher. It had been Berra who was voted Most Valuable Player by the baseball writers; he had been a favorite in the balloting, beginning in the early 1950s. Nevertheless, there was no mistaking Mantle's worth to the Yankees. Mickey led the league in on-base percentage, walks, home runs, and triples, and he was third in runs scored. In early January, the Yankees had presented Mickey with a new contract that would pay him thirty thousand dollars for the 1956 season. But even before Mantle signed the contract on January 24, the Yankees got an indication of a new maturity to Mickey. He pulled the Yankees' assistant general manager, Bill DeWitt, aside and asked him for some advice on something that had been bothering him.

"Look," Mantle began, "I was glad to see Yogi got the Most Valuable Player Award. There's no better guy in the world than Yogi. But I'm just wondering: What's a guy have to do to be considered Most Valuable?"

"Well, Mickey, I'm glad you asked me this," DeWitt said. "You may not know this, Mickey, but when the baseball writers are deciding who's been most valuable, they take other things into account. Maybe a ballplayer has to do more than have a good season on the field. Maybe he has to win a little personal popularity. Maybe he has to put out a little effort. Maybe he can't brush off every newspaperman who approaches him, or just clam up on him. Maybe he must make a real effort to be a little cooperative. . . . You've got to come out of that shell."

DeWitt as much as anyone in the Yankees' front office was aware of Mantle's bad reputation with the country's baseball writers. Part of Mantle's problem was his shyness and his lifelong discomfort in talking publicly about himself. Mickey, however, was no longer a rookie. Not only was he making no effort to cooperate with the writers, but he had grown increasingly rude and unfriendly in his dealings with the press. Sometimes he would cut off reporters with curt, one-word answers. Sometimes he would ignore their questions altogether and walk away. Sometimes he would simply disappear into the trainer's room, which was off-limits to the writers. At his worst, however, Mantle would tell a writer to "fuck off" or "go fuck yourself."

When spring training began, Mantle also began making some noticeable changes in his approach at the plate. Players and writers thought they saw Mickey becoming more patient and selective in the pitches he was swinging at, although statistics did not completely bear this out. In 1953, for instance, Mantle had a strong on-base percentage of .398. In 1954, he had been third in the American League in on-base percentage. No one in the league had been better at getting on base in 1955. However, it may have been that people had begun perceiving him differently. Also, many may have been judging his progress based on his strikeouts, because in his first thirty-six at-bats in the spring of 1956 Mickey struck out only once. Among those who took notice that spring was Stan Musial. "I saw Mantle looked different down in St. Petersburg," said Musial. "It was the first time [since 1951] that he'd ever looked real sharp in the spring. He'd always struck out a lot before, but this year he was letting the bad pitches go by. And he hit a lot of real long homers even down there, where the background isn't good for hitting. If he hits .400 or 60 home runs this season, I can't say I'll be surprised. He has all the qualifications."

Always the student and admirer of hitters, Ted Williams had been following Mantle's steady progress since his rookie season. Unlike DiMaggio,

Williams was unselfish in his admiration of Mantle and his potential. "As far as I can see," he told reporters during that season, "Mickey has improved every year, and he will continue to improve. My guess is that he's now definitely headed for his peak. Why shouldn't he be great? He has good speed, good swing, good power. There's no reason in the world why he can't be a .340 hitter and a forty-homer slugger or maybe better. I'll tell you one thing: He's the only guy in this league who has a chance of breaking Babe Ruth's home run record."

Shirley Povich of the *Washington Post*, one of the few writers who would develop a friendship with Mantle over the years, was among those who took note of the changes in Mickey that spring. "In Florida," he wrote in one piece, "one feeling has been inescapable for the past month. This is Mickey Mantle's year. This is the one when he'll burst into full magnificence, hit more and longer home runs than anybody else, lead the league in batting, perhaps, and certainly get more extra-base hits than anybody else."

The Yankees opened that season at Griffith Stadium in Washington, home of the Senators—famed as "first in war, first in peace, and last in the American League." Mantle wasted little time in showing he was ready to fulfill Povich's prediction. On opening day, Mickey launched two five-hundred-foot home runs over the center-field fence. "I'd say that Mickey attained maturity on Opening Day," recalled teammate Jerry Coleman in the weeks that followed. "It was boom-boom, and he had two tremendous homers without even trying. It gave him confidence. I've noticed since that he's going with the pitches. If they pitch him inside, he'll pull the ball. But if they pitch him outside, he'll slice to the opposite field. Last year he'd have tried to overpower them by pulling the ball anyway. The boy has come of age."

Mantle's impressive start also elevated the hitting of Yogi Berra, who was not known as a quick starter. With Mantle hitting behind him in the cleanup spot, pitchers began worrying about walking Berra and then having to face the league's most powerful hitter with a runner on base. Getting better pitches to hit, Berra got off to a career-best start, hitting twelve home runs and batting near .350 through the first weeks of the season. With Mantle and Berra becoming the most explosive batting duo since Ruth and Gehrig, the Yankees took quick control of the American League pennant race. On May 16, the Yankees took the lead by defeating the Indians and were never out of first place again. Mantle would go on to have a year for the ages. On May 18, he hit home runs from both sides of the plate. On June 18, he hit a ball over the roof at Briggs Stadium in Detroit, becoming just the second player to accomplish that feat (Ted Williams was the first). Over the season, he made the tape-measure home run seem almost routine, hitting five-hundred-foot shots on more than a handful of occasions.

But Mantle's most memorable home run of the season was undoubtedly the one he hit on Memorial Day against the Washington Senators at Yankee Stadium—a prodigious blast that would land him on the covers of *Time* and *Newsweek* magazines and signal his arrival on the national landscape as the American hero for his age. Yankee historian Peter Golenbock would offer perhaps the best description of Mantle's nineteenth home run of that season:

"Right-hander Pete Ramos, pitching for the Senators, tried to throw a fast ball by Mantle. Batting left-handed, Mantle took his usual vicious swing, and when the ball hit the bat, it rocketed toward the outfield so fast that the Yankees sitting on the bench almost got whiplash jerking their heads to the right. As the ball reached the apex of its flight, it looked like it was going to be the first fair ball ever hit out of Yankee Stadium. The soaring baseball appeared to be at a point higher than the Stadium roof, 120 feet from the ground. When it finally began descending near where the three-tiered grandstand stopped and the low one-story bullpen and bleachers began, it struck the grandstand's filigreed façade only eighteen inches from the top of the Stadium roof. The ball was going so fast when it struck the façade that it still had enough momentum to rebound more than 100 feet back onto the playing field. Had the façade not stopped it, the ball would have traveled more than 600 feet. It just didn't seem possible that a baseball could be hit that hard."

Although Mickey would be credited with "inventing" the tape-measure home run, it might be better to say that he made the tape-measure home run a conversation item, in large part because of heavy television and national media coverage of his exploits. Certainly Ruth and Gehrig had hit home runs every bit as prodigious as Mantle's. Gehrig's most talked-about blast had been a 611-foot home run hit in a 1929 exhibition at Clark Field in Princeton, New Jersey. In the 1950s, however, Mantle's home runs became a part of the pop culture lore, like Davy Crockett and coonskin caps. Fans would exaggerate, some claiming that one of Mantle's home runs off the façade at Yankee Stadium would have traveled over seven hundred feet if not impeded.

In the second game of that Memorial Day double-header, Mantle tagged pitcher Camilo Pascual with yet another tape-measure home run. Mantle finished May with twenty home runs, and he was leading the majors with a .414

batting average. By June 6, Mantle was the runaway league leader in five batting categories. By the time the Yankees had played sixty games, Mantle had hit twenty-seven home runs and was on pace to hit sixty-nine for the season and break Ruth's record. Throughout the first half of the season, newspapers tracked Mantle's home run pace alongside Ruth's home runs in the 1927 season.

With his majestic home runs and pursuit of Ruth's record, Mantle was the story on the sports pages and throughout most of America as well. In the spring of 1951 he had become a brief national phenomenon, his arrival heralded by hype about the coming of the next Ruth and DiMaggio. Now in 1956, Mantle's emergence as a bona fide sports star had transcended baseball and made him a national pop icon. Later that year, promoting the first of his autobiographies, *The Mickey Mantle Story*, Mantle would cause a mob scene when he appeared at a Long Island book signing. New York police, fearing problems controlling crowds in Manhattan or the Bronx, had convinced the publisher to move Mantle's appearance into the suburbs. It had made no difference. Police had to escort Mantle into and out of the bookstore, whose windows had been boarded up for precaution. "The mob scene was beating at the door," the Long Island paper *Newsday* reported. "Pretty teen-age girls were squealing and swooning for a glimpse of the Yankee slugger." According to the newspaper account, Mantle found himself that day the adoring object of "1,000 fanatics ranging from 8-year-old Little Leaguers to pretty bobby-soxers to their mothers, fathers, grandfathers, and grandmothers. . . . It wasn't Elvis [The Pelvis] Presley, it was Mickey (The Bomber) Mantle."

Mantle's exploits in 1956 made him not only a national hero but the front-runner in the ongoing debate among fans as to who the best center fielder in New York was. New York was home to three of the most prominent franchises in the history of the sport, each with its own set of stars, and each with its own legion of devoted fans who proudly identified with their respective teams every bit as much as they did with their faiths or their ethnicities. Just as Yankee fans swore by Mantle, if sometimes at him, so too would Dodgers fans claim that Duke Snider was the best center fielder in the game, and Giants fans argue that the title rightly belonged to their own Willie Mays. There was really no contest, though Mantle personally deferred to Mays. "You watched Willie play, and you laughed because he made it look fun," recalled *The New Yorker's* Roger Angell. "With Mantle, you didn't laugh. You gasped." Neither Snider nor Mays faced the pressure and demands that confronted Mantle that season. The chase of Ruth's home run record focused daily national attention on Mantle. Duke Snider later recalled that even at the height of their fame in New York, he and Mays both could still go out in public without being mobbed; Mantle could not. The demands from the press and fans were understandable, and Mickey's experience over the previous five seasons was invaluable in helping him handle the attention. "I just wish that people wouldn't expect me to hit a home run every game," he said at the height of the running day-to-day comparisons with Ruth's 1927 record season. "I know I can't keep up the pace. I wish people would realize this and not expect too much from me."

But the deeper pressure was personal. Merlyn had given birth to their second son, David, the day after Christmas, and Mickey had spent only a few weeks with them before reporting to spring training. He felt torn by guilt at his absence from his young family, especially as he recalled his own father's dedication to him. Four years after Mutt's death, "Not a day went by that year, especially on the days when I had hit [a home run] or did something special, that I didn't think of him and wished he'd gotten to live long enough to see it," Mantle would say years later. Mickey believed that his remarkable season was almost completely the product of his father's work to help him develop as a hitter.

His father's dedication to him, almost to the exclusion of his other children, weighed on him that season. His twin brothers had signed Yankee contracts, but their fortunes in the game were quite different from Mickey's. Mantle occasionally expressed hope of one day being part of an all-Mantle Yankee outfield, but his brothers never made it to the majors. Mickey's optimism had been sparked by the twins' performance in semipro baseball in 1953, after which he had asked the Yankees to give them a look. In the spring of 1954, Ray and Roy drove to New York, where they impressed the Yankees and signed minor league contracts. They played with McAllister in the Class D Sooner State League in Oklahoma, where they continued to show promise. Roy hit .325 in forty-five games and Ray .324 in twelve games. The next spring both were invited to the Yankees' instructional camp, where, according to Mickey, they were faster than everyone except him. They were assigned to Class C teams, but their careers were short-lived. Roy injured a leg, and Ray was drafted into the army. "When I got back I tried to play [again], but I couldn't do it," Ray recalled many years later. "Roy never did come back from his injury, and I think Mickey was more disappointed than we were that we didn't make it to the Yankees to play in the outfield with him." The only baseball the twins would play again was on a semipro weekend team back home in Commerce. Mantle knew it was the fate that would have awaited him had his father not kept him from quitting and returning home during the funk of his rookie season. The twins, he knew, had not had the benefit of their father's obsessive training when they were young; Mutt was no longer there to keep them from quitting the game he had loved so much.

However, no one saw the personal strains tugging on Mickey, least of all Merlyn. To her and to most of the people around him, Mantle's personal maturity reflected his growth as a ballplayer. "The death of his father has had a lot to do with it," Merlyn told one reporter. "It really affected him. He's had a lot of responsibility since then, and I think he's grown up quite a lot. He's sent three brothers and his sister through school."

A sign that Mantle had become the dominant player in the game was the All-Star balloting that year. Mantle was the top vote-getter in the fan balloting and enjoyed the luxury of simply staying over in Washington, home of the 1956 All-Star Game, after a Yankee series in town. It gave Mickey that much more time for the long-running parties that the All-Star breaks usually became. By his own admission, Mantle never took the All-Star Games seriously, except for the parties and the camaraderie with some of the game's other top players. That year's game was an especially eventful one for Mantle, however. He and Williams hit back-to-back home runs in the sixth inning in the American League All-Stars' loss. The only other homers in the game were hit by Stan Musial and Willie Mays for the National League, putting Mantle in distinguished company. Mantle also spent considerable time during that All-Star break talking to Williams about hitting—or, as Mantle himself was quick to describe his occasional discussions with Williams, *listening* to the Splendid Splinter talk about hitting.

"Ted liked to talk to other hitters and ask them their theories, things that he might be able to apply and use himself," recalled Mantle. "He was always asking questions, looking for new theories on hitting, telling his own theories, anything to learn more about hitting and maybe improve. One time, he started asking me which was my power hand, which hand did I use to guide the bat. And when I left him, I started thinking about all the things he told me, and I didn't get a hit for about twenty-five at-bats."

Whether he was confused by Williams's theories on hitting or stressed by chasing Babe Ruth's ghost, or because of increasing pain in his chronically ailing right knee, the month after the All-Star Game was not a good one for Mickey. In the twenty-nine years since Ruth's record-setting season with the 1927 Yankees, several players had challenged the home-run mark, but all had faded during the second half of the season. In 1932, Jimmy Foxx had forty-one home runs by the end of July, but had finished with only fifty-eight. Ruth himself had thirty home runs by the end of June in two other seasons but had been unable to surpass his own record. By mid-summer, Mantle's pace began to slacken; in July, he hit only a handful of home runs. He bounced back in August by hitting twelve. In August, even President Dwight Eisenhower joined the Mantle frenzy. He attended a Yankees game against the Senators at Griffith Stadium, where he asked Mantle to hit a home run for him. In the seventh inning, Mantle obliged. Mickey went into September with forty-seven home runs, needing only fourteen homers to break Ruth's record.

Meanwhile, no one watched Mantle as closely as the man who had staked so much on Mickey's developing as one of the game's all-time greats, Casey Stengel. It was his pregame ritual to talk to the writers from the New York newspapers as well as the writers from whatever city the Yankees happened to be playing. However, Stengel would always stop to watch Mantle take batting practice. In late summer, while watching Mickey hit ball after ball into the seats during batting practice, he muttered to writers from New York and Washington, "He's something odd. I was thinking the other night, that guy rarely or never hits a line drive back at the pitcher. [Paul] Waner used to say he aimed at 'em."

Mantle was almost always a topic in these pregame conversations between Stengel and the writers. It was as if in Stengel's mind Mantle's fate in baseball and his own were connected. Once that season, discussing his concerns about keeping Mickey healthy, Casey said to Joe Phelan of United Press International, "If anything happens to Mantle, what happens to me then?"

Later that summer in Boston, as Mantle's onslaught against American League pitching continued, Phelan became the first writer to champion Mickey as the next player to make a hundred thousand dollars—the salary then being paid to Ted Williams and the highest salary paid DiMaggio, at the end of his career. At one of these pregame discussions, Phelan got Stengel involved in the hundred-thousand-dollar salary issue, which Casey himself appeared to support.

"When," said Joe Phelan, "will the Yankees pay Mantle $100,000 a year?"

Casey looked taken aback. But his good humor was not impaired.

"Why," he said pleasantly, "I think you got a right to ask that question, young fella. It just ain't a question to ask *me*. That's a question to ask Mr. George Weiss."

Phelan eyed him coldly.

"Will the Yanks ever pay Mantle $100,000 if they can avoid it?"

The Boston writers watching the exchange were visibly embarrassed. "Ted Williams," one of them blurted, "didn't get $100,000 right away."

"Now wait," said Casey easily to Phelan, his humor intact. "You ask a question. I say you got a right to ask it, a right to your opinion. Now I say this—this fella is liable to get $100,000 sooner 'n you think—this is just my guess now—providing, I say providing he was to do these three things—break the Ruth record and lead in RBIs and batting."

A healthy Mantle might have risen to the challenge of Ruth's record, but in the first week of September he pulled a groin muscle running the bases. He failed to hit a home run in the first ten games of the month and was overtaken by Ted Williams in the batting-average race. Suddenly, not only were Mantle's chances of breaking Ruth's record diminishing but also his shot at winning the Triple Crown—leading the league in batting average, runs batted in, and home runs. Mickey began pressing. Opposing pitchers refused to give him strikes to hit, so Mantle began chasing high fastballs out of the strike zone, with disastrous results. His strikeouts were followed by profanity-laced temper tantrums that often ended with kicking over the dugout water cooler. Mantle went five for thirty-four that month, his worst slump of the season; it guaranteed that Ruth's single season home run record was safe once again. Mantle did not hit his fiftieth home run, his third of the month, until September 17, off White Sox left-hander Billy Pierce in Comiskey Park. That eleventh-inning shot broke a 2–2 pitching duel between Pierce and Whitey Ford and clinched the pennant for the Yankees.

With another berth in the World Series in hand, Mantle went on a tear despite the pulled groin. It was as if Mantle relaxed and began to enjoy his incredible year the moment the pressure of Ruth's record was lifted from him. On September 16, photographer Ray Gallo found Mantle surprisingly at ease before a game with the Red Sox in Boston. Gallo asked Mickey to pose on the bench of the visitors' dugout at Fenway Park. Mantle graciously consented. The result was what Mickey was to call "the greatest photograph I've ever seen of myself." The photographer had captured the essence of the young confident hero—Mantle, his right arm resting on the back of the bench and his golden locks showing under the front of his cap, is resplendent even in the Yankees' gray traveling uniform. The photograph was originally taken in black and white, but a hand-painted version by artist Yvette Andreoni would later be the picture of Mantle selected by the Hall of Fame from over twenty-five years' worth of entries.

Fittingly, the batting contest between Mantle and Williams came down to the final series of the season, with the Yankees hosting the Red Sox. Mantle led Williams by four percentage points, .354 to .350, going into the first game of the three-game series. Still nursing the muscle pull, Mantle insisted to Stengel that he was ready to play. "I didn't want to be sitting on the bench with the batting title at stake," Mantle said afterward. He connected for his fifty-second home run in the first game but was hitless in three other at-bats; his batting average dropped a point. Williams failed to capitalize, going zero for three and dropping his average to .348. With his groin muscle tightening up again, Mantle did not start the second game, but he pinch-hit, drawing a bases-loaded walk. Williams again failed to take advantage of the opportunity offered by Mantle's absence from the lineup. In the sweltering heat of New York in September, Williams could get only one hit in three at-bats and saw his batting average fall to .345. At the age of thirty-eight, Williams had made an amazing run at the batting championship—and would have an even more incredible season the following year. But even he sensed that 1956 was meant to be Mickey's year. Williams conceded the batting title by sitting out the final game. Mantle also did not start the season finale, but he drove in a run on a pinch-hit grounder, ending the season at .353, eight points ahead of Williams. The run he drove in with his ground ball gave him 130 RBIs for the season. Detroit's Al Kaline, going into his final game, had 126 RBIs and a chance to tie or overtake Mantle. Mickey had to wait out nervously the news from Detroit to learn that Kaline had driven in only two runs. Mantle had won the Triple Crown.

He was only the twelfth Triple Crown winner and he had the highest figures for both the American and National Leagues—only the fourth player to do so in a season. Rogers Hornsby had first done it, for the St. Louis Cardinals, in 1925; Lou Gehrig did it in 1934; and Williams had been the last to accomplish it, in 1942. Williams had also been baseball's last Triple Crown winner, in 1947. Despite the two Triple Crowns, Williams would command greater fame for being the last hitter to hit .400 in a season. For Williams, the magical .406 batting average of his 1941 season would be his own personal hallmark. The challenge of hitting .400 again was often on his mind, as it would be again in evaluating Mantle at the end of the 1956 season. "If I could run like that son of a bitch," said Williams, "I'd hit .400 every year." Mantle later agreed that his speed had probably been responsible for winning the batting title. "I don't know how many bunt hits and leg [infield] hits I got that season," he said, "but it must have been at least twenty. I know it was enough to give me my eight-point margin over Williams."

At the end of the season, Mantle became only the second man in history to win the league's Most Valuable Player award unanimously. The *Sporting News* named him the major leagues' player of the year. By World Series time, at age twenty-four, Mickey Mantle had become the most famous man in base-ball at a time when no other sport in America rivaled baseball. He appeared on the Perry Como television show, sharing the stage with starlet Kim Novak, later known for her performance in Alfred Hitchcock's dizzying thriller *Vertigo*. Mantle also joined popular singer Teresa Brewer in recording "I Love Mickey," a catchy tune that further cemented Mantle as a pop figure in the nation's consciousness. In a pre–World Series production, the highly popular *Kraft Television Theater* show aired "The Mickey Mantle Story," with an actor named Jim Olson playing Mantle. It would become the source of a story told often over the next few years by Billy Martin. "How could they have done that show about Mick," Martin would ask, "without having Marlon Brando play me?"

After Mantle's banner year, the 1956 World Series might have seemed anticlimactic, except that Mickey and the Yankees had waited a full year to avenge the 1955 loss to the Brooklyn Dodgers. Not only had Mantle fulfilled the promise he had shown in the spring of his rookie season, but he had made the team "Mantle's Yankees." Pitcher Bob Turley would later note, "There was verbal leadership coming from guys like Hank Bauer, who would remind everyone that they'd have to play hard to make the World Series. Then there was silent leadership from guys who would go out there and bust their asses every day. Mantle was a silent leader. He loved to play baseball and would do his best every day."

The 1956 World Series, the last "subway series" for forty-four years, would be remembered for Don Larsen's perfect game in game five—the only perfect game in World Series history. The twenty-seven-year-old Larsen was the un-likeliest of heroes. He was a journeyman pitcher with a reputation for wild partying, and he had failed to make it through the second inning of game two in the series, which the Dodgers won, 13–8. In game one, Sal Maglie—a thirty-nine-year-old former New York Giant who had pitched a no-hitter down the stretch of a heated pennant race with the Philadelphia Phillies— beat Whitey Ford, 6–3, supported by home runs from Jackie Robinson and Gil Hodges. After game two, when the Dodgers pounded Larsen and six other pitchers, the Yankees were forced to attempt a comeback. A solo home run by Billy Martin and a three-run shot by forty-year-old Enos Slaughter gave Ford a 5–3 win in game three. The Yankees evened up the Series at 2–2 in game four, when Tom Sturdivant pitched a six-hitter and got home runs from Mantle and Hank Bauer for a 6–2 win. In game five, Maglie would exceed his Series-opener performance; this would be the best-pitched game in World Series history. Through three innings, both Larsen and Maglie were perfect. Arthur Daley of the *Times* would even wonder in the press box if this would be "the first double no-hitter since Fred Toney of the Cincinnati Reds and Hippo Jim Vaughn of the Chicago Cubs had tangled almost forty years ago." (Vaughn lost that 1917 game on an unearned run in the tenth inning.)

In 1956, however, the double no-hitter in game five would last only until Mantle's second at-bat. In addition to his home run in game four, Mantle had also homered in the Series opener. He had hit both home runs using one of Hank Bauer's bats, something he had been doing for the last few weeks of the season. Although he had numerous bats specially crafted for him by the Louisville Slugger Company, Mantle was notorious for using other team-mates' bats, to the delight of those teammates. At the batting cage before game five, Bauer saw Mickey taking several practice swings with a different bat than the one he had been borrowing from him.

"He's quit on me," Bauer announced to everyone gathered around the batting cage at home plate. "Now he's using Joe Collins's bat, ain'tcha, Mick?"

"Nope," said Mickey. "I'm using Jerry Lumpe's bat today."

"You're nuts," said Bauer good-naturedly. "All a guy on this team has to say is, 'Hey, Mickey, I got a good bat,' and Mickey will say, 'Let me try it.'"

Lumpe, a utility infielder, was not on the World Series roster, but his bat would be a major contributor that day. In the fourth inning, Mantle broke up Maglie's perfect game when he pulled a curveball down the right-field line, barely inside the foul pole at the 296-foot mark, to put the Yankees ahead. In the fifth inning, the Dodgers' Gil Hodges almost spoiled Larsen's masterpiece when he slugged a 2–2 fastball into deep left center field; Mantle, running at full speed, made what he called "the best catch I ever made" on a four-hundred-foot-plus fly ball that would have been a home run in the Dodgers' Ebbets Field. "There would have been no perfect game for Larsen without what Mantle did to catch Hodges's line drive," the *Washington Post's* Shirley Povich would later write. "That ball was certain to fall in until a flying Mantle reached the scene from nowhere and speared it backhanded. Larsen should have blown him a kiss."

Mantle had been involved in three no-hitters during his career—Allie Reynolds's two gems in 1951 and Virgil Trucks's no-hit game in 1952. He knew, as did almost everyone, the baseball superstition of not talking about a no-hitter for fear of jinxing it. After the fifth inning, Mantle tried to stay as far away from Larsen as possible, but Goony Bird—as his teammates called Larsen—sauntered over to Mickey.

"Hey, Slick," he said, using the nickname Ford had given Mantle, "wouldn't it be funny if I pitched a no-hitter?"

Mantle almost spit out the sip of water he had just taken and waved off his pitcher: "Get the hell outta here!"

Maglie would go on to give up another run in the sixth. Larsen's perfection, however, continued. Using just ninety-seven pitches, Larsen closed out the only perfect game in a World Series game—and the first in major league baseball in thirty-four years.

Larsen's perfection might have immediately entered the record books, but it clearly did not deflate the Dodgers, who bounced back to tie the Series at 3–3 behind reliever Clem Labine in game six. Making a rare start, Labine shut out the Yankees for ten innings. Jackie Robinson's line drive scored Jim Gilliam from second in the tenth for a 1–0 Dodger win. That run would be the last the Dodgers scored in 1956. On paper, it would have seemed that game seven favored the Dodgers, playing at home and going with ace Don Newcombe, a twenty-seven-game winner and the first Cy Young recipient. The Yankees started second-year right-hander Johnny Kucks. However, Kucks would pitch the game of his career, a three-hitter, while the Yankees pounded Newcombe, chasing him in the fourth inning. Berra hit a pair of two-run homers, Elston Howard slugged a solo round-tripper, and Moose Skowron sealed the Yankees' seventeenth World Series championship with a seventh-inning grand slam off Brooklyn's Roger Craig.

Larsen was named the Most Valuable Player of the Series, and with his sixth World Series title Casey Stengel was being acclaimed a baseball genius, even by some of his strongest critics. But 1956 would ultimately be remembered as Mickey Mantle's Triple Crown year—a season when he had dueled with Ted Williams down the stretch and won, a season when he had chased Babe Ruth only to come up short, but in the end, a season that had proven that he belonged in the pantheon of the greats.

When it came to giving Mantle his due, however, Stengel could be devastatingly unsentimental. At the end of Mantle's brilliant 1956 season, a reporter asked Stengel, "Who is the greater center fielder, Mantle or DiMaggio?"

"I'd have to say DiMaggio," Stengel answered, "because he played right-handed and the park wasn't built for him, and he didn't need a manager."

Years later, Mantle was kinder in his own assessment of Stengel and of the role he had played in shaping his career. "In 1956 I had the Triple Crown year, and I credit Casey with all that," Mantle would recall. "To me . . . he was a better manager than everybody [said]. Everybody said he was a push-button manager, but I always felt like he was a great psychologist, too. He knew when to bawl you out, when to fine you, and stuff like that. I think he was better than everybody thought he was."

"It was a year I'll never forget. My favorite year."

13

Success in sports, especially in baseball, is transient. Baseball, by its very nature, is a humbling game, reminding players that while they may strive for perfection, most must learn to be content with mere achievement, at best.

For Mickey, the unparalleled highs of his Triple Crown season were, as Merlyn would say, "fantasy time. . . . There is nothing quite like it, the status, the attention, the power of being a New York icon. It really is true. If you can make it there, you can make it anywhere. . . . We were having our babies, going to some really neat places, and, in my imagination, having breakfast at Tiffany's. I thought I had the perfect marriage. Look at me, I thought. I'm married to Mickey Mantle. Who wouldn't want to be married to Mickey Mantle?"

Mickey certainly did not want anyone married to him. He had fallen for the nightlife and for the glory showered upon New York's latest prince of the city, the same way he had fallen for the high fastball as a rookie. Behind the scenes, the 1956 season had been one continuous extramarital affair for Mickey. Mickey's teammates would joke and marvel at his sexual prowess, in much the same way as Babe Ruth's once had. One running line among his teammates that season was that Mickey might be losing ground on Ruth's record on the field but was still well ahead of his home-run pace off the field. In June, Mantle had all but refused to cooperate with the FBI in an investigation of a blackmail threat for having an affair with a married woman. Mantle denied having been threatened or being involved with a married woman, but the general manager, George Weiss, and other Yankee executives suspected he was lying. They remembered the shy, humble youngster from Oklahoma who had been a naïve rookie only a few seasons earlier and wondered what had happened to him. Instead of looking to Mantle himself for the answers, they looked to the company Mickey was keeping and blamed the irascible Billy Martin. Focusing on Martin's influence, unfortunately, only took attention from the real cause—drinking, which had already become a problem in Mantle's life. Understandably, like most people with growing addictions, Mantle thought he had his drinking under control.

"Back then I could quit drinking when I went to spring training," he would recall years later. "I got myself into shape. Then when the season started I went back to drinking again—Billy, Whitey Ford and me. Hell, we played mostly night games. We'd be home by 1 A.M. and sleep until 9 or 10. I never used to have hangovers. I had an incredible tolerance for alcohol, and I'd always look and feel great in the morning. I don't think I ever blew a game because I was drunk or hung over. Maybe I hurt the team once or twice, but if I wasn't feeling right, I got myself out of the game early. When my dad died, Casey became like a father to me. He'd call me in sometimes and say, 'Look, I know we don't have a curfew, but you're overdoing it a bit. Besides, it's not helping you any.' I couldn't fool Casey."

Casey Stengel might not have been the best of influences on Mantle and on his development, which was important to the Yankees, considering Mantle was regarded as the team's future. In his younger days as a player, Stengel had been a partier and a drinker himself—and he became, in that sense, the consummate player's manager, especially with the Yankees. He imposed no curfew on his players, nor did he assess fines for showing up for games hung over, as Mantle sometimes did. Instead of benching Mickey or imposing any kind of disciplinary action, Stengel would play Mantle—conveying the problematic message to his superstar that he could do whatever he wanted and not pay a price, either then or later in his career. By 1956, with Stengel failing to intervene, Mantle was as much on his way to becoming a veteran drinker as a veteran player. The routine of excessive drinking and not taking care of himself had begun in 1952, after his father died, and had gone on virtually unchecked. It continued during the off-season in Commerce when Martin made extended visits and intensified in the years to follow, as Mantle became more self-assured around New York and in the cities to which the Yankees traveled during the season.

Mantle himself was still too immature and too intoxicated with his success—especially in 1956—and already too dependent on alcohol to see the impact that his lifestyle was having on his career. "You know," Mantle would later say when recalling his Triple Crown season, "I thought I would have ten more seasons like that. Maybe if I'd taken care of myself a little better, I would have."

It wasn't that his years after 1956 were bad. In 1957, he would achieve a career-high batting average, .365, and would exceed a .500 on-base percentage—as did Ted Williams that same year. Mantle and Williams were the last to record on-base percentages of .500 or better in a season until the 2001 season when Barry Bonds would accomplish the feat. Although he lost the batting title to Ted Williams, who hit an amazing .388, Mantle would win his second straight Most Valuable Player award—which many thought should have gone to Williams. Mickey led the league in runs, was second in total bases, and led in bases on balls. Williams finished first in on base percentage and slugging percentage, but the Red Sox finished twelve games behind the Yankees.

Still, Mantle's home-run production fell by eighteen, to thirty-four homers, and his ninety-four RBIs were also down dramatically from the Triple Crown season. In fact, except for his batting average, Mantle's 1957 hitting statistics were also down, below the thirty-seven home runs and ninety-nine RBIs of his 1955 season. The Yankee front office had its pulse close to the Mantle barometer and was concerned. In his own way, Weiss tried unsuccessfully to steer Mantle off his fast-lane nightlife. After the 1956 season, Mantle demanded that his salary be doubled. In response, Weiss threatened to reveal the private-eye reports of Mickey's adulterous affairs and unrestrained nightlife that he had been accumulating over the past few seasons. Perhaps if the Mantle after-hours dossier had been used outside the context of contract negotiations, the embarrassing revelations might have had an impact on changing Mickey's ways. But in negotiating Mantle's 1956 contract, in the wake of one of the best seasons in baseball history, Weiss apparently went overboard, threatening to trade Mantle to Cleveland for slugger Rocky Colavito and pitcher Herb Score. Co-owner Del Webb was not about to lose his franchise player and intervened on his star's behalf. Mantle wound up getting the sixty-five thousand dollars he wanted, and any leverage Weiss might have had in curbing Mickey's nightlife was lost.

The inferno of celebrity and self-destruction seductively beckoned. Other celebrities, unable to deal with the burden of fame, have experienced the same pattern of self-destruction. Some have become captives in the prison of their fame and have ultimately destroyed themselves and their careers. However, the course of the self-destruction Mantle was following had far less to do with celebrity and fame than with an impending sense of doom that would become part of the Mantle legend, even as he attempted to downplay its significance in later years. Having watched so many male members of his family, including his father, succumb to Hodgkin's disease, Mantle was haunted by the fear of an early death. Hank Bauer would later recall having once confronted Mickey after seeing him arrive for a game hung over from yet another of his late-night drinking binges. Bauer tried to have a big-brother talk with Mantle, suggesting that he be more serious and stop abusing his body. "My father died young," Mantle said, looking up at Bauer through bloodshot eyes. "I'm not going to be cheated."

For years, Mantle would be consumed by thoughts of his father and the feeling that Mutt had been cheated by his early death—cheated of seeing Mickey win the Triple Crown and his every accomplishment, cheated of seeing the grandchildren he had asked for, cheated of the chance to grow old and resolve all the issues shared by fathers and sons. Years later, researching *Dynasty*, his history of the 1949–64 Yankees, Peter Golenbock got Mantle to reminisce about his father and their relationship—something Mickey often refused to do with Yankee beat writers.

"Do you still miss him?" Golenbock asked. "Do you still think about him?"

Mantle nodded. "Oh, yes," he said. "I dream about him all the time."

Mantle, in a sense, not wanting to get "cheated," was living out not only the dream his father had for him but the life his father had been denied. As psychiatrists and Shakespeare would have it, a son comes into his own when he surpasses his father. In Mantle's case, he continued the race with his father still a prominent figure in his psyche. Mutt would forever be present in Mickey's life, not simply as a memory but as a patriarchal figure to whom Mantle never broke the ties of a child. Invariably, the tension between fathers and sons requires some form of release, physical and emotional, and with Mickey there had been neither. His carousing, his sexual infidelity, his showing up hung over for games—it may have been Mantle not wanting "to be cheated," but it also was the rebellion of a son seeking that release.

Meanwhile, Mantle's extracurricular activities continued to turn up in the files of the FBI—including an association with gamblers that undoubtedly would not have been looked upon favorably by baseball. In June 1957, according to an FBI file, a Washington "gambler and bookmaker" bought an undisclosed number of Yankees a night in a local brothel. "Allegedly, Mr. Mantle was one of the members of the team who was entertained at this house of prostitution," the FBI memo states. In another instance mentioned in the file, a "well-known Texas gambler who frequently made 'heavy bets' on professional football games and other athletic contests" got information on upcoming games. The FBI's memo stated that "some of the professional atheletes [sic] contacted by this individual allegedly included Mickey Mantle of the New York Yankees."

Mantle apparently had neither the appetite nor the penchant for gambling that ensnared other players, although he did have the money. In 1956, for instance, Mantle's total earnings had been almost a hundred thousand dollars—including his thirty-thousand-dollar annual salary, his World Series winning share of nine thousand, and fifty-nine thousand from Mickey Mantle Enterprises, the company that was handling his promotions, endorsements, and other business deals. Mantle was the highest-paid Yankee and, as such, had begun regularly picking up bar, restaurant, and taxicab bills for his teammates. Veterans like Yogi Berra and Hank Bauer, who had played with DiMaggio—whose annual salary had been a hundred thousand dollars in his last seasons—could recall only an instance or two when the Yankee Clipper had shown that kind of generosity. Mantle, on the other hand, treated his teammates like extended family members. In the summer of 1957, when Jerry Lumpe was called up from the minors, the young infielder was having a difficult time finding a house for his family that he could afford. With the school year about to start, Merlyn Mantle had just returned to their home in Commerce with their two boys, leaving Mickey alone with their rented house in River Edge, New Jersey. When Mantle heard of Lumpe's housing problems, he moved into a hotel and gave the Lumpe family the house—refusing to accept payment of any kind from his teammate.

Unfortunately for the Yankee closest to Mickey, however, there was little that Mantle could do to save himself from himself. Billy Martin celebrated his twenty-ninth birthday on May 15, 1957, with a party that began with dinner at a mid-Manhattan restaurant, Danny's Hideaway; continued at the Waldorf Astoria, where singer Johnny Ray was performing; and ended at the famous Copacabana, where Sammy Davis Jr. was the attraction. Martin, the carefree divorced bachelor, was being treated by longtime teammates Mantle, Ford, Berra, and Bauer and their wives, as well as young pitcher Johnny Kucks and his wife. Accounts of what happened at the Copacabana vary, except that all hell broke loose. Led by Bauer, the Yankees apparently got into an argument with a group of bowlers seated at the next table. According to the players, the drunken bowlers began heckling Davis, calling the entertainer "a jungle bunny," which touched a raw nerve among the Yankees after the racial harassment that Elston Howard had often had to endure, especially during spring training. The argument continued near the men's room, where, though bowlers and Yankees tried to hold back their more combative friends, scuffling broke out. It ended with a fat, drunk bowler knocked out cold on the floor, with a broken nose and other facial injuries.

Mantle recalled leaving Merlyn at their table to check on Martin, who had gone to the men's room. "I heard a loud crash," Mickey later said. "The next moment one of the drunks was lying in a heap by the cloakroom, knocked cold. I thought it was Billy. I turned around and saw a couple of other bowlers near the kitchen spitting curses at Hank. Whitey had a lock on his arms. I know this. Bauer never laid a hand on anybody. Neither did Billy. And the only thing I touched during the entire uproar was scotch and soda."

The Yankee players were quickly escorted out the back kitchen exit but were spotted by a *New York Post* entertainment columnist, who tipped off fellow reporters. It was generally believed that Bauer, who was being restrained in the men's room by his teammates, had been the Yankee who landed the punch—although Bauer vehemently denied it. Several players and other witnesses claimed the bowler had been beaten up by a couple of bouncers from the club, but the issue was irrelevant. The newspapers sensationalized the story in typical large, tabloid headlines that infuriated the Yankee front office, especially Weiss. In a way that had become common after such incidents, Weiss summoned all the players involved for early-morning meetings at the stadium. He refused to believe the Yankees, especially Martin, had not been at fault. Dan Topping also felt that his players had done something unseemly and fined them a thousand dollars apiece, except Kucks, whom he fined only five hundred, because his pay was significantly less than the others'. It made the Yankees look all the more guilty, especially after the injured bowler filed a criminal complaint that led to the Yankee players' testifying before a grand jury.

"At the grand jury, I remember Mantle standing in the middle of the room giving his testimony," Ford would later recall. "There was no chair, nothing. He was standing there and chewing gum and one of the jurors asked him, 'What are you chewing, Mr. Mantle?' 'Gum,' Mick said. 'Would you mind taking it out of your mouth?' Mick took the gum out of his mouth and there was no place to put it, so he had to hold it in his hand for the rest of the time he was being questioned."

Mantle elaborated in one of his autobiographies, repeating that he had not seen anyone throw any punches.

"Well," asked a grand juror, "did you see a gentleman lying unconscious on the floor near the Copa entrance?"

"Yes, I did," Mantle answered.

"All right. Do you have an opinion as to how this could have happened?"

Mantle thought about the question and then, with a serious look on his face, said, "I think Roy Rogers rode through the Copa, and Trigger kicked the man in the head."

The grand jury broke out laughing, and an hour later the district attorney threw out the case for insufficient evidence. However, the damage to Billy Martin's career as a Yankee was done. On June 15, a month to the day after the Copacabana incident, Martin was traded to the Kansas City Athletics. George Weiss had finally succeeded in getting Martin away from his young star, but he would soon learn that Martin had merely been a symptom of Mantle's off-the-field behavior and not the source.

"With Billy and me, drinking was a competitive thing," Mantle would recall. "We'd see who could drink the other under the table. I'd get a kick out of seeing him get loaded before me. Alcohol made him so aggressive. He's the only person I knew who could *hear* a guy give him the finger from the back of a barroom. We had some wild times."

The Yankees, meanwhile, continued to win. They won their eighth and ninth American League pennants in ten years under Stengel in 1957 and 1958. They lost the World Series in seven games in 1957 to the Milwaukee Braves but reclaimed the championship in 1958, when they became baseball's first team to come back after trailing 3–1 in the Series. Baseball, however, was entering a new era. When the 1957 season ended, the Dodgers announced they were abandoning Brooklyn for Los Angeles. The Giants too were leaving New York for the West Coast, heading to San Francisco. Suddenly, in one swift postseason move, the debate that had raged for most of the fifties over who the best center fielder in New York was had been settled, not on the field by Mickey, the Duke, and Willie Mays, but in the executive offices, by men recognizable only to their bankers and their accountants. Mantle was now the center-field prince of the city, and the fame and glory he had previously had to share were now his alone. But so were the expectations and the dashed hopes that were inevitably part of the game. In the years to follow, the booing that had always existed as a backdrop to Mantle's at-bats would actually worsen.

Years later Mantle would talk openly about needing the competition with Snider and Mays to push him, just as he had blossomed in his Triple Crown season and again in 1957 when pressed by Ted Williams. There was a part of Mickey that wished he were Snider, hitting half the season in Ebbets Field, which could have fit inside Yankee Stadium. While the right-field fence at 297 feet was almost identical, straight-away center field was only 389 feet deep. Mantle's power was in the right and left center-field alleys, and Yankee Stadium annually turned a dozen or more of Mickey's drives into long outs. Snider, on the other hand, had the benefit of the shallow power alleys at Ebbets Field. Other home-run hitters who played at Yankee Stadium would leave swearing at its Ruthian demands. "How can you play here?" the Twins' Harmon Killebrew asked Mantle after he caught three 450-foot fly balls for outs. Similarly, after playing in Yankee Stadium in the 1957 World Series, Hank Aaron said to Mantle, "I'm sure glad this isn't my home ball park."

The way Mickey figured, anywhere from a dozen to fifteen of his four-hundred-foot-plus drives that died in the stadium's power alleys each year would have been home runs in Ebbets Field. In a career of eighteen years, that would have meant 270 additional home runs—a number that would have pushed him close to an unimaginable eight hundred homers. Mickey was almost certainly overstating his case, but he did end up hitting slightly more than half of his career home runs on the road, 270 versus 266 Yankee Stadium shots.

But, of course, this was booze talk. It was the "one that got away," crying-in-your-beer talk that all drinkers indulge. Mickey might just as easily have left that many home runs each season in the bars, or at the parties, or perhaps even in foolishness, such as what happened in late August of 1957 as he was chasing Williams for the batting title. On an off-day, Mantle and pitcher Tom Sturdivant went to play eighteen holes of golf—violating one of the few prohibitions that Stengel had for his players on off-days. Angry at missing a putt, Mantle took a wild swing at a low-hanging tree branch and succeeded only in driving his putter at full speed into his shin. Mickey was hobbled for days, but no one—least of all Stengel—knew the real story of what had happened. The story that was reported for days on end in the newspapers was that Mantle had aggravated a shin-splints condition by accidentally kicking the corner of a door with his shin. To his adoring public, Mantle thus remained the injury-plagued star, enduring and overcoming through yet one more affliction. Playing in pain had become as much a part of being Mickey Mantle as the majestic home runs that seemed to disappear as quickly as they were hit. Mickey, in high and low, had become both an icon and a metaphor for New York and New Yorkers.

Among them would be the young son of a jazz-promoter father who also managed the Commodore Music Shop on 42nd Street. From the age of five, Billy Crystal had been steeped in show business. He would spontaneously jump up on stage and tap dance with some of the nation's top jazz talents, many of whom the Crystal family called friends. One such fond associate was jazz luminary Billy Holliday, who would frequently baby-sit young Billy; she affectionately referred to her precocious charge as "Face." But Crystal's real dream, since the spring day in 1956 when his father walked him down Jerome Avenue for his first Yankees game, was to be a professional baseball player—and literally to follow in Mickey's footsteps.

"I felt that when I went to a game at Yankee Stadium that Mickey Mantle knew that I was in the ballpark," Crystal said years later, looking back on that time. "I strongly felt that he was saying to himself, 'I better have a good day today. Bill's here. Damn, I don't feel good either. I better get a hit, steal a base or throw somebody out. He paid his $3.50.' Mickey Mantle was everyone's hero. He was who you wanted to be. I walked like him. I talked like him. I did my bar mitzvah with a drawl. He was a stunning athlete to watch."

In DiMaggio's era, and certainly in Ruth's, a youngster like Billy Crystal would have had to live in New York to be able to see in person how his Yankee hero looked, how he walked, how he swung the bat, how he ran the bases. But now, no verbal description on the radio, no matter how vivid the broadcaster, could compare to the real images of ballplayers transmitted across the country through television broadcasts of games. The phenomenon of fans outside major league baseball cities seeing their heroes as a game unfolded began near the end of DiMaggio's career, when television sets started being mass produced. The Giants-Dodgers 1951 playoff series, ending dramatically with Bobby Thomson's home run, was the first to be televised across America. The impact on the fans' perception of players they might previously have only read about or seen in newsreels at theaters was as visceral as what Crystal experienced his first time at Yankee Stadium, multiplied over and over. In 1946, there were seventeen thousand television sets in the country. By 1950, Americans had 4.4 million television sets. Then TV exploded, with fifteen million sets sold in 1951 alone. By 1953, two-thirds of American homes had at least one TV. By 1960, there were more than fifty million television sets throughout the land, influencing what Americans wore, did in their leisure time, bought, and talked about. Like radio before it, the development of broadcast television during the 1950s helped baseball immensely. Television not only brought the games into the fans' homes but allowed the kids to see their favorite players in action. The fact that two of baseball's "golden eras" coincided, respectively, with the advent of radio in the 1920s and television in the 1950s is probably not a coincidence. Unlike the 1920s, this era also featured a healthy baseball-card market. The influence of TV was so evident by 1955 that Bowman's final set of trading cards was designed to show its players inside a television screen.

For Mantle, the television boom coincided with the best six-year period of his career, from 1953 to 1958, when he established himself as the most feared hitter in the game and arguably its best player. In that stretch, Mickey averaged thirty-six home runs, 102 RBIs, 123 runs, 114 walks, and a .320 batting average; he also played in five of his twelve World Series. Mantle and the Yankees seemed to be regulars on the nationally televised *Game of the Week*, which began as a Saturday event and eventually included Saturday games and occasional doubleheaders. While the telecasts included most of the top major league teams, the Yankees appeared most often. Hall of Fame Cardinals pitcher Dizzy Dean was one of the announcers, along with Buddy Blattner, who was later replaced by Pee Wee Reese. With Mantle in his glory years, they had a ready-made star attraction ideal for a medium designed for Saturday afternoon heroes. The intricacies involved with Mantle's switch-hitting talents were often dissected and explained to an enthralled national audience who had never seen ballplayers close up in their dens and living rooms. Every Mantle at-bat invariably included a close-up shot of the unique way he held his bat, with the little finger of the bottom hand curled up underneath the knob.

"I wonder why he don't just use a longer bat," Dean once observed.

"Dizzy," shot back his sidekick Blattner, "that's why you were a pitcher and not a hitter."

"Yo're right, pahd'ner. Yo're right!"

Coming into tens of thousands of American homes on Saturday and Sunday afternoon via their television sets, Mickey Mantle established himself as every bit as much a cultural hero as Lucy, the Lone Ranger, or the Beaver. Mantle's swing, whether he was hitting a home run or striking out, was simply another of the fast-moving images on the small screen. There is a certain mystique of genuine Americana surrounding classic '50s television hits, a mystique that lives on to this very day. It is easy to forget that the comparatively crude technology of black-and-white television was, in the 1950s, every bit as cutting-edge and exciting as the Internet half a century later. The beautiful, rhythmic performers who inhabited this domain became the new cultural heroes. The electronic media made it possible to preserve each facial expression and each inflection of a singer's voice as well as each nuance of a baseball hitter's stance. Celebrity, too, was born of exposure to audiences upon a vast stage. The public became consumers of popular culture, connoisseurs of its various kinds of rhythms. Millions watched Mantle hit home runs or just strike out, but always with that famous swing that seemingly began behind his muscular shoulders, uncoiled from his legs and trunk in a movement of sheer power, and finished as if he had swung from his soul. No other player did that.

"When Little League uniforms were handed out every spring, the only real fight was for Number 7, everything else was afterthought," syndicated Texas columnist Mike Leggett reminisced about his boyhood, in a recollection that undoubtedly could be shared by the millions of youngsters who grew up in awe of Mantle. "You could wear Yogi's No. 8 or Hank's 44, but that was still second place. When my brother and I played home-run derby in the yard or batted rocks across Highway 79, we argued over who got to be Mickey, driving one eight rows deep in right field to win the World Series.

"It was as if wearing that number, which I did for several years and on several all-star teams, or invoking the name in a whiffle-ball game could somehow conjure up within each of us the power and grace of Mickey Mantle. Mickey was the ball player we all wanted to be and he was the first sports phenomenon created by the same electronic monster that would make Elvis a household name. Television gave Mickey Mantle a face and a name for East Texas kids by showing us his exploits on the Game of the Week.

"Mickey became a hero on television. We knew nothing of his drinking and carousing, his surliness when his head was hurting or his lack of charm when the cameras were turned off. Those days were different for several reasons. Mickey burst on the scene at just the right moment in history and the television treatment took. He could do no baseball wrong in the eyes of a Little Leaguer. We lived through his TV heroics the way Santiago [in Hemingway's *The Old Man and the Sea*] did [through] DiMaggio's box scores. Mantle's impact on baseball and on the first television sports generation transcends any negatives his personal life may thrust upon us."

For Mantle, however, no amount of hero worship could soften the bumps of real life. By 1958, two years after the most glorious season in Mickey's career, Merlyn had come to see that the "fantasy time," as she called it, had extracted a high price. The previous year, she and Mickey had moved their family to Dallas—to a four-bedroom home on an acre of land, costing $59,500, in the Preston Hollow section of the city—in part to be closer to a major airport but also because life in Commerce had become a three-ring circus, with little chance for privacy. "People were knocking at their door all hours of the night, wanting to borrow money," recalled Marshall Smith. "They'd come over and use their bathroom. Can you believe that? People just wouldn't leave them alone." Merlyn was also realizing that she not only took a back seat to baseball and to her husband's fame but also to anything else Mickey wished to put ahead of her and their family. If there was any doubt, the birth of their third son dispelled it. For several years, Mickey had been spending each Thanksgiving week hunting with Billy Martin and Harold Youngman on a ranch outside Kerrville, Texas, that belonged to another of Mickey's friends, Hamilton Wilson. That year Whitey Ford joined them, even though Merlyn had believed that Mickey would cancel the trip or delay it at least. Merlyn was nine months pregnant, and she thought she might be going into labor the night before Mickey left on the hunting trip. Merlyn complained of discomfort, but Mickey misread not only her symptoms but also her wish that he stay with her. Mickey would later say that she had not insisted that he cancel the trip or appeared especially upset when he left. Years later Merlyn lamented that throughout much of their marriage, she had been unable to communicate adequately her feelings and wishes to Mickey. Indeed, on the day Mickey left on his hunting trip, Merlyn checked herself into a hospital in Joplin, Missouri. She gave birth to Billy Giles Mantle, named after Billy Martin and her father Giles, while Mickey was hunting. Youngman flew Mickey back in his private plane, but he found Merlyn in tears, crying, "You could've waited a few more days before taking off like that!"

14

In 1960, owner Dan Topping had began taking more and more control of club operations. Topping had concluded that both his manager, Casey Stengel, who was now seventy, and his general manager, George Weiss, who was in his sixties, had reached the age when they should retire. Moreover, Stengel had never been as popular with Topping as he had been with co-owner Del Webb. Topping had even gone so far as to have his personal attorney, Arthur Fried-lund, offer the managing job to Chicago White Sox skipper Al Lopez, who, as a loyal friend of Stengel's, rejected the overture. Sadly for Stengel, despite his dozen years with the Yankees and the success of his teams, he had inspired little loyalty among his players. One of the reasons was roster turnover. Stengel had even cut loose Billy Martin, when push came to shove. Stengel put winning first, cutting and trading players who didn't help him as much as he and Weiss wanted. That inspired little loyalty, though it was successful. Stengel was also not well thought of by some of his players, because of his often unkind motivational methods—especially his treatment of Mantle, who by this time had become a hero to his teammates as well as to his fans.

Topping was convinced that Stengel had lost his touch as a manager as far back as the end of the 1958 season. Except for their comeback from a three-games-to-one deficit against Milwaukee in the World Series, the Yankees had staggered through the final two months of that season, losing twenty-five of their last forty-four games. In May of 1959, the mighty Yankees fell into last place; they eventually finished a disappointing third, barely four games above .500. Pitching coach Jim Turner wound up being the scapegoat; Eddie

Lopat replaced him at the start of the 1960 season. The fall into mediocrity continued at the start of the 1960 season, when the Yankees lost twenty of their first forty-one games, floundering in fourth place. The turnaround came in early June, coinciding with Stengel's return to the dugout after a week's illness. The Yankees began winning again, Mantle snapped out of one of the worst slumps of his career, and the Yankees took control of the pennant race.

But as well as Mantle played at midseason, it was doubtful that the Yankees would have been in first place were it not for their new power-hitting right fielder, Roger Maris, who had been obtained in a winter trade. Maris was twenty-five, three years younger than Mickey. Weiss had previously tried to deal with the Indians for Maris, but they wouldn't trade him to a contender, choosing to deal him to the seventh-place Kansas City team in 1958. This was a break for the Yankees, as they had helped Kansas City's owner Arnold Johnson to get into baseball, and with that leverage they persuaded him to trade Maris. The Yankees gave up four players, including Don Larsen and longtime fan favorite Hank Bauer. "For the first few games, I used to hear guys yelling for Bauer," Maris said that summer, "but not much anymore."

Like Mickey Mantle, Roger Maris had been an outstanding high school football player. As a senior he had set a national high school record, scoring four touchdowns on kickoff returns in a single game. As he had with Mantle, University of Oklahoma coach Bud Wilkinson had tried to recruit Maris for his football program. But Maris, like Mantle, was obsessed with playing professional baseball. Under the supervision of Hank Greenberg, he had tried out for the Cleveland Indians and signed for a five-thousand-dollar bonus, with another ten thousand promised if he made the majors. During the Indians' minor league camp, Maris displayed the stubbornness that was an integral part of his personality—he refused assignment to any Class D team and would accept Class C only if he were sent to the Indians' team in his hometown of Fargo, North Dakota. Cleveland farm director Mike McNally told him, "We never let a boy play in his hometown. It subjects him to too much pressure." But Maris stood his ground. "I'm going to Fargo," he told McNally. "That's definite. Now it's up to you to decide whether I go there just to live on my own or whether I go there to play ball for Cleveland."

Maris spent four years in the minor leagues, playing for Fargo-Moorhead, Keokuk, Tulsa, Reading, and Indianapolis before making it to the major leagues in 1957, at the age of twenty-two. At the time, Maris's star appeared to be an ill-fated one. At one point in 1957 he seemed headed for Rookie of the Year honors, leading the American League in home runs and runs batted in, when he broke three ribs making a headfirst slide. He finished with a .235 average, fourteen home runs, and fifty-one RBIs. The following year, he was splitting time in the outfield with another promising young player, Rocky Colavito, and made his disappointment and displeasure about the situation known. He was traded to Kansas City, where he played amid the mediocrity that marked the Athletics, until his trade to the Yankees.

Starting his career with the Indians, Maris had been hailed as "Cleveland's future Mickey Mantle." In his fourth major league season with New York, Maris was having a spectacular year. Batting in the cleanup slot behind Mantle, Maris led the league in home runs and runs batted in, and he made fans forget about Bauer in right field with his outstanding defensive play. The feeling was mutual. Although he did not like the big city atmosphere of New York, Maris was happy to be with the Yankees. "Don't ever let anybody tell you they don't like coming to a team like the Yankees," said outfielder Bob Cerv, Maris's roommate who had also come to the Yankees from Kansas City. "The Yankees are over the track and up the hill."

With Mickey rebounding to his old form, the Mantle-Maris combination in the number-three and number-four spots of the order quickly became fodder for Ruth-Gehrig comparisons and a slew of nicknames. One Detroit writer called them "the buzz-saw team." Another dubbed them "Double M for Murder." Yankee announcer Mel Allen referred to them as "the gold dust twins" and "those magic marvels." Then there was Stengel's own description of the pair: "The fella in right does the job if the other fella doesn't."

For Mantle, getting himself mentally into the 1960 season had been one of the most difficult challenges of his career to that time. The 1959 season had been one of his toughest; fans had placed much of the blame for the team's disappointing performance on his shoulders. The booing of Mickey by Yankee fans became so strong that at one point he simply gave up. After striking out twice in one game, on his third time up he intentionally took three straight strikes. The displeasure of fans in the stadium was matched only by Stengel's own outrage. Mantle on several occasions had shown his own disgust at the booing by saluting his tormentors with a defiant middle finger of an upraised fist. In this instance, however, a subdued Mickey knew he had been wrong and apologized to his teammates. But once again, the Yankees' fortunes in the middle of the season were crippled by injuries to Mantle. During one stretch, Mickey came up to bat with fifty-seven men on base—and drove in only four of them. Mantle drove in only two runs in the entire month of August.

Throughout the slump, Mickey never slowed down his drinking, his nightlife, or his emotional outbursts against the fans and the press. Exasperated, Stengel publicly referred to Mantle as his "greatest disappointment." It was not surprising, except to Mickey, that Weiss opened the Yankees' 1960 contract negotiations by demanding that Mantle take a seventeen-thousand-dollar pay cut from his salary of seventy-two thousand. Mantle responded by holding out during the first two weeks of spring training, before finally agreeing to a seven-thousand-dollar pay cut. Trying to make up for the lost training time, Mickey aggravated the old injury to his right knee. He also was bothered by a right-shoulder injury from the 1957 World Series, suffered when Braves' second baseman Red Schoendienst had fallen on him during a botched pickoff play. It was an injury that affected his hitting and would reduce the strength of his once-powerful throwing arm for the remainder of his career.

Hurt and embittered as he might have been, Mantle still found time to unwind. That spring training, he and Whitey Ford were among a group who were rescued naked and treading water in St. Petersburg Bay after a boat on which they had been partying caught fire and sank. Among Yankee management, only Stengel may have been amused. He had been drinking more himself in recent years, often staying up until the early hours of the morning entertaining writers with his stories. Stengel had been known to doze off occasionally in the dugout in the middle of games, but now players noticed that it was happening more frequently. Now even the old Stengel charm had worn thin, particularly with his players, although writers continued to be fascinated by his double-talk and the lively copy it made. Often it amounted to little more than stream-of-consciousness rambling.

The best example of it in a public setting may have been his 1958 testimony before Senator Estes Kefauver's subcommittee looking into proposed legislation exempting baseball from antitrust laws. Stengel was among a number of baseball people called to testify, including Mantle, Ted Williams, Stan Musial, and the Yankee's Del Webb. But it was Stengel who would be remembered for his answer about whether the Yankees would continue to monopolize the World Series.

"I got a little concerned yesterday," Stengel began, "in the first three innings when I saw the three players I had gotten rid of, and I said, 'When I lose nine what am I going to do?' And when I had a couple of my players I thought so great of that did not do so good up to the sixth inning, I was more confused. But I finally had to go and call on a young man from Baltimore that we don't own, and the Yankees don't own him, and he is doing pretty good. And I would actually have to tell you that I think we are more the Greta Garbo type now from success. We are being hated. I mean from the ownership and all, we are being hated. Every sport that gets too great, or one individual."

The senators, unsure what to make of what Stengel had just said, called on Mantle. Mickey was nervous, and when he was asked his views on applying antitrust laws to baseball, he said the first thing that came to mind. "Well," Mickey began in that country drawl of his, "after hearing Casey's testimony, my views are about the same." The straitlaced Capitol Hill hearing room erupted in laughter.

In 1960, despite the comeback of the Yankees, Mantle's performance switched between being fabulous and in a funk until a turnaround began on August 14. On that day, in a doubleheader with the Senators, Mantle failed to run out a routine double-play ground ball. Mantle's gaffe was in stark contrast with the all-out effort by Maris, who, running from first base, had barreled into the knees of the second baseman. Maris was injured on the play, bruising his ribs so badly that he would be out of the lineup for weeks. The loss seemed completely wasted, in that Mickey hadn't bothered to move beyond a few feet from the batter's box. Disgusted with himself as the double-play ended the inning, Mantle waited near the first-base foul line for someone to bring him his glove. Instead, he saw Bob Cerv emerge from the dugout. Stengel was pulling Mickey out of the game. The chorus of boos grew even louder as Mantle, humiliated in front of his home fans, walked back to the dugout. "It don't look very good, us trying to win when the man hits the ball to second or third and doesn't run it out," an exasperated Stengel told reporters after the game. "That's not the first time he's done that. If he can't run, he should tell me. If he wants to come out, all he has to do is tell me. Who the hell does he think he is, Superman?"

With Maris injured and sidelined, the anti-Mantle fans at the stadium had all the more reason to boo and jeer him, as they did when Mickey's name was announced in the lineup the next day. Veteran Yankee followers believe it was the loudest, fiercest booing ever heard at the ballpark; Stengel would later say, "In all my years in baseball, I never saw a city that booed a man so much before he went to work." For years, beginning with his rookie season, Mantle had endured an unprecedented amount of booing, heckling, and abuse, a glimpse into the dark side of sports fanaticism. Dick Schaap, in his early biography of Mantle, tells of an incident in which a young teen-aged woman waited for Mantle outside the player's entrance to the stadium before a game. When Mickey arrived in a cab, the young woman ran up to him and began punching him and pulling his hair, explaining later, "We don't like him because he's stuck up." Other angry fans would greet him with derisive remarks, like "Look, here comes the All-American out."

Announcer Red Barber believed that Mantle was paying the price for all the premature praise that Stengel had heaped on him, including the comparison to Yankee legends like Babe Ruth, that Mantle had been unable to live up to on the field. "He's booed," Barber theorized, "because he's not a colorful player like Babe Ruth. Ruth was a freewheeling guy on and off the field. He had magic, but Mantle's isn't a showman." But sportscaster Mel Allen, the "voice of the Yankees," felt that the booing had less to do with ancient Yankee history than with the more recent Yankee legend, Joe DiMaggio. Mantle was playing in a stadium at a position still haunted by the memory of DiMaggio; the adoration of fans for the Yankee Clipper at times approached idolatry.

DiMaggio, though a son of San Francisco, had come to personify New York's ethnic diversity; his popularity had been a bond for the melting pot's confluence of cultures. DiMaggio had also had the luxury of not having to play in the era of television, as Mantle did. The magic and mystique of the game and its heroes could often be stripped away by televised pictures, which left little to the imagination. As David Halberstam would write in *Summer of '49*, about a pennant race in which DiMaggio figured prominently, "Radio was an instrument that could heighten the mystique of a player; television [through overexposure] eventually demythologized the famous." Allen would feel the same way. "The unfortunate thing about Mickey," he said, "is that he followed DiMag in center field. No matter who played center field after DiMaggio, that person would be booed. Fans resented that Mantle was supposed to be another DiMaggio. DiMaggio fans believed nobody could ever be another DiMaggio. When Mickey came up at nineteen, they started booing. They're still booing."

The booing and heckling of Mantle was not just from Yankee fans. Once Mantle glanced into a section of the stands from where the verbal abuse was especially bad and noticed that it was coming from several vendors. Former stadium vendor Curt Schleier later recalled a gracious incident between Mantle and some autograph seekers, an incident that had surprised him. "Even

Mickey Mantle stopped for me," he said. "He first gently inquired if I was 'one of the bastards that was booing me yesterday?' After I assured him I wasn't part of a group of vendors that had razzed him the day before, he signed too."

The day after the worst episode of booing in 1960, Mantle rose to the occasion in a game that many Yankee writers believe ultimately changed the minds of some of his harshest critics in the stands. Mantle hit a game-tying home run in the fourth inning against the Orioles, eliciting some cheers among the boos and leading Mickey to do something that was extremely un-Mantle-like. As he trotted from home plate back to the dugout, Mickey tipped his cap to the fans—something he rarely did, because, he said, he never liked to show up a pitcher off whom he had homered. When Mantle came up to bat in the eighth inning, the Yankees again trailed. The Orioles had a chance to retire him on a pop-up behind the plate; however, the ball was dropped, and Mickey had one more chance. Mantle then drove a Hoyt Wilhelm knuckleball into the right-field seats for a two-run home run that put the Yankees back on top; it proved to be the game-winner. Peter Golenbock singles out that game and those Mantle heroics—rising up after the disastrous performance of the day before—as the day that the booing of Mickey at Yankee Stadium stopped.

"I wanted to be good tonight more than I ever wanted to be good in my life," Mantle said after that game. "I don't know what I would have done if I had had another bad day like yesterday."

This would also be the beginning of one of the Yankees' most fabled periods. The Yankees would close out the 1960 season by winning their final fifteen games. They featured a revived pitching corps led by Ford, Ralph Terry, Art Ditmar, and Bob Turley; revived defensive play in the infield, with Bobby Richardson, Tony Kubek, and Clete Boyer; and a power-hitting game spearheaded by Mantle and Maris. Mickey hit forty home runs to lead the league; Maris finished one homer behind him—and would edge out Mantle for the league's Most Valuable Player award in the closest balloting up to that time. At season's end, Stengel lavished more praise on Mantle that at any time since spring training of his rookie season: "I believe the most powerful factor has been Mickey Mantle who hit forty home runs and drove in ninety runs and played fifty hours through three doubleheaders on a bad knee without asking for relief or flinching. He has worked hard and hustled and in my mind he is the most valuable player."

After a long decade, however, the Stengel-Mantle relationship was nearing its end. Shortly before the end of the season, in the middle of the Yankees' fifteen-game winning streak, Webb had informed Stengel that this season would be his last as manager. Stengel did not want to retire, but Webb insisted. The plan was to make Ralph Houk the new Yankee manager, and to make the transition as smooth as possible. Houk was one of Stengel's coaches and had been a minor league manager in Denver when Webb had been president of that team. Stengel agreed to go quietly—though Webb might have been better off to wait until after the World Series to tell Stengel that he was going to dump him. The Series, against the Pittsburgh Pirates, would spoil an otherwise magnificent season finish for the Yankees and for Mantle. It is generally acknowledged by players and reporters who covered the Yankees that Stengel mismanaged his final World Series.

"He didn't start Whitey in [the opening game of] the series," Mantle would later recall. "Whitey shut them out twice. We outscored them something like 58 runs to 23, something like that. We surely had the best team. That was the only time that we got beat in the World Series where I felt that the best team lost, and I believe it was because Casey didn't start Whitey in the first game."

One could argue that Stengel had mismanaged Whitey Ford throughout his career. Over the course of his fifteen-year career, Ford had compiled a 236–106 record and the second-best winning percentage in the history of the game, at .690. But Mantle and others generally agreed that Whitey's record might have been even better had Stengel used him in a normal pitching rotation like most teams with strong pitching staffs used. Instead, Stengel used Ford every fifth day, sometimes holding him back from a rotation start against a weak team to use him against the best teams in the league. Not only was Ford not reaping the benefit of some easy starts, he also wasn't getting enough starts to have a chance at winning twenty games. The result was that Ford never had a twenty-game season under Stengel; Ford's best record under Casey was in 1956, when he won nineteen games. He enjoyed his greatest success the year after Casey was ousted, posting a Cy Young Award–winning 25–4 record in 1961. Mantle often blamed himself for costing Whitey a twenty-win season in 1956, by committing a costly error that decided a 1–0 loss to the Orioles in Ford's last start. "I didn't have the heart to face Whitey after the game," Mantle would recall years later. "I was almost in tears. I dreaded the thought of facing Whitey, but he made it easy for me. He came up to me in the clubhouse, put his hand on my shoulder and said, 'Forget it, Mick. Let's have a beer!'"

Customarily, the ace of the staff gets the starting nod in the World Series opener, as the Pirates' Vernon Law did in the first game, at Forbes Field in Pittsburgh. Ford was ready to start for the Yankees. "I was sure I was going to pitch the first game of the World Series," Whitey would recall. "But Casey started Art Ditmar instead. He said he wanted to save me for the first game at Yankee Stadium [game three of the Series], which really ticked me off. It was the only time I ever got mad at Casey. I felt I should have pitched the first game, so that I could pitch three times if it became necessary."

Ditmar never made it out of the first inning, and the Yankees lost a 6–4 game that Ford was confident he could have won. The Yankees won the next two games by scores of 16–3 and 10–0. Ford's start in game three was the first of two shutouts in the Series. Mantle hit two home runs in game two and another in game three. Mantle's home runs at Forbes Field included a tape-measure blast to a desolate part of center field where only Babe Ruth had ever hit a ball. Pittsburgh bounced back from being nearly pummeled out of contention with 3–2 and 5–2 victories in Yankee Stadium before Ford came back to shut them out, 12–0, at Forbes Field to force game seven. But for all the power shown by the Yankees, the Series was decided by second baseman Bill Mazeroski's dramatic home run in the bottom of the ninth inning, giving Pittsburgh a 10–9 victory in the slugfest and one of the most unlikely World Series championships.

The Yankees were stunned. They had outscored the Pirates, 55–27, out-homered them 10–4, and outpitched them with Ford's two shutouts. The Yankees' Bobby Richardson was named the Most Valuable Players of the series, not a Pirate. Mantle, in addition to his three home runs, had batted .400, driven in eleven runs, scored eight runs, and walked eight times. The loss was a bitter disappointment. In the clubhouse, Mantle retreated to the trainer's room, where he cried uncontrollably, unable to reconcile himself with the defeat. "I was so disappointed," said Mickey, "I cried on the plane ride home."

Ford wouldn't talk to Stengel on the flight back to New York. "The way I was pitching," said Ford, "I know I would have beaten them three times, and we would have been world champs again. But Stengel was stubborn."

The mismanagement of his pitching rotation and ultimately the squandering of the 1960 World Series would tarnish Stengel's legacy. So too would his treatment of his players. Mantle and Ford would look back upon their years with Stengel with fondness, but they had been among his pets—players whom he had shielded and favored, for obvious reasons. Along with Berra, they had been the backbone of his glory years through the 1950s. Stengel would be remembered among many of his other players, those who were not the stars of the team, for cruelty and insensitivity. The World Series against the Pirates provides an example. In the second inning of the opening game, after Berra and Bill Skowron had singled, Clete Boyer was called back to the dugout as he walked to the plate to bat. Boyer, about to have his first at-bat in his first World Series, was shocked to learn that, so early in the game, Stengel was pulling him for a pinch-hitter. Stengel later explained that he was playing for a big inning; as it happened, pinch-hitter Dale Long flied out, and the Yankees did not score in that inning. Boyer left the dugout for the clubhouse, where he cried at his locker for half an hour while his teammates tried vainly to console him.

Perhaps it was poetic justice that two days after losing the World Series, Stengel was dismissed as manager in an equally heartless manner. Although Stengel was being "retired," to keep successor Ralph Houk from possibly going to another team, the Yankees did not announce the changing of the guard in that context. Instead, at a press conference at the Savoy Hotel, Dan Topping told reporters that Stengel was being replaced because he was too old to manage. Stengel had been given a prepared text by the Yankees to read, but the charade quickly fell apart when Joe Reichler, the Associated Press baseball beat writer, demanded of Stengel, "Casey, tell us the truth. Were you fired?"

"You're goddamn right I was fired," Stengel snapped.

Despite the World Series humiliation and his inept management that had led to the loss, Stengel came to be viewed as a sympathetic figure unjustly fired by the world's richest sports franchise. Stengel had spent much of his twelve years with the Yankees winning over baseball beat writers. He drank with them, was always accessible to them, and provided them with daily arsenals of delightful quotes and stories. As Topping would point out, the Yankees had been criticized twelve years earlier when they hired Stengel by the very writers whom he then seduced, and who were now criticizing the Yankees for firing Stengel.

A month after Stengel's departure, George Weiss retired after twenty-nine years with the Yankees. When he heard the news, Mantle cheerfully poured himself a drink. Like most Yankee players, Mantle had a genuine dislike of Weiss. For Mantle, however, the negative feelings toward Weiss weren't simply the result of the acrimonious dealings of the late 1950s over his contracts; as the player around whom the franchise revolved, Mickey had been able to appeal to Webb and Topping in his disputes, with favorable results. What Mantle found unforgivable in Weiss was the manner in which he had treated the players who did not have that kind of value to the organization. Most prominent among those, of course, had been Mickey's close friend Billy Martin. But Mantle remembered others who had received similar treatment from the Yankee general manager. Weiss had sold veteran pitcher Vic Raschi for holding out before the 1954 season, and he had released Phil Rizzuto on Old Timers' Day in 1956 in a manner that had been especially humiliating for the proud Yankee shortstop. Now, finally, it looked as if Weiss had gotten his comeuppance. Mickey didn't see that Stengel had in his own way been just as manipulative, nor did he yet realize that Stengel's moving on would be the best thing that could have happened to his own career.

15

The 1961 season marked the beginning of a new, if brief, period in the country's history—the Kennedy years. President John F. Kennedy was an avid fan of his hometown Boston Red Sox, but even he couldn't ignore the specialness of the Yankees. Shortly after his inauguration, as spring training in 1961 began, the country's new president wanted to cheer up his father, Joseph P. Kennedy, who was recovering from a stroke in Palm Beach. President Kennedy dispatched a couple of Secret Service agents to nearby West Palm Beach, where the Yankees were playing an exhibition game, to ask Mantle, Berra, Ford, and Tony Kubek if they would kindly pay a visit on the elder Kennedy, whose stroke had left him unable to speak. The four Yankees obliged and spent part of an afternoon with the Kennedy patriarch; they talked baseball among themselves, and Kennedy listened attentively. Ford later recalled, "You could tell he was interested in what we had to say and grateful for our visit." While in office, Kennedy saw Mantle play in person only once—in the 1962 All-Star Game, where he threw out the first pitch, shook hands with many of the players, including Mickey, and said to Stan Musial, "A couple of years ago, they told me I was too young to be president and you were too old to be playing baseball. But we fooled them."

The 1961 spring training became a reintroduction of sorts for Mantle. His relationship with Stengel had begun as one of surrogate father–adoptive son, and it had never changed. Mantle had been twenty-eight years old in his last season under Stengel, but the "Old Perfessor"—as Stengel had enjoyed being called—had still treated him the way he had at nineteen. Berra, Ford, and Mantle, grown men playing a boys' game, had still been treated as young-sters in the patriarchal environment that existed under Stengel. There had been no players' union, and no players' representative on the team—and no openly designated player in a leadership or captain's role. The impact on Mantle, especially, had been severe. Years later Mantle would acknowledge that his father had died before Mickey had come to terms with him or their relationship. As Mutt had always dealt with him on an adult-child basis, so too had Stengel, both on the field and off. In the spring training of 1961, a new manager, Ralph Houk, would help Mickey to break free of his childhood. In one of their first meetings, Houk took Mantle aside and said, "Mickey, I want you to become the leader of this team. It's your team."

Mantle had never been the rah-rah type, one to give clubhouse speeches; Houk explained that what he wanted and expected of him was to lead by example. To some extent, Mantle had already been doing this. His unselfish-ness in playing in pain, helping younger players with their transition to the big leagues, and being "one of the guys" instead of the isolated icon he could have been had made him the most beloved teammate on the Yankees. In his self-deprecating way, Mickey would later say that he suspected that Houk had also privately asked Ford and Berra to become leaders of the team. But Houk had not. Houk himself had been a rarely used reserve catcher with the Yankees from 1947 to 1954. He had gone on to manage a farm team before becoming a Yankee coach and had seen firsthand the love and admiration Yankee play-ers had for Mantle. Houk had been in the same clubhouse with DiMaggio and knew the selfish, self-absorbed side of the Yankee Clipper that had remained hidden from the public. He knew that DiMaggio had been the fans' favorite, but he also knew that Mantle was a players' player.

Houk would also begin changing the way Stengel had run the team. Casey's platoon system, which had diminished or ruined careers, was dis-carded. A regular four-man pitching rotation was implemented; it would make Ford a twenty-game winner for the first time in his career. Gone too was the "doghouse" in which Stengel had put players, as well as his manner of criticizing players or destroying their confidence, as he had done to Clete Boyer in the 1960 World Series. It can be argued that without Houk at the helm, the 1961 home-run derby in which Mantle and Maris both chased Ruth would never have taken place.

The 1961 season did not begin with any hint of an assault on Ruth's 1927 record. In 1927, Babe Ruth himself had had an unspectacular start, mustering only four home runs in April. Mantle got off ahead of that pace, hitting seven home runs in the season's first month. Maris, on the other hand, hit his first and last home run of April on the 26th and was batting a lowly .204 at the end of the month. Maris's Most Valuable Player season in 1960 had established him as a legitimate star in the league, but no one had been ready to place him on the same level as Mantle. What turned Maris's fortunes around was Houk's decision to switch Mantle and Maris in the batting order. The number-three spot in the batting order is usually reserved for the team's best hitter (that is, the batter most likely to get on base and advance runners), the cleanup slot for the team's most powerful hitter. Mantle was comfortable in either slot. However, it's generally believed that putting Mantle in the cleanup spot made Maris the beneficiary of good pitches to hit. Opponents would pitch to Maris rather than around him, for fear of putting him on base and having to pitch to Mantle with a runner on base. In 1961, Maris never received an intentional base on balls. Moreover, he immediately broke out of his slump, hitting eleven home runs in May. Mantle continued his good start and had fourteen home runs at the end of May. At the same point of the season in 1927, Ruth had had sixteen home runs.

Mantle, of course, had made his own chase of Ruth's record in 1956. He had a decade's worth of familiarity with the New York press, and he had been through the tedious, trying business of being asked the same question dozens of times after ball games—questions that often were silly or naïve, sometimes stupid, and seemed intended to goad players into brash comments that would make good copy for the next day's newspapers. More importantly, Mantle had come to understand that in the world of journalism there are rarely embarrassing questions, only embarrassing answers. Mickey had learned through experience what to say and what not to say. Mickey also knew, as do most ballplayers, that the pressures related to breaking records are not self-imposed but are imposed on them by the constant attention to them and the records by the news media. On top of it all, Mantle had learned to court the writers, much as Stengel had. Sportswriter Bert Sugar was among those who noticed the growth and change in Mantle. "Particularly at a bar," said Sugar, "where he liked his scotch. Mickey had no pretense. He wasn't hung up on being Mickey Mantle. I'd run into him in places like Mr. Laff's, Bunyan's, Tucker's—bars where sports guys hung out. And he's always saying, 'Hey, why don't you come over and say hello?' In a bar, Mickey was quiet—he wasn't a noisemaker. He was very comfortable being in a crowd. He was happy being accepted as a person rather than Mickey Mantle. We'd tell one another jokes. He loved jokes, the longer the better. He didn't like one-liners. He went for good ol' boy humor—I'm framing this, pre-1990s—you know, politically incorrect women jokes were the brunt of it. Mickey Mantle was a frat boy at heart."

Mantle thus was fairly well prepared for the media onslaught that hit the "M&M Boys," as he and Maris came to be called. They finished June with Mantle taking the home-run lead on an inside-the-park home run at Yankee Stadium. It had been a "moon shot" to dead center, landing about fifteen feet to the right of the 461-foot sign. "I made up my mind when I reached second that I'd go all the way," Mantle said afterward. "But I sure wish I'd hit it in the stands. Too much running on this type of homer."

On the other hand, few would have been less able to handle the media pressures associated with chasing the Babe than Roger Maris. Maris, like Mantle, was a small-town boy. He had been born in Hibbing, Minnesota, on September 10, 1934. His father, who worked for the Great Northern Railroad, had moved the family to North Dakota in 1942, where Roger and Rudy, his older brother by one year, had grown up. The Maris brothers had played sports and attended Shanley High School in Fargo, North Dakota, where Roger and Rudy had excelled in football and basketball. It was in the tenth grade, at a high school basketball game, that Roger had met Patricia, his future wife. Roger had played baseball in the American Legion program during the summers, since the North Dakota high schools, because of the cold weather, did not have a program. Roger had led his team to the state championship and had drawn the attention of professional scouts. But unlike Mantle, Maris had remained rooted in his small-town mind-set even after arriving in the big leagues. New York was hardly where he would have chosen to play. He was suspicious of the big city and its ways and uncomfortable with the demands of the swarm of reporters who covered the Yankees, especially when the team played at home.

Fortunately, one of Maris's best friends from his time with the Athletics was now a Yankee again. In 1961 Bob Cerv was in his third stint with the Yankees. He had been a rookie with Mantle in 1951 but had been dealt away to the Athletics in 1957, traded back to the Yankees in 1960, and traded to the Los Angeles Angels, where he played eighteen games in 1961 before returning to the Yankees again. He was one of those players who had had no chance to blossom under Stengel's platoon system. In Kansas City, however, he had gotten a chance to play regularly over three full seasons, during which time he hit sixty-nine home runs; his best year was 1958, when he hit .305, slugged thirty-eight homers, and drove in 104 runs. By 1961, now in his mid-thirties and a year away from retirement, Cerv was best suited to serve the talent-rich Yankees as a pinch-hitter and occasional outfielder.

When Cerv rejoined the Yankees early that season, he and Maris began sharing an apartment in Queens, away from the spotlight of Manhattan. "The first year Roger was [in New York], 1960, Maris was starting to get recognized," Cerv later recalled, "and it was starting to be too much downtown." They were joined in the apartment later in the season by Mickey, though exactly how that came about is not altogether clear. The popular story surrounding Mantle's moving in—and repeated again in Billy Crystal's film 61*, recounting the Mantle-Maris home-run derby—was that it had been Maris's idea, a way to save Mickey from his drinking and carousing. Cerv and fellow Yankee Tony Kubek, however, remember it differently. According to Cerv, Mantle one day said, "'Hey, can I move out with ya?' Just like that. Nothing more. 'Sure,' I said, 'we don't care.'" Mickey, Kubek felt, was spending too much money living at the St. Moritz Hotel in Manhattan. Kubek also believed that Mantle was concerned about the pressure being placed on Maris and wanted to help out. "Mickey had been through it so many times," Kubek recalled, "that I really believe he thought he could help Roger by moving in and giving support."

In the course of being roommates, a deep friendship developed between Mantle and Maris, despite their difference in personalities and habits. Part of their bonding was through being teammates, but obviously the key ingredient in their friendship was their chase of Ruth's home-run record. At various times reports circulated that their on-field rivalry had developed into a feud. It was little more than New York tabloid sensationalism. Those "feud" stories rarely, if ever, mentioned that the two men were roommates—for the obvious reason that such a detail would have seriously lessened the validity of those accounts.

"It seemed the more pressure was on Maris, the closer he and Mickey became," Whitey Ford would recount. "Not that there wasn't a good-natured rivalry between them, a sense of competition. That was only natural. They both wanted to lead the league in home runs, and they both wanted to break Ruth's record. This was normal, and the competition brought the best out of both of them. Then, when Mantle got hurt and he knew his chances of breaking the record were over, he rooted for Roger as much as anybody."

What Mantle couldn't help Maris with, however, was his actual day-to-day handling of reporters' questions. Where Mantle's answers were now often short, humorously self-deprecating, or mundane, Maris would make the mistake of being too honest, even brutally frank. He would be noticeably impatient at answering the same question over and over. At other times, he would become verbally combative but lacked the intimidating presence that Mantle could muster when he didn't want to answer a reporter's question. Journalists like Newsday's Steve Jacobson believe that the growth of television changed the attitudes of newspapers at the time. Newspapers, seeking to combat the popularity of television, decided that they must not only report about the game but that "an effort had to be made to delve into what the athlete was thinking and what his response was." In the days of Ruth, baseball writers had written about what happened at the park and nothing else. Perhaps that has something to do with the fact that Ruth, a man with infinitely more bad habits than Maris, had been viewed as someone who could do no wrong, while Maris, a family man, was now treated as a pariah. The harshest articles written about Maris were in a series by Jimmy Cannon, who was irked that Maris had missed an appointment with him, and a piece by UPI's Oscar Fraley, who thought Maris had snubbed a child asking for an autograph. Cannon ripped Maris in 1962, calling him "the whiner" and accusing him of "treacherous smallness," "lingering rudeness," and "self-worship." Fraley called him a one-year wonder and a "zero."

Unfortunately for Maris, he was not protected by the Yankees from the media the way that Mark McGwire would be by the Cardinals in 1998 when he broke Maris's home-run record—setting a new record that would be broken by Barry Bonds of the Giants three years later. Maris's experience, in fact, would serve as a negative lesson for how the news media's demands on McGwire would be handled by his team. But in 1961, the Yankee beat reporters were virtually unchecked in their freedom in the team clubhouse after each game, with only the trainer's room and the showers off limits.

Maris would ultimately become the public's whipping boy, taking the onus of great expectations off of Mantle. Robert Creamer was among those who would personally witness the transformation in Mickey. "Mantle changed quite a bit in 1961," Creamer recalled years later. "Mantle hit 54 home runs himself, but now it was Maris who was hounded by reporters. As Roger bore the brunt of the media pressure, Mickey became almost genial and was much more responsive to questions from reporters he knew." In the past, Mantle had been almost impossible to interview at length, a point that was underscored in a story Creamer recounted about fellow *Sports Illustrated* writer Gerald Holland: "Holland had run into the same wall of indifference that Mantle habitually erected against writers. But Holland had understood that Mantle was a country boy and country people tend to dislike pushy strangers. So he visited Mantle at home in Oklahoma, but he stopped asking questions, stopped talking to him almost entirely, except for perfunctory remarks like 'Yup' and 'Nope' and 'Pass the sugar.' He was getting Mantle used to him. Finally one day Mickey said, 'Well, are you going to ask me questions or what?' Holland's story was a gem."

As the home-run derby intensified, so too did Maris's unpopularity among some of the writers and among some longtime Yankee fans, undoubtedly including many who had previously booed Mantle. When Maris took the lead in the home-run race, it may have been the best thing that ever happened to Mantle. The fans had found a new scapegoat and began booing Maris, who happened to play the position that Ruth had. Clete Boyer was among the Yankees who saw this incredible turnaround in the way fans had suddenly became Mantle supporters in the pursuit of Ruth's record. "Mickey got booed because Casey Stengel built him up to be something he wasn't," said Boyer. "Mickey was supposed to hit 1,000 home runs. When he didn't, the fans got on him. Roger took the pressure off Mickey. They never booed Mickey again. It became good guy–bad guy. The press, everybody, wanted Mickey Mantle to break Babe Ruth's record."

Historically, Ruth's record was the most sacred in the game. The Babe was credited with revolutionizing the game with his power; his name was part of the nation's language. He was a sports icon, larger than the game itself. Perhaps no one inside of baseball held Ruth in higher esteem than the commissioner, Ford Frick. A personal friend of Ruth's who had even been his ghostwriter, Frick became concerned midway through the season that Babe's record might finally be broken. His concern was not without merit, beyond loyalty to Ruth's memory. In 1961, baseball experienced its first expansion, the American League adding the Los Angeles Angels and a new Senators franchise in Washington to replace the club that had moved to Minnesota. Frick and others worried that expansion, with the introduction of at least twenty more pitchers, had weakened the overall level of pitching in the league. Additionally, expansion had meant increasing the number of games each team played to 162, eight more games than in the season in which Ruth had hit sixty home runs. Frick could do little about the allegedly weaker pitching that Mantle and Maris were facing, except to lament the situation. The expanded schedule was another matter. On July 17, Frick ruled that anyone who broke Ruth's home run record—or any other record as well—would have to do it in 154 games if it was to be considered as having bettered Ruth's mark; otherwise it would be regarded as an altogether separate record in the books. Practically speaking, it would be a record with an asterisk.

The additional pressure of the commissioner's decree was yet another distraction in the media circus that had formed around the two sluggers. The frenzy surrounding them was not limited to Yankee Stadium but extended throughout the league. Security guards had to escort Mantle and Maris in and out of ballparks. The lobbies of the Yankees' hotels were regularly filled with journalists not only from newspapers but also from radio and television stations, each reporter wanting an interview with the duo.

Through mid-August they were even, with forty-five home runs apiece; then Maris surged ahead. On September 2, Maris hit his fifty-second and fifty-third home runs. The next day, Mantle hit two home runs, to pull within three homers of Maris. A week later Maris hit his fifty-sixth, followed the next day by Mantle's slugging his fifty-third home run of the season. The M&M Boys had eighteen games in which to catch Ruth, but the pressure was almost unbearable. Maris was chain-smoking Camels, and his hair began falling out in patches. Pressure and criticism was coming from unexpected sources. Hall of Famer Rogers Hornsby, considered by some at the time to be the greatest pure hitter ever to play the game, entered the fray, telling reporters, "Maris has no right to break Ruth's record." For the most part, Maris internalized the pressure. "He became a nervous wreck," said longtime friend Whitey Herzog.

Houk recalled that "Roger'd say things honestly, without thinking about them, and they'd be exaggerated. Somebody asked him if he really wanted to break Babe Ruth's record and Roger said, 'Hell, yes' and that was big news. Why wouldn't he want to break the record? Rogers Hornsby, I think it was, said, 'Wouldn't it be a shame for a hitter like Maris to break Babe's record?' And Roger said, 'Screw Hornsby.' He said it half kidding, but the writers were jumping on things like that, and now that's in the headlines: Maris Rips Hornsby."

Mantle was also feeling the pressure. He became run down physically, developing a cold and flu symptoms on a road trip to Cleveland and Boston.

Mel Allen, a Yankee broadcaster who was privately pulling for Mantle in the home-run derby, saw Mickey and urged him to see his doctor, Max Jacobson, immediately. Jacobson's patients included Elizabeth Taylor and Eddie Fisher, and he specialized in giving vitamin shots that Allen said would "fix you right up." Upon returning to New York, Mickey hurried to an appointment with Dr. Jacobson that Allen had made for him, not suspecting that he would regret that visit for the rest of his life. Jacobson gave Mantle a shot in his hip that Mickey later said made him scream in pain. No one is certain what went wrong, but something had. Walking back to his hotel on Jacobson's advice, Mantle became delirious. He eventually made it into bed with a fever, feeling worse than before he had visited the doctor. He couldn't play in the next day's game and eventually wound up at Lenox Hill Hospital. An infection formed, and doctors had to lance the area with a three-inch star-shaped incision over the hip to permit the area to drain. The hole was big enough to fit a golf ball. Mantle's part in the chase of the Babe was effectively over. After the shot, he started only two more games, in the postseason, finishing with fifty-four home runs.

For Maris, however, the season would be a triumph that would not be fully appreciated until years later. On the 154th game of the season he hit number fifty-nine, in Baltimore against pitcher Milt Pappas, and barely missed another home run that would have tied the Babe's record. He had failed in his record-setting quest with respect to the time frame set up by the commissioner, but the season was not over. The media and national attention on Maris continued unabated. The pursuit of the Babe, much to Frick's chagrin, was still on. In the 158th game, in New York, with Ruth's widow in attendance, Maris tied the record with his sixtieth home run. Maris took a day off, then went hitless on Friday and homerless on Saturday. On Sunday, October 1, facing Boston in the final game of the season, Maris broke the record in his second at-bat, planting a 2–0 pitch from Tracy Stallard ten rows deep in the right-field stands. "It was," remembered Kubek in his book *Sixty-One*, "as if all the pressure he had been carrying around with him for months was finally off."

Mantle watched Maris hit the record breaker from his hospital room. Years later, he would acknowledge having envied Maris for breaking Ruth's record. "Everyone always thought it would be me who'd do it," he said. "But it wasn't. The only regret I have about it was that I wish I'd been healthy enough to give him a better run. In my heart, I have to think I'd been there myself, but that's not to take anything away from Roger because he's the one who broke it."

Not since the days of Ruth and Gehrig had two players, or any team, exhibited the kind of power that the Yankees unleashed that year. Together, Maris and Mantle's 115 combined home runs broke Ruth and Gehrig's record of 107 set in 1927. In 1961, the Yankees also had four other players hit twenty or more home runs; together they set a team record, with 240 home runs.

Mantle struggled out of the hospital to play in the World Series against the Cincinnati Reds, in a display of courage that won him even more admirers. Backup catcher Johnny Blanchard was among those who saw Mantle's infected hip in the clubhouse dressing room. He later said, "[The surgical wound] was from the bone up, not from the skin down. The way the wound was dressed was first with a coating of sulfur right down on the bone, by the hip where it was, then it was covered with gauze and then bandaged over. It was unbelievable this guy could walk, much less play."

Play Mickey did. Mantle didn't get into either of the first two games of the Series at Yankee Stadium, which the Yankees and Reds split. Whitey Ford pitched a two-hit shutout in the opener for his third consecutive Series shutout, including the two from 1960—which made Stengel's questionable pitching decisions seem that much more ludicrous. Mickey finally started in the third game, at Cincinnati's Crossley Field. He went hitless in four at-bats, though the Yankees won, taking the Series lead. "When he came to bat," Blanchard recalled, "you could see a spot of blood on his uniform by his hip. We could all see it." Mantle started again in game four, but he opened the wound in the first inning while making a catch in right-center field. It was especially important for Mickey to be in this game, however, because Whitey was going after yet another of Babe Ruth's records—consecutive scoreless innings pitched in the World Series. Mantle came up for his second at-bat of the scoreless game in the top of the fourth inning. "He could barely stand," *Los Angeles Times* columnist Jim Murray would write. "He hit one off the center field fence but barely made first base like a guy crawling with an arrow in his back. 'Look at his pants!' someone cried. They were covered with blood. He was hemorrhaging." With Ford having broken the Babe's pitching record, Mantle came out of the game for a pinch-runner, who would score the first run of another Yankee victory. The Yankees would win the Series the next day and fly home with yet another championship.

It had been a glorious season for Mickey, second only to his Triple Crown year. Perhaps even more significantly, it had changed the public perception of him. Having tested Mantle through a decade of boos and indifference, New York was finally ready to accept him as its hero. For Mantle, this newfound popularity was an important crossing of a personal threshold—the acceptance of himself.

"After Roger beat me in the home run race in 1961," Mickey said, "I could do no wrong. Everywhere I went I got standing ovations. All I had to do was walk out on the field. Hey, what the hell? It's a lot better than having them boo you. . . . I became the underdog. They hated him and liked me."

The fans' resentment of Maris would build over the coming years. Part of it was over breaking Babe Ruth's home-run record. Part of it, too, was over surpassing Mantle—at least, one of the expectations of Mantle. Mickey had been the prodigal son who could abuse his gifts and disappoint his great expectations, but some New Yorkers had adopted him as their native son—a Yankee, who, like DiMaggio and Berra and Gehrig, had been with the team from the start of his major league career. However, the feeling toward both Maris and Mantle was not limited to New York. Maris had broken one of the game's most enduring records, and the next spring he would be booed by the hard core of Babe Ruth fans around the league. In Detroit he would be pelted with garbage from the right-field seats.

In spring training in 1962, Maris stuck to his brooding, antipress stance. He caught new barbs when he refused to pose for a picture with Rogers Hornsby, the three-time .400 hitter of another era. "He called me a bush leaguer," said Maris. It was true. Hornsby took a dim view of a player who had never hit .300 in his life now being called the new home-run champion. Hornsby said bluntly, "He has no right to break Babe Ruth's record." The 1961 season had also brought out Mantle's utter unpretentiousness. Both Maris and Mantle had come to the major leagues as small-town kids. However, in his record-setting season, Maris came off in public as sullen and spoiled—Mantle as an "aw shucks" kind of guy, unaffected. Mantle could be endearing without even trying. On a visit to Disneyland, Mickey agreed to pose for publicity photos with a menagerie of Disney characters. All smiles and cooperative, Mantle heard the photographer say, "Goofy, move a little to the right, please." Mickey gladly obliged, only to have the photographer quickly say, "No, not you, Mr. Mantle. I meant *Goofy*."

Ultimately, it may have been part of Maris's legacy to make Mantle finally appreciated by even his critics, who could have more easily accepted Mickey breaking Ruth's record—Stengel had said he was the next Ruth, hadn't he?—than someone they considered, as sportswriter Frank Deford described Maris, an "impostor."

"Ironically, Mantle was always going to be a Hall of Famer, a great Yankee," observed broadcaster Bob Costas. "Maris needed the record, this season, to have a place in history."

16

The life of a big league baseball player is almost Odyssean in nature. Including spring training, he is away from home more than half the year. The 162-game schedule takes up the months from April to September. Spring training wipes out March. Add another two weeks for reporting early to spring training. The World Series—and Mantle played in a dozen of them—eats up the early part of October. Then there are the postseason tours of Japan and Hawaii, which Mickey did several times. Altogether, it adds up to at least two-thirds of the year in which baseball occupied all of Mantle's time. Over the eighteen seasons that Mantle played in the majors, he spent a cumulative twelve years playing ball, away from his wife Merlyn, away from his sons. After 1961, he was the hero of New York but a virtual stranger to his family. But there was no breaking the cycle of the ballplayer's life, especially when he had finally come into his own but still had that priceless baseball skill that Mickey possessed: the ability to hit the ball, hit it far, and excite grown men and children alike.

It was no coincidence that the last three good years of Mantle's career were also the last three good ones of the Yankee dynasty that Mickey helped sustain. In 1962, he would win his third Most Valuable Player award, though he did not lead the league in home runs, batting, average, or runs batted in. However, Yankee publicist Jackie Ferrell may have summed up Mantle's impact when he said, "What did he lead the league in? He led the league in manhood, that's what." Playing in only 123 games because of various injuries, Mantle still hit thirty home runs, collected a .321 average, and drove in eighty-nine runs. It was enough to make Mickey the team's first $100,000-a-year player since DiMaggio.

The 1963 season, however, turned out to be almost a microcosm of Mickey's career, filled with great promise and dashed by injury. That spring was one in which Mantle befriended Pete Rose, a young Cincinnati Reds rookie who impressed Mickey by running to first base on a walk during an exhibition game. Mickey called Rose "Charlie Hustle"—a nickname that would stick to the future all-time hits leader throughout his career. Despite Mickey's increasing pain and swelling in his legs, the season started off solid and seemed likely to be another MVP-caliber year. On May 22 that season, Mantle hit a pitch from Bill Fischer of the Athletics off of the façade of the right-field roof, a blast similar to the one he had hit off the Senators' Pedro Ramos in 1956. However, on June 5, Mantle broke his foot when he caught it on a chain-link fence in Baltimore as he tried to make a leaping catch of a ball hit by the Orioles' Brooks Robinson.

Mickey had typically misused his rehabilitation time when he was on the disabled list, in part because his great athletic ability allowed him to get away with it. The 1963 injury was another example. Two months after the injury, as he was completing his halfhearted rehabilitation, Mickey and Whitey went to have dinner outside Baltimore at a farm that belonged to friends of the Mantles. Mickey and Whitey drank into the night, slept there, and had to drive straight to the ballpark the next morning. At the park, Whitey put Mickey in the showers and then in the whirlpool trying to get him presentable enough just to sit on the bench. During batting practice, former teammate Hank Bauer, now coaching for the Orioles, couldn't help but notice that Mickey was in terrible shape. Mantle assured him he would be okay, he wouldn't be playing. Both Mickey and Whitey stayed far away from Yankee manager Ralph Houk. When the game began, Mantle wore a pair of sunglasses and napped at the far end of the bench. But in the ninth inning, Mickey was awakened by Whitey, who was sitting next to him.

"Wake up, wake up," Whitey whispered to him. "Houk's coming."

Houk walked down from the other end of the bench. "Can you hit, Mick?" he asked.

"I'm not eligible," Mickey replied. "I'm on the disabled list."

"No, you're not," Houk said. "You went on the active list today."

Mickey began preparing to pinch-hit. He didn't want to tell his manager that he was too hung over to see straight, and Houk hadn't picked up that

Mickey was in no shape to play. Mickey couldn't find his cap until Whitey realized he had been sitting on it. Mickey's cap looked as rumpled as he felt, and he found a batting helmet to put over it. Whitey was behind him when Mickey picked out a bat.

"Mick," Ford said, "hit the first pitch you see."

In the Orioles' dugout, Bauer walked over to Billy Hitchcock, Baltimore's manager, to confer about Mickey. Moments later, with Mickey at the plate, the Orioles called a time-out so that Bauer could talk to pitcher Mike McCormick on the mound. Bauer advised McCormick that Mantle was just off of the disabled list and hung over to boot—Mickey would never be able to get around on a fastball.

Following Whitey's advice, Mantle swung at McCormick's first pitch—a head-high fastball—and hit it out of the park. He circled the bases with Bauer looking on from the Orioles' dugout in stunned silence. In the Yankee dugout, Mickey slumped back down on the bench next to Whitey.

"Kid, great hit," said Whitey. "I dunno how you hit that."

"Hitting the ball was easy," Mickey murmured. "Running around the bases was the tough part."

Though he played in only sixty-five games in 1963, Mantle batted .314 and hit fifteen home runs—including another homer that almost cleared Yankee Stadium. Collectively, Mantle and Maris played in a total of only 155 games, but the Yanks persevered behind Whitey Ford, a twenty-four-game winner, and even prospered, capturing the American League pennant by ten and a half games. In the World Series, the Yankees faced the Los Angeles Dodgers, whom they had beaten six out of seven times in the Series while they were in Brooklyn. These Dodgers, however, were different. They had possibly the best pitcher in baseball, left-hander Sandy Koufax, who in 1963 posted a 25–5 record and a 1.88 earned-run average—throwing eleven shutouts and striking out 306 batters in 311 innings while giving up only 1.7 walks per game. He was backed up by side-wheeling right-hander Don Drysdale, a twenty-five-game winner in 1962, who had nineteen victories and a 2.63 ERA in '63; crafty veteran Johnny Podres, who won fourteen games, with five shutouts; and relief ace Ron Perranoski, who made sixty-nine appearances and went 16–3 with a 1.67 ERA. From his experience against him in All-Star Games, Mantle especially disliked hitting against Drysdale. Mickey would later recall, "Whenever he hit you, he'd come around, look at the bruise on your arm and say, 'Do you want me to sign it?'"

Koufax outdueled Ford in game one, striking out fifteen and breaking Dodger Carl Erskine's ten-year-old World Series strikeout record. Like Erskine's, Koufax's record was set in a game played October 2. The only common strikeout victim for the Dodgers pitchers was Mantle, who had fanned four times against right-hander Erskine and now twice against Koufax. In winning 5–2, Koufax and the Dodgers got out to a 4–0 second-inning lead on a run-scoring single by Bill Skowron, obtained from the Yankees after the 1962 season, and John Roseboro's three-run home run. Skowron singled home another run in the third. The Yankees didn't touch Koufax until the eighth, when Tom Tresh slugged a two-run home run with Tony Kubek on base.

Podres, with two-out relief help from Perranoski, beat the Yankees 4–1 in game two. Willie Davis's two-run double in the first inning got Los Angeles rolling, and Skowron provided Podres with another run on a home run in the fourth. Maris had a chance to catch Davis's drive but slipped on the Yankee Stadium grass. Maris injured his knee and elbow in the third when he ran into a railing pursuing a Tommy Davis triple and left the game. Maris never played another inning in the Series.

Los Angeles took its two games-to-none lead to Dodger Stadium, a palatial estate that made for a dramatic contrast to the Dodger park that Mantle and many of the Yankees remembered from World Series past, Ebbets Field. Drysdale made the first Series game at the glittering park one to remember, pitching a three-hitter and striking out nine batters in a 1–0 triumph. Tough-luck loser Jim Bouton surrendered the game's only run in the first inning on a walk to Jim Gilliam, a wild pitch, and a single by Tommy Davis, who had just captured his second straight National League batting championship

Ford and Koufax faced each other again in game four, a scoreless contest until the fifth inning, when Frank Howard, the Dodgers' six-foot seven-inch, 250-pound right fielder, blasted a mammoth home run to left, one of only two hits the Dodgers got in the game. Mantle got the run back in the seventh when, having managed only one hit in thirteen Series at-bats, Mickey rocketed a home run to left-center against Koufax. It was Mantle's fifteenth World Series home run, tying him with Babe Ruth. But the Dodgers regained the lead in the bottom of the inning—without getting a hit. Jim Gilliam led off with a high bouncer that was speared by third baseman Clete Boyer, but first baseman Joe Pepitone lost Boyer's on-target throw against the background of the white-shirted crowd, and Gilliam scooted all the way to third base. Willie

Davis then drove Gilliam home with a sacrifice fly to deep center field for a 2–1 victory that did to the Yankees what had never been done to them in all their storied World Series history. The Yankees had been swept.

Mantle would follow his shortened 1963 season with his last big year. On August 12, 1964, Mantle hit the longest measured drive in Yankee Stadium history—a 502-foot shot to dead center field. At the age of thirty-three, he hit .303 with thirty-five home runs and 111 RBIs. But the Yankees' dominance was slipping.

Great players have rarely made great managers, and Yogi Berra—who replaced Ralph Houk, who in turn became general manager—was an example. The 1964 season was his first as a manager, and his mistakes were magnified by the fact that he was managing the most famous baseball team in the biggest city in the country. Berra's biggest headache appeared to be that he literally couldn't communicate with his players. Once on a bus ride to O'Hare International Airport after losing a four-game series to the White Sox, Berra became so sick of utility player Phil Linz's harmonica rendition of "Mary Had a Little Lamb" that he yelled to the back of the bus ordering him to stop. Linz failed to understand what Berra had said and asked Mantle. Mantle, of course, was the wrong person to ask. (Dick Schaap would recall once observing Mantle on the team bus reading aloud portions of Henry Miller's *Tropic of Cancer,* a highly controversial book by the standards of the time.) Always the practical joker around his teammates, Mickey yelled back to Linz, "He said to play it *louder.*" When Linz did just that, Berra stormed to the back of the bus, chewed him out, and fined him. The incident may have had a silver lining. The Yankees won twenty-two of their next thirty games.

The Yankees were in a particularly good groove at the end of the 1964 season, earning their fourteenth Series berth in sixteen years by winning the American League pennant by one game over the Chicago White Sox. The 1964 World Series—matching the Yankees against the Cardinals—would be the fifteenth Fall Classic for Berra, who had first appeared in the Series in 1947, last played in it in 1963, and along the way had established the record for most Series games played, seventy-five. Mantle was about to play in his twelfth Series for the Yankees, Ford in his eleventh, and Howard in his ninth. Up and down the lineup, the Yankees clearly were a veteran team, with extensive World Series experience.

In the Cardinals, the Yankees faced a team that had overcome the mid-August turmoil surrounding the ouster of their general manager, Bing Devine, and had come back from fifth place to first, as the Philadelphia Phillies blew a six-and-a-half-game league lead with twelve games to play.

The Series opener would be a bad omen for the Yankees. New York carried a 4–2 lead behind Whitey Ford into the sixth inning, when the wheels came off the thirty-five-year-old left-hander. Cardinal right fielder Mike Shannon hit a long two-run home run, and catcher Tim McCarver followed with a double. Ford was finished for the day and, because of arm problems, for the World Series as well. The Cardinals went on to win 9–5.

However, the Yankees bounced back in game two by beating Cardinal ace Bob Gibson, 8–3, behind the pitching of rookie Mel Stottlemyre. Game three at Yankee Stadium, a 1–1 pitcher's duel between the Yankees' Jim Bouton and Cardinals veteran Curt Simmons, became a dramatic stage for Mantle in the bottom of the ninth. When Cardinals manager Johnny Keene brought thirty-eight-year-old knuckleball artist Barney Schultz to pitch to Mantle, Mickey turned to Elston Howard, who was in the on-deck circle, and said, "Ellie, you might as well go on to the clubhouse and start getting dressed, 'cause I'm ending this game right here." A Yankee scouting report had noted that Schultz usually tried to throw his first pitch across the plate to try to get ahead in the count, and now Mantle hit Schultz's first pitch for a home run—what later became known as Mickey's "called shot." It won the game, 2–1, and broke the Series home run record, which Mickey had shared with Ruth.

Ahead two games to one in the Series, the Yankees scored three first-inning runs and led game four until the sixth inning, when St. Louis third baseman Ken Boyer connected on a grand-slam home run off lefty Al Downing. With Roger Craig and Ron Taylor combining for eight and two-thirds innings of two-hit, scoreless relief, St. Louis evened the Series with a 4–3 victory. The next day Gibson came back and prevailed 5–2; in the tenth inning battery mate McCarver hit a three-run, game-winning home run. Game six was a 1–1 tie going into the sixth inning, but Simmons yielded consecutive-pitch home runs to Maris and Mantle. Joe Pepitone then sealed the game with a bases-loaded home run in the eighth, giving the Yankees an 8–3 win.

The climactic game, featuring a Stottlemyre-Gibson pitching matchup, was scoreless through three innings before the Cardinals scored three runs in the fourth and three more in the fifth. Mantle responded with a three-run home run in the sixth, his eighteenth career Series home run. Clete Boyer and Phil Linz hit solo home runs in the ninth, but Gibson held on for a complete game, a 7–5 win that gave the Cardinals their first World Series championship in eighteen years.

This would be Mantle's last World Series. In addition to his three home runs, he had driven in a record-tying eight runs—and his eighteen World Series home runs would stand as a record longer than Ruth's mark had stood. It would also be the last Series for Ford, Richardson, Kubek, and Clete Boyer. Howard would play in one more Series, with the Boston Red Sox. Maris would play in two more Series after his trade to the Cardinals. The Yankees themselves would not be back in the World Series for twelve years.

"You kind of took it for granted around the Yankees that there was always going to be baseball in October," Whitey Ford later said about the end of the dynasty in 1964. "Things just seemed to fall apart after that. Everybody got old at once and then, later, in an effort to compensate, trades began breaking up the Yankees gang and the Yankee spirit, at least as I knew it."

Indeed, through the early part of the 1960s few questioned the inevitability of the Yankees' playing October baseball. Mantle had made the transition to the leadership role that Houk had asked him to assume in 1961, and he continued to provide power along with Maris. Ford had backed his twenty-five-win season in 1961 with seventeen wins in 1962, a twenty-four-win year in 1963, and yet another seventeen victories in 1964. At the end of 1964, the backbone of the Yankee dynasty still seemed to be in place, apparently ready to continue its winning ways. Then, almost without warning, it all fell apart.

Some blamed the Yankee decline on the organization's failure to develop black ballplayers, with Elston Howard being the notable exception. In this, the Yankees were like their American League brethren generally. It had been National League teams that signed Willie Mays, Hank Aaron, Ernie Banks, Frank Robinson, Roberto Clemente, and many more in order to stay competitive with Jackie Robinson's Brooklyn Dodgers. This led to an unprecedented dominance in All-Star competition for the National League. Others attributed the Yankees' collapse to the forced retirement of George Weiss as general manager. Without Weiss's direction, it was believed, the Yankee farm system had deteriorated and not stockpiled the talent he had secured in years past. Moreover, Weiss's successor had been unable to make the kinds of midseason player deals that had historically benefited the Yankees. Houk would do no better; the brilliance he had shown in managing and handling players on the field did not translate into success in the front office. The Yankees' losing their predatory dominance over the Kansas City Athletics when Charles O.

Finley bought the club in 1960 didn't help either. However, if any one decision can be singled out as a turning point in the Yankees' fortunes, it may well be the decision to fire Berra as manager the day after the end of the World Series.

By most accounts, Houk had decided to fire Yogi in August but held off because the man he wanted to hire (and eventually did hire), Johnny Keane, was managing the Cardinals. A day after the Series ended, the Yankees fired Berra, and Keane resigned in St. Louis. Four days later, the Yankees hired Keane. It would prove to be a disaster for both Keane and the Yankees.

"He was absolutely the wrong guy," said Yankee pitcher—and later *Ball Four* author—Jim Bouton. "The players hadn't respected Yogi, but at least they liked him. Keane they didn't like or respect. Johnny was too old for us and too much of a traditionalist, and he never could get used to our outrageous habits and lifestyle."

Keane's fatal mistake with the New York players may have been not getting off to a good start with their hero and leader. Mantle's stature had grown not only among his own teammates but among opponents as well. In part this was because of his personality, but it was also because of the sportsmanship that marked his mature years, his utter refusal to strut or show off in any way. "Baseball has an unwritten law against such behavior," George F. Will would note years later. "Etched on every fan's mental retina is the archetypal sight of Mickey Mantle in his home run trot, with his head down, so as not to show up the pitcher." Once, when Detroit's Al Kaline was taunted by a youngster who said, "You're not half as good as Mickey Mantle," he replied, "Son, nobody is half as good as Mickey Mantle."

By the spring of 1965, Mickey was set in his ways, especially his drinking and partying, which even Stengel had never seriously tried, or wanted, to change. Keane was a devout man who wanted his teams to comply with curfews and who took spring training games with the seriousness of a rookie. When he saw that the Yankees, with the exception of Bobby Richardson and Tony Kubek, followed Mantle's example of after-hours carousing, he decided to make an example of Mickey. Seeing Mantle hung over after a night of partying, Keane grabbed a fungo bat and a bag of balls and sent Mickey out to center field to shag some flies. Keane emptied the ball bag, hitting ball after ball and forcing Mantle to run in all directions. "I had been playing center field in the major leagues for fifteen years—I knew how to catch fly balls," Mantle recalled. "I knew he wasn't providing instruction. He was trying to make me sick, trying to set an example. And I didn't like it."

Eventually Mickey tired of it. Keane happened to hit him a short fly ball that the hustling Mantle fielded on the run—and then threw as hard as he could at the head of his manager. The startled Keane ducked just in time and figured that Mantle knew how to play center field under any conditions. "I kept my distance," said Mantle. "When we did talk, there were no arguments. More often than not, we had staring contests. Eventually, the situation got so bad that if I had been financially set, I would have retired at the end of the season."

That season the Yankees were also plagued by injuries, which wasn't unusual. What *was* unusual was the manner in which Houk and Keane handled the injury situation and the team. When Roger Maris broke his hand, management deliberately kept the extent of the injury from him so that he would continue playing. Elston Howard was kept behind the plate despite an injured arm. Tony Kubek developed chronic back problems that forced him to retire at the end of the season, at the age of twenty-nine.

"Keane thought the players were babying themselves too much," recalled Bouton, "so he started making guys play with injuries. He would always try to get Mickey to play in a game. I used to make up this conversation where I was Keane [whose nickname was "Skip"] and Mantle, and Mickey used to get a big kick out of it. I'd say, 'How's your leg, Mick?' And I'd say, 'Not too good, Skip. It's broken in four places.' 'But Mick, can you set the bones in time for the game? We sure could use you.' 'If I can set the bone, I can play, Skip.' 'Good. How's your back?' 'Skip, my back fell clean off.' 'Can you get another back, Mick? We can probably find one for you before the game starts.' 'That will be fine, Skip. If you find me another back, I guess I can play. Shit. I can play, Skip.' 'Good, Mick, I knew you could.' And he played Maris when he was injured, and he should not have been playing. And, of course, Houk backed Keane on that when he should have backed Maris, and Ellie played when he shouldn't have, and I pitched when I shouldn't have been pitching. The year was a disaster."

Other than 1963, when he played in only sixty-five games, the 1965 season turned out to be Mickey's worst year to date. His .255 average and forty-six RBIs were below even the modest figures of his rookie season, and his nineteen home runs were only six more than he hit in his 1951 season. The season was equally disappointing for the team. Having come within a game of the world championship the year before, the Yankees plunged all the way to sixth place. For the first time in its long history, the Yankee organization appeared to be in disarray. Casey Stengel had become the manager of the expansion New York Mets and hired Berra as a coach in 1965. Even the public voice of the Yankees had changed; at the end of the 1964 season the Yankees had fired their famed broadcasting team of Mel Allen and Red Barber, whose voices had been synonymous with the Yankee dynasty.

It was an altogether new Yankee organization. In the middle of the 1964 season, after nineteen years as the owners, Del Webb and Dan Topping had sold their team to CBS for $11.2 million, the most expensive franchise deal ever at the time. Mickey had become disillusioned with the front office, compounding his frustration over his injuries and his disappointing season, a season in which Keane at one point moved the injury-slowed Mantle to left field. Rumors that Mantle might retire sent shivers up through the Yankee front office, which began a public relations drive to woo him back for the following season.

On September 18, 1965, Mantle played in his two-thousandth game, celebrated as Mickey Mantle Day at Yankee Stadium. It would be the first of four celebrations in Mantle's honor at the stadium (he would become the only player for whom that has been done): Mickey Mantle Day in 1965, Mickey Mantle Fan Appreciation Day in 1966, Mickey Mantle Day after his retirement in 1969, and Mickey Mantle Day in 1997, two years after his death. On that first Mickey Mantle Day, a sellout crowd packed the stadium. Mickey was presented with a new car; two quarter horses; vacation trips to Rome, Nassau, and Puerto Rico; a mink coat for Merlyn; a six-foot, hundred-pound Hebrew National salami; a Winchester rifle; and more—as well as the adoration of the city, the fans, and the Yankee organization. Large banners read "Don't Quit, Mick" and "We Love the Mick." Author Gay Talese, in his *Esquire* profile of Joe DiMaggio, would call the celebration—which even the archbishop of New York, Francis Cardinal Spellman, had helped promote— "an almost holy day for the believers who had crammed the grandstands early to witness the canonization of a new stadium saint."

DiMaggio flew to New York to make the introduction of Mantle. Mickey had long ago reached an understanding with the Clipper; the two men would never be friends, but they would be friendly. They would see each other not only at the annual Yankee Old Timers' Day games but also almost every spring, because DiMaggio attended the Yankees' spring training camps as a special instructor. Invariably, photographers would flock to them, and they were regularly photographed together. In 1961, photographer Ozzie Sweet, whose portraits often graced the cover of *Sport* magazine, arranged to photograph the two legendary Yankee center fielders together. His account of the photo session contradicts any notion that Mantle felt uncomfortable in DiMaggio's presence. On the contrary, according to Sweet, it was Mantle who looked "relaxed and confident" and DiMaggio who appeared "antsy and uncomfortable." DiMaggio was his typical distant self, causing Sweet to tread lightly. "With anyone else, I might say, 'Adjust your cap. . . .'" said Sweet. "But with Joe, I didn't dare. I just wanted to quickly get some images of the two of them together. In one photograph from that session, DiMaggio can be seen straining his neck as he tried to move his head closer to Mantle's. "I didn't' know what the heck he was doing there," said Sweet. "But with Joe, I didn't want to fool around for long. I didn't want to say, 'Mr. DiMaggio, could you please change the angle of your neck so you don't look like a turtle?' I think he might have walked away!"

DiMaggio was also one to brood at small slights, or even perceived slights. In one Old-Timers' Game at Yankee Stadium, the public-address announcer made an unintentional protocol gaffe and introduced the great Yankee Clipper ahead of Mantle, instead of last, as was customary. With Mickey introduced at the end, with the fans' energy and enthusiasm at a fever's pitch, it appeared that Mantle had received the biggest and loudest ovation. Mickey himself was aware of it and even remarked with great satisfaction, "I heard Joe was pissed off about it."

The rivalry, of course, worked both ways. Songwriter Paul Simon told author David Halberstam how amid the social and political upheaval of the 1960s he came to write the lyric, "Where have you gone, Joe DiMaggio? A nation turns its lonely eyes to you." Simon said Mickey Mantle asked why he'd used DiMaggio and not him. Rather than get into the complex idea of the simpler times DiMaggio symbolized, Simon said, "It was syllables, Mickey. The syllables were all wrong."

Mantle had matured professionally—he had a healthy hold on his working life—but his personal life was, at best, a denial of his increasing drinking problem. He continued to drink heavily, although it wasn't talked about outside the clubhouse or outside his home. Sports journalism at the time was continuing to evolve as far as the professional relationships between writers and players, but the personal lives of the players were still off limits. Robert Creamer, who ghostwrote Mantle's book *The Quality of Courage* in 1964, would write years later that the only time he ever saw Mickey drunk was in New York in 1963, after the Yankees had been swept in the World Series by the Dodgers. "It was late at night," said Creamer, "and he was standing in the downstairs lobby of a hotel with a drink in his hand, talking with a small group of baseball people. He wasn't loud or belligerent, just a little sodden and a little wistful about the defeat." Creamer said it did not take long to understand that more than a dozen years after his death, Mutt Mantle still remained foremost in Mickey's thoughts—and that it was an issue that still affected him deeply. "[Mickey] said, 'What about this book?' It was about courage, I said," Creamer recalled, "and Mantle began talking about his father. He described his strength in holding his family together during the Depression and his courage in the last year of his life, when he knew he was dying of Hodgkin's disease but did not tell Mickey, who was in his precarious rookie season with the Yankees. 'My father was the bravest man I ever knew,' he said. I learned that Mantle was more sensitive than I had imagined from the surly image he had been projecting, and I found he had a subtle sense of humor. After our book was published, I took a copy to Yankee Stadium and asked him to autograph it for my children. When he handed it back, he had a little grin. In his strong, clear hand he had written, 'To Jim, Tom, John, Ellen and Bobby, my best wishes—from the man who taught your father a few lessons in journalism—Your friend, Mickey Mantle.' That was a nice little zinger, and I got a kick out of it."

DiMaggio would never have allowed a journalist to get that close to him. For years, all the public saw was the DiMaggio with the packaged grace and magnanimity, the exquisitely tailored pin-striped suits, the regal image of suave detachment, an American hero transformed into a national aristocrat. That is how DiMaggio came off at that first Mickey Mantle Day, with the Yankee franchise in decline and Mickey already talking about retirement. When DiMaggio was introduced to the packed Yankee Stadium that afternoon, he walked with his customary grace from the dugout on to the field. Then, as he waved to the cheering crowd, DiMaggio noticed Mickey's mother Lovell standing, almost ignored, to one side. DiMaggio unexpectedly took her elbow and escorted her to where all the players and dignitaries were lined up along the infield grass. As he stood near home plate acknowledging the fans and the dignitaries on the field, DiMaggio happened to glance back at Mantle, who was still in the Yankee dugout with Merlyn and the boys. But what caught his eye was the figure of Senator Robert F. Kennedy, who was walking back and forth in the dugout, anticipating his own introduction.

DiMaggio despised both Bobby Kennedy and his brother, the late president, for their romantic involvements with Marilyn Monroe. He blamed them, among others, for her demise. Marilyn had been the love of Joe's life, and his devotion to her had continued long past their nine-month marriage in 1954. DiMaggio had reportedly told close friends that he had believed a reconciliation might be possible and was shocked when she was found dead of an overdose in 1962. DiMaggio had vowed never to have anything to do with the Kennedys, but now he was faced with the prospect of exchanging at least cordial greetings with one of them. This was a stadium filled with people still enamored with him, and he would not disappoint. DiMaggio turned his attention to Mickey and the fans there to honor him. "I'm proud," he announced, "to introduce the man who succeeded me in center field in 1951."

The applause in the stadium was thunderous and sustained for Mickey as he and his family walked on to the field. Mantle waved to the crowd, which was on its feet, then posed with his wife and sons for the photographers kneeling in front of them. Mantle then gave a typically short speech. "A lot has been written about the pain that I've played with," he said. "When one of the fans says, 'Hi, Mick, how ya doin'? How's the leg?' It makes it all worth it. I just wish I had fifteen more years to play here."

Moved almost to tears, Mantle turned and began shaking hands with all the dignitaries standing nearby. "Among them now," wrote Talese, "was Senator Kennedy, who had been spotted in the dugout five minutes before by Red Barber, and had been called out and introduced. Kennedy posed with Mantle for a photographer, then shook hands with the Mantle children, and with Toots Shor and [New York political leader] James Farley and others. DiMaggio saw him coming down the line and at the last second he backed away, casually, hardly anybody noticing it, and Kennedy seemed not to notice it either, just swept past shaking more hands."

Even Mickey Mantle Day, however, couldn't detract from the Yankees' most horrendous season since the early days of the Babe. The Yankees finished 1965 with a 77–85 record, their first losing season since 1925. It would get worse. That November, Mantle tore up his right shoulder in a backyard football game in which he and Mickey Jr. were taking on the twins, Ray and Roy. Mickey underwent surgery and got himself ready for his sixteenth season. Twenty games into the 1966 season, after a 4–16 start, Houk would have no choice except to fire Keane and step back into the manager's role.

The exhibition season began with a burst of glory, with the Yankees opening Houston's Astrodome where, with President Lyndon B. Johnson looking on, Mantle became the first player to hit a home run in the first domed stadium in the world. Injuries limited Mickey to 108 games that season, but even so Mickey's numbers were slightly up from 1965—twenty-three home runs, fifty-six RBIs, and a .288 batting average. But 1966 would end with the Yankees humiliated, finishing dead last in the American League.

Mantle got into 144 games in both 1967 and 1968, but statistically he would not measure up to his numbers of 1966, or to his own standards. His production those final two seasons were be almost identical. In 1967, he hit twenty-two home runs, drove in fifty-five runs, and batted .245. In 1968, he hit eighteen home runs, drove in fifty-four runs, and batted .237. Moreover, Mantle's slugging percentages in those two seasons—.434 in 1967 and .398 in 1968—were the two lowest of his career. Ford retired in the second month of the 1967 season. He had had a circulatory problem in his left shoulder that required a vein-graft operation that winter, but what finally forced him into retirement was a painful bone spur in his left elbow. With Ford went Mantle's last link to his glory years with the Yankees. As bad as Mickey felt for Whitey, he felt just as bad for himself, coming to grips with the fact that the end of his own career was near. As if to underscore that, Mantle in 1967 was switched from center field to first base. The move was intended to take the strain off his knees and prolong his career, but at first base, by Mickey's own admission, he had to settle for being not great but simply adequate.

Mickey never felt comfortable at the position. Everyone, especially Yankee opponents, knew that and, in respect, rarely attempted to exploit Mantle's limitations there. Cleveland Indians rookie Dave Nelson recalled the time he laid a bunt down first base to capitalize on Mickey's limited mobility. "I had no clue at the time that other clubs had decided some things for themselves out of reverence for him," said Nelson. "I had great speed, so [my bunt] was a base hit. I turn around halfway down the right field line, and there's our first base coach walking towards me, and he stops me and tells me, 'Hey, Dave, we don't bunt on Mick out of respect for him.' I go to myself, 'Oh-kayyy.' So then I walked back to first base and I'm standing next to Mickey Mantle. I'm looking at this guy's arms, and they look like tree trunks, and I'm saying, 'Man, he's gonna pinch my head off,' and then he pats me on the butt and he says, 'Nice bunt, rook.' And I look at him and say, 'Thanks, Mr. Mantle.'"

Perhaps only Mickey Mantle, with his unique sense of humor, could appreciate the irony that the most popular player in the game, cheered and celebrated not only in New York but in all the American League cities, now played for the worst team in baseball.

"It's all sentiment," said Mantle. "I'm not sure I like that. They sure as hell aren't cheering me for my batting average."

17

"I can't see the ball anymore. I can't steal second when I need to anymore. I can't go for from first to third anymore, and I think it's time to quit trying."

With those words, reflecting the homespun manner he had come to cultivate, Mickey Mantle announced his retirement on the afternoon of March 1, 1969, before a group of reporters at, appropriately, the Yankee Clipper Hotel in Fort Lauderdale. Mantle had gone to spring training early that year to see if he could turn back time but knowing deep down that his career was over. The mounting injuries and years of fast living had taken their toll. Marvin Miller, the president of the fledgling baseball players' association, had called him "a gimpy 36-year-old first baseman with 66-year-old legs."

In 1968, Whitey Ford was hired to coach first base by manager Ralph Houk. It would be a job that left Whitey with mixed emotions, because it forced him to watch his longtime friend in the twilight of his career. "One of the sad things about coaching first base was that I was witnessing, firsthand, the demise of Mickey Mantle as a ballplayer," Whitey said. "It was sad to see him struggling to hit .240 because I knew how proud Mick was, and it hurt him not to be able to help the Yankees. . . . The worst thing about watching Mickey that year was to see him in such pain. I knew his legs were killing him, but he would never complain. Sometimes he wouldn't even want to go out, he was hurting so much."

But the incident that may have ultimately convinced Mickey that it was time to leave the game may have come in Detroit near the end of the 1968 season, when he came to bat against Tigers' ace Denny McLain. McLain won thirty-one games that season, and the Tigers had already clinched the pennant and would go on to win the World Series. McLain was also a Mantle fan and would later say, "I think everyone then wanted to be Mickey Mantle for at least one day in their lives." As Mantle came to the plate, McLain called his catcher Bill Freehan to the mound.

"What the hell's going on?" asked Freehan. "There's two outs. Let's go home."

McLain shook his head. "I got an idea," he told his catcher. "This is Mantle's last at-bat in Tiger Stadium. Let's see if he can whack one."

"You've got to be kidding," said Freehan.

"No, let's let him hit one. Let's at least let him try. You go back there, and you tell Mr. Mantle to be ready."

When Freehan set up behind the plate and told Mantle to "be ready," Mickey didn't know what to think. McLain grooved the first pitch perfectly down the middle, and the unbelieving Mantle took it for a strike. Mickey looked at Freehan. "Don't shit me, Bill. Is he setting me up for something?"

"No, Mick. He wants you to hit one out."

This had happened to Mantle only once before. In 1952 against the Philadelphia Athletics, Mickey found himself with an admirer of his long home runs in catcher Joe Tipton, a country boy from Georgia. That day, in a low voice out of the umpire's range, Tipton had said to Mickey: "Hi, big guy, what would you like to have?"

"How 'bout a change-up?" Mantle said.

"You got it," said Tipton.

The first pitch was a change-up that Mantle immediately sent to the bleachers. As he crossed home plate, Mickey saw Tipton with his mask off. The catcher looked at him and winked.

So now, at the end of his career, Mickey was getting another gift pitch—and from arguably the best pitcher in the league. McLain's next pitch was a fastball no more than fifty miles an hour, and Mantle fouled it off.

"Where the hell do you want the pitch?" McLain asked.

Mantle put his left hand over the plate. "I want it here, belt high inside part of the plate. Put it there."

McLain complied, and Mantle hit a line drive into the upper deck of Tiger Stadium. Knowing it was probably Mickey's swan song, the Detroit crowd gave Mantle a standing ovation, as did the Tiger infielders and players as he circled the bases. It was Mickey's 535th home run, putting him ahead of Jimmie Fox into third place at that time in career home runs, behind only Babe Ruth and Willie Mays. Mickey would hit his final home run on September 20—his 266th homer in Yankee Stadium, seven more than Ruth's total there.

If there was one regret above others, it was that in 1968 he had hit a paltry .237, worse even than the .244 of the 1967 campaign. In 1968 he collected only 103 hits in 144 games, a performance over which Mantle would agonize for years. That season dropped his career average below .300. Mickey would finish his career with a .298 batting average, which pained him, because he considered himself a .300 hitter. "God damn, to think you're a .300 hitter and end up at .237 in your last season, then find yourself looking at a lifetime .298 average—it made me want to cry," Mickey would say. Hitting .300 has been a symbolic benchmark in baseball, and Mickey was disappointed that his career record would show that he had failed to attain it. Realistically, of course, in what seemed to be a dead-ball period in the 1960s, it was difficult to keep his average up when all of baseball was down, from the American League's .248 mark in 1964 to .231 in 1968. Nevertheless, in the years following his retirement, Mantle would briefly consider making a comeback, partly motivated by wanting to raise his career batting average to .300 or better. But thoughts of a comeback were daydreams and fantasies that Mickey would indulge in when feeling sorry for himself about his final years. Like his fans, Mickey would often dwell on what might have been.

"If I had gotten more rest, worked out more, lived a drier life," Mantle said looking back on his career, "I might not have been injured as much. I didn't lose any enthusiasm for the game, I just lost the ability to do the things I used to do. I could have played a few more seasons if I had just taken my injuries more seriously. I'm not sure if I was lazy or didn't know better, but I didn't go to the trouble of doing the rehab on my leg as I was supposed to do. . . .

"And there is no doubt in my mind that alcohol hurt my career terribly. In the end, all you really have are the memories and the numbers on paper. The numbers are important because baseball is built on them, and this is the way you are measured. And the point is, I played in more than 2,400 games, more than any Yankee player in history, and I hit 536 home runs, and I shouldn't be griping about my career. But I know it should have been so much better, and the big reason it wasn't is the lifestyle I chose, the late nights and too many empty glasses."

If any player's career transcended numbers, however, that player was Mickey. By the end of his career, he had evolved into a sports figure of mythic proportions. He hadn't become Ruth, he hadn't been DiMaggio; he had etched his own identity into the game. Newspapers and radio exalting their heroic exploits to readers and listeners had built the legends of Ruth and DiMaggio. Mantle, however, had been *seen* in households across America. The pain, the misery, the frustration had been there for all to see, but so had the power and majesty of his swing, his home runs, his triumphs. Mickey Mantle had been baseball's first televised sports hero. In a sense, television did for his career the same thing it did for John F. Kennedy's—it elevated them both beyond their accomplishments and their circumstances.

"He's the last of the Yankees," *Los Angeles Times* columnist Jim Murray wrote. "He might have been the best of them, considering night games, the slider, the big parks, the trappers' mitts, and the fact that he would have been a certified cripple in any other industry. He was rejected four times by the military, afraid he couldn't keep up with a Fourth of July parade. I know one thing: those monuments in center field are going to be awfully lonely this summer. Their last link to the present is gone."

On June 8, three months after Mantle announced his retirement, the Yankees honored Mickey for the second time at Yankee Stadium, this time to retire his uniform, with a crowd of 61,157 looking on. The cheering and the applause were even louder than on the first Mickey Mantle Day, four years earlier. For a few moments, it was as if the stadium had been transported back through time to the 1950s. Many of Mantle's teammates from those great Yankee teams joined him on the field, and DiMaggio had been flown in to present him a plaque that would be hung on the center-field wall. Mickey himself would later present DiMaggio a similar plaque that would be hung next to his.

"When I walked into the stadium eighteen years ago," Mickey said that day, "I guess I felt the same way I feel now. I can't describe it. I just want to say that playing eighteen years in Yankee Stadium for you folks is the best thing that could ever happen to a ballplayer. Now having my number join 3, 4, and 5 kind of tops everything. I never knew how a man who was going to die [Lou Gehrig] could say he was the luckiest man in the world. But now I can understand."

Mantle later waved to his adoring fans as he rode around the perimeter of the stadium in a golf cart with Yankee pinstripes on the sides and personalized license plates that read "MM-7." Mickey was visibly moved and struggled to hold back tears. So too, high up in his stadium booth, was Eddie

Layton, who had become the Yankee organist in 1967 and who later would write "Blues for Mickey" as a tribute to his favorite Yankee, even though he had not known much about baseball when he had first taken the job. "I never saw a baseball game in my life," he recalled. "I didn't know where first base was. "My first game [playing the organ] Mickey Mantle hit a home run and started running around the bases. I yelled, 'He's running around the bases the wrong way!' thinking you were suppose to run them clockwise."

Waving to his fans that day, Mickey had come to the end of his life as a Yankee and as a professional ballplayer, but he had also come to the end of the dream that his father had envisioned for him. For Mutt, back in those dark days struggling to survive in the black mines of Oklahoma, the only vision of escape he had had for his oldest son had been baseball. He had endowed Mickey with enormous talent to play the game and the confidence to go forth and to succeed. However, the result was that Mickey had been prepared for little else, especially in his personal life. As he rode around the stadium that afternoon, Mantle was filled with sadness at the passing of his time on the field but also with uncertainty about his future—a future he feared he was completely unprepared to deal with.

Mantle's retirement did not go unnoticed by one fan who that same year had assumed the highest office in the country. Six weeks after Mantle's uniform was retired at Yankee Stadium, President Richard Nixon invited Mickey and Merlyn to a White House reception whose guest list also included Billy Martin and Mrs. Branch Rickey. The FBI routinely checks its files for arrest information on any White House guest, and on July 24, 1969, presidential counselor John Ehrlichman forwarded a letter to Nixon on the FBI's four-page file on Mantle—the alleged blackmail over a relationship with a married woman, the connection with the Washington gambler who treated Yankees to a night at a brothel, and the threat against his life. Mickey had his photograph taken with Nixon and talked baseball for a few minutes with the president, who was an avowed sports fan. Three years later, Mantle joined a group of "Athletes for Nixon" who supported the president's 1972 reelection campaign.

In retirement, Mantle would acknowledge that he had played the last two years at least for the money, for the hundred-thousand-dollar contracts that provided for the family—because Mickey's businesses and investments certainly didn't, nor would they in the years after his playing days. These were the days before the lucrative endorsement contracts with shoe companies and sporting goods giants. Fortunately for Mickey, he had deferred some of his money during his last few years. This would be the source for much of Mantle's income in the years after his retirement, along with payments from the Yankees for being a special coach during spring training and fees for speaking engagements that his lawyer, Roy True, arranged. The other businesses associated with Mantle simply had not paid off. The bowling alley in Dallas had faded along with the bowling craze. The employment agency with New York Jets star Joe Namath in Manhattan never seriously took off—despite its Madison Avenue name, "Mantle Men and Namath Women." The motel and chicken restaurant in Oklahoma bearing Mantle's name were short-term successes that failed the test of time. Mickey often jokingly blamed himself for the demise of the chicken restaurant. "I came up with the slogan 'to get a better piece of chicken, you'd have to be a rooster,'" Mantle recalled. "Business kinda went downhill after that." After a while, Mantle began looking at all potential business opportunities with gallows humor. About one business endeavor, Mickey remarked, "People are gonna say, 'My God, is Mantle in it? It'll go belly up for sure.'"

Mantle seemed snake bitten in business, as he had from the early days of his career as a rookie. Mickey's business luck was bad even when he became involved with others who generally had been successful in their own ventures. One of these people was Cleveland pitching ace Bob Feller, who had a reputation throughout the league of doing well with his business investments. In 1959, while in Cleveland for a series with the Indians, Mickey and Whitey Ford received a phone call from Feller with a tip on what he told them was a "terrific investment." Mickey and Whitey met Feller in his room at the Hotel Cleveland. The two Yankees were introduced to a businessman from Toronto named Ted Boomer. Boomer said he was the founder and president of the Canadian Bomb Shelter Survival Corporation, and, he told them, he was going to make them rich and secure their futures financially. Boomer said his company was building bomb shelters throughout Canada and would soon be expanding into the United States. Boomer told them that for a ten-thousand-dollar investment, each of them would become partners in his company. That evening, Mickey wrote Boomer a ten-thousand-dollar check and left. Whitey stayed around to talk pitching with Feller and soon thought it had been fortunate that he hadn't left.

"Whitey," Boomer said to him, "you and Mickey now own ten thousand shares each. I'm going to give you another twenty-five thousand shares for nothing, if you will agree to serve on our board of directors."

Whitey walked away that night with stock certificates for forty-five thousand shares of the Canadian Bomb Shelter Survival Corporation, and couldn't wait to tell Mickey. They waited to hear from Ted Boomer, who cashed their checks, but they had been fleeced. Neither Mickey nor Whitey ever bothered to report the scam to law enforcement authorities, and they never mentioned it to Feller until years later, when they treated the name Ted Boomer and the Canadian Bomb Shelter Survival Corporation as an inside joke.

Fortunately for Mickey, his business associations had started taking a positive, if slow, turn the year before his retirement. In 1968, Mantle met Roy True. It would be a fortuitous meeting, because at the time Mantle was involved with the Mickey Mantle's Country Cookin' franchises, which were about to go public. When True examined the paperwork for the stock offering, he uncovered some matters that he believed to be fraudulent, reported them to the Securities and Exchange Commission, and kept Mickey out of trouble. True soon began helping right Mickey financially, connecting him to Allied Chemical and Fuji Photo.

"When Mickey and I first started out together, everybody told me I ought to make sure Mantle's name was kept before the public or they'd forget," True later said with some amusement. "This didn't make sense to me. How was anybody going to forget Mickey Mantle? Remember, he was essentially a shy and retiring person, a laid-back type of guy. We picked his appearances carefully. Little by little, he became acquainted with the TV medium. He saw when he made a positive impression and when he didn't. And it turned out that he was a quick study. When I first got commercials for him, the producers would tell me, 'Better get this guy in a day ahead of time so we can work with him.' I knew this was ridiculous. Mick went in the day of the commercial and in fifteen minutes he had it cold. What's more, he had patience—which you need a lot of when you work with TV and advertising people. I had producers call me later and say, 'Mickey was tremendous. You can't believe the trouble we'd had with other jocks.'"

But even in retirement, long after his baptism by the hustlers of Manhattan, Mickey remained at heart the naïve country boy, unsuspecting of sharp practice. One of Mickey's most endearing qualities to his friends like Roy True was his willingness to trust people, even complete strangers. "He would call me some mornings," says True, "and say, 'I met a helluva guy last night. A terrific guy. He says he can make me ten million dollars. Will you talk to him?'" According to True, it was a long time before Mantle finally learned to be suspicious of strangers and their business propositions.

As he ended his career, however, business was the last thing Mantle had on his mind. Instead, his mind was on his father and on how the end of his career had now brought them full circle. "The beauty of the game," Roger Rosenblatt would write a year after Mantle's death, "is that it traces the arc of life. Until mid-August, baseball was a boy in shorts whooping it up in the fat grass. Now it becomes a leery veteran with a sunbaked neck, whose main concern is to protect the plate. In its second summer, baseball is about fouling off death."

The end of Mickey Mantle's career also marked the close of an era that had begun when life in the United States seemed simple; now it ended as America appeared to the world to be a society at war with itself. Harry S Truman had been in the White House when Mantle arrived in the majors as an innocent-eyed rookie. Richard Nixon had been inaugurated as president just forty days before Mickey uttered his departing line that seemed to come from a country song: "I think it's time I just quit trying." The 1950s sentiments of American nationalism and untroubled Norman Rockwell portraits had given way to a national psyche fractured over civil rights and antiwar protests. The sense of domestic security that had lulled the nation in the age of Eisenhower had forever been destroyed by the assassination of President Kennedy. Now, the onetime symbol for the promise and hope of the 1950s had become, through his own two decades of rebelliousness, just another reflection of the anger and frustration in the 1960s. In that context, Mantle's often crude, sometimes obscene, conduct perhaps took on larger meaning. *New York Times* columnist Robert Lipsyte would recall his own first meeting with Mantle, when he asked him a question he obviously did not want to answer. Without looking up from his locker, Mickey said: "Why don't you go fuck yourself?"

Mickey Mantle had not wanted to be Ruth or DiMaggio. He had not wanted to measure up to anyone else's expectations. He was, in that sense, like the generation that grew up looking to him as one of its heroes while at the same time thumbing its nose at the mores and values of the society that bred it. All Mickey Mantle had ever wanted was to be allowed to be himself.

December 26, 1951. Mickey and Merlyn get married at her family's home in Picher, Oklahoma. *The Mickey Mantle Museum, Cooperstown, N.Y., and Mr. Tom Catal and Mr. Andrew Vilacky*

Mickey flings his batting helmet in disgust, showcasing his temper after one of his 1,710 career strikeouts, the record until Reggie Jackson came along. *The Mickey Mantle Museum, Cooperstown, N.Y., and Mr. Tom Catal and Mr. Andrew Vilacky*

Mickey poses for Boston photographer Ray Gallo at Fenway Park in 1956 while pursuing the Triple Crown. Mantle called it "the greatest photograph I've ever seen of myself." *The Mickey Mantle Museum, Cooperstown, N.Y., and Mr. Tom Catal and Mr. Andrew Vilacky*

To Merlyn's regret, Mick spent much of his time at home during the offseasons either fishing with Billy Martin or just saying he was. *Randall Swearingen and www.mickey-mantle.com*

Mickey would popularize the "tape-measure home run" with his mammoth blasts during his career. *The Mickey Mantle Museum, Cooperstown, N.Y., and Mr. Tom Catal and Mr. Andrew Vilacky*

Mickey shakes hands with President Eisenhower prior to Game 1 of the 1956 World Series at Ebbets Field. *The Mickey Mantle Museum, Cooperstown, N.Y., and Mr. Tom Catal and Mr. Andrew Vilacky*

Manager Casey Stengel adorns Mickey's head with a crown in honor of Mantle winning the 1956 Triple Crown. The three bats over Mick's shoulder bear the numbers that won him the Crown. *The Mickey Mantle Museum, Cooperstown, N.Y., and Mr. Tom Catal and Mr. Andrew Vilacky*

Mickey with his two drinking buddies, Whitey Ford (left) and Billy Martin (right) in 1956. *Randall Swearingen and www.mickey-mantle.com*

THE AUTUMN
OF THE LEGEND

CHAPTER

18

Mickey Mantle had grown up with the stories of Babe Ruth partying long and hard, then going to the ballpark hung over and with little sleep, and hitting game-winning home runs. Jimmy Reese, later the coach of the Anaheim Angels, who roomed with Ruth for one season, was once asked what the Babe had really been like. "I dunno," answered Reese. "Mostly, I roomed with his suitcase." The prototypical Yankee slugger, cut from Ruth's pattern, was one who hit long home runs, stayed out long hours, and drank long into the night. Mantle came to fit it perfectly, although he fell into the lifestyle for reasons different from Ruth's. The Babe, an orphan, had simply been a man of gargantuan appetites. Mantle would look back and know that the turning point in his personal life, and the way it affected his professional career, had been the day his father died.

"If he had lived longer," Mantle said, "I don't think the problem would have gone as far as it did. I couldn't have faced my dad if he knew I was drinking. When I lost him, I didn't have anyone to answer to except Casey Stengel, and the truth is he could outdrink most of his players.

"After I retired in 1969, my drinking got steadily worse. I have always been proud of the fact that all my life I have always been honest with people. I wish I had been more honest with myself. . . . I started going to a lot of banquets and cocktail parties, and the drinking came easy. The next day someone might call and ask if I could remember what I had said to someone. And sometimes I couldn't. And yet up until [1994] I didn't believe I was an alcoholic. I always thought I could take it or leave it."

Mickey had also been a product of his times, the much-ballyhooed golden years of baseball. Drinking was the macho thing to do, and Mantle had more than enough free time on his hands, as well as all the temptations that present themselves to a major league baseball player. It was a time when the measure of a man was often how well he could hold his liquor. As Mantle was later to put it: "I drank because I thought we were having fun. It was part of the camaraderie, the male bonding thing. If you were going to be The Man on the field, you had to be The Man off the field. The choice was mine. That was the era, the culture. Fast-buck promoters waved their deals at you, and women waltzed in and out the revolving door. It was a macho time. If you could drink all night, get a girl, get up the next day, and hit a home run, you passed the test."

"When Mickey retired, a big chunk of his self-esteem went out the window," Merlyn wrote in *A Hero All His Life*. "I question whether he ever had much to begin with. People may find it amazing that I could say such a thing; here is someone who was celebrated, who was a hero to a generation of baseball fans, and who rubbed elbows with the rich and famous. But Mick was hiding behind alcohol. When he stopped hitting home runs, the only time he had any self-esteem was after a drink or two."

Part of Mickey's way of denying his drinking problem was to make fun of it. In a television commercial they once made, Mickey and Whitey Ford belittled their 1974 induction into Baseball's Hall of Fame by joking that they probably belonged to the beer drinker's hall of fame. In *The Mick*, published in 1985, Mickey had gone so far as to marvel at what he considered his "incredible tolerance" for alcohol during his playing days. All the while, however, the problem was worsening. He needed a drink to get going early in the day, and the drinking continued as the day wore on.

Fortunately for Mickey's image, his heavy drinking was not common knowledge. Numerous incidents of alcohol-induced rude and crude behavior, often at banquets and other public events, went unreported by the news media. Reporters, like his immediate family, seemed overly protective of Mickey and the Mickey Mantle image. For many of them, Mickey had been a boyhood hero; they chose to ignore the incidents or consider them isolated and unimportant. Also, the news media still considered the personal lives of politicians and other public figures off limits. There were no tabloid television shows reporting nightly on celebrities, and the influence of gossip and tabloid journalism had not yet become as prevalent and infectious as it would become in the 1990s.

There was one group of people, however, who could not escape knowledge of Mantle's drinking—his family. Holidays were especially difficult in the Mantle household, particularly Christmas, which was his least favorite holiday. "He was always sad," said golfing buddy and longtime friend Marshall Smith. "He always put on the biggest drunk at Christmas time, and stayed that way." Smith's wife Corrine believes she knew why. "I think," she said, "it was because he missed his father." There was the Christmas morning in 1964 when Mickey, hung over from too much drinking on Christmas Eve, tried to assemble a bicycle for son David, who was turning eight the next day. Mickey finished and flashed that silly crooked smile as David took the bike outdoors for his first ride. But the moment David pushed the pedals, the bike moved backward. Mickey had installed the bike chain in reverse.

"It's okay, dad," David said. "I can fix it."

Mickey would later observe of his life: "It has been this way most of my life: If I said or did something wrong, the people who might have suffered for it would worry about hurting *my* feelings. Even eight-year-olds made excuses for me."

One of David's most vivid memories of that time was his concern over his alcoholic father's safety behind the wheel: "I remember going to sleep when I was a kid and saying, 'Dear God, let dad get home safe.'"

Had he not been Mickey Mantle, in short, he would have been regarded as nothing more than a broken-down drunk. In fact, in retirement in Dallas, that is what he became. Jickey Harwell, a teaching pro at the South Oak Cliff Golf Course in the early 1970s, recalled the day he received a telephone call alerting him that Mantle would be in a foursome playing in a charity event at his course. "I was excited beyond belief because Mickey Mantle had been my hero growing up," said Harwell, a onetime baseball phenom himself in Central Texas. "So can you imagine my disappointment when Mickey arrived drunk and not very friendly either. We were all taken aback. *This* was Mickey Mantle? *This* was the guy who had been our hero?"

Mantle was also capable of enormous pettiness, which, like his drinking, was rarely seen by his adoring public. After his retirement, Mantle compiled what he called a "scratch list"—what amounted to a blackball list—with Marshall Smith. "We listed the people we thought weren't true-blue," recalled Marshall. "Sometimes Mickey would call me and say, 'Take that guy off the scratch list because we're back together.' He had a heart of gold. There was a long scratch list, and a short list of those you could trust." Among those on the scratch list was Milwaukee pitching great Warren Spahn, whose crime had been refusing to sign an autograph for Mantle's friend Darrell Royal, the former University of Texas coach.

Until his induction into the Hall of Fame in 1974, retirement was not kind to Mickey. He spent his days in Dallas playing golf, drinking, and seemingly serving out time until he could celebrate taking his rightful place in Cooperstown. In 1970 he had accepted a coaching position with the Yankees; it turned out to be short-lived. Mantle felt he had been hired as a public relations move to boost attendance for a struggling franchise. At one point he put his hand through a glass door attempting to get into his suite at the St. Moritz Hotel, showing up the next day in the first base coaching box with his stitched-up hand in bandages. "I wasn't naïve—I put extra people in the stands, that's all," Mantle said of his days as a Yankee coach. "There I was, pacing back and forth in the [first base coaching] box, and saying, 'Let's get it going now!' and feeling like a fool when Bobby Murcer drew a leadoff walk in the fourth inning, called time and asked me what the signs were. I said, 'Mine look good. I'm a Libra.' I was nothing more than a public relations gimmick."

In Dallas he lived in virtual anonymity except among his fellow members of the Preston Trail Golf Club in North Dallas. "It was like Mickey Mantle had died," he said about life after retirement. "It was weird. I'm thinking, 'Geeze, what did I do?' It seemed nobody cared what I was doing."

For Mantle, Dallas at this period was like a man-made baseball purgatory—a big city in America without a major league baseball team. As the country finally exited the troubled sixties and entered the seventies, Dallas was also a city still in mourning over the most defining event of the recently completed decade. The Kennedy assassination had left Dallas not only with a civic black eye but also at a loss for a national identity, beyond the Dallas Cowboys. That alone said volumes. Dallas was not a baseball town. Dallas was a big enough city to have its own professional football franchise—two of them, in fact, when the Dallas Texans of the old American Football League had been around before the move to Kansas City—but it wasn't a big enough city to have its own major league franchise. When big league baseball did come to the area in 1972 with the move of the Washington Senators, Dallas would share the franchise with Fort Worth and Arlington.

Moreover, Mickey's image had taken a devastating blow in the first year after his retirement with the publication of former Yankee pitcher Jim Bouton's tell-all book *Ball Four*. In retrospect, Bouton appears to have been fair in his brief portrayal of Mantle. He alluded to Mickey's sense of humor, including his pools for golf matches and horse races. "I once invested a dollar when Mantle raffled a ham," Bouton wrote. "I won, only there was no ham. That was one of the hazards of entering a game of chance, Mickey explained." Bouton also remembered with fondness Mantle's kindness in laying out a white-towel-carpet welcome in the clubhouse after he had pitched and won his first game. All that remembrance, however, was undone by the one paragraph that followed: "On the other hand, there were all those times he'd push little kids aside when they wanted his autograph, and the times when he was snotty to reporters, just about making them crawl and beg for a minute of his time. I've seen him slam a bus window on kids trying to get his autograph. And I hated that look of his, when he'd get angry at somebody and cut him down with a glare. Bill Gilbert of *Sports Illustrated* once described that look as flickering across his face 'like the nictitating membrane in the eye of a bird.' And I don't like the Mantle that refused to sign baseballs in the clubhouse before games. Everybody else had to sign, but [clubhouse man] Little Pete [Previte] forged Mantle's signature. So there are thousands of baseballs around the country that have been signed not by Mickey Mantle but by Pete Previte."

Marshall Smith confirms Bouton's account as well as the frustration of those around Mickey about his attitude on signing autographs. "I could go over and over it with him, but up until the day he died, Mickey never understood why someone would want his autograph," recalled Smith. "He would ask, 'Why do you think they make such a fuss over me like that?' I'd tell him, 'Because you look like an All-American boy. You've never lifted a weight in your life, but you have a 19-$\frac{1}{2}$ inch neck and they can hardly take your blood pressure because your forearms and arms are so solid. The speed and talent you have is something else. You play hard when you can hardly even walk. Plus you hit the ball a country mile. That's why they want your autograph.'"

Smith said Mantle called the autograph seekers "eyeballers." "They would sit there and eyeball him while he was eating dinner or something," Smith said. "They'd come over and just about the time he was taking a bite, they'd say, 'Would you sign this?' Or when he went to the bathroom. It was awful hard for him just to go somewhere, even back home [in Commerce]. That's why when he came to visit we'd just drive around and stay in the car most of the time. I'd not let anyone know he was around. He couldn't go anywhere, really. He couldn't go to Six Flags. He couldn't go to a football game. He had to hide. He wished he could go in freedom just like everybody else. One time it was suggested that he wear a disguise. But Mickey said, 'Oh, no. If someone found out I did that. . . .' He didn't want a scandal or anything, no matter how small. He cared what people thought about him. He cared a great deal. He enjoyed being Mickey Mantle, but I don't think he liked having to hide. He was never more at ease than when he was on the golf course or in the clubhouse. People didn't bother him there. What really stressed him out was when he would treat kids badly when they tried to get his autograph. He'd say 'no' and it bothered him when he did. He kept adding to his drinking. It hurt him. He'd say something to someone later. He'd say, 'Why'd I do that? Do you think I upset them?' That would really bother him. It bothered him his whole life."

In Bouton's book, a national best-seller, Mantle's treatment of autograph-seeking young fans suddenly became inescapable fodder for reviewers and for feature stories about Bouton and his unprecedented behind-the-scenes look at the Yankees and life in the majors. Understandably, Mantle's most loyal friends—especially Whitey Ford and Elston Howard—rallied to his defense. Bouton, a twenty-one-game winner in 1963, would be blackballed in numerous baseball circles, including the Yankees, who banned him from festivities at Yankee Stadium until the 1998 Old Timers' Day Game. His book, however, broke new ground for sports journalism and for the way professional athletes would be viewed outside the lines—in particular, Mickey Mantle. "It was the age of the antihero," wrote Mantle biographer David Falkner, "and Bouton's irreverence fit the times perfectly. . . . [A]s far as Mantle was concerned, the uncritically adoring view the public had of him began to fade. In the years following, the public's image of Mantle was as someone who surfaced for a few weeks each spring to stand around for several hours in his old uniform and then to carouse at night."

Mantle would never get the opportunity to manage in the majors, and it is unclear whether he would ever know or understand the reason. By the time of Mickey's retirement, most of the teams' front offices were aware of his worsening drinking problem as well as of his undisciplined work habits. George Weiss's dossier on Mantle's extracurricular activities had been widely circulated by word of mouth, and by Weiss himself, who after being dumped by the Yankees had become the general manager of the Mets. Ironically, Mickey was suffering the same fate as had befallen Babe Ruth when he attempted to get himself seriously considered as a major league manager. Mantle himself believed that the new major league franchise coming to the Dallas–Fort Worth area would be the perfect opportunity for him to return to the game as a manager, like Billy Martin, who at the time was the skipper of the Detroit Tigers. "They might make my whole salary back in one series if I brought a team into Yankee Stadium to play the Yankees," Mantle told *Dallas Times Herald* columnist Blackie Sherrod. "And how about if I was managing a team and took it to Detroit to play Billy Martin's team? That might draw quite a few at the gate. It ought to be good for something."

Mickey was further excited when Bob Short, the owner of the Washington team moving to Dallas–Fort Worth, contacted him. The Senators were managed by Ted Williams, but there were rumors that the former Red Sox star wanted to step down. Mantle's best chance of making a personal case for himself as a manager came at a breakfast meeting with Short that the Senators' owner had arranged. "Mickey," Short began, "I need a new manager, and I wondered if you had anyone in mind?" Short may have simply been playing coy, trying to get a sense of Mantle. Mickey, however, was never one to toot his own horn—an obvious miscalculation here. Mantle served up the name of Billy Martin, and Mickey's name never again came up. A year later, after Williams completed his final season as manager, Short followed Mantle's suggestion and hired Martin as skipper of the Rangers.

Mantle, meanwhile, began looking ahead to the one career certainty that he knew lay ahead. In 1974, after waiting the required five years, Mickey was elected to the Hall of Fame at the same time as Whitey Ford, who had not been enshrined at Cooperstown in his first year of eligibility. Mantle received 322 out of the 365 votes cast. Getting elected with 88 percent of the votes was especially pleasing to Mickey, considering some of his strained relations with baseball writers in the early part of his career and in the wake of the Bouton book. No player had ever been unanimously elected to the Hall of Fame, and a number of the writers who vote have traditionally refused to vote for anyone in their first year of eligibility. Fittingly, Mantle became only the seventh player to be elected to the Hall of Fame in his first year of eligibility.

Perhaps it was prophetic, but the day that Mantle and his friends boarded a charter bus for the trip to Cooperstown, the *New York Daily News* carried a headline that read: "Drinks Are on Mickey and Whitey." It would be the crowning achievement in Mantle's professional career, and he would celebrate it as he had all of his triumphs. Reports on a press conference Mickey and Whitey held in New York noted how they had held court with Bloody Marys in their hands. The days of celebration leading up to the charter bus ride to Cooperstown were filled with merriment and drinks. Mantle's Hall of Fame induction speech has been categorized by some baseball writers as one in which a seemingly scatterbrained Mickey dwelled on his strikeouts and some of the other shortcomings of his life and career. The speech, however, is characteristically Mickey Mantle—a shy public speaker humbled and perhaps even overwhelmed by a moment few from his background could have ever imagined. He followed baseball commissioner Bowie Kuhn, who in his introduction read all of Mantle's career achievements, which were engraved on the plaque that would hang in the Hall of Fame—among them his Triple Crown year, his three Most Valuable Player Awards, his record eighteen World Series home runs, and more. For Mantle, it was almost like the great expectations in his rookie season. There was nothing more he could do. He felt there was more he should have accomplished. In any case, talking about himself was something he had not been comfortable with during his career or in retirement. That is why, in his country-bumpkin fashion, he blurted out, "I was the world champion in striking out and everything I'm sure. I don't know for sure, but I must have had that record in the World Series, too. I broke Babe Ruth's record for all-time strikeouts."

But Mickey knew whom he had to thank, the people who had sacrificed—his mother and father and his siblings, Merlyn, Tom Greenwade, Casey Stengel, and, of course, Harold and Stella Youngman, who attended the ceremony. The Holiday Inn in Joplin, Missouri, which Harold Youngman had built with Mantle's name on it, had been one of the few successful business ventures in Mickey's life up until that time. When Youngman sold the motel after eight years, Mickey walked away with another hundred-thousand-dollar payday and an additional thousand dollars a month for the next twenty years.

Some of Mickey's friends saw another side of Harold Youngman that they didn't like—the side that sometimes exploited Mantle. They point to the disappearance of Mantle memorabilia that was kept at the Mickey Mantle Holiday Inn as an example. Marshall Smith said that before his death in 1990, Youngman pawned numerous items Mickey had presented to him as gifts, while other important pieces of Mantle memorabilia were sold.

"[Youngman] sold Mickey's 1956 World Series ring to a collector for $8,000," said Smith. "That guy sold it to Upper Deck for $65,000, then they sold it for $285,000."

Mike Samara, the Mantle Holiday Inn's first manager, also recalled, "We had this trophy case at the Holiday Inn that was filled with various awards Mickey won—the Hickok Belt, the Gold Glove, things like that. When we left the hotel, all that stuff had disappeared. You know who took it? Harold Youngman, that's who."

"That's Harold Youngman," said Smith. "I used to call him 'Mr. 20 Percent.' Mickey got so mad at him, they didn't talk for years and years."

Mantle and Youngman had made up by the time Mickey was enshrined into the Hall of Fame. In his Hall of Fame induction speech, Mickey thanked Youngman and his wife for their years of support and spoke of them in glowing terms. But the most moving part of Mantle's Hall of Fame speech was what he had to say about his childhood and his father, "probably the most influential thing that ever happened to me in my life."

"Before I was born," Mickey said, "my father lived and died for baseball and he named me after a Hall of Famer: Mickey Cochrane. I'm not sure if my dad knew it or not, but his real name was Gordon. I hope there's no Gordons here today, but I'm glad that he didn't name me Gordon. He had the foresight to realize that someday in baseball that left-handed hitters were going to hit against right-handed pitchers and right-handed hitters were going to hit against left-handed pitchers; and he taught me, he and his father, to switch-hit at a real young age, when I first started to learn how to play ball. And my dad always told me if I could hit both ways when I got ready to go to the major leagues, that I would have a better chance of playing. And believe it or not, the year that I came to the Yankees is when Casey started platooning everybody. So he did realize that that was going to happen someday, and it did. So I was lucky that they taught me how to switch-hit when I was young."

Mickey had the Cooperstown audience in stitches as well as tears. He repeated the slogan he had made up for the chicken at the Holiday Inn in Joplin; former umpire Jocko Conlan, one of the other four inductees, laughed so hard that Whitey sitting next to him was afraid he might be having a heart attack. Just minutes earlier, the seventy-five-year-old Conlan had grabbed Ford's arm and complained, "I'm getting pains in my chest." It turned out that Conlan's symptoms were from the heat that August day. Even DiMaggio, sitting with the other living members of the Hall of Fame on the veranda outside the library in Cooperstown, managed a smile at some of Mantle's remarks.

Whitey, who spoke ahead of Mantle, had been nervous for Mickey—and for good reason. Like most of the inductees over the years, Ford had prepared a speech and had fretted for days over what he would say. In his speech he had even dropped in a clever line: "This is a great week for the Fords"— Richard Nixon, culminating the long national drama over the Watergate scandal, had resigned four days earlier, and Gerald Ford had succeeded him as president. But on the night before the Hall of Fame induction, Whitey Ford had learned that Mickey not only hadn't yet written a speech but that he planned to speak off the cuff. While Whitey spent the night working on his speech, Mickey stayed up most of the evening playing pool and drinking beer with his four sons—Mickey Jr., Danny, David, and Billy—and with Whitey's son, Tommy.

After the ceremonies, photographers gathered Mantle and Ford to pose with their former manager, who had been elected to the Hall of Fame by the Veterans Committee in 1966. Stengel was eighty-four years old, and he would die the following year. "Casey never congratulated us for getting in the Hall of Fame," Ford later recalled. "He didn't have to. When photographers asked him to pose with Mickey and me with our plaques, you could just see by the look in his eyes how proud he was that we both got in. He would never say so because that just wasn't his way. But I could tell."

For Mickey, too, making the Hall of Fame was more than words could describe, except perhaps the words that always seemed to come out of him whenever he had reached a milestone: "I wish my dad could've been here to see this."

19

In 1982, Merlyn Mantle discovered what she believes to have been the first of a series of affairs Mickey had in the years after his retirement. In fact, Mickey had had numerous other affairs throughout his life, and it appears that Merlyn was aware at the time of at least some of them. Stories abound in almost every American League city of Mantle's flings at whatever hotels the Yankees happened to be staying during their road trips in the 1960s. In Kansas City, Mantle often stayed at the home of businessman Don Tanner, whom he had met through friends at the Brookridge Country Club in Overland Park, Kansas. Tanner was a witness to many of Mantle's sexual trysts during Yankee road trips to Kansas City and to a bizarre collection of provocative women's underwear that Mickey kept as trophies of those conquests.

"Merlyn was aware of it—had to be aware of it," recalled Tanner. "I remember once being at a dinner with a number of other people. Everyone had been drinking, maybe too much, including Mickey and Merlyn. And Merlyn finally blurted out at the dinner table, 'I'm just trying to figure out how many of the women at this table my husband has slept with?' Mickey got angry and said, 'Shut up! What are you going to do about it anyway? Go back to Commerce, Oklahoma?'"

Mantle made no secret of how much he missed baseball and his life in baseball. In Mickey's mind, the women and the drinking were parts of his baseball life he could take with him into retirement. As his body broke down, his ego still needed the sense of conquest that came from being with adoring women. Mickey found plenty of opportunities. His name and image survived the *Ball Four* tempest well enough to continue being attractive for engagements as a speaker and corporate public relations man, jobs that Mantle came to do quite well. As a speaker, he evolved into baseball's version of Will Rogers; colorful anecdotes about his career and about the game became his stock in trade, no matter how often he told the same stories. In many instances, Mantle had ready-made audiences of baby boomers who had grown up idolizing him. By now, many of them were in corporate positions that allowed them to hire their hero for appearances at company golf tournaments, banquets, and sales meetings. Mantle was even a special guest at a state dinner for the president of France during the Ford administration. Mickey's place-setting was next to President Ford, with whom he talked about golf the entire evening, while Merlyn was entertained by Vice President Nelson Rockefeller.

In the 1980s, Mickey Mantle began a comeback that would make him what *New York Times* sports writer William C. Rhoden would describe as "larger now, if not more popular than the nineteen-year-old kid who arrived in New York as the embodiment of springtime, the symbol of innocence not yet lost. . . . He has survived to become a national treasure." What was the reason for the comeback? "It may have been the bubble gum card craze," said Mantle. "I don't know why my rookie card was worth $12,500 and somebody else's $200 or $300. I just know I'm more popular now than I've ever been in my life. I'm very pleased. I love my life, and I'm really happy."

Another part of the reason may have been the wave of nostalgia—especially for the 1950s—that had swept the country; yet another might have been America's insatiable need for heroes. In 1981 balladeer Terry Cashman's "Talkin' Baseball" with lyrics immortalizing "Willie, Mickey and the Duke" had underscored the country's sentimental longing for the bygone era.

But undoubtedly, a major boost in Mantle's comeback was the world of sports memorabilia, which became a cottage industry at this time, boosted by the renewal of the trading card industry. Since 1951, Mickey's rookie season, the Topps Chewing Gum Company of Brooklyn had had the corner on the production of baseball trading cards. But on August 15, 1980, a federal court ruled that Topps's stranglehold on that market violated the nation's antitrust laws, effectively opening the way for the multimillion-dollar business that was about to emerge. As the trading card boom unfolded, Mantle's trading-card values steadily increased. Dealers also soon realized that Mantle's autograph alone could make ordinary photographs or bats instant collectibles that would fetch high prices.

It would be a while, however, before Mantle began realizing the fortune to be made in the memorabilia and autograph business. In 1983, to maintain a steady source of income, he signed on as a hundred-thousand-dollar-a-year "corporate greeter"—a promotions and public relations position—with the Claridge Hotel and Casino in Atlantic City. Willie Mays took a similar position at about the same time. Baseball has historically maintained a careful watch over any appearance of gambling in the game, as a result of the infamous 1919 scandal in which the Chicago White Sox threw the World Series to the Cincinnati Reds; eight members of the White Sox team, including the legendary Shoeless Joe Jackson, had been banned for life from the game. Mantle's and Mays's positions with Atlantic City hotels and casinos hardly appeared to approach the so-called Black Sox Scandal, and their presence in those establishments did not threaten the integrity of baseball. However, Commissioner Bowie Kuhn, who was nearing the end of his tumultuous fifteen-year tenure, chose a course of action that would forever make him a figure of scorn among most baseball fans. He banned both Mantle and Mays from baseball. Although its only real impact was to keep the two baseball greats away from spring training and Old Timers' Games, the ban infuriated fans who were only too ready to welcome Mantle and Mays back when Kuhn's successor, Peter Ueberroth, nullified the action less than two years later.

It was around this time that the final strands of Mickey and Merlyn's marriage began to unravel. Merlyn could not put up with the way Mickey shamelessly flaunted his latest affair, with a woman who traveled regularly with him as a secretary to card shows and to Atlantic City. Mantle loaned her his car, invited her to parties at his home, and even got two-bedroom hotel suites in which she was to use one of the bedrooms and Merlyn and Mickey the other. After that affair ended, Mickey was careless in keeping flings secret—affairs with girlfriends of millionaire high-rollers, the wife of a famous Nashville country singer, and finally a ten-year relationship with Greer Johnson, a former school teacher who became Mickey's personal manager.

In 1988, Mickey left Merlyn; the separation would last the rest of his life. He had been with Greer Johnson for the past three years, but he would never acknowledge publicly the relationship. He would openly admit to having "had relationships with many women, two or three that were important to me, that lasted a period of years." Publicly, he also said all the politically correct things about his broken marriage and his estrangement from his wife: he loved Merlyn and had never stopped loving her; she was the woman to whom he had given his last name; he would never divorce her unless she wanted a divorce; he felt tremendous guilt over the way he had treated her and their children and over the pain he had caused them. Mickey essentially shouldered all the blame for everything that had gone wrong in their marriage and relationship.

In fact, however, both Mickey and Merlyn would later blame the failure of their marriage and the dysfunctionality of their family on alcohol. At the time, however, as we have seen, Mickey was in denial about his alcoholism and personal problems, even in the third autobiography, written in 1985 with Herb Gluck. In it Mantle wrote: "I'll say this, in the last few years my drinking has been confined to social occasions. Merlyn has been highly successful in re-minding me if I forget. As a matter of fact, if it wasn't for her, I probably would have wound up an alcoholic like so many other ball players who did come to a tragic end that way." On another occasion, Mickey said, "It amazed me sometimes how much liquor I could hold."

When he began working with Mantle on their *All My Octobers* book, writer Mickey Herskowitz said he was advised by Kathy Hampton, the admin-istrator at Roy True's law firm, which handled Mantle's business dealings, that all their interviews should be done by eleven in the morning. Afternoons were blocked off for Mickey's golf game, and he would be completely unavailable at night. "There was a hint in this instruction that I missed," Herskowitz would later write in a tribute to Mantle. "I did not yet know about the seri-ousness of the drinking, the 'Breakfast of Champions' in the morning—Kah-lua, brandy, and cream—or the four to five glasses of wine for lunch, the vodka dinners." Herskowitz would recall watching Mickey drink but never actually seeing him drunk. "He was not an angry drinker, he did not turn phys-ical and start looking for an argument. His laugh got louder, his jokes cruder, but if he seemed anything, it was content—to stay put, whooping it up with his pals."

Throughout this period, Mantle was also having to deal with real life, beyond the booze and the women. In 1977 his son Billy, then nineteen years old, was diagnosed with Hodgkin's disease, the illness that had killed Mick-ey's father and several uncles years ago. It was the disease that Mantle always feared would eventually strike him down too at an early age. Instead, it had skipped him and attacked one of his children. Mantle was overwhelmed with guilt and helplessness as he watched Billy undergo radiation and chemo-therapy treatments, extensive hospital testing, spleen removal surgery, excru-ciatingly painful experimental drugs, remission, and more illness. Billy was also fighting addictions to prescription drugs and alcohol. All the Mantle sons, in fact, were having alcohol problems. Mickey blamed himself for turning them into what he called his "saloon buddies." Meanwhile, Merlyn had developed a serious drinking problem of her own. She blamed her alcoholism on trying to keep up with her husband, in an attempt to save their marriage. She wrote in *A Hero All His Life*, "I decided that if he needed someone who parked her butt on a barstool and drank with him all night, I could be that person. I started to travel with him more, but I knew I couldn't be a guard dog the rest of my life."

Amazingly, no one in the inner circle of Mickey's friends stepped forward to help him confront the drinking that had put his personal life into a downward spiral. Perhaps they expected the family members to initiate the process. Maybe too, the idea of admitting that one of America's heroes was drinking himself to death was impossible to acknowledge. Certainly the public incidents in which Mantle in effect cried out for help were clear and numerous. Once Mickey flew from Florida into Love Field at Dallas, drinking hard most of the way. Fortunately for Mantle, pro golfers Tony Lema and Jackie Cupit were on the same flight and saw that he needed help. It was a wet winter night, and the roads were dangerously slick with sleet. When Mickey refused their offers to drive him home, the golfers followed him in their car. They saw Mickey's car go out of control, go over a curb, and blow a tire. Lema and Cupit then drove him home and left the Mantle house only after Mickey promised not to go out in his condition to retrieve his car. The moment they left, Mickey hopped on the motorcycle the Yankees had given him on one of the Mickey Mantle Days, taking Mickey Jr. along. After Mickey Jr. put the spare tire on the car, Mantle got behind the wheel and drove home, his nervous son following on the motorcycle.

Another time, Mickey suffered an anxiety attack, in an incident that made the national news. On a flight home to Dallas, Mickey began to hyperventilate. Believing he was having a heart attack, Mantle asked a flight attendant to see if there was a doctor on the plane. The flight attendant immediately snapped an oxygen mask over Mickey's face, and the pilot radioed ahead to have paramedics meet the plane upon its arrival at Love Field. Mantle was taken away from the terminal in a stretcher. He later tried to make light of the incident by saying a fan had stuck a ball in his face and asked for his autograph despite his condition. Fortunately, Mickey had not had a heart attack, nor was there anything wrong with his heart; the problem was in fact related to Mickey's excessive drinking. In New York, some thirty years after tearing up a knee slipping on a Yankee Stadium drainage gutter, a drunken Mickey Mantle stepped out of a limousine and tripped and fell into a gutter outside the St. Moritz Hotel. A friend kneeled down to help; Mickey looked up with a crooked grin and cracked, "A helluva place for America's hero, ain't it?"

Meanwhile, Mantle was becoming the premier name in the sports memorabilia industry. He was traveling to card shows and memorabilia conventions all over the country; sometimes he was paid as much as fifty thousand dollars per weekend just to sign his autograph. The travel only intensified his drinking. For a while, his sons Danny and David helped him, including the grueling task of traveling and drinking with their father. For a while, the boys even opened a memorabilia shop, which was more of a family tavern. "We didn't take that too serious," recalled Danny Mantle. "I look back and it wasn't funny at all, but we were in the middle of the disease [alcoholism] and didn't care. It was sad, but dad would say, 'Close down, we're leaving,' and we couldn't say no." Eventually, burned out and with drinking problems of their own, the boys left the job of taking care of their father on the road to a series of hangers-on and friends. Among the most faithful of those was former stock broker Tom Catal, who in 1978 had organized one of Mantle's first autograph-signing shows and to whom Mantle gave many of the items he received on Mickey Mantle Days—items that became the backbone of the Mickey Mantle Museum, up the street from the Baseball Hall of Fame in Cooperstown.

It was through the card-show business that Mantle developed his relationship with the woman for whom he ultimately left Merlyn. Greer Johnson was a divorced, thirty-four-year-old elementary teacher from Georgia when she met Mantle in 1983 while on a date with a high-roller at the Claridge Hotel, where Mickey's job was to entertain such guests. Mantle not only fell in love with her but also convinced her to become a celebrity agent for himself and a number of other former Yankee teammates. Johnson gave up her teaching career and began traveling around the country with Mantle, learning the memorabilia business and watching over Mickey's business interests and his drinking.

"When I met Mick I knew he drank," Johnson recalled, "and it seemed like it got progressively worse. At first I didn't realize there was a problem. Finally, I did realize it, so I'd talk to him. I tried to have an intervention with him, and he would balk at that. We would go out and, first of all, if we were at places where I knew the bartenders, I'd talk to them and tell them to make his drinks real light. Then he got wise to that. So I came up with a way of mixing a drink that he thought was a great drink. I'd fill the glass with ice, then three-fourths was a chaser, then just a splash of alcohol, whatever it was, right on top, and when he took a drink that's what he tasted—the alcohol—so he thought it was a great drink. I played all kinds of mind games with him. I'd fake headaches, tell him I needed to go home. Sometimes it worked, and sometimes I'd get so upset and angry with him, I'd just walk out and leave him. Usually that would make him go home, too."

The year that Greer met Mickey would be one of the most difficult ones for Mantle. It was a year when Mickey again came face to face with his mortality, this time through the teammate who had come to be associated with him in the chase of Babe Ruth—Roger Maris. On December 14, 1985, at the age of fifty-one, Maris died of lymphatic cancer. According to Bob Costas, Mantle was broken up by Maris's death: "Roger was a better person than me . . . a better family man than me. If anyone went early, I should have been the guy."

"The only time I saw Mickey get physically sick was the day he learned that Roger had been admitted to the hospital again," recalled Greer Johnson. "Mickey knew that his condition must have worsened, and it upset him tremendously. He got so sick that I had to put him to bed that night—and we learned the next morning that Roger had died that night."

Mantle's separation from Merlyn, though it was he who walked out, worsened his drinking problem: "As my drinking increased, after my separation from Merlyn, I would get paranoid." As Mickey Herskowitz recalled, "Almost no one outside his inner circle knew that he and Merlyn lived apart for their last seven years, not even in Dallas, where he sometimes had more privacy than he really wanted." When he moved out, Mickey began living in an apartment in Dallas and at the Regency Hotel in New York. Later he built a house in Dallas, which he shared with son Danny and Danny's fiancée, Kay Kollars. Outside the Mantle household in Dallas, however, the Mickey Mantle public persona took on a life of its own. It was said that while Mantle lived his personal life in Dallas, he parked his image in New York. In 1987, Mickey lent his name to a restaurant on Central Park South. Developed by two businessmen and Mantle fans, Bill Liederman and John Lowry, it eventually became part of the Mantle legacy in Manhattan. Its immediate success in the late 1980s typified the magic that had come to surround Mickey's name.

For many, Mantle had come to embody the game as it once had been but no longer was. Indeed, successful baby-boomers with money to spend on memorabilia had created the demand. The original painting of Mantle that was used for his 1953 Topps baseball card sold for $110,000 at auction. A rare Mantle rookie card in perfect condition would sell for a hundred thousand dollars. One of the country's top memorabilia promoters, Alan Rosen, even paid Mickey $150,000 for a three-day reunion of the 1961 Yankees at Trump Castle in Atlantic City. But there was more, too. Fans had grown weary of the greed that began overrunning the sport in the 1980s, especially the perception that free agency was turning team rosters into a game of musical chairs while creating a runaway salary structure that isolated players from the average person. Mantle, however, continued to be in high demand. The aging star had also mellowed considerably from his younger days, knowing that his good image had become an extremely valuable commodity. For instance, whenever he traveled, Mickey made sure to have baseball cards of himself already signed and ready to distribute to adoring fans just in case he was in a hurry to make a flight.

Mantle's biggest deal in the memorabilia industry would cement his reputation as king of the "hobby" business, as it came to be known in the trade. Upper Deck, which in 1989 began revolutionizing the appearance of baseball cards and was moving quickly to establish itself as the leader in the collectibles market, signed Mantle to an exclusive multimillion-dollar deal that would guarantee the authenticity of Mickey's signature on its memorabilia while securing his own financial future. At the time, the Internal Revenue Service had begun cracking down on the largely cash market of the memorabilia industry. Pete Rose would eventually be sentenced to five months in a minimum-security federal prison for tax evasion related in part to card-show earnings. Duke Snider and Darryl Strawberry were also among the former and active players who had legal problems stemming from memorabilia earnings. One card-show promoter, William Hongach, indicted for tax evasion, claimed that in 1989 he had paid several players in cash after one show, including a box with twenty-seven thousand dollars that went to Mantle. Mickey's attorney's denied the allegation, insisting that Mantle had declared all his income. Mantle never became the target of any investigation from the card-show business; Greer Johnson and Mickey's lawyers became even more diligent in watching his business dealings.

"We became the first to get his deals in writing," said Johnson. "It had been a business that had been very casual, but common sense told me that Mickey needed to treat it as a serious business because Mickey had never had a very good business head. Money didn't mean that much to him. But when I got involved in helping him [with his business], I made sure we were keeping good records. I found that in business, so much of it was just using good common sense about what you do."

Meanwhile, Mantle's drinking continued unabated. Not even Billy Martin's death appeared to diminish Mickey's obsession with the bottle. Martin was killed on Christmas Day 1989 when his pickup truck skidded off a snowy road. Although there was some question over whether Martin was behind the wheel, there was no doubt that he had been drinking. One year after Mantle had been the best man at Billy's fourth marriage, he was a pallbearer at his funeral. Mantle was deeply saddened by Martin's unexpected death, but the two had drifted apart and didn't talk for months on end during the final year of Billy's life. But Mantle had also become distant with many of his former teammates. Whitey Ford and Mantle were business partners for several years in a fantasy baseball camp, but otherwise Mickey's ties to his old teammates were limited to rendezvous at Yankee spring training and Old Timers' Days at Yankee Stadium. Promoter Alan Rosen claimed that Mantle had been late to the 1961 Yankee reunion for which he was paid $150,000—and that he had steadfastly refused to sign a bat for Moose Skowron, even though all the other Yankees from that team had autographed it.

Mantle's drinking, of course, was the principal reason for his crude and sometimes profanity-laced behavior. It was also slowly destroying his memory. He was surprisingly clear, however, about stories and anecdotes, possibly from the endless retelling of them and from watching films of himself playing, and from hearing accounts from others. But Mickey painfully confessed in several interviews during this time that the actual memories themselves were gone. He told one interviewer, "When I see, even as late as 1968, but all the way back to 1951 when I was really young, I can be watching these things and I keep thinking, you know, that I can't really hardly remember playing. It's like it's somebody else. At home in my trophy room, we have a den that we call a trophy room that's got all the Most Valuable Player [awards] and the silver bats and pictures all over the walls and everything. It's like it's somebody else. I mean, it's not like it's me, you know. I can hardly remember it."

Mickey Mantle couldn't remember why he was America's hero. He felt anything but heroic, especially in retirement, living day to day with a family that was, in many ways, a set of strangers. "I don't think I was a very good father," he would ultimately admit. "I was never there." He tried to make up for it. He helped Mickey Jr., probably the best ballplayer of Mantle's sons, get a minor league contract with the Yankees. Mickey Jr. was not his father, and called it quits after a few months. A part of Mickey, however, had not wanted to place the same expectation on his sons that his own father had placed on him. He expressed regret over naming his oldest son "Mickey Jr." for that very reason. Both he and Merlyn had been upset by an incident that occurred on a plane flight when fellow passenger asked young Mickey Jr. what his name was. "Mickey Mantle," little Mickey had answered. "Isn't he cute? He thinks he's Mickey Mantle," the passenger laughed. Mickey Jr. burst into tears. In 1962, Mickey Jr. and David had small roles in the Mantle-Maris film *Safe at Home;* the director had been impressed with David and offered to give him the name of an agent. "No, thanks," Mantle said, scuttling the idea. "One star in the family is enough." Mickey knew all too well the personal demands and expectations of being a star, and he wanted to protect his loved ones from what he had been through. In retirement, Mantle and his sons continued to reach out to each other, even to the exclusion of their mother. They were aware of Mickey's infidelities and, of course, of his relationship with Greer Johnson. They wanted to protect their mother, but Danny Mantle later said they also feared losing the relationship they had always longed for with their father.

Meanwhile, Mickey was being torn apart emotionally by the two women in his life, and by the schism between the public image of his marriage and the private reality that it was failing. His public devotion to Merlyn was extraordinary in light of their tumultuous history, Mickey's own cheating past, and the fact that he was living with a woman who considered herself the second Mrs. Mickey Mantle. "I've been asked what it felt like to be the other woman," said Greer Johnson, "and the truth is that I've never felt like the 'other woman' because I've felt like I've been *the* woman in Mickey's life." Yet Mickey publicly maintained that he would never marry anyone else, that he was married for life to Merlyn—who understandably was not happy with the arrangement forced upon her. "There were times I could have killed him," she said. "If I could have wished anything, I would have wished him to be hit by a big Mac truck." Instead of killing Mickey, Merlyn might have come close to killing herself. In 1985, as she dealt with the knowledge of Mantle's affairs, she had a mild stroke that she later said was stress related.

Mickey had plunged headlong into depression over a life over which he seemed to have lost control, a family that he feared he continued to disappoint, and unceasing pain from degenerative arthritis in his legs, a pain that served as a constant reminder of a career of which otherwise he could remember little. The panic-attack disorder that he had experienced at times throughout his career was now magnified by the worsening drinking, which was affecting his overall health. He was suffering panic attacks with more frequency and insisted on having someone with him, especially when he traveled. Mickey was also having dreams—recurring nightmares, actually. In one dream, he was still playing baseball; he had arrived at Yankee Stadium for a game that was about to begin but could not get inside. In another dream, he had died, and the epitaph on his tombstone read, "Mickey Mantle—Banned from Baseball." Mickey would awaken in a cold sweat and blame the nightmares on the alcohol and his stomach problems. Mantle had been diagnosed with a stomach disorder and an ulcer, which the drinking exacerbated. There were moments when depression gave way to despair and thoughts of suicide. "At times," Mickey later admitted, "I thought about killing myself."

"I think Mick was always plagued by a sense that he did not have enough strength of character," said broadcaster Bob Costas, who from his youth had carried a 1958 Mantle baseball card in his wallet and who later befriended his boyhood hero. "But even so, for ten years or more, without the press ever paying attention—you know, it wasn't like he saw the light only in the year before he died—he was out there preaching to kids to stay away from alcohol and not use him as a role model. He did a video in the late '80s where he made that a special point. He and I also did a video together called the 500 Home Run Club, and he went out of his way to say it again. . . .

"I think the low moments became lower and lower and worse and worse, and I think what was torturing him all along was that he understood what he should be and what he was."

What Mantle thought himself to be was a hell-bound sinner, even though religion had not played any role in his life. He would joke about a dream in which he died and went to heaven, where he was met at the gates by St. Peter, who would say to him, "Mick, we can't let you in on account of the kind of life you've lived down on earth. But before you go to that other place, God wanted to know if you'd sign these two dozen balls for him."

Growing up in the heart of the Bible Belt, as Mantle did in Oklahoma, can have strange effects on people. Religion was ingrained in the social fabric of the community in which Mantle grew up. All of Mantle's childhood friends belonged to God-fearing, churchgoing families. Merlyn herself had been raised in a heavily religious environment. Both her grandfather and her father were deacons in the Baptist Church. Mutt Mantle, however, believed in base-ball and little else, a value system that seemed to work well for him at the time. When he arrived in New York at the age of nineteen, Mantle not only was a country bumpkin but a youth unprepared for the personal challenges and temptations in the world he had been set to conquer. Just as nothing had prepared him for New York, little had been done to develop in Mickey any sense of personal moral values and social responsibility, beyond what was right or wrong in his father's judgment. For Mantle, then, the death of his father in 1952 was also the death, in a sense, of the moral and ethical force holding him in check. He had no other value system than his father. Thus, finally, a little more than forty years after Mutt's death, Mickey found himself floundering in a crisis of booze and a broken family, reluctantly and angrily seeking redemp-tion and at last crying out for help from a higher force.

The turning point came in two separate incidents. In September 1993, Mickey and Danny flew to Los Angeles for an autograph-signing date for Upper Deck. While there, Danny disappeared from Mickey's side and couldn't be located. Seeking help for his own addiction, Danny had checked himself into the Betty Ford Center in Rancho Mirage, California, where he was even-tually joined in rehabilitation by his wife Kay. Mickey was furious with Danny and refused to attend the designated "family week" at the center. Mantle would not acknowledge his own role in his son's problems.

"For all those years, I'd make [Danny] go to lunch and dinner with me," Mantle would say after his own visit to the Better Ford Center. "I'd get Mickey Jr., and my next oldest son, David, to go too. I'd say, 'Hey, what are you guys doing tonight? Let's go eat.' Which would mean, 'Let's go drink.' They all drank too much because of me. We don't have normal father-son relationships. When they were growing up, I was playing baseball and after I retired, I was too busy traveling around being Mickey Mantle. We never played catch in the backyard. But when they were old enough to drink, we became drinking buddies. When we were together, it kind of felt like the old days with Billy and Whitey. I had no idea that I was making my kids drink like that."

Meanwhile, in Los Angeles that September, Mantle's condition was ob-vious to officials of the Upper Deck Company. Mickey's speech was slurred, and he spent much of his time at the event drunk. A few weeks later, Mantle hit perhaps an all-time low at a charity golf tournament for the Harbor Club Children's Christmas Fund near Atlanta. After drinking all day, he made a public spectacle of himself in a drunken display of vulgarity at the event's dinner finale. From his dinner table, as if to leave no doubt of the antihero he could be, Mantle referred to the Reverend Wayne Monroe, who was in charge of the charity tournament, as "that fucking preacher."

The next day, after learning how he had behaved and what he had said, Mantle was "absolutely horrified"—although this had been a pattern for the past ten years of his life. At first, Mantle had thought the stories of past behavior were exaggerated. Slowly, however, he became troubled. "The stories bugged the hell out of me," he said. "That wasn't like me. I wasn't that guy they were talking about. . . . I'm sure over the years, people have put up with a lot from me because I was Mickey Mantle. But after this episode, I couldn't believe I'd been so disrespectful. When I got back to Dallas, I approached Danny about the Betty Ford Center."

20

In late December 1993, Mickey made plans to have a knee-replacement operation on his left leg, and possibly on his right one as well. Those plans were quickly and suddenly postponed after one of Mickey's daily rounds of golf just before Christmas. At the Preston Trail Golf Club, with an exclusive membership of Dallas's elite, Mantle was often surrounded by playing partners who were among the best doctors in Texas. They knew Mickey as a fun-loving guy who sometimes gave them some unexpected awkward moments. Mickey, for instance, had a tendency to walk into the club's restaurant to order a drink completely naked. Mantle had also on occasion shocked members of a nearby country club by going skinny-dipping in the club's pool. At Preston Trail, the members committee finally instituted "The Mickey Mantle Rule," prohibiting anyone from entering or lounging in the club's restaurant in the nude. Otherwise, Mickey was one of the most popular members. He often would solicit free advice from the doctors he played with, such as when he worried that he was losing his memory. "I'd forget what day it was, what month it was, what city I was in," Mantle recalled. "The loss of memory really scared me. I told a couple of the doctors I play golf with at Preston Trail Golf Club . . . that I thought I had Alzheimer's disease, and they said, 'Well you're probably not there yet.'. . . I was scared that alcohol had changed my brain.'

A doctor who happened to be one of Mickey's golf partners at Preston Trail that December day in 1993 saw in Mantle's bloodshot eyes and jaundiced-looking skin something that worried him. The next day Mickey had a complete physical examination; the results alarmed his doctor. Mantle's red-blood-cell count was at a dangerously low level, and preliminary tests showed that he had done serious damage to his liver. The doctor was concerned enough to order a magnetic resonance imaging (MRI) scan, which would allow a thorough assessment of the condition of Mickey's liver. The experience would prove cathartic, as Mantle would later explain to Jill Lieber of *Sports Illustrated:*

"For an hour and fifteen minutes, I lay in that MRI tube, and I thought, 'What am I doing here? This must really be serious.' It was hard to keep from crying, thinking about the bad shape I was in, how I had abused myself with alcohol for forty-two years, all the people I'd let down. I was worried that fans would remember Mickey Mantle as a drunk rather than for my baseball accomplishments. I had always thought I could quit drinking by myself, and I'd do it for several days or a couple of weeks, but when I got to feeling good again, I'd go back to getting loaded. I was physically and emotionally worn out from all the drinking. I'd hit rock bottom."

The next day, Mantle's doctor called him into his office. "Mickey, your liver is still working," the doctor said, "but it has healed itself so many times that before long, you're just going to have one big scab there. Eventually you'll need a new liver. Look, I'm not going to lie to you. The next drink might be your last."

Mickey Mantle finally realized that what he was doing amounted to the suicide he had occasionally thought about. He was killing himself. He knew he needed help, or he would die.

In a mild panic, Mickey called upon Roy True and asked for help with checking into the Betty Ford Center in Palm Springs. At the same time, Mickey sought out Danny and Kay, as well as Pat Summerall, a broadcaster and former professional football player whom Mickey had known from their playing days in New York. Like Danny and Kay, Summerall had had a drinking problem; he had finally conquered it at the Betty Ford Center. Mickey wanted to know how the program at Betty Ford worked, and he got an earful. Mickey cringed at having to share his story with complete strangers, who would also be getting help at Betty Ford. The answers were not quite what Mickey wanted to hear, and he feared he had more reasons for not going through with his plans than for getting the help he so desperately needed.

Still, three days after Christmas, Mickey checked into the Betty Ford Center, where he was assigned room 202. In the 1980s, the Betty Ford Center had become the highest-profile substance-addiction rehabilitation program in the country, largely because of its clientele of Hollywood stars and celebrities. The treatment program at Betty Ford is based on the Alcoholics Anonymous approach, with its fabled twelve-step program. It involves regular meetings in which the people are forced to confront their problems by talking openly about them. For Mickey, it was thirty-two days of talking tearfully about his failure as a father and husband, his drinking addiction, and his behavior while drunk, his bouts with depression and thoughts of suicide.

"I don't think I was ever really nervous on a baseball field, in any league, in any situation," Mickey would write in his portion of the family confessional, *A Hero All His Life*. "But I thought I might pass out the first time I stood up in a meeting at the Betty Ford Center and said, 'I'm Mick and I'm an alcoholic.'"

In an interview several months after his Betty Ford Center stay, Mantle elaborated: "It took me a couple of times before I could talk without crying. You're supposed to say why you're there, and I said because I had a bad liver and I was depressed. Whenever I tried to talk about my family, I got all choked up. One of the things I really screwed up, besides baseball, was being a father. I wasn't a good family man. I was always out, running around with the guys. Mickey Jr. could have been a helluva athlete. If he'd had *my* dad, he could have been a major league baseball player. My kids have never blamed me for not being there. They don't have to. I blame myself."

Finally, at age sixty-two, Mantle was also being forced to confront his unfinished relationship with his father. In his preadmission interview at Betty Ford, Mickey had told his counselor that "I drank because of depression that came from feeling I'd never fulfilled my father's dreams." Days later, Mantle had the most important breakthrough of his rehabilitation stay. "I had to write my father a letter and tell him how I felt about him," said Mickey. "You talk about sad. It took me ten minutes to write the letter, and I cried the whole time. But after it was over, I felt better. I said I missed him, and I wish he could have lived to see that I did a lot better after my rookie season with the Yankees. I told him I had four boys—he died before my first son, Mickey Jr., was born—and I told him that I loved him. I wish I could have told him that when he was still alive."

Family and friends wondered about the contents of his letter to his father, but Mickey insisted on not sharing it with anyone else. "He wouldn't tell me what it said because he said it would have embarrassed him," said Marshall Smith. "I asked him if he still had the letter. He said he took it out and burned it. He didn't want anybody to see what he wrote."

Mickey later told *Sports Illustrated,* "Dad would be proud of me today, knowing that I've completed treatment at Betty Ford and have been sober for three months. But he would have been mad that I had to go there in the first place. He would have forgiven me, but it would have been hard to look him in the eye and say, 'Dad, I'm an alcoholic.' I don't think I could have done it. I would feel like I'd let him down. I don't know how you get over that. I can't hit a home run for him anymore."

Suddenly sober, Mantle's guilt about how he had neglected his family intensified. He felt so guilty that he chose not to have them come visit him during family week. He spent that time instead with Greer Johnson. Toward the end of his stay, Mickey called Summerall and said to him, "Pat, if you ever see me start to take a drink, I want you to promise to put a bullet in my head." Moved, Summerall told Mantle he could not promise that—and urged him to turn to a higher power.

Mickey would soon have his own inner strength and ability to maintain his sobriety. In March, only just weeks after Mantle left the Betty Ford Center, his son Billy died of a heart attack, at age thirty-six. Billy had complicated his fight with Hodgkin's disease with drug and alcohol problems. He had been in addiction rehab treatment four times in four years, and he had undergone heart-bypass surgery in 1993. Danny Mantle brought the news to his father at the locker room at Preston Trail, where Mickey had just finished his daily round of golf. "We were worried that the news might send him back [to drinking]," said Danny.

Mantle, however, was finally ready to be the head of his family. He insisted on being the one to break the news to Merlyn, knowing that of all the family members she had been the closest to Billy. Mickey called it "the most agonizing thing I've ever had to do." Merlyn had herself checked into a rehab center in Wilmer, Texas, and had to deal with news of her son's death while she was struggling to regain control of her own life. Mickey, meanwhile, maintained his sobriety through the loss of his son and through the death of his mother a year later. If his son's premature death hadn't driven him to drink again, he knew, nothing would.

Mickey now was determined to rededicate himself to his family, to his fans, to his image and reputation, and to baseball. In perhaps the most moving interview of his life, Mantle discussed his career and his addiction on national television with Bob Costas. Few watching the interview could have been untouched by the sight of tears streaming down Mickey's cheeks as he talked about his life. Costas may have been one of the few who had seen behind the Mantle facade a man who was never really at peace with himself. He brought it up.

"I've always had the sense that there was a sadness about you," Costas said "Was that true?"

"Yeah," Mantle answered wistfully. "I think that when I did drink a little too much or something, it kind of relieved the tension that I felt within myself maybe because I hadn't been what I should have been."

"Because you hadn't been the ballplayer you thought you should have been?"

"Or the daddy."

"Did you ever say to yourself, 'Wait a minute. I'm one of the best ball-players of all time. I've made a significant amount of change doing this. I'm financially secure. People seem to love me. Why don't I feel better?'"

"Maybe I do, in the back of my mind, feel like I've let everybody down some way or other. I know there is something in there that's not fulfilled or something. I don't know what it is. . . . I can't explain it."

Mantle's emotional confession strengthened the loyalty of his fans and connected him with a new following. He was, if the imperfect man, indeed the perfect hero for a nation now accustomed to forgiving the contrite and welcoming back the repentant. Once the crude and carousing embodiment of the American Dream, Mickey Mantle had grown up to become America's prodigal son.

Mantle could even joke about it. "If I had known I was gonna live this long," he said, "I would have taken better care of myself."

Not everyone, however, was as understanding or perhaps as convinced that there was a new Mick in Mantle. The Upper Deck Company had had its fill of the old Mick, whom company officials had been forced to deal with and apologize for at signings and shows. The company was also concerned about its own image in what had developed into a highly competitive industry. Also, if the interview with Costas had portrayed Mantle sympathetically, the *Sports Illustrated* story "My Life as an Alcoholic" did not. In it, and in his own words, Mantle had painted a dark self-portrait that made him look tragic at best and, at worst, like an abusive father who had made alcoholics of his sons. Upper Deck moved to distance itself from Mantle by scaling back his contract and his association with the company. In November 1994, Mickey filed a multimillion-dollar lawsuit, claiming the trading-card maker would not ful-fill its contract with him because of his alcohol problems. Mantle alleged that

Upper Deck said it wanted out of its 1992 contract with him unless he agreed to take a pay cut. According to the lawsuit, the company said Mickey's public admission earlier that year had diminished his marketability. Roy True argued that Mickey had made several contractual concessions to help Upper Deck with cash-flow problems. "Mickey is hurt and disappointed that Upper Deck would attempt to stoop to this level in order to deprive him of the money guaranteed him," True said in an interview at that time. Upper Deck blamed Mickey for creating the problem, saying in a statement: "The discussions regarding restructuring Mr. Mantle's contract were the product of his disability and other performance-related concerns. In short, Mr. Mantle has failed to live up to his commitments as effective spokesperson for the company."

In 1998, Mantle's estate received $4.9 million from an arbitration panel, which ruled that Upper Deck had breached its contract with Mickey. The following year, the estate signed a new deal with Upper Deck to produce Mickey Mantle cards. True said that even before the Upper Deck arbitration award, the Mantle estate "had amassed substantially more millions."

But contrary to Upper Deck's fears, Mantle's marketability remained as strong as ever in the early 1990s. He was still the top draw in the memorabilia industry, and his demand among show promoters increased after his Betty Ford stay. Mickey was also enjoying his life as never before. He marveled at his own new sense of the world around him and at his physical condition. He had dropped ten pounds while at Betty Ford and had managed to keep it off. Mantle's outlook remained positive, and for the first time in his life he felt a spiritual awakening. He began a series of conversations with Summerall about his religious beliefs, especially baptism. "They do something with water, don't they?" said Mickey. "Well, you know, I can't even swim." But Mickey, who had never been baptized, decided it was time.

Mantle had also mapped out a set of personal goals. He had promised Joe DiMaggio, now a broadcaster, to assist him with the Baseball Assistance Team, known as BAT, to help old ballplayers with their problems. He wanted to campaign among young people against alcohol and drug abuse. "It used to be said that I was a role model," Mantle recalled, "and kids, even older guys looked up to me. Maybe I can truly be a role model now—because I admitted I had a problem, got treatment, and am staying sober—and maybe I can help more people than I ever helped when I was a famous ballplayer. I feel more important as Mickey Mantle now than I did when I was playing for the Yankees." Finally, he had dedicated himself to starting the Mickey Mantle Foundation, in memory of his late son Billy.

However, Mickey's concerns for his family were far from over. Lovell Mantle, who was suffering from Alzheimer's disease, had been placed in a nursing home in Jay, Oklahoma, where Mickey often visited. "It was so warm to watch him with his mama," recalled Marshall Smith. "Every time he'd leave, he'd seem so sad. He thought it was too bad she was still living because of her state of mind. He would always talk about that death doctor, Dr. Jack Kevorkian, who assists terminally ill patients with suicide. Mickey always thought that was right, the right thing to do. He couldn't stand to see his mother like that. She'd remember me as 'the golfer,' but half the time she didn't remember him. When you're that sick and you don't remember things, that's sad to see. But when she did recognize Mickey, she'd perk up. Late in her life, Mickey would say, 'I just wish she'd go ahead and die. It's too painful to deal with.' Mickey never wanted to go to the nursing home alone. Someone, either me or [my wife] Corinne, always went with him." Mickey's mom died on March 19, 1995, at the age of ninety-two.

In the spring of 1995, Mickey began suffering from stomach pains. He thought they were acid indigestion. He had always had a high tolerance for pain and was not alarmed at first. But on May 28, a Sunday, Mickey was admitted to the Baylor University Medical Center for tests. Although his stomach pains had worsened, Mantle at first had hesitated about going to the hospital, because he didn't want to disrupt plans that Merlyn had made with Danny and his wife Kay. The Mantles' daughter-in-law was pregnant, and she and Danny had invited Merlyn on a trip to visit Kay's parents. Merlyn might not have gone except that Danny and Kay, aware of her long-standing fear of flying, had decided to make the trip by car. As soon as Mickey knew that they were on the road, he had David drive him to the hospital for what he believed would be only a couple of days of tests. Nine days later, however, Mickey was still in the hospital, feeling worse than when he had been admitted. The tests confirmed that he was as sick as he felt. That day, with his lawyer and friend Roy True in the room, Dr. Daniel DeMarco, Mickey's gastroenterologist, and other specialists from the center informed Mickey that his liver was beyond healing. The tests, they told him, had revealed that he had cirrhosis, hepatitis C, and cancer of the liver. The hepatitis, which was dormant, probably stemmed from a blood transfusion during one of the operations during his baseball career. The immediate threat to his life was the cancer, and only a liver transplant would save his life. When the doctors left the room, Mickey turned to his lawyer.

"Well," Mickey said, "it looks like I've really done it *this* time."

That night David telephoned Danny in South Dakota. The next day, Danny, Kay, and Merlyn were on a flight back to Dallas. Merlyn's acrophobia was the least of her concerns. News of Mickey's illness had become public, but not its severity. Having seen the public interest and furor over the revelation of his Betty Ford Center stay a year earlier, Mickey didn't want a repeat of the pity and sympathy that he knew would pour out if it were disclosed he had cancer. So the first reports that came out of Baylor Medical Center suggested that he would be released in a day or so and downplayed any seriousness in his condition. In fact, however, the tumor was blocking the bile duct, leaving his stomach swollen from bacteria and pus. Mickey was badly jaundiced, and the liver failure had shut down his kidneys. A week later, doctors finally announced that Mickey had liver cancer and needed a transplant to live. Out of respect for his privacy, Mickey's doctors still did not reveal how close Mickey already was to death—he was sinking into a coma and might not live another forty-eight hours without a new liver. Ironically, the family's reluctance to disclose fully the gravity of Mickey's condition was probably responsible for the public outcry that would erupt over how quickly he received the transplant.

There was also a measure of concern over whether giving a liver to an old alcoholic was appropriate. Nationally, the average wait for a new liver is 130 days. In Texas, however, the waiting period is 3.3 days for someone in the condition Mickey was in. Given that 804 patients died in 1995 while awaiting a liver transplant, Mantle's case raised justifiable questions about which of the 7,400 liver patients on the waiting list should have received the 3,900 livers that became available that year.

Mickey received his new liver on June 8, the second day after being placed on the transplant waiting list. Until the surgery, none of the tests had shown any indication that the cancer had spread beyond the liver. Even the early probing during the surgery failed to show any signs of new cancer cells. It was not until Mickey's diseased liver was removed that surgeons discovered microscopic evidence of new cancer cells in the blood vessels around the bile duct. It was an unfavorable sign in an operation that otherwise was a success, and it was not a topic the doctors immediately discussed.

Nor were they given much chance. At the news conference following the surgery, reporters appeared outraged at the suddenness with which Mickey received the new liver, and they challenged the doctors as to whether Mantle had received preferential treatment for being a celebrity and a sports hero. Deciding what is fair and who should be first in line for organ transplants is especially troubling and difficult. Dr. Mark Siegler, who directs the University of Chicago clinical ethics program, has stated that "all alcoholics should go to the bottom of the transplant list . . . yet Dr. Siegler [also] said he would exempt Mickey Mantle from his rule because the baseball legend is 'a real American hero'. . . [We] have got to take them with all their warts and failures and treat them differently."

Dr. Goran Klintmalm, the head of the Baylor Transplant Institute, later would say that Mickey probably would have died had he not received the new liver when he did. "Mick was extraordinarily sick," said Klintmalm. "He was the only one here in North Texas waiting for a liver who was that sick. The donor liver was the right blood group. You cannot ethically deny a patient what may be the only chance he has. You don't know if or when you will get another one. So obviously we did the transplant."

Almost immediately after the transplant operation, the Mantle family and the hospital were deluged with calls and telegrams wishing Mickey a speedy recovery. Months later, the United Network for Organ Sharing issued a report on Mickey's case and concluded that he had been fairly given a liver transplant and that no selection procedures had been waived in his favor. Only when he was released from the hospital on June 28, a month after being admitted, did Mickey fully understand the accusations of favoritism in his liver transplant. He may have argued his own defense best. "People think I got that liver because of who I am," he said in an interview, "but they have rules they go by. They told me I had one day to live. If I hadn't got this one, I wouldn't have made it."

Mantle's sense of humor had been unaffected. At a press conference a month after the transplant, Mantle spotted collector Barry Halper and said, "Hey Barry, want to buy my liver?" Halper declined. He told Mickey he was just there to see how he was doing. Mantle and Halper had become friends over the years, and Mickey had been a visitor to his home, where Halper had showed him a collection that would be sold for close to twenty-two million dollars in 1999. Later, when Halper spoke to Mantle's doctor, he was offered Mantle's liver again. Halper again declined. After some prodding from the doctor to take something for his collection, Halper asked for the scalpel used to operate on Mickey. The doctor no longer had the scalpel, but said he would come up with something. Halper left his business card and Federal Express account number, and a week later a package arrived at Halper's house. Inside was a pair of stained surgical gloves. "Mickey had complained of hemorrhoids in the last week of his life," recalled Halper. After a doctor examined him, Mantle insisted that the gloves be sent to Halper. "I didn't ask him for that," said Halper. "But he sent it to me." Halper did not include the gloves in the auction of his collection but kept them, along with a statement of authenticity from the doctor and the Federal Express label. "I keep it in the garage because my wife said, 'If you even think of bringing that in the house. . . .'"

Unfortunately, medical complications began almost as soon as Mickey received the new liver. He had immediately been placed on drugs to keep his body from rejecting the new liver, as well as on chemotherapy to fight the cancer. Unfortunately, the antirejection medication made his body more sus-ceptible to cancer cell growth. Even after his release, Mickey had to return regularly to Baylor Medical Center for a series of chemotherapy treatments and blood transfusions. The chemotherapy made Mickey anemic, and his weight quickly dropped almost forty pounds from the 208 pounds he had weighed when admitted. The weight loss made him look old. Compared to the strong figure he had cut in the nationally televised interview with Bob Costas in early 1994, Mickey now looked skeletal. His condition was never more evident than at a press conference he gave three days after his trans-plant operation; Mickey looked gaunt and weak. Even an adjustable com-memorative baseball cap from the All-Star Game, played at nearby Arlington that month, looked several sizes too big for him. It may have been the ulti-mate insult to the heroic image of Mickey. But Mickey had never been more alive or more eloquent.

"I owe so much to God and to the American people," he told reporters. "I'm going to spend the rest of my life trying to make it up. It seems to me like all I've done is take. Have fun and take. I'm going to start giving some-thing back. I'd like to say to kids out there, if you're looking for a role model, this is a role model." Mickey pointed at his chest with his thumb. "Don't be like me. God gave me a body and an ability to play baseball. God gave me everything, and I just . . . pfffttt!" He had kissed off his talents, as he had much of his life.

"It's dangerous to make cardboard figures out of people," Bob Costas would later say in assessing Mantle's life. "You're always going to be wrong.

He was neither entirely this or entirely that. But there's always the possibility for redemption. There's always the possibility that the better angels of your nature will take over in the end."

There was a fragility to Mantle that had never been seen before. He appeared to be dying even as he talked enthusiastically about promoting, in unprecedented fashion, an organ-donor campaign within the Mickey Mantle Foundation. Yet, perhaps overcompensating for their fears, both Mickey and those around him exuded a sense of confidence about his condition. Once out of the hospital, Mantle and Greer Johnson moved into Pat Summerall's house, which he generously loaned to them for as long as they needed. Summerall's home also served as a hideaway from reporters and the incessant phone calls, although Ted Williams and Harmon Killebrew managed to get through with calls wishing Mickey well. Johnson would later say that she had been unaware of the true seriousness of Mantle's condition; she and Mickey had been making plans to return to her home in Georgia and for him to resume cancer treatments at nearby Emory University. According to Greer Johnson, she and Mantle also had several conversations about baptism during their last week together. Over their years together, she had seen Mantle slowly come around to embracing a spiritual life. He had finally begun attending services with her at the church she belonged to in Greensboro, Georgia.

Then, almost as suddenly as he had received the new liver, Mickey got bad news. An X ray showed that the cancer had spread to his lungs. A few days later, his stomach pains returned. On July 28, two months to the day of his admission to Baylor Medical, Mickey was readmitted to the hospital. Once again, at Mickey's request, doctors did not reveal how ill Mickey truly was, although rumors that the cancer had spread began circulating. Mantle had committed himself to appear on ABC's *Good Morning, America,* and he had to cancel. Instead, he videotaped a statement, which the show aired August 1; in it Mickey finally acknowledged how sick he was. "Hi, this is Mick," he said on the videotape. "When I left Baylor University Medical Center about a month ago, I felt great. I have been [coming back] to the hospital for checkups every once in a while and, about two weeks ago, the doctors found a couple of spots of cancer in my lungs. Now I'm taking chemotherapy to get rid of the new cancer. I hope to get back to feeling as good as when I first left here. If you'd like to do something really great, be a donor."

It was a similar message to the one he delivered at Old Timers' Day at Yankee Stadium that summer. Too sick to travel to New York, Mickey had videotaped a message to his fans; it was played on the stadium's large scoreboard screen. Mantle was wearing ill-fitting Yankee pinstripes and looked weak.

"How 'bout this uniform?" Mickey said in his familiar Oklahoma drawl. "I feel like Phil Rizzuto in Babe Ruth's uniform. But like I said, I'm lucky to be in any uniform. I just want to thank God, the American people, and all you Yankee fans who sent cards and flowers with all my heart. I was really lucky to have played in New York City, for all you folks, the New York press and especially all the great teammates I've had over the years. I said one time I didn't know how Lou Gehrig could stand at home plate, knowing he was dying and say he was the luckiest man on the face of the earth. Now I think I know how he felt. I've always said when I die, I told one guy this, a sportswriter, when I die, I want it on my tombstone, 'A great teammate.' But I didn't want it this soon. To all my little teammates out there, please don't do drugs and alcohol. God only gave us one body, and keep it healthy. We really need it. If you want to do something great, be an organ donor. Thanks again. I'll see you all next year, maybe, hopefully. Bye."

"Good-bye, Mickey," Mel Allen said in narrating a memorial video of Mantle, "We had hoped we'd see you again next year, too. But you will always live in our minds and surely in our hearts."

Mantle's final days became a sad national deathwatch. Former teammates poured into Dallas to say their farewells. Mickey's hospital room resembled a Yankee reunion at times, especially when Hank Bauer, Moose Skowron, and Johnny Blanchard visited him together. They nursed Mantle during their visit—even helping him stand during an exhausting walk to the bathroom, dragging the wheeled intravenous-drip rack, with the tubes still attached to him. Some familiar faces, of course, had already passed on: Billy Martin in 1989, Roger Maris to cancer in 1985, and Casey Stengel well before that. Mantle's first professional manager, Harry Craft, would die ten days before Mickey, at the age of eighty.

Mantle had been a pallbearer at Maris's funeral and afterward had asked Bobby Richardson, the former Yankee turned evangelical lay minister, if he would officiate at his own services as he had at Roger's. Richardson was taken aback at the time, but he came to Dallas after receiving a call from Roy True, to be with his friend and to offer his prayers. No two players on the Yankees teams, of course, could have been more different than Mantle and Richardson. Of Richardson Stengel had once said, "He don't smoke, he don't drink, and he still can't hit .250." Over the years, Mantle had never been receptive to Richardson's attempts to talk to him about his faith and Christianity. On his deathbed, however, Richardson was one of the people Mickey wanted most to see. His visit followed that of Whitey Ford, whose presence had lifted Mantle's spirits. By this time, Mickey was drifting in and out of a peaceful sleep. At Mickey's bedside, Richardson took his friend's hand and prayed silently. Mantle awoke.

"Mickey, I love you," Richardson told him, "and I want you to spend eternity in heaven with me."

Mantle smiled back. "Bobby," he said, "I've been wanting to tell you that I have received Jesus Christ as my savior."

Richardson and his wife Betsy visited Mantle again later that day. Kneeling beside Mickey, Betsy Richardson shared her testimony with him and asked him how he knew for sure that he had been born again.

"Mickey," she said, "if God were to stand before you today and say, 'Why should I let you into my heaven?' what would you say?"

Mantle then quoted to them the words of John 3:16, in which Jesus summarizes God's plan of salvation: "For God so loved the world that he gave his only begotten Son, that whosoever believeth in him should not perish, but have everlasting life."

Bobby Richardson sensed that Mickey knew he was dying, that it was only a matter of time. Merlyn and the family had already been advised by Mickey's doctors that Mantle's death was imminent. Perhaps the last of those close to Mickey to learn the gravity of his condition was Greer Johnson, who was informed by Mantle's lawyer on Saturday, just hours before his death. Although she lived with Mantle that final week at Pat Summerall's house, it appears that the Mantle sons and the family lawyer withheld from her the gravity of Mickey's condition when he was readmitted to the hospital.

In Mantle's final days, Merlyn began reassuming what she felt was her rightful place in Mickey's life. She could finally keep the other women away— or perhaps more correctly, keep Mickey away from the other women. Merlyn had spoken to Greer Johnson only once, in the mid-1980s, not long after she learned of her relationship with Mickey. "She called," Johnson recalled. "It was civil. She said I was not the first girlfriend. She and Mickey had gotten married straight out of high school. They grew apart. I never felt that I had taken Mickey from her. . . . He said many times: 'If it weren't for you, I'd be dead right now.' . . . Had I been bad for Mickey, I could see them treating me this way. But I did everything in my power to help his career—which benefited [the family.]" Merlyn was given an adjoining room to Mantle's suite at Baylor Medical Center, from where she could monitor Mickey's visitors. Johnson spoke to Mickey for the last time on the Thursday before he died, but she was not told by Roy True that Mickey was dying until two days later. Johnson was stunned. "Neither Mickey nor I really knew how bad it was," she recalled. "We were still making a lot of plans. We were going back to Georgia, then to Hawaii. He wanted us to go to Hawaii because we'd never been there."

The final hours were especially difficult on Mickey's son David. Recalling a famous photograph of a frustrated Mantle flipping away his batting helmet as he walked back to the dugout after striking out, he was moved to write an ode to his dad: "Can I touch your face? Can I hold your hand? Can I give you a hug again and again? Can I say I love you, you're also my friend, my father?"

"Just seeing that picture," said David, "I wish I could have been there at that moment just to kind of say, 'That's life and you're gonna strike out.'"

In the final hours it fell upon David to shoulder a responsibility that would leave him guilt ridden. "I was the one who told them to take him off life support," David acknowledged in an interview six years later. "I felt like I killed dad, and maybe I OD'd him on morphine."

On Sunday, August 13, at 1:10 A.M., at the age of sixty-three, Mickey died, Merlyn holding one hand and son David holding the other. As Mantle's death was reported around the country—and around the world—millions of fans began mourning his passing. There were memorials and tributes at every major league park where games were played that Sunday. At Yankee Stadium, flags were at half-staff; a moment of silence was followed by a two-minute standing ovation. Organist Eddie Layton played "Somewhere, over the Rainbow" in tribute to Mickey. Highlights from Mantle's career were played on the score-board, which flashed the words "With Us Forever." All the Yankees wore black armbands, and some had number seven on their caps. They beat the Cleveland Indians, 4–1, with Paul O'Neill hitting a home run and the crowd roaring as it had when Mickey homered. The day after Mickey's death, a *Dallas Morning News* editorial cartoon paid tribute to Mantle with a fitting play on the joke he often told about being denied entrance into heaven by St. Peter at the gates. The cartoon showed St. Peter with his arm around Mickey walking together in heaven, with Christ's greatest disciple telling Mantle, "Kid, that was the most courageous ninth inning I've ever seen."

"Just before he died, Mickey Mantle gave us a reason to love him," said sportswriter Robert Lypsyte. "He was willing to use himself as an almost anti–role model in a very heroic way."

The funeral was held two days after Mickey died, at the Lovers Lane United Methodist Church in Dallas. The family had wanted a private service but, understanding the nationwide interest in Mickey, agreed to a public one, after a private wake. All 1,500 seats inside the church sanctuary were filled, as were an additional 1,500 in adjoining chapels, where the service was seen on video monitors. Greer Johnson was relegated to a seat near the back of the church, where she was joined by Pat Summerall. Summerall declined an usher's request that he move to the front of the church, where a seat had been reserved for him.

Until the last week of Mickey's life, Johnson's relationship with Mantle's sons had always been cordial. Just the previous Christmas, Mickey's sons had given her an engraved silver platter with an inscription that read: "To Greer, Thanks for being there during the tough times. Love, The Mantle Boys." Mickey's death, however, signaled a change. In the coming years, a growing conflict between Greer Johnson and the Mantle family would play out in the courts over the fortune involved in Mickey's memorabilia. It would also play out in an ugly scene at Mickey Mantle's Restaurant, where, on orders from the family, the manager refused to serve Johnson.

The Mantles were understandably upset at how big of a treasure in autographed bats, balls, and other valuable items he had given Johnson and others in contrast to the modest amount he had left his family: 110 signed balls, twenty-four signed bats, four signed gloves—hardly a DiMaggio-like trove. The Mantles have none of Mickey's game-worn uniforms. They say many were stolen and that Mickey gave others away. An indication of the value of Mantle items came at the 1999 auction of the Barry Halper Collection, widely acknowledged as the world's finest and largest private collection of baseball memorabilia. At that auction, Billy Crystal paid $239,000 for a glove used by Mantle in 1960. Merlyn did have one of Mickey's gloves and a pair of spikes bronzed because, she said, "He would've given them away without regard to their future value." "If he was drunk," said son David, "he'd say, 'You like it, you take it.'" Ironically, when Mickey died, a cottage industry based on fraud arose almost directly from his ashes. Fly-by-night companies rushed to flood the marketplace with Mantle-signed baseballs, photos, and plaques, trying to capitalize on Mickey's death. Many of those items, according to Mantle's family and closest associates, were absolute fakes. "The day after Mickey passed away, people came out of the woodwork, each with 2,000 or 3,000 items all 'signed' by Mickey," said Johnson. "There's absolutely no way anyone could have that kind of inventory."

At the funeral, Johnson at least had gotten a seat in the church. Mantle's childhood baseball idol, Stan Musial, had had to settle for a place outside the church among the two thousand mourners who gathered to pay their respects. The pallbearers were all former Yankee teammates: Whitey Ford, Yogi Berra, Bill Skowron, Hank Bauer, John Blanchard, and Bobby Murcer. Years earlier, Mickey had been moved at hearing country recording artist Roy Clark sing "Yesterday When I Was Young," and had asked that he perform it at his funeral. The song seemed to capture Mantle's life and squandered opportunities, especially the final line: "The time has come to pay for yesterday when I was young." Clark had been flattered but never truly expected he would be singing as he did at the service that afternoon. The main eulogy was delivered by Bob Costas. For all of his adult life, Costas had carried Mantle's 1958 Topps All-Star card in his wallet as a symbolic connection to his childhood, "when baseball meant nearly everything to me, and Mantle was as much a symbol of baseball as Cracker Jacks."

Costas's eulogy would be fitting; it would stand as a benchmark for memorializing heroes whose personal lives had been fraught with problems. "I felt that if I didn't in some way acknowledge the complexity of his character—the flaws as well as the more appealing parts of him—then the appreciation would sound just like hero worship," Costas would later say. "The facts of his life did not render untrue what was magnificent about him. If anything they made it more poignant." So Costas spoke to Mickey's magnificence as well as his darker side: "There was greatness in him, but vulnerability, too. . . . God knows no one is perfect. God also knows there's something special about a hero." Much like the baseball card he carried in his wallet did for him, Costas's eulogy connected Mantle to pieces of our childhood— and to the belief that baseball, like mankind, perseveres in the face of life's challenges.

"In a very different time than today," Costas said, "the first baseball commissioner, Kenesaw Mountain Landis, said every boy builds a shrine to some baseball hero, and before that shrine a candle always burns. For a huge portion of my generation, Mickey Mantle was that baseball hero. And for reasons that no statistics, no dry recitation of facts can possibly capture, he was the most compelling hero of our lifetime. And he was our symbol of baseball at a time when the game meant something to us that perhaps it no longer does. Mickey Mantle had those dual qualities so seldom seen, exuding dynamism and excitement, but at the same time touching your heart—flawed, wounded."

Noticeably absent from the funeral was Joe DiMaggio, who issued a statement of tribute in which, in typical fashion, he found it necessary to mention that Mantle had been demoted to the minors in his rookie season, as if this somehow diminished his career. In his later years, becoming even more protective of his place in Yankee and baseball history, DiMaggio had developed a one-sided rivalry with Mantle. He resented Mantle's resurgence and popularity with the rise of the memorabilia business. DiMaggio especially could not understand the hoopla over Mantle's baseball cards, especially the high prices paid in the late 1980s and early 1990s for Mantle's 1951 Bowman rookie card. At times, it seemed, DiMaggio would go out of his way to make certain that Mickey—and all other great players of the modern era—were placed at a level beneath the Yankee Clipper. Once, not long after the Yankees won back-to-back World Series in 1977–78, DiMaggio was asked to compare the star of that Yankee team, Reggie Jackson, with other Yankee greats. DiMaggio could have compared Reggie to himself, as indispensable to their respective Yankee championship teams. Instead, he compared Reggie to Mickey, and in such a way as to disparage their accomplishments. "Reggie is a lot like Mantle," said DiMaggio. "They think a 380-foot homer doesn't count. They both tried to hit the ball 500 feet." Mantle never saw that side of DiMaggio, who would remain, for him, the consummate hero and role model. "Heroes are people who are all good with no bad in them," Mickey said in an interview a year after his retirement. "That's the way I always saw Joe DiMaggio."

Morris Engelberg, DiMaggio's lawyer in later years, who attended to all of his needs and whims, recalled how shortly before Mickey's death Joe's "mood brightened during Old Timers' Day in 1995, when he got more applause from the fans than Mantle—even though Mantle . . . was so sick he could only appear on the scoreboard screen in a videotaped message to the fans." DiMaggio had a big smile on his face after that, Engelberg remembered. "Sitting in George Steinbrenner's private box at the stadium, he was talkative and happy and cut into his hot dogs in his patented style, using a fork and knife to eat them and throwing away the buns." Not long after Mickey's death, DiMaggio had to return again to Yankee Stadium when the Yankees dedicated to Mantle the fourth monument in the history of the stadium. "Joe resented that. When had Mantle ever showed up for him?" wrote DiMaggio biographer Richard Ben Cramer. "But what really griped him wasn't Mickey's monument in left center field. . . . No, what set Joe to seething was the special ball they used in that day's game. It was a regulation Rawlings game-ready Mickey Mantle Commemorative Ball, authorized by Major League Baseball. Right away the collectors and dealers in memorabilia bid those balls up to three hundred per. That was twice as much as Joe was getting for his balls—which were autographed!"

From the grave, Mickey Mantle was having the last laugh.

"In the last year," Costas said in his eulogy, "Mickey Mantle, always so hard on himself, finally came to accept and appreciate that distinction between a role model and a hero. The first he often was not, the second he always will be."

Mickey was interred in a crypt next to his son Billy inside a huge concrete mausoleum, at the Sparkman-Hillcrest Memorial Park in Dallas. The inscription underneath Mickey's name on the outside of the crypt reads simply, as he wanted, "A Great Teammate." His oldest son Mickey Jr., who died of non-Hodgkin's lymphoma five years later at the age of forty-seven, would also be laid to rest there, next to his father. Merlyn, who never remarried, has a space reserved for herself in the same crypt. In 2001, youngest son Danny, then forty-one, had precancerous polyps removed from his colon, and at the time faced the possibility of prostate cancer.

"Why my children?" Merlyn lamented in an interview. "I'm not wishing cancer on anyone's children. But why mine?"

"I don't know how she does it," said Pat Summerall. "I get the sense from Merlyn that she feels there's a hex."

David, who is healthy, and Danny manage Four M Enterprises, the Mantles' licensing business, as well as the Mickey Mantle Foundation, which raises organ-donation awareness and has distributed eight million donor cards. "It's what dad wanted us to do," said Danny. "If we've done any good, that makes us feel good."

David and his wife Marla have one child, Marilyn, born the year before Mickey died. Danny and his wife have a son, Will, and a daughter, Chloe, born after their grandfather's death. In the year after Mickey Jr. died, Merlyn was raising his twelve-year-old daughter Mallory, until a custody case with Mickey Jr.'s ex-wife was settled.

In September of 2001, Roy Mantle, one of Mickey's twin brothers, died of Hodgkin's disease in Las Vegas. He was sixty-five. Summerall, who played minor league ball against Roy, said, "I'd be haunted. Wouldn't you?"

Mickey has three surviving siblings, all in their sixties. Ray Mantle, Roy's twin, lives in Las Vegas. Larry Mantle and Barbara Delise live in Oklahoma. Delise, who has not been touched with cancer, agrees with Summerall—that the Mantle men have been haunted. "It's just everybody on the male side," he said. "It's difficult. My grandpa, my dad, Mickey, Billy, little Mickey. . . . The men never talked about it, except for Mickey."

Mickey and Merlyn pose with their four boys in 1961 outside the Mickey Mantle Holiday Inn in Joplin, Missouri. Shown left to right with their parents: Danny, Mickey Jr., Billy, and David. *The Mickey Mantle Museum, Cooperstown, N.Y., and Mr. Tom Catal and Mr. Andrew Vilacky*

Mickey and Mickey Junior pose back to back at the beach. Later in life Mickey would help his son get a minor-league contract with the Yankees, but Mickey Jr. would call it quits after a few months. *Randall Swearingen and www.mickey-mantle.com*

Roger Maris and Mickey Mantle. Together, the two would break Ruth and Gehrig's combined home run record with 115- including Maris's then-record 61-in 1961. *The Mickey Mantle Museum, Cooperstown, N.Y., and Mr. Tom Catal and Mr. Andrew Vilacky*

Mickey and his companion for the last ten years of his life, Greer Johnson, sitting with Billy and Jill Martin. *The Mickey Mantle Museum, Cooperstown, N.Y., and Mr. Tom Catal and Mr. Andrew Vilacky*

Mickey Mantle speaks to the crowd at the first of four Mickey Mantle Days, in 1965. The Yankees held this day, celebrating Mantle's 2000th game, in an effort to convince Mantle not to retire. *The Mickey Mantle Museum, Cooperstown, N.Y., and Mr. Tom Catal and Mr. Andrew Vilacky*

Old Timers Day, 1972. The uneasy relationship between Mantle and DiMaggio lasted into their retirements and their lifetimes. *The Mickey Mantle Museum, Cooperstown, N.Y., and Mr. Tom Catal and Mr. Andrew Vilacky*

Mickey stands between
George Steinbrenner and
Richard Nixon at Billy
Martin's funeral
December 29, 1989. One
year after Mantle had
been the best man at
Billy's fourth marriage,
he was a pallbearer at his
funeral. *The Mickey
Mantle Museum,
Cooperstown, N.Y., and
Mr. Tom Catal and Mr.
Andrew Vilacky*

Mickey speaks at a press
conference three days
after his liver transplant
operation in 1995. *The
Mickey Mantle Museum,
Cooperstown, N.Y., and
Mr. Tom Catal and Mr.
Andrew Vilacky*

EPILOGUE

Mickey Mantle's life matched his appropriation of his father's dream to be the best in the game. However, it may be said that in a sense, Mutt Mantle never became an adult, and Mickey Mantle never became a child. Unlike his father, Mickey may have realized that this dream was exactly that—an impossibility, perhaps much like the country's own naïve belief of unchallenged, untroubled greatness. Yet Mantle, like the country, would carry on in pursuit of that dream—playing hurt when others would not have, pursuing Ruth's record, which he personally thought would never be broken, or if so, not by him.

"I was supposed to be the next Ruth, the next DiMaggio," Mantle was to recall in later years. "Casey told the writers that. The writers wrote that, and everyone believed it. But I knew it wasn't true. How could anyone live up to those expectations? When I didn't, and the fans booed, I kinda felt that they weren't really booing at me but at someone else who was suppose to live out their dreams."

Mantle's life, in fact, followed a dual narrative, one in which Mantle's movement away from his small-town roots corresponded with his quiet raging against the big-city microscope placed on his life and those of other sports figures, particularly Roger Maris in 1961. Mantle later was to feel indebted to Maris for taking the media spotlight off of his shoulders, although ultimately it would lead to the end of Maris's career in New York. For Mickey Mantle, as well as for others for whom baseball was a world unto itself, the game represented a symbol of all that was right and true about the midcentury America in which he was raised—but it had now become threatened by the machinations of an increasingly commercialized world. Television and modern media had begun to change the game. Willingly or not, Mickey Mantle, as the game's first television-era hero, found himself at the heart of these forces tugging on baseball and the country. For generations, baseball had been viewed as working to implant certain specific "American cultural values" into the national landscape as a means to preserve what had been self-promoted as inherent American qualities. But in the eyes of some, the century's move toward capitalist democracy served to corrupt the ideals behind baseball. The 1919 Black Sox scandal was the best example of this—Chicago, as the epitome of the new urban America, polluting the purest symbol of American individuality.

If baseball represents the American experience in its purest form, then it has been its historians—from sportswriters to filmmaker Ken Burns, producer and creator of the magnificent PBS documentary on the game—who have assigned a divine quality to it. In that mind-set, the America in which Mickey Mantle grew up playing baseball was a freshly painted one, with the dew still on it and the autumn fields of the Oklahoma farmland glowing with the same iridescence as Mantle's golden hair—the reality of the Depression notwithstanding. Within reason, the portrayal of Mantle as the all-American Adonis displays perfectly a deflowering element of New York in myth and society— the innocence of the Midwest and Mantle, who had "never been on a plane before going to spring training"; the establishing relationship of the young Mickey Mantle with his father, Mutt; the high school sweetheart, Merlyn; and baseball. All were irrevocably lost as Mantle's adventures, athletic and personal, unfolded in the big city.

The Midwest from which young Mickey Mantle emerged saw New York as a decadent collection of transients and alienated, lost souls, whose faltering lives were attributable to the damaging effects of the city, especially in terms of the decline or loss of familial ties. Merlyn Mantle was later to even suggest that all of these people plotted Mickey's downfall, most notably those who shared Mantle's New York nightlife in the 1950s, when boozing and carousing undermined his ability to achieve his father's dreams. It is fair to suggest that New York's unfocused and mystical landscape, matching the alienating quality of a rite of passage to manhood, swamped the young Mickey Mantle and left him the way we often came to read about him in the 1950s: hung over at games, surly to sportswriters, unfriendly to fans. Sportswriter Mike Lupica remembered that "the summer before Mantle died, he told me that when he was a kid, when he hit New York as hard as one of his home run balls hitting the seats, he knew the strike zone about as well as he knew when it was time to leave the bar and go home."

Today a professional athlete's personal life is grist for the news media's daily mill. That was unheard of in Mantle's day, in the 1950s and 1960s, except perhaps when DiMaggio married Marilyn Monroe. Mickey Mantle, as the reigning king of sports heroes in his day, was the first professional athlete to be the target of such scrutiny. In fact, it can be argued that more media attention was paid to his personal life in some of those years than to the personal lives of American presidents. The sexual and personal escapades of John F. Kennedy as senator and later as president went unmentioned for almost twenty years, though many reporters covering him were aware of them. There is perhaps no greater symbol of what Americans believe to be the inherent truth about themselves—baseball, as a sport of pace, exuberance, the family, driving spirit, and opportunity for the best and most worthy individuals to excel. Mark Twain once said that baseball became the "outward and visible expression of the drive and push and rush and struggle of the raging, tearing and booming 19th century." But all that began changing in the time of Mantle, in the era of modern media. The game had become inextricably entangled and muddied with the economics of the sport; it had become a marketable commodity—a process that has continued through to the Pete Rose scandal and the pervasion of multimillion-dollar contracts, legal suits, and media advertising today.

For some Americans of his generation, Mickey Mantle was a stronger influence on their lives than perhaps even God or family. Billy Crystal, the actor and producer of *61**, a film about the Mantle-Maris chase of Babe Ruth's home-run record, talks of having tried not only to run like Mantle but to use an Oklahoma twang when he recited from the Torah at his bar mitzvah. Howard Schultz, a typical New York youngster who grew up in awe of Mantle, would remember being at Yankee Stadium on Mickey Mantle Days in 1968 and 1969, feeling deeply sad as he listened to the tributes to his hero. "Baseball was never the same for me after that," recalled Schultz. "The Mick was such an intense presence in our lives that years later, when he died, I got phone calls of consolation from childhood friends I hadn't heard from in decades." Even writers, grown men who were groomed in skepticism, found themselves furthering the myth. "There is no sound in baseball akin to the sound of Mantle hitting a home run," wrote Arnold Hano in his 1958 book *Baseball Stars*. "The crunchy sound of an axe biting into a tree, yet magnified a hundred times in the vast, cavernous, echo making hollows of a ball field."

Today, evidence of Mickey as a hero and a symbol of his age may be even stronger than it was at the height of his career. One need look no farther than the memorabilia and collector industry, where Mantle items continue to be the most coveted, especially his rookie cards and his other cards from the 1950s. The visual image of Mantle endures almost as if it was carefully constructed from the start. Sifting through the visual glut of Mantle items at any major collectors' show, one finds evidence of how fans collect, arrange, and display Mantle memorabilia, make Mantle artwork, and participate in annual rituals celebrating Mantle in his Oklahoma hometown. By engaging in these acts, fans continually reinvent Mickey in their own ways to keep his memory alive. The demand for Mantle cards and autographed bats and balls also strikingly shows the power of the visual image in our culture and reveals much about American attitudes toward sports heroes and celebrities—as well as about the construction of American identity in the late twentieth and early twenty-first centuries. It may also be proof that the love we bear our cultural icons is as complex and life-enhancing as those icons themselves. It is an insight, too, into how Americans use the stuff of commercial mass culture to make their lives meaningful—something that Mantle himself had difficulty understanding.

Why is Mickey Mantle so ubiquitous a presence in our culture? Why would Al Gore, in his 2000 presidential campaign, compare Bill Clinton to DiMaggio and himself to Mantle—"It's two great players, but one era takes over for the other"? Why does Mantle continue to enjoy a cultural prominence that would be the envy of the most heavily publicized living celebrities? Could it be that Mickey, like other pop culture touchstones, has helped provide a common understanding about our world? "Popular culture has become part of the common language of American life," asserts Stewart Hoover, a professor of mass communication at the University of Colorado who researches media audiences. "Popular culture provides our metaphors and our symbols and our myths, and when people search for a way of describing something that's happened to them, the most florid way of doing that is always a metaphor."

A *Sports Illustrated* article summing up Mickey's impact described a woman beseeching Mantle to make an appearance and surprise her husband. "Mantle materializes at some cocktail party, introductions are made, and the husband weeps in the presence of such fantasy made flesh." To his fans, especially those whose boyhood spanned his glory years, Mantle was Elvis in pin-stripes at the fountainhead of contemporary American culture. Even to some contemporary baseball stars, Mickey Mantle exists on another level. In 1992 Chipper Jones, then a hot-shot minor leaguer in the Atlanta Braves organization, looked forward with excitement to meeting Mantle at an off-season card show. Jones had grown up hearing about Mantle all his life and had even become a switch-hitter himself. "The night before [the card show], I found myself in front of the mirror, rehearsing how I'd approach this baseball legend," Jones recalled. "I wanted to tell him how much I looked up to him, respected him and tell him about the influence on my career. None of which came out of my mouth at the time." Jones was dumbstruck at the sight of Mantle sticking his hand out, a smile on his face. Mickey, in short, has become inseparable from many of the defining myths of our culture, enmeshed with the American Dream and the very idea of the "United States," caught up in debates about what the country means and over what constitutes a national culture.

To be sure, unfamiliar prosperity and expansion tested the ideals of America at the time that Mickey Mantle became a star. As new institutions like television networks were constructed and old ones like racism were radically altered, the idea of an American hero as a civilizing force, whether John Wayne on the screen or Mantle on the ball field, could be held up against concrete social forms—forms of our own making, with the growth of American pop culture at the center—that seemed very defective as reflections of civilization. America and Americans, in a sense, were trying to humanize the success of a grand new nation, buoyed by triumph in war and unaware of the coming social strife that would signal an end to the postwar prosperity and cultural hegemony ahead. A wide discrepancy existed between the America that came to cheer and jeer Mantle, and the articulated values and ideas that Americans adopted and developed during the postwar period. Ultimately, within that climate of ideas, the country would be forced to examine itself. Some of these ideas were the cultural myths that we grew up with; they were the accompaniment to still another rite of passage, for the country as well as for Mantle, as he settled into retirement and cult mythology. "When he couldn't play ball anymore, a whole generation felt older," said author Roger Kahn. "When he got cancer, a whole generation felt the fear of death."

Mickey Mantle need not be elevated to anything beyond what he deserves to be. But he was also a close observer of the country around him. He arrived in New York as a country bumpkin—but all of us who have arrived in a big city wide-eyed and naïve take in the scene and the world in ways in which the native never can. Mickey would also maintain that small-town-boy aspect throughout his life. Marty Appel, former publicity director of the Yankees, started his career with the Yankees at age nineteen, answering Mickey's fan mail. Appel remembered Mantle crying at a showing of *The Last Picture Show*, a Peter Bogdanovich study of life in a small Texas town.

"That reminded you of home?" Appel asked.

"Hell," said Mickey, "we even had a village idiot like that one."

Mickey would never fully acclimate to New York and the awakening it could bring. In one of his reminiscences about New York, Mantle talked about seeing one day a group of Japanese women who were survivors of the atomic bomb. Presumably these were the "Hiroshima Maidens"—a group of young Japanese women who had been grotesquely disfigured in the atomic holocaust of Hiroshima and who were brought in the mid-1950s to the United States for plastic surgery at New York's Mount Sinai Hospital. They were followed everywhere by the press. Mantle said he didn't know what all the fuss about the atomic bomb was until that moment, when he realized the horrible reality of it.

What may have been most refreshing about Mickey Mantle, ultimately, was that he combined the irrepressible hope of each spring training with our blind nostalgia for an age that probably never was in the first place. Mantle just happened to come along at a time that became the game's golden age for a generation. "It's funny," said Yogi Berra, thinking back on his teammate, "when I remember him, I remember him young." Indeed, Mantle's career and life produce a kind of wistful remorse grounded within a specific historical circumstance, the great American hopes of the 1950s and the failed promises of the 1960s, the immense disillusionment with politics after Watergate and Vietnam. Mickey Mantle serves as a memory for many Americans, as a wish-fulfillment not for Mickey himself but for what he represented, and for what he reminds them of—a celebration, a rite both of communion and of redemption.

AUTHOR'S NOTE

On my drive home from work on a June day in 1995, I found myself breaking down and sobbing like a small child over the human frailty of a little boy's hero. I had just learned from a radio newscast that Mickey Mantle was in a Texas hospital, doomed to die of liver failure if he didn't have an organ transplant. When I arrived home, my lack of composure must have been obvious.

"Why are you crying, dad?" my ten-year-old son Trey asked. "Is it Goppy? Did Goppy die?"

My son called his grandfather "Goppy" when he first learned to talk, and the nickname had stuck.

"No, it's not Goppy," I said, calming his own fears. "It's Mickey Mantle. He's in the hospital, and he's very sick."

My son, who in previous conversations had expressed serious doubts that The Mick could ever have been as good as Ken Griffey Jr. or Mark McGwire are today, couldn't understand my highly emotional state.

"You haven't cried over Goppy," he said. "And he's been much, much sicker."

He was right, of course. I was all broken up over the possibility that Mickey Mantle might die, but I hadn't once shed a single tear over my father or over the series of strokes he had had over the previous two and a half years.

That night, I did what every other post–World War II baby boomer probably did in the final days of Mickey Mantle's life that summer: I retreated to my bedroom and surrounded myself with all the Mickey Mantle baseball cards and memories I could find.

The oldest of those memories was the day my father brought home a newspaper sports page that had a picture of Joe DiMaggio with his arm around a hotshot rookie who, my dad informed me, "will be even better than DiMaggio."

I could only imagine. After all, a near life-sized poster of Joe DiMaggio even dwarfed a crucifix over my bed, much to my mother's chagrin. But then, that was my father's doing. Three things had always been important to him: God, family, and baseball—though not necessarily in that order.

My father, of course, was right about Mickey Mantle. In my mind, he would wind up being greater than DiMaggio, although not for the reasons some baseball purists would argue.

DiMaggio had retired by the time I could talk baseball with my father. But in the 1950s and into the 1960s, Mickey Mantle was the centerpiece of many of the discussions my father and I had about baseball in those years. We saw The Mick play hundreds of times on Saturday and Sunday afternoon televised games broadcast by Dizzy Dean and Buddy Blattner, who was later replaced by Pee Wee Reese. But unfortunately, we never made it to Yankee Stadium to see Mickey play in person. We lived in Texas, not far from Mantle's native Oklahoma but seemingly millions of miles from New York. We kept promising ourselves that one day we would see Mickey Mantle play in the stadium.

The closest we came was seeing Mickey in an exhibition game in Houston, where he hit the first home run ever hit in the then-new Astrodome, the world's first domed stadium.

I went off to college that year; for my father, for me to have seen Mickey Mantle in person was like a celebration of seeing his son safely through passage from adolescence to manhood.

"Mickey Mantle has always been your hero," my father said to me. "But you have always been mine."

I didn't know what to say to him then, and as the years have passed, sometimes I have felt like Mickey Mantle when triumphant at the plate. But sometimes I have felt like a child who has disappointed, like Mickey Mantle having struck out.

On the night I learned that Mickey was dying, then, I relived my childhood by going through my Mickey Mantle baseball cards. I caught myself mumbling an old childhood prayer when I came to a faded sepia photograph of my father that I also keep in one of those plastic covers that protects my Mickey Mantle baseball cards and my son's Griffey and McGwire cards.

The old picture is of my father in 1942, wearing a U.S. Army baseball uniform. He had pitched and played first base on an enlisted men's team that won an armed forces championship before he went overseas.

I was overcome with guilt until the next day, when I told a friend how I had cried for Mickey Mantle but never once for my father when he had been near death.

"That's not too surprising," my friend said. "You haven't cried for your father because to do so would be an admission of his vulnerability."

My friend was right, of course. I don't want to imagine life without my father. I didn't want to miss the chance to tell my dad how special he has always been, so I immediately wrote my father a note.

"Dear Dad:

"Like Mickey Mantle, you, too, have always been my hero."

This book obviously had its genesis in a childhood in the so-called golden age of baseball years ago, but it didn't begin taking shape until Mantle and DiMaggio were both in their own golden years. I actually wanted to write a biography of Joe DiMaggio. Although Mantle had been my hero, DiMaggio had been my father's baseball idol—and I think I'd wanted to write that book for my father. So for a number of years, my idea had been to research and write the DiMaggio book.

DiMaggio, of course, wasn't an easy interview to land. It was finally in the late 1980s that I got to DiMaggio, through a strange set of circumstances. During my work as a columnist for the *Los Angeles Herald Examiner* from the late 1970s to the 1980s (and a few times in the early 1990s), I was fortunate to interview DiMaggio. I know the popular myth, especially among writers who tried to get through to DiMaggio but weren't able to, of his inaccessibility. But I found that not to be the case. I had been in Reno Barsocchini's bar several times during visits to San Francisco and had struck up a friendship of sorts with Reno. I'm not altogether sure why—a lot of reasons, I suppose. He got to know of my interest in baseball and DiMaggio. I'd told him the story of how this huge poster-size photo of DiMaggio had hung over my bed when I was young and how my mother would take it down anytime our parish priest would visit our home and replace it with a crucifix.

Anyway, back in L.A., I would occasionally get a call from Reno: "The Clipper's in town. Wanna talk to him?" I would catch a flight out of Los Angeles International after work and sometimes catch DiMaggio at Reno's that night or the next. I wouldn't say a friendship struck up with him, but I found myself serving as a kind of court in which he could talk about whatever was on his mind. Maybe I wouldn't have gotten the calls had I made my presence known as a "reporter" or had I meant to write about DiMaggio. I don't know. But I got the sense that Reno would call out to people such as myself in order to have this court there for his friend. Years later I would learn from golf writer Art Spander that he had gotten to know DiMaggio much the same way, through Reno, who would also alert him whenever Joe was in town.

However, I found that while DiMaggio could be generous with his time and observations in talking about other subjects—a diverse range of subjects, from immigrants and immigration to baseball and Mantle—he could be guarded to the point of abruptness and rudeness when the subject of conversation turned toward him. I had been told—and I knew from everything I'd read and knew about him—that DiMaggio wouldn't talk about himself, but I was able to get him to open up and talk about Mickey. Eventually I became convinced that I could write a better, more definitive biography about Mantle than I could about DiMaggio.

The problem was Mickey Mantle himself. By the early 1990s, although he was extremely popular among the memorabilia crowd, the stories about Mantle's boorish behavior and his excessive drinking were widespread; he was no longer exactly a sympathetic figure. In the vernacular of Hollywood, there wasn't a third act in his story—a redeeming ending. What ultimately changed that was his admission to the Betty Ford Center and his subsequent openness in talking about his alcoholism. Unlike American cultural icons such as Elvis, Marilyn, and JFK, Mickey had had the hero's "misfortune" of not dying young—although he always thought he would—and had to be examined in middle age and as an older man. Although his myth aged well, Mickey did not—that is, not until he got help and publicly admitted in interviews with Roy Firestone and Bob Costas and *Sports Illustrated* that he'd screwed up and would make amends. It was the mea culpas and the glimpses of sobriety and character throughout his deathwatch in 1995 that made Mickey a hero again, this time in life, as if he had been saved at the last moment.

I first met Mickey Mantle in 1970, the year after his retirement and shortly after he had returned to Dallas from a frustrating season as a coach of the New York Yankees. Mickey had lived in Dallas since the late 1950s, and only earlier that year I had joined the reporting staff of the *Dallas Times Herald*, right out of college. One of the first things I did upon going to work at the *Times Herald* was to check the Mickey Mantle files at the newspaper's morgue. I was stunned to see the scarcity of any Mantle clips since his retirement. No lifestyle pieces, no Mick-in-retirement articles—you would have thought Mantle didn't reside in Dallas. A couple of national pieces had been written about Mickey in retirement, but nothing locally. I lobbied for an assignment to interview Mantle, which came my way because no one else was interested. Heck, my editors themselves weren't interested.

When I first contacted Mantle, I started getting a sense of why no one was writing about him. Even after I explained that his home telephone number had been in our City Desk files, Mickey seemed miffed. I remember his words as something that might have come from Yogi Berra. "Well," Mickey said over the phone, "I only gave out that number so that I could be reached whenever someone needed to talk to me."

Mickey was close to an hour late to our lunch interview. He had wanted to meet at a trendy burger shop in the Turtle Creek section of North Dallas. It was one of those seventies-type restaurants with peanut shells scattered all over the floor, and where they served drinks in old jam preserve jars. If it hadn't been for all those peanut shells, which Mickey thought gave the place distinction, I would have sworn I had gone to the wrong restaurant. When he finally arrived, Mickey apologized in a matter-of-fact manner: "There was a screw-up on our tee time this morning."

I was immediately blown away. Not because I was finally meeting my boyhood hero, face to face, but because as I saw him—slightly red-eyed, smiling crookedly, slurring some of his words—I thought to myself, my God, it's like meeting my father. They both were heroes, and they both were drinkers—and not happy drunks, either. Of course, I didn't tell Mickey he reminded me of my father. Nor did I tell my father that he reminded me of Mickey. But from experience, I had an understanding of how to deal with Mantle. A formal question-and-answer interview was out of the question. Instead, over charbroiled cheeseburgers and beers, Mickey rambled in a disjointed exercise of free association for which I wasn't prepared.

We talked for close to two hours that afternoon, and I remember being panic stricken the longer the interview went on; I feared that I actually had little to use in a traditional story about Mickey in retirement. He would clam up when the conversation turned to things he was doing now. A bowling alley bearing Mickey's name in Dallas had closed down, and then reopened, and Mickey was unclear about its status. He didn't want to talk about his investments, and he was equally evasive on questions about his life with his sons. There was one comment I wrote several times in my notebook: "We're doing a lot more things together now, that's for sure."

My access to Mickey might have ended that afternoon had we not started talking about golf, one of the few things over which he showed any passion. I happened to live in a townhouse complex that was near the Preston Trails Golf Club in far North Dallas. Mickey was a member of Preston Trails. I wasn't—this was one of the most exclusive golf courses in Dallas—but I'd sneaked onto the course a few times and attended the Byron Nelson Classic there in my first year in Dallas. So when he told me of a particularly tricky par four whose length he said he had driven with a slight breeze, I knew exactly which one he was talking about. I was a duffer, but golf is the consummate game for eternal optimists. The next thing I knew, I had a golf date with Mickey a few days later. We played with two other members, from whom Mickey cajoled a stroke-per-hole handicap for me, even though I kept assuring him I wasn't *that* bad. "Believe me," he said, "you are." We won all eighteen holes at ten dollars a hole, and Mickey won a side bet with each of the two fellow members. He insisted I keep the winnings from the main bet, and I sensed that Mickey got as big a kick out of winning hundred-dollar bets from each of the two men as he would have from receiving a week's salary when he was playing baseball.

As for the interview itself, Gore Vidal, I think, described interviews like it as "encounters"—and I had several of them with Mickey in the 1970s and in the 1980s. In 1973, I was working for the PBS *Newsroom* show, which Jim Lehrer had created in Dallas, and we wanted Mantle to appear live to discuss the young Texas Rangers baseball team. Since I knew Mickey, I contacted him. Immediately there were two insurmountable problems. First, Mickey wanted to be paid. He had no idea what PBS was, but he thought if it was live he should be paid. Second, Mickey really didn't want to appear live but wanted the interview to be taped, which went against the format of the show. The whole thing was a wash.

In 1985, while at *Sports Illustrated*, I proposed and obtained approval for a Mickey Mantle profile that resulted in several phone conversations with Mickey, and as many broken dates for face-to-face meetings. As we were to learn later, Mickey was drinking himself to death during these years. His family life was also not good. There were ongoing problems with his son Billy, and he and Merlyn were breaking up. They didn't divorce, but they lived apart for the last seven years of his life. I spoke with him twice in late 1994, planning to meet with him during an upcoming card-show appearance on the West Coast. But then he had to cancel the show because of the stomach problems that worsened until his death.

The book that I ended up writing began taking final shape the year before Mickey died. It took some time to complete for several reasons, the most important one being that I didn't want this to be just another sports biography, or a fan or sportswriter's sentimental outpouring about a baseball hero. There are sufficient books like that about Mantle already. I wanted to develop and write a serious biography not only about Mickey Mantle but also about his time and about an America that shaped him and that he helped shape—a biography that transcended Mantle and that tried to explain and define him as part of our American culture.

Ultimately, the book is also about fathers and sons. What Mutt Mantle wanted for his son was not altogether different from what most fathers have always wanted for their children. In that sense, it may indeed be our fathers who are the true heroes of the game.

ACKNOWLEDGMENTS

Mickey Mantle: America's Prodigal Son would not have been possible without the assistance of many individuals.

First, acknowledgment must go to my literary agent and friend, Mike Hamilburg, of the Mitchell Hamilburg Agency in Beverly Hills, California. Without Mike's professional skills, constant encouragement, and unstinting moral support, this book would never have been completed.

Professor Bryan M. Davis, PhD., of Stephen F. Austin College in Texas, was especially generous with his time and assistance in reevaluating Mickey beyond the role of a sports and cult hero and more as an archetypical heroic figure, reflecting the hopes and fears of his times.

Professor Kevin Kerrane of the University of Delaware, author of the definitive book on scouts, *Dollar Sign on the Muscle: The World of Baseball Scouting,* was generous with his knowledge and anecdotes of the scouting wars around the time that Mantle was signed by Tom Greenwade, as well as with recollections of interviews with Greenwade and a fellow scout, Hugh Alexander.

Ivan Shouse, Mantle's childhood friend, was kind enough to assist in filling in missing pieces of Mickey's early years, Mickey's time with the Baxter Springs Whiz Kids team, and Mickey's years at Commerce High School.

Pete Rose was magnanimous in sharing his memories and recollections of the time he spent with Mantle both while Mickey was still playing in the 1960s and later on the memorabilia circuit.

Tom Catal and Andrew Vilacky of the Mickey Mantle Museum in Cooperstown were both gracious and generous in their hospitality to both me and my family.

Greer Johnson, Mantle's "soul mate" the last ten years of his life, was extremely kind and gracious in reminiscing about Mickey and trusting me with her memories, recalling Mickey's conversations with her about his father, DiMaggio, Maris, and many of the other important people in her life. This book would not be as complete in its assessment of Mantle without her assistance.

Ray Mantle took time to share his memories of growing up with Mickey, especially in clearing up discrepancies in previous accounts of Mantle's early life. Ray also offered tremendous insight into Mickey's relationship with his father and his friendship with Billy Martin.

Marshall Smith, Oklahoma golf pro and Mickey's longtime friend, provided valuable assistance in piecing together Mantle's life after his retirement and his relationship with his mother.

A number of people were helpful in providing information or putting me in touch with prospective interviewees but especially: the late Phil Berger, who graciously shared his insights and contacts on Mantle, the subject of one of his numerous books; and Michael A. Stoner, attorney for Greer Johnson.

Special thanks to these individuals for their support or assistance in tangible and intangible ways: Hank Aaron, Art Aguilar, Jim Bacon, Reno Barsocchini, Cameron Bebehani, Jim Bellows, Yogi Berra, Hollis Biddle, Alan and Jan Block, Barry Bonds, John Borunda, Jim Bouton, Brian Brassfield, Marty Brennaman, Jimmy Breslin, Tony Brooklier, Jerry Brown, Jim Brown, Jeff and Cindy Brynan, Jim Bunning, David Burke, Ken Burns, George W. Bush, Dave Campbell, Frank and Lucy Casado, Patricia Casado, Tom Catal, Rick Cerrone, Barbara Cigarroa, Paul Cohen, John B. Connally, Bob Costas, Kevin Costner, Warren Cowan, Richard Ben Cramer, Billy Crystal, Francis Dale, Teo Davis, Gavin deBecker, Mary Anne Dolan, Joe DiMaggio, Mel Durslag, Charlie Ericksen, Carl Erskine, Roy Firestone Bob Fishel, Robert Fitzgerald, Whitey Ford, Don Forst, Dudley Freeman, Glenn Frey, Randy Galloway, Peter Gammons, Art Garfunkel, Rudolph Guiliani, Kathy Griffin, Chris Gwynn, Jacleen Haber, David Halberstam, Pete Hamill, Arnold Hano, Thomas Harris, Ray Harper, Lew Harris, Jickey Harwell, Don Henley, Mickey Herskowitz, Gerald Holland, Emory Holmes, Bill Hudson, Ed Hunter, Alex Jacinto, Derek

Jeter, Don Johnson, Chipper Jones, David Justice, Ray Kelly, Kitty Kelley, Jennifer Kemp, Steve Kraly, Doug Krikorian, Sandy Koufax, Tony Kubek, Deborah Larcom, Ring Lardner Jr., Don Larsen, Lisa LaSalle, Tommy Lasorda, Tim Layana, Timothy Leary, Mike Leggett, Dana Leung, Jill Lieber, Mike Lupica, Professor Ralph Lynn, Bob Mallon, C. J. Martinez, Willie Mays, Bill McAda, Todd McClain, Julie McCullough, Mark McGwire, David McHam, Robbie Mescudi, Frank Messer, Lidia Montemayor, Jim Montgomery, Louis F. Moret, Mark Mulvoy, Stan Musial, Joe Namath, Yolanda Nava, Jack Nelson, Don Newcombe, Peter O'Malley, Edward James Olmos, Bill Orozco, Professor Thomas Pettigrew, Tony Perez, Vic Prado, Tony Pederson, George Pla, Charles Rappleye, Robert Redford, Jimmy Reese, Pee Wee Reese, Rick Reilly, Bobby Richardson, Wanda Rickerby, Phil Rizzuto, Tim Robbins, Phil Alden Robinson, Gregory Rodriguez, Jim Rome, Carol Rose, Richard Sandomir, Susan Sarandon, Dick Schaap, Larry Schwartz, Vin Scully, Gail Sheehy, Charley Sheen, Ron Shelton, Bob Sheppard, Blackie Sherrod, Ivan Shouse, Buck Showalter, John Silva, T. J. Simers, Paul Simon, Marty Singer, Bill Skowron, April Smith, Stephanie Sowa, Gary Spiecker, Ben Stein, George Steinbrenner, Jeannine Stein, Randall Swearingen, Gay Talese, Don Tanner, J. Randy Taraborrelli, Dave Thomas, Joe Torre, Nadine Tuch, John Tuthill, Peter Ueberroth, George Vecsey, Andrew Vilacky, Antonio Villaraigosa, Judy Wammack Rice, Sander Vanocur, Don Wanlass, Kurt Warner, Tommy West, Ted Williams, Tom Wolfe, Gene Woodling, Steve Wulf, Anthony Yerkovich, Don Zimmer, and members of the Beverly Hills Baseball Club and their families.

My appreciation to the entire staff of the Baseball Hall of Fame Museum Library in Cooperstown, New York, for their cooperation on so many levels. Thanks also to the library staffs of *Time* and *Sports Illustrated, The Sporting News*, Associated Press, the *Los Angeles Times*, the *New York Times*, the *New York Post*, the *New York Daily News*, *Newsday*, the *Washington Post*, the *Boston Globe*, the *Dallas Morning News*, the *Houston Chronicle*, the *Detroit Free Press*, the *Kansas City Star*, the *Oklahoman*, and the *Tulsa World*; ESPN Archives, MLB.com, the New York Yankees, TheMick.com, Susan Naulty of the Richard Nixon Presidential Library in Yorba Linda (California), the National Archives and Records Administration, the reference departments at the New York Public Library, the Beverly Hills Public Library, the Santa Monica Public Library, the Dallas Public Library, and the Library of Congress; and the administration of the Commerce (Oklahoma) Unified School District.

I want to thank, too, Chris Kahrl, my editor at Brassey's, Inc., for his sensitive editing and commentary on drafts of the manuscript. My publisher, Don McKeon of Brassey's, Inc., has been a writer's delight in his belief in the book and in his patience and support.

I am especially indebted to my parents: my mother, Maria Emma, for always encouraging my interest in heroes in general and Mickey Mantle in particular; my father, Antonio Sr., for sparking my love of baseball as a youth and spending countless hours over the years talking baseball and forever debating the merits of DiMaggio and Mantle.

Special gratitude goes out to my muse, Griffey, the king of all Labrador retrievers.

This book might never have been written without the inspiration and sacrifice of my wife and sons. Ryan, our Little League all-star and obsessive, gifted student, was especially relentless in inspiring the pursuit of the smallest details and the most obscure of anecdotes. Our oldest son Trey, our southpaw pitching and hitting star of his Beverly Hills High School baseball team—and who perhaps will one day play in Yankee Stadium himself—has been the source of my renewed interest in baseball and in Mickey Mantle. My wife Renee has been the guiding light of the Mantle book from the very beginning—willing to sacrifice vacations, movie nights, and more for whatever research and work the project required. Her devotion and love—and the love of my sons—are my proof that there is a God.

Tony Castro
Beverly Hills, California

MICKEY MANTLE'S
HALL OF FAME SPEECH

August 12, 1974, Cooperstown, New York

Thank you very much, Commissioner. I would really like to thank you for leaving out those strikeouts. He gave all those records, but he didn't say anything about all those strikeouts. I was the world champion in striking out and everything, I'm sure. I don't know for sure, but I'm almost positive I must have had that record in the World Series, too. I broke Babe Ruth's record for all-time strikeouts. He only had, like, 1,500, I think. I ended up with 1,710. So that's one that no one will ever break probably, because, if you strike out that much, you don't get to play very long. I just lucked out.

One of the reasons I'm in the Hall of Fame right now is not because of my speaking, so everybody be patient here. I know it's hot and I'll try to get through with what I gotta say real fast here. I was named after a Hall of Famer. I think this is the first time it's ever happened that a guy's ever come into the Hall of Fame that was named after one. Before I was born, my father lived and died for baseball and he named me after a Hall of Famer—Mickey Cochrane. I'm not sure if my dad knew it or not, but his real name was Gordon. I hope there's no Gordons here today, but I'm glad that he didn't name me Gordon.

He had the foresight to realize that someday in baseball that left-handed hitters were going to hit against right-handed pitchers and right-handed hitters were going to hit against left-handed pitchers; and he taught me, he and his father, to switch-hit at a real young age, when I first started to learn how to play ball. And my dad always told me if I could hit both ways when I got ready to go to the major leagues, that I would have a better chance of playing. And believe it or not, the year that I came to the Yankees is when Casey started platooning everybody. So he did realize that that was going to happen someday, and it did. So I was lucky that they taught me how to switch-hit when I was young.

We lived in a little town called Commerce, Oklahoma, and my mother, who is here today—I'd like to introduce her right now. . . . Mom. We didn't have a lot of money or anything. She used to make my uniforms and we would buy the cleats or get 'em off of somebody else's shoes or somethin' and then we would take 'em and have 'em put onto a pair of my street shoes that were getting old. So that's how we started out. We lived in Commerce till I can remember I was about in high school, then we moved out to a farm. We had 160-acre farm out in Whitebird, Oklahoma, I remember. I had three brothers, but one of them was too little. My mom used to have to make the twins come out and play ball with me. We dozed a little ballpark out in the pasture and I think that I probably burnt my twins out on baseball. I think by the time the twins got old enough to play ball they were tired of it, because I used to make 'em shag flies for me and play all day, which I'm sorry of because they could have been great ballplayers.

My dad really is probably the most influential thing that ever happened to me in my life. He loved baseball, I loved it and, like I say, he named me after a baseball player. He worked in the mines, and when he came home at night, why, he would come out and, after we milked the cows, we would go ahead and play ball till dark. I don't know how he kept doing it.

I think the first real baseball uniform—and I'm sure it is—the most proud I ever was when I went to Baxter Springs in Kansas and I played on the Baxter Springs Whiz Kids. We had—that was the first time—I'll never forget the guy, his name was Barney Burnett, gave me a uniform and it had a BW on the cap there and it said Whiz Kids on the back. I really thought I was some-thin' when I got that uniform. It was the first one my mom hadn't made for me. It was really somethin'.

There is a man and a woman here that were really nice to me all through the years, Mr. and Mrs. Harold Youngman. I don't know if all of you have ever heard about any of my business endeavors or not, but some of 'em weren't too good. Probably the worst thing I ever did was movin' away from Mr. Youngman. We went and moved to Dallas, Texas, in 1957, but Mr. Young-man built a Holiday Inn in Joplin, Missouri, and called it Mickey Mantle's

Holiday Inn. And we were doin' pretty good there, and Mr. Youngman said, "You know, you're half of this thing, so why don't you do something for it." So we had real good chicken there and I made up a slogan. Merlyn doesn't want me to tell this, but I'm going to tell it anyway. I made up the slogan for our chicken and I said, "To get a better piece of chicken, you'd have to be a rooster." And I don't know if that's what closed up our Holiday Inn or not, but we didn't do too good after that. No, actually, it was really a good deal.

Also, in Baxter Springs, the ballpark is right by the highway, and Tom Greenwade, the Yankee scout, was coming by there one day. He saw this ball game goin' on and I was playing in it and he stopped to watch the game. I'm making this kind of fast; it's gettin' a little hot. And I hit three home runs that day and Greenwade, the Yankee scout, stopped and talked to me. He was actually on his way to Broken Arrow, Oklahoma, to sign another shortstop. I was playing shortstop at that time, and I hit three home runs that day. A couple of them went in the river—one right-handed and one left-handed—and he stopped and he said, "You're not out of high school yet, so I really can't talk to you yet, but I'll be back when you get out of high school."

In 1949, Tom Greenwade came back to Commerce the night that I was supposed to go to my commencement exercises. He asked the principal of the school if I could go play ball. The Whiz Kids had a game that night. He took me. I hit another home run or two that night, so he signed me and I went to Independence, Kansas, Class D League, and started playing for the Yankees. I was very fortunate to play for Harry Craft. He had a great ball club there. We have one man here in the audience today who I played with in the minors, Carl Lombardi. He was on those teams, so he knows we had two of the greatest teams in minor league baseball at that time, or any time probably, and I was very fortunate to have played with those two teams.

I was lucky when I got out. I played at Joplin. The next year, I came to the Yankees. And I was lucky to play with Whitey Ford, Yogi Berra, Joe Di-Maggio, Phil Rizzuto—who came up with me—and I appreciate it. He's been a great friend all the way through for me. Lots of times I've teased Whitey about how I could have played five more years if it hadn't been for him, but, believe me, when Ralph Houk used to say that I was the leader of the Yankees, he was just kiddin' everybody. Our real leader was Whitey Ford all the time. I'm sure that everybody will tell you that.

Casey Stengel's here in the Hall of Fame already and, outside of my dad, I would say that probably Casey is the man who is most responsible for me standing right here today. The first thing he did was to take me off of short-stop and get me out in the outfield where I wouldn't have to handle so many balls.

At this time I'd like to introduce my family. I introduced my mother. Merlyn, my wife, we've been married 22 years. That's a record where I come from. Mickey, my oldest boy, David, Billy and Danny. That's my family that I've been with for so long.

I listened to Mr. Terry make a talk last night just for the Hall of Famers, and he said that he hoped we would come back, and I just hope that Whitey and I can live up to the expectation and what these here guys stand for. I'm sure we're going to try to. I just would—before I leave—would like to thank everybody for coming up here. It's been a great day for all of us and I appreciate it very much."

BOB COSTAS'S EULOGY

It occurs to me as we're all sitting here thinking of Mickey, he's probably somewhere getting an earful from Casey Stengel, and no doubt quite confused by now.

One of Mickey's fondest wishes was that he be remembered as a great teammate, to know that the men he played with thought well of him.

But it was more than that. Moose and Whitey and Tony and Yogi and Bobby and Hank, what a remarkable team you were. And the stories of the visits you guys made to Mickey's bedside the last few days were heartbreakingly tender. It meant everything to Mickey, as would the presence of so many baseball figures past and present here today.

I was honored to be asked to speak by the Mantle family today. I am not standing here as a broadcaster. Mel Allen is the eternal voice of the Yankees and that would be his place. And there are others here with a longer and deeper association with Mickey than mine.

But I guess I'm here, not so much to speak for myself as to simply represent the millions of baseball-loving kids who grew up in the '50s and '60s and for whom Mickey Mantle was baseball.

And more than that, he was a presence in our lives—a fragile hero to whom we had an emotional attachment so strong and lasting that it defied logic. Mickey often said he didn't understand it, this enduring connection and affection—for men now in their 40s and 50s, otherwise perfectly sensible, who went dry in the mouth and stammered like schoolboys in the presence of Mickey Mantle.

Maybe Mick was uncomfortable with it, not just because of his basic shyness, but because he was always too honest to regard himself as some kind of deity.

But that was never really the point. In a very different time than today, the first baseball commissioner, Kenesaw Mountain Landis, said every boy builds a shrine to some baseball hero, and before that shrine, a candle always burns.

For a huge portion of my generation, Mickey Mantle was that baseball hero. And for reasons that no statistics, no dry recitation of facts can possibly capture, he was the most compelling baseball hero of our lifetime. And he was our symbol of baseball at a time when the game meant something to us that perhaps it no longer does.

Mickey Mantle had those dual qualities so seldom seen, exuding dynamism and excitement but at the same time touching your heart—flawed, wounded. We knew there was something poignant about Mickey Mantle before we knew what poignant meant.

We didn't just root for him, we felt for him.

Long before many of us ever cracked a serious book, we knew something about mythology as we watched Mickey Mantle run out a home run through the lengthening shadows of a late Sunday afternoon at Yankee Stadium.

There was greatness in him, but vulnerability too.

He was our guy. When he was hot, we felt great. When he slumped or got hurt, we sagged a bit too. We tried to crease our caps like him; kneel in an imaginary on-deck circle like him; run like him, heads down, elbows up.

Billy Crystal is here today. Billy says that at his bar mitzvah he spoke in an Oklahoma drawl. Billy's here today because he loved Mickey Mantle, and millions more who felt like him are here today in spirit as well.

It's been said that the truth is never pure and rarely simple.

Mickey Mantle was too humble and honest to believe that the whole truth about him could be found on a Wheaties box or a baseball card. But the emotional truths of childhood have a power to transcend objective fact. They stay with us through all the years, withstanding the ambivalence that so often accompanies the experiences of adults.

That's why we can still recall the immediate tingle in that instant of recognition when a Mickey Mantle popped up in a pack of Topps bubble gum cards—a treasure lodged between an Eli Grba and a Pumpsie Green.

That's why we smile today, recalling those October afternoons when we'd sneak a transistor radio into school to follow Mickey and the Yankees in the World Series.

Or when I think of Mr. Tomasee, a very wise sixth-grade teacher who understood that the World Series was more important, at least for one day, than any school lesson could be. So he brought his black-and-white TV from home, plugged it in and let us watch it right there in school through the flicker and the static. It was richer and more compelling than anything I've seen on a high-resolution, big-screen TV.

Of course, the bad part, Bobby [Richardson], was that Koufax struck 15 of you guys out that day.

My phone's been ringing the past few weeks as Mickey fought for his life. I've heard from people I hadn't seen or talked to in years—guys I played stickball with, even some guys who took Willie's side in those endless Mantle-Mays arguments. They're grown up now. They have their families. They're not even necessarily big baseball fans anymore. But they felt something hearing about Mickey, and they figured I did too.

In the last year, Mickey Mantle, always so hard on himself, finally came to accept and appreciate that distinction between a role model and a hero. The first he often was not, the second he always will be.

In the end, people got it. And Mickey Mantle got from America something other than misplaced and mindless celebrity worship. He got something far more meaningful. He got love—love for what he had been; love for what he made us feel; love for the humanity and sweetness that was always there mixed in with the flaws and all the pain that wracked his body and his soul.

We wanted to tell him that it was OK, that what he had been was enough. We hoped he felt that Mutt Mantle would have understood and that Merlyn and the boys loved him.

And then in the end, something remarkable happened—the way it does for champions. Mickey Mantle rallied. His heart took over, and he had some innings as fine as any in 1956 or with his buddy, Roger, in 1961.

But this time, he did it in the harsh and trying summer of '95. And what he did was stunning. The sheer grace of that ninth inning—the humility, the sense of humor, the total absence of self-pity, the simple eloquence and honesty of his pleas to others to take heed of his mistakes.

All of America watched in admiration. His doctors said he was, in many ways, the most remarkable patient they'd ever seen. His bravery, so stark and real, that even those used to seeing people in dire circumstances were moved by his example.

Because of that example, organ donations are up dramatically all across America. A cautionary tale has been honestly told and perhaps will affect some lives for the better.

And our last memories of Mickey Mantle are as heroic as the first.

None of us, Mickey included, would want to be held to account for every moment of our lives. But how many of us could say that our best moments were as magnificent as his?

This is the cartoon from this morning's *Dallas Morning News*. Maybe some of you saw it. It got torn a little bit on the way to the hotel to here. There's a figure here, St. Peter I take it to be, with his arm around Mickey, that broad back and the number 7. He's holding his book of admissions. He says, "Kid, that was the most courageous ninth inning I've ever seen."

It brings to mind a story Mickey liked to tell on himself and maybe some of you have heard it. He pictured himself at the pearly gates, met by St. Peter who shook his head and said "Mick, we checked the record. We know some of what went on. Sorry, we can't let you in. But before you go, God wants to know if you'd sign these six dozen baseballs."

Well, there were days when Mickey Mantle was so darn good that we kids would bet that even God would want his autograph. But like the cartoon says, I don't think Mick needed to worry much about the other part.

I just hope God has a place for him where he can run again. Where he can play practical jokes on his teammates and smile that boyish smile, 'cause God knows, no one's perfect. And God knows there's something special about heroes.

So long, Mick. Thanks.

MICKEY MANTLE'S BATTING STATISTICS

MINOR LEAGUE CAREER

Year	Team		G	AB	R	H	2B	3B	HR	RBI	AVG	SLG
1949	Independence	K-O-M	89	323	54	101	15	7	7	63	.313	.467
1950	Joplin	W.A	137	519	141	199	30	12	26	136	.383	.638
1951	Kansas City	A.A.	40	166	32	60	9	3	11	50	.361	.651

MAJOR LEAGUE REGULAR SEASON

Year	G	AB	R	H	2B	3B	HR	RBI	BB	K	SB	CS	GDP	IBB	HBP	AVG	OBP	SLG
1951	96	341	61	91	11	5	13	65	43	74	8	7	3	–	0	.267	.349	.443
1952	142	549	94	171	37	7	23	87	75	111	4	1	5	–	0	.311	.394	.530
1953	127	461	105	136	24	3	21	92	79	90	8	4	2	–	0	.295	.398	.497
1954	146	543	129	163	17	12	27	102	102	107	5	2	3	–	0	.300	.408	.525
1955	147	517	121	158	25	11	37	99	113	97	8	1	4	6	3	.306	.431	.611
1956	150	533	132	188	22	5	52	130	112	99	10	1	4	6	2	.353	.464	.705
1957	144	474	121	173	28	6	34	94	146	75	16	3	5	23	0	.365	.512	.665
1958	150	519	127	158	21	1	42	97	129	120	18	3	11	13	2	.304	.443	.592
1959	144	541	104	154	23	4	31	75	94	126	21	3	7	6	2	.285	.390	.514
1960	153	527	119	145	17	6	40	94	111	125	14	3	11	6	1	.275	.399	.558
1961	153	514	132	163	16	6	54	128	126	112	12	1	2	9	0	.317	.448	.687
1962	123	377	96	121	15	1	30	89	122	78	9	0	4	9	1	.321	.486	.605
1963	65	172	40	54	8	0	15	35	40	32	2	1	5	4	0	.314	.441	.622
1964	143	465	92	141	25	2	35	111	99	102	6	3	9	18	0	.303	.423	.591
1965	122	361	44	92	12	1	19	46	73	76	4	1	11	7	0	.255	.379	.452
1966	108	333	40	96	12	1	23	56	57	76	1	1	9	5	0	.288	.389	.538
1967	144	440	63	108	17	0	22	55	107	113	1	1	9	7	1	.245	.391	.434
1968	144	435	57	103	14	1	18	54	106	97	6	2	9	7	1	.237	.385	.398
Totals	2401	8102	1677	2415	344	72	536	1509	1734	1710	153	38	113	126	13	.298	.421	.557

WORLD SERIES

Year	Opponent	G	AB	R	H	2B	3B	HR	RBI	BB	K	SB	AVG	OBP	SLG
1951	New York (N)	2	5	1	1	0	0	0	0	0	1	0	.200	.429	.200
1952	Brooklyn	7	29	5	10	1	1	2	3	3	4	0	.345	.406	.655
1953	Brooklyn	6	24	3	5	0	0	2	7	3	8	0	.208	.296	.458
1955	Brooklyn	3	10	1	2	0	0	1	1	0	2	0	.200	.200	.500
1956	Brooklyn	7	24	6	6	1	0	3	4	6	5	1	.250	.400	.667
1957	Milwaukee	6	19	3	5	0	0	1	2	3	1	0	.263	.364	.421
1958	Milwaukee	7	24	4	6	0	1	2	3	7	4	0	.250	.419	.583
1960	Pittsburgh	7	25	8	10	1	0	3	11	8	9	0	.400	.545	.800
1961	Cincinnati	2	6	0	1	0	0	0	0	0	2	0	.167	.167	.167
1962	San Francisco	7	25	2	3	1	0	0	0	4	5	2	.120	.241	.160
1963	Los Angeles	4	15	1	2	0	0	1	1	1	5	0	.133	.187	.333
1964	St. Louis	7	24	8	8	2	0	3	8	6	8	0	.333	.467	.792
Totals		65	230	42	59	6	2	18	40	43	54	3	.257	.374	.535

MICKEY MANTLE'S CAREER HOME RUNS
The Complete Year by Year List
Plus World Series and All-Star Games
Includes Date, Lefty or Righty, Location, Team, and Pitcher

1951: 13 Home Runs

1 (1). May 1, 1951, LH, Comiskey Park vs. Chicago White Sox, Pitcher: Randy Gumpert (RH)

2 (2). May 4, 1951, LH, Sportsman's Park vs. St. Louis Browns, Pitcher: Duane Pillette (RH)

3 (3). May 13, 1951, RH, Shibe Park vs. Philadelphia A's, Pitcher: Alex Kellner (LH)

4 (4). May 16, 1951, RH, Yankee Stadium vs. Cleveland Indians, Pitcher: Dick Rozek (LH)

5 (5). June 19, 1951, LH, Yankee Stadium vs. Chicago White Sox, Pitcher: Lou Kretlow (RH)

6 (6). June 19, 1951, LH, Yankee Stadium vs. Chicago White Sox, Pitcher: Joe Dobson (RH)

7 (7). July 7, 1951, LH, Fenway Park vs. Boston Red Sox, Pitcher: Ellis Kinder (RH)

8 (8). August 25, 1951, LH, Municipal Stadium vs. Cleveland Indians, Pitcher: Mike Garcia (RH)

9 (9). August 29, 1951, LH, Sportsman's Park vs. St. Louis Browns, Pitcher: Satchel Paige (RH)

10 (10). September 8, 1951, LH, Yankee Stadium vs. Washington Senators, Pitcher: Sid Hudson (RH)

11 (11). September 9, 1951, LH, Yankee Stadium vs. Washington Senators, Pitcher: Dick Starr (RH)

12 (12). September 12, 1951, Yankee Stadium vs. Detroit Tigers, Pitcher: Virgil Trucks (RH)

13 (13). September 19, 1951, LH, Yankee Stadium vs. Chicago White Sox, Pitcher: Lou Kretlow (RH)

Number of games in which Mickey homered in 1951: 13

Yankees record in 1951 in games in which Mickey homered: 11–2 (.846)

1952: 23 Home Runs

14 (1). April 21, 1952, RH, Yankee Stadium vs. Philadelphia A's, Pitcher: Bobby Shantz (LH)

15 (2). April 30, 1952, RH, Yankee Stadium vs. St. Louis Browns, Pitcher: Bob Cain (LH)

16 (3). May 30, 1952, RH, Yankee Stadium vs. Philadelphia A's, Pitcher: Bobby Shantz (LH)

17 (4). June 15, 1952, LH, Municipal Stadium vs. Cleveland Indians, Pitcher: Bob Lemon (RH)

18 (5). June 17, 1952, RH, Briggs Stadium vs. Detroit Tigers, Pitcher: Billy Hoeft (LH)

19 (6). June 22, 1952, LH, Comiskey Park vs. Chicago White Sox, Pitcher: Marv Grissom (RH)

20 (7). June 27, 1952, LH, Yankee Stadium vs. Philadelphia A's, Pitcher: Bob Hooper (RH)

21 (8). July 5, 1952, RH, Shibe Park vs. Philadelphia A's, Pitcher: Alex Kellner (LH)

22 (9). July 6, 1952, RH, Shibe Park vs. Philadelphia A's, Pitcher: Bobby Shantz (LH)

23 (10). July 13, 1952, LH, Yankee Stadium vs. Detroit Tigers, Pitcher: Marlin Stuart (RH)

24 (11). July 13, 1952, RH, Yankee Stadium vs. Detroit Tigers, Pitcher: Hal Newhouser (LH)

25 (12). July 15, 1952, LH, Yankee Stadium vs. Cleveland Indians, Pitcher: Early Wynn (RH)

26 (13). July 17, 1952, LH, Yankee Stadium vs. Cleveland Indians, Pitcher: Steve Gromek (RH)

27 (14). July 25, 1952, LH, Briggs Stadium vs. Detroit Tigers, Pitcher: Art Houtteman (RH)

28 (15). July 26, 1952, RH, Briggs Stadium vs. Detroit Tigers, Pitcher: Ted Gray (LH)

29 (16). July 29, 1952, RH, Comiskey Park vs. Chicago White Sox, Pitcher: Chuck Stobbs (LH)

30 (17). August 11, 1952, LH, Yankee Stadium vs. Boston Red Sox, Pitcher: Sid Hudson (RH)

31 (18). August 11, 1952, LH, Yankee Stadium vs. Boston Red Sox, Pitcher: Ralph Brickner (RH)

32 (19). August 30, 1952, LH, Yankee Stadium vs. Washington Senators, Pitcher: Randy Gumpert (RH)

33 (20). September 14, 1952, RH, Municipal Stadium vs. Cleveland Indians, Pitcher: Lou Brissie (LH)

34 (21). September 17, 1952, RH, Briggs Stadium vs. Detroit Tigers, Pitcher: Bill Wight (LH)

35 (22). September 24, 1952, RH, Fenway Park vs. Boston Red Sox, Pitcher: Mel Parnell (LH)

36 (23). September 26, 1952, LH, Shibe Park vs. Philadelphia A's, Pitcher: Harry Byrd (RH)

Number of games in which Mickey homered in 1952: 22
Yankees record in 1952 in games in which Mickey homered: 14–8 (.636)

1953: 21 Home Runs

37 (1). April 17, 1953, RH, Griffith Stadium vs. Washington Senators, Pitcher: Chuck Stobbs (LH)

38 (2). April 23, 1953, LH, Yankee Stadium vs. Boston Red Sox, Pitcher: Ellis Kinder (RH)

39 (3). April 28, 1953, RH, Busch Stadium vs. St. Louis Browns, Pitcher: Bob Cain (LH)

40 (4). April 30, 1953, RH, Comiskey Park vs. Chicago White Sox, Pitcher: Gene Bearden (LH)

41 (5). May 9, 1953, RH, Fenway Park vs. Boston Red Sox, Pitcher: Willie Werle (LH)

42 (6). May 25, 1953, RH, Yankee Stadium vs. Boston Red Sox, Pitcher: Mickey McDermott (LH)

43 (7). June 4, 1953, RH, Comiskey Park vs. Chicago White Sox, Pitcher: Billy Pierce (LH)

44 (8). June 5, 1953, LH, Busch Stadium vs. St. Louis Browns, Pitcher: Bobo Holloman (RH)

45 (9). June 11, 1953, LH, Briggs Stadium vs. Detroit Tigers, Pitcher: Art Houtteman (RH)

46 (10). June 18, 1953, RH, Yankee Stadium vs. St. Louis Browns, Pitcher: Bob Cain (LH)

47 (11). June 21, 1953, RH, Yankee Stadium vs. Detroit Tigers, Pitcher: Hal Newhouser (LH)

48 (12). June 23, 1953, LH, Yankee Stadium vs. Chicago White Sox, Pitcher: Virgil Trucks (RH)

49 (13). July 16, 1953, RH, Connie Mack Stadium vs. Philadelphia A's, Pitcher: Frank Fanovich (LH)

50 (14). July 26, 1953, RH, Briggs Stadium vs. Detroit Tigers, Pitcher: Al Albert (LH)

51 (15). July 26, 1953, LH, Briggs Stadium vs. Detroit Tigers, Pitcher: Steve Gromek (RH)

52 (16).   August 7, 1953, LH, Yankee Stadium vs. Chicago White Sox, Pitcher: Connie Johnson (RH)

53 (17).   September 1, 1953, LH, Comiskey Park vs. Chicago White Sox, Pitcher: Virgil Trucks (RH)

54 (18).   September 7, 1953, RH, Fenway Park vs. Boston Red Sox, Pitcher: Mel Parnell (LH)

55 (19).   September 9, 1953, RH, Yankee Stadium vs. Chicago White Sox, Pitcher: Billy Pierce (LH)

56 (20).   September 12, 1953, RH, Yankee Stadium vs. Detroit Tigers, Pitcher: Billy Hoeft (LH)

57 (21).   September 20, 1953, RH, Fenway Park vs. Boston Red Sox, Pitcher: Mickey McDermott (LH)

Number of games in which Mickey homered in 1953: 21

Yankees record in 1953 in games in which Mickey homered: 15–6 (.714)

1954: 27 Home Runs

58   (1).   April 19, 1954, RH, Fenway Park vs. Boston Red Sox, Pitcher: Mel Parnell (LH)

59   (2).   April 21, 1954, RH, Yankee Stadium vs. Boston Red Sox, Pitcher: Lou Kiely (LH)

60   (3).   May 7, 1954, RH, Yankee Stadium vs. Philadelphia A's, Pitcher: Morrie Martin (LH)

61   (4).   May 21, 1954, LH, Yankee Stadium vs. Boston Red Sox, Pitcher: Frank Sullivan (RH)

62   (5).   May 22, 1954, LH, Yankee Stadium vs. Boston Red Sox, Pitcher: Tex Clevenger (RH)

63   (6).   May 23, 1954, RH, Yankee Stadium vs. Boston Red Sox, Pitcher: Bill Henry (LH)

64   (7).   May 25, 1954, LH, Griffith Stadium vs. Washington Senators, Pitcher: Sonny Dixon (RH)

65   (8).   May 29, 1954, LH, Fenway Park vs. Boston Red Sox, Pitcher: Sid Hudson (RH)

66   (9).   May 30, 1954, LH, Fenway Park vs. Boston Red Sox, Pitcher: Willard Nixon (RH)

67 (10).   June 6, 1954, LH, Yankee Stadium vs. Baltimore Orioles, Pitcher: Don Larsen (RH)

68 (11).   June 10, 1954, LH, Yankee Stadium vs. Detroit Tigers, Pitcher: Ralph Branca (RH)

69 (12).   June 20, 1954, LH, Comiskey Park vs. Chicago White Sox, Pitcher: Mike Fornieles (RH)

70 (13).   June 26, 1954, LH, Municipal Stadium vs. Cleveland Indians, Pitcher: Bob Hooper (RH)

71 (14). June 30, 1954, LH, Fenway Park vs. Boston Red Sox, Pitcher: Willard Nixon (RH)

72 (15). July 1, 1954, LH, Fenway Park vs. Boston Red Sox, Pitcher: Frank Sullivan (RH)

73 (16). July 3, 1954, LH, Yankee Stadium vs. Washington Senators, Pitcher: Bob Porterfield (RH)

74 (17). July 5, 1954, LH, Connie Mack Stadium vs. Philadelphia A's, Pitcher: Arnie Portocarrero (RH)

75 (18). July 7, 1954, LH, Yankee Stadium vs. Boston Red Sox, Pitcher: Tom Brewer (RH)

76 (19). July 19, 1954, RH, Yankee Stadium vs. Detroit Tigers, Pitcher: Ted Gray (LH)

77 (20). July 22, 1954, LH, Yankee Stadium vs. Chicago White Sox, Pitcher: Don Johnson (RH)

78 (21). July 28, 1954, RH, Comiskey Park vs. Chicago White Sox, Pitcher: Jack Harshman (LH)

79 (22). August 5, 1954, LH, Municipal Stadium vs. Cleveland Indians, Pitcher: Early Wynn (RH)

80 (23). August 5, 1954, LH, Municipal Stadium vs. Cleveland Indians, Pitcher: Ray Narelski (RH)

81 (24). August 8, 1954, RH, Briggs Stadiums vs. Detroit Tigers, Pitcher: Billy Hoeft (LH)

82 (25). August 12, 1954, LH, Yankee Stadium vs. Philadelphia A's, Pitcher: Arnie Portocarrero (RH)

83 (??). August 15, 1954, LH, Yankee Stadium vs. Boston Red Sox, Pitcher: Hal "Skinny" Brown (RH)

84 (26). September 2, 1954, LH, Yankee Stadium vs. Cleveland Indians, Pitcher: Bob Lemon (RH)

Number of games in which Mickey homered in 1954: 26
Yankees record in 1954 in games in which Mickey homered: 21–5 (.846)

1955: 37 Home Runs (League Leader)

85 (1). April 13, 1955, LH, Yankee Stadium vs. Washington Senators, Pitcher: Ted Abernathy (RH)

86 (2). April 18, 1955, LH, Memorial Stadium vs. Baltimore Orioles, Pitcher: Harry Byrd (RH)

87 (3). April 28, 1955, LH, Municipal Stadium vs. Kansas City A's, Pitcher: Charlie Bishop (RH)

88 (4). May 3, 1955, LH, Municipal Stadium vs. Cleveland Indians, Pitcher: Mike Garcia (RH)

89 (5). May 6, 1955, LH, Fenway Park vs. Boston Red Sox, Pitcher: Frank Sullivan (RH)

90 (6). May 7, 1955, LH, Fenway Park vs. Boston Red Sox, Pitcher: Ike Delock (RH)

91 (7). May 11, 1955, LH, Yankee Stadium vs. Cleveland Indians, Pitcher: Early Wynn (RH)

92 (8). May 13, 1955, LH, Yankee Stadium vs. Detroit Tigers, Pitcher: Steve Gromek (RH)

93 (9). May 13, 1955, LH, Yankee Stadium vs. Detroit Tigers, Pitcher: Steve Gromek (RH)

94 (10). May 13, 1955, RH, Yankee Stadium vs. Detroit Tigers, Pitcher: Bob Miller (LH)

95 (11). May 18, 1955, LH, Yankee Stadium vs. Chicago White Sox, Pitcher: Mike Fornieles (RH)

96 (12). June 3, 1955, RH, Comiskey Park vs. Chicago White Sox, Pitcher: Jack Harshman (LH)

97 (13). June 5, 1955, RH, Comiskey Park vs. Chicago White Sox, Pitcher: Billy Pierce (LH)

98 (14). June 6, 1955, RH, Briggs Stadium vs. Detroit Tigers, Pitcher: Bob Miller (LH)

99 (15). June 17, 1955, LH, Yankee Stadium vs. Chicago White Sox, Pitcher: Dick Donovan (RH)

100 (16). June 19, 1955, LH, Yankee Stadium vs. Chicago White Sox, Pitcher: Sandy Consuegra (RH)

101 (17). June 21, 1955, RH, Yankee Stadium vs. Kansas City A's, Pitcher: Alex Kellner (LH)

102 (18). June 22, 1955, LH, Yankee Stadium vs. Kansas City A's, Pitcher: Art Ditmar (RH)

103 (19). July 10, 1955, RH, Griffith Stadium vs. Washington Senators, Pitcher: Dean Stone (LH)

104 (20). July 10, 1955, RH, Griffith Stadium vs. Washington Senators, Pitcher: Dean Stone (LH)

105 (21). July 10, 1955, LH, Griffith Stadium vs. Washington Senators, Pitcher: Ted Abernathy (RH)

106 (22). July 28, 1955, LH, Yankee Stadium vs. Chicago White Sox, Pitcher: Connie Johnson (RH)

107 (23). July 31, 1955, RH, Yankee Stadium vs. Kansas City A's, Pitcher: Alex Kellner (LH)

108 (24). August 4, 1955, LH, Yankee Stadium vs. Cleveland Indians, Pitcher: Ray Narelski (RH)

109 (25). August 7, 1955, LH, Yankee Stadium vs. Detroit Tigers, Pitcher: Frank Lary (RH)

110 (26). August 7, 1955, LH, Yankee Stadium vs. Detroit Tigers, Pitcher: Babe Birrer (RH)

111 (27). August 14, 1955, RH, Memorial Stadium vs. Baltimore Orioles, Pitcher: Ed Lopat (LH)

112 (28). August 15, 1955, LH, Memorial Stadium vs. Baltimore Orioles, Pitcher: Ray Moore (RH)

113 (29). August 15, 1955, RH, Memorial Stadium vs. Baltimore Orioles, Pitcher: Art Schallock (LH)

114 (30). August 16, 1955, LH, Fenway Park vs. Boston Red Sox, Pitcher: Frank Sullivan (RH)

115 (31). August 19, 1955, LH, Yankee Stadium vs. Baltimore Orioles, Pitcher: Jim Wilson (RH)

116 (32). August 21, 1955, RH, Yankee Stadium vs. Baltimore Orioles, Pitcher: Ed Lopat (LH)

117 (33). August 24, 1955, LH, Briggs Stadium vs. Detroit Tigers, Pitcher: Steve Gromek (RH)

118 (34). August 28, 1955, LH, Comiskey Park vs. Chicago White Sox, Pitcher: Connie Johnson (RH)

119 (35). August 31, 1955, LH, Municipal Stadium vs. Kansas City A's, Pitcher: Arnie Portocarrero (RH)

120 (36). September 2, 1955, LH, Yankee Stadium vs. Washington Senators, Pitcher: Bob Porterfield (RH)

121 (37). September 4, 1955, LH, Yankee Stadium vs. Washington Senators, Pitcher: Pedro Ramos (RH)

Number of games in which Mickey homered in 1955: 32
Yankees record in 1955 in games in which Mickey homered: 27–5 (.844)

1956: 52 Home Runs (League Leader)

122 (1). April 17, 1956, LH, Griffith Stadium vs. Washington Senators, Pitcher: Camilo Pascual (RH)

123 (2). April 17, 1956, LH, Griffith Stadium vs. Washington Senators, Pitcher: Camilo Pascual (RH)

124 (3). April 20, 1956, LH, Yankee Stadium vs. Boston Red Sox, Pitcher: Ike Delock (RH)

125 (4). April 21, 1956, LH, Yankee Stadium vs. Boston Red Sox, Pitcher: George Susce (RH)

126 (5). May 1, 1956, LH, Yankee Stadium vs. Detroit Tigers, Pitcher: Steve Gromek (RH)

127 (6). May 2, 1956, LH, Yankee Stadium vs. Detroit Tigers, Pitcher: Frank Lary (RH)

128 (7). May 3, 1956, RH, Yankee Stadium vs. Kansas City A's, Pitcher: Art Ceccarelli (LH)

129 (8). May 5, 1956, LH, Yankee Stadium vs. Kansas City A's, Pitcher: Lou Kretlow (RH)

130 (9). May 5, 1956, LH, Yankee Stadium vs. Kansas City A's, Pitcher: Moe Burtschy (RH)

131 (10). May 8, 1956, LH, Yankee Stadium vs. Cleveland Indians, Pitcher: Early Wynn (RH)

132 (11). May 10, 1956, LH, Yankee Stadium vs. Cleveland Indians, Pitcher: Bob

Lemon (RH)

133 (12). May 14, 1956, LH, Municipal Stadium vs. Cleveland Indians, Pitcher: Bob Lemon (RH)

134 (13). May 16, 1956, RH, Municipal Stadium vs. Cleveland Indians, Pitcher: Bud Daley (LH)

135 (14). May 18, 1956, RH, Comiskey Park vs. Chicago White Sox, Pitcher: Billy Pierce (LH)

136 (15). May 18, 1956, LH, Comiskey Park vs. Chicago White Sox, Pitcher: Dixie Howell (RH)

137 (16). May 21, 1956, LH, Municipal Stadium vs. Kansas City A's, Pitcher: Moe Burtschy (RH)

138 (17). May 24, 1956, LH, Briggs Stadium vs. Detroit Tigers, Pitcher: Duke Mass (RH)

139 (18). May 29, 1956, LH, Yankee Stadium vs. Boston Red Sox, Pitcher: Willard Nixon (RH)

140 (19). May 30, 1956, LH, Yankee Stadium vs. Washington Senators, Pitcher: Pedro Ramos (RH)

141 (20). May 30, 1956, LH, Yankee Stadium vs. Washington Senators, Pitcher: Camilo Pascual (RH)

142 (21). June 5, 1956, LH, Yankee Stadium vs. Kansas City A's, Pitcher: Lou Kretlow (RH)

143 (22). June 14, 1956, LH, Yankee Stadium vs. Chicago White Sox, Pitcher: Jim Wilson (RH)

144 (23). June 15, 1956, LH, Municipal Stadium vs. Cleveland Indians, Pitcher: Mike Garcia (RH)

145 (24). June 16, 1956, RH, Municipal Stadium vs. Cleveland Indians, Pitcher: Herb Score (LH)

146 (25). June 18, 1956, LH, Briggs Stadium vs. Detroit Tigers, Pitcher: Paul Foytack (RH)

147 (26). June 20, 1956, RH, Briggs Stadium vs. Detroit Tigers, Pitcher: Billy Hoeft (LH)

148 (27). June 20, 1956, RH, Briggs Stadium vs. Detroit Tigers, Pitcher: Billy Hoeft (LH)

149 (28). July 1, 1956, RH, Yankee Stadium vs. Washington Senators, Pitcher: Dean Stone (LH)

150 (29). July 1, 1956, LH, Yankee Stadium vs. Washington Senators, Pitcher: Bud Byerly (RH)

151 (30). July 14, 1956, RH, Yankee Stadium vs. Cleveland Indians, Pitcher: Herb Score (LH)

152 (31). July 18, 1956, LH, Yankee Stadium vs. Detroit Tigers, Pitcher: Paul Foytack (RH)

153 (32). July 22, 1956, LH, Yankee Stadium vs. Kansas City A's, Pitcher: Art Ditmar (RH)

154 (33). July 30, 1956, LH, Municipal Stadium vs. Cleveland Indians, Pitcher: Bob Lemon (RH)

155 (34). July 30, 1956, LH, Municipal Stadium vs. Cleveland Indians, Pitcher: Bob Feller (RH)

156 (35). August 4, 1956, LH, Briggs Stadium vs. Detroit Tigers, Pitcher: Virgil Trucks (RH)

157 (36). August 4, 1956, LH, Briggs Stadium vs. Detroit Tigers, Pitcher: Virgil Trucks (RH)

158 (37). August 5, 1956, LH, Briggs Stadium vs. Detroit Tigers, Pitcher: Jim Bunning (RH)

159 (38). August 8, 1956, LH, Griffith Stadium vs. Washington Senators, Pitcher: Camilo Pascual (RH)

160 (39). August 9, 1956, LH, Griffith Stadium vs. Washington Senators, Pitcher: Hal Griggs (RH)

161 (40). August 11, 1956, LH, Yankee Stadium vs. Baltimore Orioles, Pitcher: Hal Skinny Brown (RH)

162 (41). August 12, 1956, RH, Yankee Stadium vs. Baltimore Orioles, Pitcher: Dan Ferrarese (LH)

163 (42). August 14, 1956, RH, Yankee Stadium vs. Boston Red Sox, Pitcher: Mel Parnell (LH)

164 (43). August 23, 1956, RH, Yankee Stadium vs. Chicago White Sox, Pitcher: Paul LaPalme (LH)

165 (44). August 25, 1956, LH, Yankee Stadium vs. Chicago White Sox, Pitcher: Dick Donovan (RH)

166 (45). August 28, 1956, LH, Yankee Stadium vs. Kansas City A's, Pitcher: Art Ditmar (RH)

167 (46). August 29, 1956, LH, Yankee Stadium vs. Kansas City A's, Pitcher: Jack McMahan (RH)

168 (47). August 31, 1956, LH, Griffith Stadium vs. Washington Senators, Pitcher: Camilo Pascual (RH)

169 (48). September 13, 1956, LH, Municipal Stadium vs. Kansas City A's, Pitcher: Tom Gorman (RH)

170 (49). September 16, 1956, LH, Municipal Stadium vs. Cleveland Indians, Pitcher: Early Wynn (RH)

171 (50). September 18, 1956, RH, Comiskey Park vs. Chicago White Sox, Pitcher: Billy Pierce (LH)

172 (51). September 21, 1956, LH, Fenway Park vs. Boston Red Sox, Pitcher: Frank Sullivan (RH)

173 (52). September 28, 1956, LH, Yankee Stadium vs. Boston Red Sox, Pitcher: Bob Porterfield (RH)

Number of games in which Mickey homered in 1956: 45

Yankees record in 1956 in games in which Mickey homered: 30–15 (.667)

1957: 34 Home Runs

174 (1). April 22, 1957, RH, Griffith Stadium vs. Washington Senators, Pitcher: Chuck Stobbs (LH)

175 (2). April 24, 1957, LH, Yankee Stadium vs. Baltimore Orioles, Pitcher: Connie Johnson (RH)

176 (3). May 5, 1957, RH, Comiskey Park vs. Chicago White Sox, Pitcher: Billy Pierce (LH)

177 (4). May 8, 1957, LH, Municipal Stadium vs. Cleveland Indians, Pitcher: Early Wynn (RH)

178 (5). May 12, 1957, LH, Memorial Stadium vs. Baltimore Orioles, Pitcher: Hal Skinny Brown (RH)

179 (6). May 16, 1957, RH, Yankee Stadium vs. Kansas City A's, Pitcher: Alex Kellner (LH)

180 (7). May 19, 1957, LH, Yankee Stadium vs. Cleveland Indians, Pitcher: Bob Lemon (RH)

181 (8). May 25, 1957, LH, Yankee Stadium vs. Washington Senators, Pitcher: Pedro Ramos (RH)

182 (9). May 26, 1957, LH, Yankee Stadium vs. Washington Senators, Pitcher: Camilo Pascual (RH)

183 (10). May 29, 1957, LH, Griffith Stadium vs. Washington Senators, Pitcher: Pedro Ramos (RH)

184 (11). June 2, 1957, LH, Yankee Stadium vs. Baltimore Orioles, Pitcher: Hal Skinny Brown (RH)

185 (12). June 5, 1957, LH, Municipal Stadium vs. Cleveland Indians, Pitcher: Early Wynn (RH)

186 (13). June 6, 1957, LH, Municipal Stadium vs. Cleveland Indians, Pitcher: Mike Garcia (RH)

187 (14). June 7, 1957, LH, Briggs Stadium vs. Detroit Tigers, Pitcher: Jim Bunning (RH)

188 (15). June 10, 1957, LH, Briggs Stadium vs. Detroit Tigers, Pitcher: Frank Lary (RH)

189 (16). June 11, 1957, LH, Comiskey Park vs. Chicago White Sox, Pitcher: Jim Wilson (RH)

190 (17). June 12, 1957, RH, Comiskey Park vs. Chicago White Sox, Pitcher: Jack Harshman (LH)

191 (18). June 12, 1957, LH, Comiskey Park vs. Chicago White Sox, Pitcher: Bob Keegan (RH)

192 (19). June 14, 1957, RH, Municipal Stadium vs. Kansas City A's, Pitcher: Gene Host (LH)

193 (20). June 22, 1957, RH, Yankee Stadium vs. Chicago White Sox, Pitcher: Jack Harshman (LH)

194 (21). June 23, 1957, LH, Yankee Stadium vs. Chicago White Sox, Pitcher: Dick Donovan (RH)

195 (22). July 1, 1957, LH, Memorial Stadium vs. Baltimore Orioles, Pitcher: George Zuverink (RH)

196 (23). July 11, 1957, LH, Municipal Stadium vs. Kansas City A's, Pitcher: Tom Morgan (RH)

197 (24). July 12, 1957, LH, Municipal Stadium vs. Kansas City A's, Pitcher: Ralph Terry (RH)

198 (25). July 21, 1957, LH, Municipal Stadium vs. Kansas City A's, Pitcher: Ray Narelski (RH)

199 (26). July 23, 1957, LH, Yankee Stadium vs. Chicago White Sox, Pitcher: Bob Keegan (RH)

200 (27). July 26, 1957, LH, Yankee Stadium vs. Detroit Tigers, Pitcher: Jim Bunning (RH)

201 (28). July 31, 1957, RH, Yankee Stadium vs. Kansas City A's, Pitcher: Wally Burnette (LH)

202 (29). August 2, 1957, RH, Yankee Stadium vs. Cleveland Indians, Pitcher: Don Mossi (LH)

203 (30). August 7, 1957, LH, Yankee Stadium vs. Washington Senators, Pitcher: Tex Clevenger (RH)

204 (31). August 10, 1957, LH, Memorial Stadium vs. Baltimore Orioles, Pitcher: Ray Moore (RH)

205 (32). August 13, 1957, LH, Fenway Park vs. Boston Red Sox, Pitcher: Frank Sullivan (RH)

206 (33). August 26, 1957, LH, Briggs Stadium vs. Detroit Tigers, Pitcher: Frank Lary (RH)

207 (34). August 30, 1957, RH, Yankee Stadium vs. Washington Senators, Pitcher: Chuck Stobbs (LH)

Number of games in which Mickey homered in 1957: 33

Yankees record in 1957 in games in which Mickey homered: 20–13 (.613)

1958: 42 Home Runs (League Leader)

208 (1). April 17, 1958, LH, Fenway Park vs. Boston Red Sox, Pitcher: Tom Brewer (RH)

209 (2). May 9, 1958, LH, Yankee Stadium vs. Washington Senators, Pitcher: Pedro Ramos (RH)

210 (3). May 18, 1958, LH, Griffith Stadium vs. Washington Senators, Pitcher: Pedro Ramos (RH)

211 (4). May 20, 1958, LH, Comiskey Park vs. Chicago White Sox, Pitcher: Dick Donovan (RH)

212 (5). June 2, 1958, LH, Yankee Stadium vs. Chicago White Sox, Pitcher: Jim Wilson (RH)

213 (6). June 3, 1958, LH, Yankee Stadium vs. Chicago White Sox, Pitcher: Dick Donovan (RH)

214 (7). June 4, 1958, RH, Yankee Stadium vs. Chicago White Sox, Pitcher: Billy Pierce (LH)

215 (8). June 5, 1958, LH, Yankee Stadium vs. Chicago White Sox, Pitcher: Early Wynn (RH)

216 (9). June 6, 1958, RH, Yankee Stadium vs. Cleveland Indians, Pitcher: Dick Tomanek (LH)

217 (10). June 6, 1958, RH, Yankee Stadium vs. Cleveland Indians, Pitcher: Dick Tomanek (LH)

218 (11). June 8, 1958, LH, Yankee Stadium vs. Cleveland Indians, Pitcher: Jim Mudcat Grant (RH)

219 (12). June 13, 1958, RH, Yankee Stadium vs. Detroit Tigers: Billy Hoeft (LH)

220 (13). June 24, 1958, LH, Comiskey Park vs. Chicago White Sox, Pitcher: Early Wynn (RH)

221 (14). June 29, 1958, LH, Municipal Stadium vs. Kansas City A's, Pitcher: Ralph Terry (RH)

222 (15). July 1, 1958, LH, Memorial Stadium vs. Baltimore Orioles, Pitcher: Connie Johnson (RH)

223 (16). July 1, 1958, RH, Memorial Stadium vs. Baltimore Orioles, Pitcher: Jack Harshman (LH)

224 (17). July 3, 1958, LH, Griffith Stadium vs. Washington Senators, Pitcher: Russ Kemmerer (RH)

225 (18). July 3, 1958, LH, Griffith Stadium vs. Washington Senators, Pitcher: Russ Kemmerer (RH)

226 (19). July 4, 1958, RH, Griffith Stadium vs. Washington Senators, Pitcher: Chuck Stobbs (LH)

227 (20). July 5, 1958, LH, Yankee Stadium vs. Boston Red Sox, Pitcher: Dave Sisler (RH)

228 (21). July 6, 1958, LH, Yankee Stadium vs. Boston Red Sox, Pitcher: Ike Delock (RH)

229 (22). July 11, 1958, LH, Yankee Stadium vs. Cleveland Indians, Pitcher: Ray Narelski (RH)

230 (23). July 14, 1958, LH, Yankee Stadium vs. Chicago White Sox, Pitcher: Early Wynn (RH)

231 (24). July 15, 1958, LH, Yankee Stadium vs. Detroit Tigers, Pitcher: Frank Lary (RH)

232 (25). July 23, 1958, LH, Briggs Stadium vs. Detroit Tigers, Pitcher: Bill Fischer (RH)

233 (26). July 24, 1958, LH, Briggs Stadium vs. Detroit Tigers, Pitcher: Paul Foytack (RH)

234 (27). July 28, 1958, RH, Municipal Stadium vs. Kansas City A's, Pitcher: Dick Tomanek (LH)

235 (28). July 28, 1958, LH, Municipal Stadium vs. Kansas City A's, Pitcher: Ray Herbert (RH)

236 (29). August 4, 1958, LH, Memorial Stadium vs. Baltimore Orioles, Pitcher: Charlie Beamon (RH)

237 (30). August 5, 1958, LH, Memorial Stadium vs. Baltimore Orioles, Pitcher: Connie Johnson (RH)

238 (31). August 9, 1958, LH, Yankee Stadium vs. Boston Red Sox, Pitcher: Dave Sisler (RH)

239 (32). August 11,1958, LH, Yankee Stadium vs. Baltimore Orioles, Pitcher: Connie Johnson (RH)

240 (33). August 12, 1958, RH, Yankee Stadium vs. Baltimore Orioles, Pitcher: Ken Lehman (LH)

241 (34). August 16, 1958, LH, Fenway Park vs. Boston Red Sox, Pitcher: Tom Brewer (RH)

242 (35). August 17, 1958, LH, Fenway Park vs. Boston Red Sox, Pitcher: Ike Delock (RH)

243 (36). August 22, 1958, LH, Yankee Stadium vs. Chicago White Sox, Pitcher: Early Wynn (RH)

244 (37). August 27, 1958, LH, Yankee Stadium vs. Kansas City A's, Pitcher: Tom Gorman (RH)

245 (38). September 2, 1958, LH, Yankee Stadium vs. Boston Red Sox, Pitcher: Dave Sisler (RH)

246 (39). September 3, 1958, LH, Yankee Stadium vs. Boston Red Sox, Pitcher: Frank Sullivan (RH)

247 (40). September 9, 1958, LH, Municipal Stadium vs. Cleveland Indians, Pitcher: Cal McLish (RH)

248 (41). September 17, 1958, LH, Briggs Stadium vs. Detroit Tigers, Pitcher: Jim Bunning (RH)

249 (42). September 24, 1958, LH, Fenway Park vs. Boston Red Sox, Pitcher: Tom Gorman (RH)

Number of games in which Mickey homered in 1958: 38 (plus one game suspended)

Yankees record in 1958 in games in which Mickey homered: 26–12–1 (.605)

1959: 31 Home Runs

250　(1). April 21, 1959, LH, Griffith Stadium vs. Washington Senators, Pitcher: Pedro Ramos (RH)

251　(2). April 23, 1959, LH, Griffith Stadium vs. Washington Senators, Pitcher: Russ Kemmerer (RH)

252　(3). April 29, 1959, LH, Comiskey Park vs. Chicago White Sox, Pitcher: Ray Moore (RH)

253　(4). May 10, 1959, RH, Yankee Stadium vs. Washington Senators, Pitcher: Chuck Stobbs (LH)

254　(5). May 12, 1959, LH, Yankee Stadium vs. Cleveland Indians, Pitcher: Cal McLish (RH)

255　(6). May 20, 1959, LH, Yankee Stadium vs. Detroit Tigers, Pitcher: Frank Lary (RH)

256 (7). May 23, 1959, LH, Memorial Stadium vs. Baltimore Orioles, Pitcher: George Zuverink (RH)

257 (8). May 24, 1959, RH, Memorial Stadium vs. Baltimore Orioles, Pitcher: Billy O'Dell (LH)

258 (9). May 30, 1959, LH, Griffith Stadium vs. Washington Senators, Pitcher: Dick Hyde (RH)

259 (10). June 3, 1959, Briggs Stadium vs. Detroit Tigers, Pitcher: Ray Narelski (RH)

260 (11). June 9, 1959, Yankee Stadium vs. Kansas City A's, Pitcher: Murray Dickson (RH)

261 (12). June 11, 1959, LH, Yankee Stadium vs. Kansas City A's, Pitcher: Ned Garver (RH)

262 (13). June 13, 1959, LH, Yankee Stadium vs. Detroit Tigers, Pitcher: Jim Bunning (RH)

263 (14). June 17, 1959, LH, Yankee Stadium vs. Chicago White Sox, Pitcher: Ray Moore (RH)

264 (15). June 18, 1959, LH, Yankee Stadium vs. Chicago White Sox, Pitcher: Jerry Staley (RH)

265 (16). June 22, 1959, LH, Municipal Stadium vs. Kansas City A's, Pitcher: Ray Herbert (RH)

266 (17). June 22, 1959, LH, Municipal Stadium vs. Kansas City A's, Pitcher: Bob Grim (RH)

267 (18). June 23, 1959, RH, Municipal Stadium vs. Kansas City A's, Pitcher: Rip Coleman (LH)

268 (19). July 16, 1959, LH, Yankee Stadium vs. Cleveland Indians, Pitcher: Gary Bell (RH)

269 (20). July 19, 1959, RH, Yankee Stadium vs. Chicago White Sox, Pitcher: Billy Pierce (LH)

270 (21). August 4, 1959, LH, Yankee Stadium vs. Detroit Tigers, Pitcher: Frank Lary (RH)

271 (22). August 5, 1959, RH, Yankee Stadium vs. Detroit Tigers, Pitcher: Don Mossi (LH)

272 (23). August 16, 1959, LH, Yankee Stadium vs. Boston Red Sox, Pitcher: Jerry Casale (RH)

273 (24). August 16, 1959, LH, Yankee Stadium vs. Boston Red Sox, Pitcher: Bill Monbouquette (RH)

274 (25). August 26, 1959, LH, Municipal Stadium vs. Cleveland Indians, Pitcher: Gary Bell (RH)

275 (26). August 29, 1959, LH, Griffith Stadium vs. Washington Senators, Pitcher: Hal Griggs (RH)

276 (27). September 7, 1959, LH, Fenway Park vs. Boston Red Sox, Pitcher: Jerry Casale (RH)

277 (28). September 10, 1959, LH, Yankee Stadium vs. Kansas City A's, Pitcher: Ray Herbert (RH)

278 (29). September 13, 1959, RH, Yankee Stadium vs. Cleveland Indians, Pitcher: Jack Harshman (LH)

279 (30). September 15, 1959, RH, Yankee Stadium vs. Chicago White Sox, Pitcher: Billy Pierce (LH)

280 (31). September 15, 1959, LH, Yankee Stadium vs. Chicago White Sox, Pitcher: Bob Shaw (RH)

Number of games in which Mickey homered in 1959: 29

Yankees record in 1959 in games in which Mickey homered: 19–10 (.652)

1960: 40 Home Runs (League Leader)

281 (1). April 22, 1960, LH, Yankee Stadium vs. Baltimore Orioles, Pitcher: Hoyt Wilhelm (RH)

282 (2). May 13, 1960, RH, Griffith Stadium vs. Washington Senators, Pitcher: Jim Kaat (LH)

283 (3). May 17, 1960, LH, Municipal Stadium vs. Cleveland Indians, Pitcher: Gary Bell (RH)

284 (4). May 20, 1960, LH, Comiskey Park vs. Chicago White Sox, Pitcher: Early Wynn (RH)

285 (5). May 29, 1960, RH, Yankee Stadium vs. Washington Senators, Pitcher: Jim Kaat (LH)

286 (6). May 29, 1960, RH, Yankee Stadium vs. Washington Senators, Pitcher: Hal Woodeschick (LH)

287 (7). June 1, 1960, LH, Memorial Stadium vs. Baltimore Orioles, Pitcher: Hal Skinny Brown (RH)

288 (8). June 5, 1960, LH, Yankee Stadium vs. Boston Red Sox, Pitcher: Tom Brewer (RH)

289 (9). June 8, 1960, LH, Yankee Stadium vs. Chicago White Sox, Pitcher: Bob Shaw (RH)

290 (10). June 8, 1960, LH, Yankee Stadium vs. Chicago White Sox, Pitcher: Ray Moore (RH)

291 (11). June 9, 1960, RH, Yankee Stadium vs. Chicago White Sox, Pitcher: Frank Baumann (LH)

292 (12). June 10, 1960, RH, Yankee Stadium vs. Cleveland Indians, Pitcher: Dick Stigman (LH)

293 (13). June 17, 1960, LH, Comiskey Park vs. Chicago White Sox, Pitcher: Turk Lown (RH)

294 (14). June 18, 1960, LH, Comiskey Park vs. Chicago White Sox, Pitcher: Bob Rush (RH)

295 (15). June 21, 1960, LH, Briggs Stadium vs. Detroit Tigers, Pitcher: Frank Lary (RH)

296 (16). June 21, 1960, LH, Briggs Stadium vs. Detroit Tigers, Pitcher: Frank Lary (RH)

297 (17). June 28, 1960, RH, Yankee Stadium vs. Kansas City A's, Pitcher: Bud Daley (LH)

298 (18). June 30, 1960, LH, Yankee Stadium vs. Kansas City A's, Pitcher: Bob Trowbridge (RH)

299 (19). July 3, 1960, RH, Yankee Stadium vs. Detroit Tigers, Pitcher: Pete Burnside (LH)

300 (20). July 4, 1960, RH, Griffith Stadium vs. Washington Senators, Pitcher: Hal Woodeschick (LH)

301 (21). July 15, 1960, RH, Briggs Stadium vs. Detroit Tigers, Pitcher: Don Mossi (LH)

302 (22). July 18, 1960, RH, Municipal Stadium vs. Cleveland Indians, Pitcher: Dick Stigman (LH)

303 (23). July 20, 1960, LH, Municipal Stadium vs. Cleveland Indians, Pitcher: Gary Bell (RH)

304 (24). July 24, 1960, LH, Yankee Stadium vs. Chicago White Sox, Pitcher: Russ Kemmerer (RH)

305 (25). July 26, 1960, RH, Yankee Stadium vs. Cleveland Indians, Pitcher: Dick Stigman (LH)

306 (26). July 28, 1960, LH, Yankee Stadium vs. Cleveland Indians, Pitcher: Jim Perry (RH)

307 (27). July 31, 1960, LH, Yankee Stadium vs. Kansas City A's, Pitcher: Johnny Kucks (RH)

308 (28). August 15, 1960, LH, Yankee Stadium vs. Baltimore Orioles, Pitcher: Jerry Walker (RH)

309 (29). August 15, 1960, LH, Yankee Stadium vs. Baltimore Orioles, Pitcher: Hoyt Wilhelm (RH)

310 (30). August 26, 1960, LH, Yankee Stadium vs. Cleveland Indians, Pitcher: Jim Perry (RH)

311 (31). August 28, 1960, LH, Yankee Stadium vs. Detroit Tigers, Pitcher: Phil Regan (RH)

312 (32). September 6, 1960, LH, Yankee Stadium vs. Boston Red Sox, Pitcher: Billy Muffett (RH)

313 (33). September 10, 1960, LH, Briggs Stadium vs. Detroit Tigers, Pitcher: Paul Foytack (RH)

314 (34). September 11,1960, RH, Municipal Stadium vs. Cleveland Indians, Pitcher: Carl Mathias (LH)

315 (35). September 17,1960, LH, Yankee Stadium vs. Baltimore Orioles, Pitcher: Chuck Estrada (RH)

316 (36). September 20, 1960, RH, Yankee Stadium vs. Washington Senators, Pitcher: Jack Kralick (LH)

317 (37). September 21,1960, LH, Yankee Stadium vs. Washington Senators, Pitcher: Pedro Ramos (RH)

318 (38). September 24, 1960, RH, Fenway Park vs. Boston Red Sox, Pitcher: Ted Williss (LH)

319 (39). September 28, 1960, RH, Griffith Stadium vs. Washington Senators, Pitcher: Chuck Stobbs (LH)

320 (40). September 28, 1960, RH, Griffith Stadium vs. Washington Senators, Pitcher: Chuck Stobbs (LH)

Number of games in which Mickey homered in 1960: 36

Yankees record in 1960 in games in which Mickey homered: 28–8 (.778)

1961: 54 Home Runs

321 (1). April 17, 1961, LH, Yankee Stadium vs. Kansas City A's, Pitcher: Jerry Walker (RH)

322 (2). April 20, 1961, LH, Yankee Stadium vs. Los Angeles Angels, Pitcher: Eli Grba (RH)

323 (3). April 20, 1961, LH, Yankee Stadium vs. Los Angeles Angels, Pitcher: Eli Grba (RH)

324 (4). April 21, 1961, RH, Memorial Stadium vs. Baltimore Orioles, Pitcher: Steve Barber (LH)

325 (5). April 23, 1961, LH, Memorial Stadium vs. Baltimore Orioles, Pitcher: Chuck Estrada (RH)

326 (6). April 26, 1961, LH, Tiger Stadium vs. Detroit Tigers, Pitcher: Jim Donahue (RH)

327 (7). April 26, 1961, RH, Tiger Stadium vs. Detroit Tigers, Pitcher: Hank Aguirre (LH)

328 (8). May 2, 1961, LH, Metropolitan Stadium vs. Minnesota Twins, Pitcher: Camilo Pascual (RH)

329 (9). May 4, 1961, LH, Metropolitan Stadium vs. Minnesota Twins, Pitcher: Ted Sadowski (RH)

330 (10). May 16, 1961, RH, Yankee Stadium vs. Washington Senators, Pitcher: Hal Woodeschick (LH)

331 (11). May 29, 1961, LH, Fenway Park vs. Boston Red Sox, Pitcher: Ike Delock (RH)

332 (12). May 30, 1961, LH, Fenway Park vs. Boston Red Sox, Pitcher: Gene Conley (RH)

333 (13). May 30, 1961, LH, Fenway Park vs. Boston Red Sox, Pitcher: Mike Fornieles (RH)

334 (14). May 31, 1961, LH, Fenway Park vs. Boston Red Sox, Pitcher: Billy Muffett (RH)

335 (15). June 5, 1961, LH, Yankee Stadium vs. Minnesota Twins, Pitcher: Don Lee (RH)

336 (16). June 9, 1961, LH, Yankee Stadium vs. Kansas City A's, Pitcher: Ray Herbert (RH)

337 (17). June 10, 1961, LH, Yankee Stadium vs. Kansas City A's, Pitcher: Bill Kunkel (RH)

338 (18). June 11,1961, LH, Yankee Stadium vs. Los Angeles Angels, Pitcher: Eli Grba (RH)

339 (19). June 15, 1961, LH, Municipal Stadium vs. Cleveland Indians, Pitcher: Jim Mudcat Grant (RH)

340 (20). June 17, 1961, LH, Tiger Stadium vs. Detroit Tigers, Pitcher: Paul Foytack (RH)

341 (21). June 21, 1961, LH, Municipal Stadium vs. Kansas City A's, Pitcher: Bob Shaw (RH)

342 (22). June 21, 1961, LH, Municipal Stadium vs. Kansas City A's, Pitcher: Bob Shaw (RH)

343 (23). June 26, 1961, LH, Wrigley Field vs. Los Angeles Angels, Pitcher: Ken McBride (RH)

344 (24). June 28, 1961, LH, Wrigley Field vs. Los Angeles Angels, Pitcher: Ryne Duren (RH)

345 (25). June 30, 1961, LH, Yankee Stadium vs. Washington Senators, Pitcher: Dick Donovan (RH)

346 (26). July 1, 1961, RH, Yankee Stadium vs. Washington Senators, Pitcher: Carl Mathias (LH)

347 (27). July 1, 1961, RH, Yankee Stadium vs. Washington Senators, Pitcher: Carl Mathias (LH)

348 (28). July 2, 1961, LH, Yankee Stadium vs. Washington Senators, Pitcher: Johnny Klippstein (RH)

349 (29). July 8, 1961, LH, Yankee Stadium vs. Boston Red Sox, Pitcher: Tracy Stallard (RH)

350 (30). July 13, 1961, LH, Comiskey Park vs. Chicago White Sox, Pitcher: Early Wynn (RH)

351 (31). July 14, 1961, RH, Comiskey Park vs. Chicago White Sox, Pitcher: Juan Pizarro (LH)

352 (32). July 16, 1961, RH, Memorial Stadium vs. Baltimore Orioles, Pitcher: Steve Barber (LH)

353 (33). July 17, 1961, LH, Memorial Stadium vs. Baltimore Orioles, Pitcher: Milt Pappas (RH)

354 (34). July 18, 1961, LH, Griffith Stadium vs. Washington Senators, Pitcher: Joe McLain (RH)

355 (35). July 18, 1961, LH, Griffith Stadium vs. Washington Senators, Pitcher: Joe McLain (RH)

356 (36). July 19, 1961, LH, Griffith Stadium vs. Washington Senators, Pitcher: Dick Donovan (RH)

357 (37). July 21, 1961, LH, Fenway Park vs. Boston Red Sox, Pitcher: Bill Monbouquette (RH)

358 (38). July 25, 1961, RH, Yankee Stadium vs. Chicago White Sox, Pitcher: Frank Baumann (LH)

359 (39). July 26, 1961, LH, Yankee Stadium vs. Chicago White Sox, Pitcher: Ray Herbert (RH)

360 (40). August 2, 1961, RH, Yankee Stadium vs. Kansas City A's, Pitcher: Jim Archer (LH)

361 (41). August 6, 1961, LH, Yankee Stadium vs. Minnesota Twins, Pitcher: Pedro Ramos (RH)

362 (42). August 6, 1961, LH, Yankee Stadium vs. Minnesota Twins, Pitcher: Pedro Ramos (RH)

363 (43). August 6, 1961, LH, Yankee Stadium vs. Minnesota Twins, Pitcher: Al Schroll (RH)

364 (44). August 11, 1961, RH, Yankee Stadium vs. Washington Senators, Pitcher: Pete Burnside (LH)

365 (45). August 13, 1961, LH, Griffith Stadium vs. Washington Senators, Pitcher: Bennie Daniels (RH)

366 (46). August 20, 1961, LH, Municipal Stadium vs. Cleveland Indians, Pitcher: Jim Perry (RH)

367 (47). August 30, 1961, RH, Metropolitan Stadium vs. Minnesota Twins, Pitcher: Jim Kaat (LH)

368 (48). August 31, 1961, RH, Metropolitan Stadium vs. Minnesota Twins, Pitcher: Jack Kralick (LH)

369 (49). September 3, 1961, LH, Yankee Stadium vs. Detroit Tigers, Pitcher: Jim Bunning (RH)

370 (50). September 3, 1961, LH, Yankee Stadium vs. Detroit Tigers, Pitcher: Jerry Staley (RH)

371 (51). September 5, 1961, LH, Yankee Stadium vs. Washington Senators, Pitcher: Joe McLain (RH)

372 (52). September 8, 1961, LH, Yankee Stadium vs. Cleveland Indians, Pitcher: Gary Bell (RH)

373 (53). September 10, 1961, LH, Yankee Stadium vs. Cleveland Indians, Pitcher: Jim Perry (RH)

374 (54). September 23, 1961, LH, Fenway Park vs. Boston Red Sox, Pitcher: Don Schwall (RH)

Number of games in which Mickey homered in 1961: 47
Yankees record in 1961 in games in which Mickey homered: 39–8 (.830)

1962: 30 Home Runs

375 (1). April 10, 1962, LH, Yankee Stadium vs. Baltimore Orioles, Pitcher: Hoyt Wilhelm (RH)

376 (2). April 19, 1962, LH, Memorial Stadium vs. Baltimore Orioles, Pitcher: Chuck Estrada (RH)

377 (3). May 5, 1962, LH, Yankee Stadium vs. Washington Senators, Pitcher: Marty Kutyna (RH)

378 (4). May 6, 1962, LH, Yankee Stadium vs. Washington Senators, Pitcher: Dave Stenhouse (RH)

379 (5). May 6, 1962, RH, Yankee Stadium vs. Washington Senators, Pitcher: Pete Burnside (LH)

380 (6). May 6, 1962, LH, Yankee Stadium vs. Washington Senators, Pitcher: Jim Hannan (RH)

381 (7). May 12, 1962, LH, Municipal Stadium vs. Cleveland Indians, Pitcher: Barry Latman (RH)

382　(8).　June 16, 1962, Municipal Stadium vs. Cleveland Indians, Pitcher: Gary Bell (RH)

383　(9).　June 23, 1962, LH, Tiger Stadium vs. Detroit Tigers, Pitcher: Paul Foytack (RH)

384 (10).　June 28, 1962, RH, Yankee Stadium vs. Minnesota Twins, Pitcher: Jack Kralick (LH)

385 (11).　July 2, 1962, LH, Yankee Stadium vs. Kansas City A's, Pitcher: Ed Rakow (RH)

386 (12).　July 3, 1962, LH, Yankee Stadium vs. Kansas City A's, Pitcher: Jerry Walker (RH)

387 (13).　July 3, 1962, LH, Yankee Stadium vs. Kansas City A's, Pitcher: Gordon Jones (RH)

388 (14).　July 4, 1962, RH, Yankee Stadium vs. Kansas City A's, Pitcher: Dan Pfister (LH)

389 (15).　July 4, 1962, LH, Yankee Stadium vs. Kansas City A's, Pitcher: John Wyatt (RH)

390 (16).　July 6, 1962, LH, Metropolitan Stadium vs. Minnesota Twins, Pitcher: Camilo Pascual (RH)

391 (17).　July 6, 1962, LH, Metropolitan Stadium vs. Minnesota Twins, Pitcher: Camilo Pascual (RH)

392 (18).　July 18, 1962, LH, Fenway Park vs. Boston Red Sox, Pitcher: Galen Cisco (RH)

393 (19).　July 20, 1962, RH, Yankee Stadium vs. Washington Senators, Pitcher: Steve Hamilton (LH)

394 (20).　July 25, 1962, LH, Yankee Stadium vs. Boston Red Sox, Pitcher: Earl Wilson (RH)

395 (21).　July 28, 1962, LH, Yankee Stadium vs. Chicago White Sox, Pitcher: Eddie Fisher (RH)

396 (22).　August 17, 1962, LH, Municipal Stadium vs. Kansas City A's, Pitcher: Bill Fischer (RH)

397 (23).　August 18, 1962, LH, Municipal Stadium vs. Kansas City A's, Pitcher: Diego Segui (RH)

398 (24).　August 19, 1962, LH, Municipal Stadium vs. Kansas City A's, Pitcher: Jerry Walkerv

399 (25).　August 28, 1962, LH, Yankee Stadium vs. Cleveland Indians, Pitcher: Jim Mudcat Grant (RH)

400 (26).　September 10, 1962, RH, Tiger Stadium vs. Detroit Tigers, Pitcher: Hank Aguirre (LH)

401 (27).　September 12, 1962, LH, Municipal Stadium vs. Cleveland Indians, Pitcher: Pedro Ramos (RH)

402 (28).　September 18, 1962, LH, D.C. Stadium vs. Washington Senators, Pitcher: Tom Cheney (RH)

403 (29).　September 18, 1962, LH, D.C. Stadium vs. Washington Senators, Pitcher: Tom Cheney (RH)

404 (30).   September 30, 1962, LH, Yankee Stadium vs. Chicago White Sox, Pitcher: Ray Herbert (RH)

Number of games in which Mickey homered in 1962: 25
Yankees record in 1962 in games in which Mickey homered: 18–7 (.720)

1963: 15 Home Runs

405   (1).   April 10, 1963, RH, Municipal Stadium vs. Kansas City A's, Pitcher: Ted Bowsfield (LH)
406   (2).   April 11, 1963, LH, Yankee Stadium vs. Baltimore Orioles, Pitcher: Milt Pappas (RH)
407   (3).   May 4, 1963, RH, Metropolitan Stadium vs. Minnesota Twins, Pitcher: Jim Kaat (LH)
408   (4).   May 6, 1963, RH, Tiger Stadium vs. Detroit Tigers, Pitcher: Hank Aguirre (LH)
409   (5).   May 11, 1963, LH, Memorial Stadium vs. Baltimore Orioles, Pitcher: Milt Pappas (RH)
410   (6).   May 15, 1963, LH, Yankee Stadium vs. Minnesota Twins, Pitcher: Camilo Pascual (RH)
411   (7).   May 21, 1963, LH, Yankee Stadium vs. Kansas City A's, Pitcher: Orlando Pena (RH)
412   (8).   May 21, 1963, LH, Yankee Stadium vs. Kansas City A's, Pitcher: Diego Segui (RH)
413   (9).   May 22, 1963, LH, Yankee Stadium vs. Kansas City A's, Pitcher: Bill Fischer (RH)
414 (10).   May 26, 1963, RH, Yankee Stadium vs. Washington Senators, Pitcher: Don Rudolph (LH)
415 (11).   June 4, 1963, RH, Memorial Stadium vs. Baltimore Orioles, Pitcher: Steve Barber (LH)
416 (12).   August 4, 1963, RH, Yankee Stadium vs. Baltimore Orioles, Pitcher: George Brunet (LH)
417 (13).   September 1, 1963, RH, Memorial Stadium vs. Baltimore Orioles, Pitcher: Mike McCormick (LH)
418 (14).   September 11, 1963, LH, Municipal Stadium vs. Kansas City A's, Pitcher: Ed Rakow (RH)
419 (15).   September 21, 1963, LH, Yankee Stadium vs. Kansas City A's, Pitcher: Moe Drabowsky (RH)

Number of games in which Mickey homered in 1963: 14
Yankees record in 1963 in games in which Mickey homered: 11–3 (.786)

1964: 35 Home Runs

420   (1).   May 6, 1964, LH, D.C. Stadium vs. Washington Senators, Pitcher: Bennie Daniels (RH)

421 (2). May 6, 1964, RH, D.C. Stadium vs. Washington Senators, Pitcher: Bob Meyer (LH)

422 (3). May 8, 1964, RH, Municipal Stadium vs. Cleveland Indians, Pitcher: Tommy John (LH)

423 (4). May 9, 1964, LH, Municipal Stadium vs. Cleveland Indians, Pitcher: Pedro Ramos (RH)

424 (5). May 16, 1964, LH, Yankee Stadium vs. Kansas City A's, Pitcher: Moe Drabowsky (RH)

425 (6). May 17, 1964, RH, Yankee Stadium vs. Kansas City A's, Pitcher: John O'Donoghue (LH)

426 (7). May 23, 1964, RH, Yankee Stadium vs. Los Angeles Angels, Pitcher: Bo Belinsky (LH)

427 (8). May 24, 1964, LH, Yankee Stadium vs. Los Angeles Angels, Pitcher: Fred Newman (RH)

428 (9). June 11, 1964, LH, Fenway Park vs. Boston Red Sox, Pitcher: Bill Monbouquette (RH)

429 (10). June 11, 1964, LH, Fenway Park vs. Boston Red Sox, Pitcher: Bill Monbouquette (RH)

430 (11). June 13, 1964, RH, Yankee Stadium vs. Chicago White Sox, Pitcher: Don Mossi (LH)

431 (12). June 17, 1964, LH, Yankee Stadium vs. Boston Red Sox, Pitcher: Dick Radatz (RH)

432 (13). June 21, 1964, RH, Comiskey Park vs. Chicago White Sox, Pitcher: Juan Pizarro (LH)

433 (14). June 23, 1964, LH, Memorial Stadium vs. Baltimore Orioles, Pitcher: Chuck Estrada (RH)

434 (15). June 27, 1964, LH, Yankee Stadium vs. Detroit Tigers, Pitcher: Denny McLain (RH)

435 (16). July 1, 1964, RH, Yankee Stadium vs. Kansas City A's, Pitcher: John O'Donoghue (LH)

436 (17). July 4, 1964, LH, Yankee Stadium vs. Minnesota Twins, Pitcher: Al Worthington (RH)

437 (18). July 13, 1964, LH, Municipal Stadium vs. Cleveland Indians, Pitcher: Gary Bell (RH)

438 (19). July 24, 1964, RH, Tiger Stadium vs. Detroit Tigers, Pitcher: Hank Aguirre (LH)

439 (20). July 28, 1964, LH, Chavez Ravine vs. Los Angeles Angels, Pitcher: Dean Chance (RH)

440 (21). August 1, 1964, RH, Metropolitan Stadium vs. Minnesota Twins, Pitcher: Dick Stigman (LH)

441 (22). August 4, 1964, RH, Municipal Stadium vs. Kansas City A's, Pitcher: John O'Donoghue (LH)

442 (23). August 11, 1964, RH, Yankee Stadium vs. Chicago White Sox, Pitcher: Juan Pizarro (LH)

443 (24). August 12, 1964, LH, Yankee Stadium vs. Chicago White Sox, Pitcher: Ray Herbert (RH)

444 (25). August 12, 1964, RH, Yankee Stadium vs. Chicago White Sox, Pitcher: Frank Baumann (LH)

445 (26). August 22, 1964, LH, Fenway Park vs. Boston Red Sox, Pitcher: Jack Lamabe (RH)

446 (27). August 23, 1964, LH, Fenway Park vs. Boston Red Sox, Pitcher: Earl Wilson (RH)

447 (28). August 29, 1964, LH, Yankee Stadium vs. Boston Red Sox, Pitcher: Pete Charlton (RH)

448 (29). September 4, 1964, RH, Municipal Stadium vs. Kansas City A's, Pitcher: John O'Donoghue (LH)

449 (30). September 5, 1964, LH, Municipal Stadium vs. Kansas City A's, Pitcher: John Blue Moon Odum (RH)

450 (31). September 17, 1964, LH, Yankee Stadium vs. Los Angeles Angels, Pitcher: Bob Duliba (RH)

451 (32). September 19, 1964, LH, Yankee Stadium vs. Kansas City A's, Pitcher: Diego Segui (RH)

452 (33). September 22, 1964, LH, Municipal Stadium vs. Cleveland Indians, Pitcher: Dick Donovan (RH)

453 (34). September 27, 1964, LH, D.C. Stadium vs. Washington Senators, Pitcher: Bennie Daniels (RH)

454 (35). September 30, 1964, RH, Yankee Stadium vs. Detroit Tigers, Pitcher: Mickey Lolich (LH)

Number of games in which Mickey homered in 1964: 33
Yankees record in 1964 in games in which Mickey homered: 25−8 (.758)

1965: 19 Home Runs

455 (1). April 17, 1965, LH, Municipal Stadium vs. Kansas City A's, Pitcher: John Wyatt (RH)

456 (2). April 18, 1965, LH, Municipal Stadium vs. Kansas City A's, Pitcher: Moe Drabowsky (RH)

457 (3). April 21, 1965, LH, Yankee Stadium vs. Minnesota Twins, Pitcher: Camilo Pascual (RH)

458 (4). April 25, 1965, RH, Yankee Stadium vs. Los Angeles Angels, Pitcher: Rudy May (LH)

459 (5). May 10, 1965, LH, Fenway Park vs. Boston Red Sox, Pitcher: Jim Lonborg (RH)

460 (6). May 11, 1965, RH, Fenway Park vs. Boston Red Sox, Pitcher: Arnold Earley (LH)

461 (7). May 15, 1965, LH, Memorial Stadium vs. Baltimore Orioles, Pitcher: Dick Hall (RH)

462 (8). May 30, 1965, RH, Comiskey Park vs. Chicago White Sox, Pitcher: Gary Peters (LH)

463 (9). June 5, 1965, RH, Yankee Stadium vs. Chicago White Sox, Pitcher: Gary Peters (LH)

464 (10). June 18, 1965, RH, Yankee Stadium vs. Minnesota Twins, Pitcher: Mel Nelson (LH)

465 (11). June 22, 1965, RH, Yankee Stadium vs. Kansas City A's, Pitcher: John O'Donoghue (LH)

466 (12). July 15, 1965, LH, Yankee Stadium vs. Washington Senators, Pitcher: Phil Ortega (RH)

467 (13). July 25, 1965, LH, Municipal Stadium vs. Cleveland Indians, Pitcher: Lee Stange (RH)

468 (14). August 6, 1965, RH, Tiger Stadium vs. Detroit Tigers, Pitcher: Mickey Lolich (LH)

469 (15). August 7, 1965, LH, Tiger Stadium vs. Detroit Tigers, Pitcher: Fred Gladding (RH)

470 (16). August 10, 1965, RH, Yankee Stadium vs. Minnesota Twins, Pitcher: Jim Kaat (LH)

471 (17). August 18, 1965, LH,Yankee Stadium vs. Los Angeles Angels, Pitcher: Dean Chance (RH)

472 (18). September 2, 1965, RH, Chavez Ravine vs. Los Angeles Angels, Pitcher: Marcelino Lopez (LH)

473 (19). September 4, 1965, RH, Yankee Stadium vs. Boston Red Sox, Pitcher: Dennis Bennett (LH)

Number of games in which Mickey homered in 1965: 19

Yankees record in 1965 in games in which Mickey homered: 12–7 (.632)

1966: 23 Home Runs

474 (1). May 9, 1966, LH, Metropolitan Stadium vs. Minnesota Twins, Pitcher: Jim Perry (RH)

475 (2). May 14, 1966, LH, Municipal Stadium vs. Kansas City A's, Pitcher: Fred Talbot (RH)

476 (3). May 25, 1966, LH, Yankee Stadium vs. California Angels, Pitcher: Dean Chance (RH)

477 (4). May 25, 1966, LH, Yankee Stadium vs. California Angels, Pitcher: Lew Burdette (RH)

478 (5). June 1, 1966, RH, Comiskey Park vs. Chicago White Sox, Pitcher: Juan Pizarro (LH)

479 (6). June 16, 1966, RH, Yankee Stadium vs. Cleveland Indians, Pitcher: Sam McDowell (LH)

480 (7). June 23, 1966, LH, Yankee Stadium vs. Baltimore Orioles, Pitcher: Jim Palmer (RH)

481 (8). June 28, 1966, LH, Fenway Park vs. Boston Red Sox, Pitcher: Jose Santiago (RH)

482 (9). June 28, 1966, LH, Fenway Park vs. Boston Red Sox, Pitcher: Jose Santiago (RH)

483 (10). June 29, 1966, LH, Fenway Park vs. Boston Red Sox, Pitcher: Roland Sheldon (RH)

484 (11). June 29, 1966, LH, Fenway Park vs. Boston Red Sox, Pitcher: Lee Stange (RH)

485 (12). July 1, 1966, LH, D.C. Stadium vs. Washington Senators, Pitcher: Phil Ortega (RH)

486 (13). July 2, 1966, RH, D.C. Stadium vs. Washington Senators, Pitcher: Mike McCormick (LH)

487 (14). July 2, 1966, RH, D.C. Stadium vs. Washington Senators, Pitcher: Mike McCormick (LH)

488 (15). July 3, 1966, RH, D.C. Stadium vs. Washington Senators, Pitcher: Pete Richert (LH)

489 (16). July 7, 1966, LH, Yankee Stadium vs. Boston Red Sox, Pitcher: Don McMahon (RH)

490 (17). July 8, 1966, LH, Yankee Stadium vs. Washington Senators, Pitcher: Dick Bosman (RH)

491 (18). July 8, 1966, RH, Yankee Stadium vs. Washington Senators, Pitcher: Jim Hannan (RH)

492 (19). July 23, 1966, RH, Yankee Stadium vs. California Angels, Pitcher: Marcelino Lopez (LH)

493 (20). July 24, 1966, RH, Yankee Stadium vs. California Angels, Pitcher: George Brunet (LH)

494 (21). July 29, 1966, LH, Comiskey Park vs. Chicago White Sox, Pitcher: Bruce Howard (RH)

495 (22). August 14, 1966, RH, Yankee Stadium vs. Cleveland Indians, Pitcher: Jack Kralick (LH)

496 (23). August 26, 1966, RH, Yankee Stadium vs. Detroit Tigers, Pitcher: Hank Aguirre (LH)

Number of games in which Mickey homered in 1966: 18

Yankees record in 1966 in games in which Mickey homered: 11–7 (.611)

1967: 22 Home Runs

497 (1). April 29, 1967, LH, Yankee Stadium vs. California Angels, Pitcher: Jack Sanford (RH)

498 (2). April 30, 1967, LH, Yankee Stadium vs. California Angels, Pitcher: Minnie Rojas (RH)

499 (3). May 3, 1967, LH, Metropolitan Stadium vs. Minnesota Twins, Pitcher: Dave Boswell (RH)

500 (4). May 14, 1967, LH, Yankee Stadium vs. Baltimore Orioles, Pitcher: Stu Miller (RH)

501 (5). May 17, 1967, LH, Yankee Stadium vs. Cleveland Indians, Pitcher: Steve Hargan (RH)

502 (6). May 19, 1967, RH, Tiger Stadium vs. Detroit Tigers, Pitcher: Mickey Lolich (LH)

503 (7). May 20, 1967, LH, Tiger Stadium vs. Detroit Tigers, Pitcher: Denny McLain (RH)

504 (8). May 21, 1967, LH, Tiger Stadium vs. Detroit Tigers, Pitcher: Earl Wilson (RH)

505 (9). May 24, 1967, RH, Memorial Stadium vs. Baltimore Orioles, Pitcher: Steve Barber (LH)

506 (10). May 27, 1967, LH, Municipal Stadium vs. Cleveland Indians, Pitcher: Sonny Siebert (RH)

507 (11). May 28, 1967, LH, Municipal Stadium vs. Cleveland Indians, Pitcher: Gary Bell (RH)

508 (12). June 5, 1967, RH, Yankee Stadium vs. Washington Senators, Pitcher: Darold Knowles (LH)

509 (13). June 15, 1967, RH, D.C. Stadium vs. Washington Senators, Pitcher: Frank Bertaina (LH)

510 (14). June 24, 1967, LH, Yankee Stadium vs. Detroit Tigers, Pitcher: Fred Gladding (RH)

511 (15). July 4, 1967, LH, Metropolitan Stadium vs. Minnesota Twins, Pitcher: Jim Mudcat Grant (RH)

512 (16). July 4, 1967, LH, Metropolitan Stadium vs. Minnesota Twins, Pitcher: Jim Mudcat Grant (RH)

513 (17). July 16, 1967, LH, Yankee Stadium vs. Baltimore Orioles, Pitcher: Bill Dillman (RH)

514 (18). July 22, 1967, LH, Tiger Stadium vs. Detroit Tigers, Pitcher: Earl Wilson (RH)

515 (19). July 25, 1967, RH, Yankee Stadium vs. Minnesota Twins, Pitcher: Jim Kaat (LH)

516 (20). August 7, 1967, LH, Anaheim Stadium vs. California Angels, Pitcher: Minnie Rojas (RH)

517 (21). September 2, 1967, LH, Yankee Stadium vs. Washington Senators, Pitcher: Bob Priddy (RH)

518 (22). September 3, 1967, LH, Yankee Stadium vs. Washington Senators, Pitcher: Dick Bosman (RH)

Number of games in which Mickey homered in 1967: 20 (plus one game suspended)

Yankees record in 1967 in games in which Mickey homered: 9–11–1 (.450)

1968: 18 Home Runs

519 (1). April 18, 1968, LH, Anaheim Stadium vs. California Angels, Pitcher: Jim McGlothlin (RH)

520 (2). April 24, 1968, LH, Oakland Coliseum vs. Oakland A's, Pitcher: Jim Nash (RH)

521 (3). April 26, 1968, LH, Yankee Stadium vs. Detroit Tigers, Pitcher: Earl Wilson (RH)

522 (4). May 6, 1968, RH, Yankee Stadium vs. Cleveland Indians, Pitcher: Sam McDowell (LH)

523 (5). May 30, 1968, LH, Yankee Stadium vs. Washington Senators, Pitcher: Joe Coleman (RH)

524 (6). May 30, 1968, LH, Yankee Stadium vs. Washington Senators, Pitcher: Bob Humphreys (RH)

525 (7). June 7, 1968, LH, Yankee Stadium vs. California Angels, Pitcher: Jim McGlothlin (RH)

526 (8). June 11, 1968, LH, Yankee Stadium vs. Chicago White Sox, Pitcher: Joel Horlen (RH)

527 (9). June 16, 1968, RH, Anaheim Stadium vs. California Angels, Pitcher: Clyde Wright (LH)

528 (10). June 22, 1968, RH, Metropolitan Stadium vs. Minnesota Twins, Pitcher: Jim Kaat (LH)

529 (11). June 29, 1968, LH, Yankee Stadium vs. Oakland A's, Pitcher: John Blue Moon Odum (RH)

530 (12). August 10, 1968, RH, Yankee Stadium vs. Minnesota Twins, Pitcher: Jim Merritt (LH)

531 (13). August 10, 1968, RH, Yankee Stadium vs. Minnesota Twins, Pitcher: Jim Merritt (LH)

532 (14). August 12, 1968, RH, Anaheim Stadium vs. California Angels, Pitcher: George Brunet (LH)

533 (15). August 15, 1968, LH, Oakland Coliseum vs. Oakland A's, Pitcher: John Blue Moon Odum (RH)

534 (16). August 22, 1968, RH, Metropolitan Stadium vs. Minnesota Twins, Pitcher: Jim Merritt (LH)

535 (17). September 19, 1968, LH, Tiger Stadium vs. Detroit Tigers, Pitcher: Denny McLain (RH)

536 (18). September 20, 1968, LH, Yankee Stadium vs. Boston Red Sox, Pitcher: Jim Lonborg (RH)

Number of games in which Mickey homered in 1968: 16 (plus one game suspended)

Yankees record in 1968 in games in which Mickey homered: 8−8−1 (.500)

CAREER TOTALS

Home Runs Hit Left-handed: 372

Home Runs Hit Right-handed: 164

Number of Games in which Mickey Homered: 487 (plus three games suspended)

Yankees record in games in which Mickey homered: 344–143–3 (.706)

MICKEY MANTLE'S WORLD SERIES HOME RUNS (18)

1. October 6, 1952, Ebbets Field vs. Brooklyn Dodgers
2. October 7, 1952, Ebbets Field vs. Brooklyn Dodgers
3. October 1, 1953, Yankee Stadium vs. Brooklyn Dodgers
4. October 4, 1953, Ebbets Field vs. Brooklyn Dodgers
5. September 30, 1955, Ebbets Field vs. Brooklyn Dodgers
6. October 3, 1956, Ebbets Field vs. Brooklyn Dodgers
7. October 7, 1956, Yankee Stadium vs. Brooklyn Dodgers
8. October 8, 1956, Yankee Stadium vs. Brooklyn Dodgers
9. October 5, 1957, County Stadium vs. Milwaukee Braves
10. October 2, 1958, County Stadium vs. Milwaukee Braves
11. October 2, 1958, County Stadium vs. Milwaukee Braves
12. October 6, 1960, Forbes Field vs. Pittsburgh Pirates
13. October 6, 1960, Forbes Field vs. Pittsburgh Pirates
14. October 8, 1960, Yankee Stadium vs. Pittsburgh Pirates
15. October 6, 1963, Dodger Stadium vs. Los Angeles Dodgers
16. October 10, 1964, Yankee Stadium vs. St. Louis Cardinals
17. October 14, 1964, Busch Stadium vs. St. Louis Cardinals
18. October 15, 1964, Busch Stadium vs. St. Louis Cardinals

Total: Left-handed–10/Right-handed–8

MICKEY MANTLE'S ALL STAR GAME HOME RUNS (2)

1. July 22, 1955, County Stadium, Milwaukee–Pitcher Robin Roberts
2. July 10, 1956, Griffith Stadium, Washington–Pitcher Warren Spahn

Total: Left-handed–1/Right-handed–1

BIBLIOGRAPHY

Berger, Phil. *Mickey Mantle*. New York: Park Lane, 1998.

Canale, Larry. *Mickey Mantle: The Classic Photography of Ozzie Sweet*. Richmond, Va.: Tuff Stuff, 1998.

Cramer, Richard Ben. *Joe DiMaggio: The Hero's Life*. New York: Simon and Schuster, 2000.

Creamer, Robert W. *Babe: The Legend Comes to Life*. Evanston, Ill.: Holtzman, 1974.

———. *Stengel: His Life and Times*. New York: Simon and Schuster, 1984.

Creamer, Robert W., and *Sports Illustrated*. *Mantle Remembered*. SI Presents. New York: Warner, 1995.

Durso, Joseph. *Casey: The Life and Legend of Charles Dillon Stengel*. Upper Saddle River, N.J.: Prentice Hall, 1967.

Falkner, David. *The Last Hero: The Life of Mickey Mantle*. New York: Simon and Schuster, 1995.

Flynn, George. *Lewis B. Hershey, Mr. Selective Service*. Chapel Hill: University of North Carolina Press, 1985.

Ford, Whitey, and Mickey Mantle. *Whitey and Mickey: A Joint Autobiography of the Yankee Years*. New York: 1987.

Golenbock, Peter. *Dynasty: The New York Yankees, 1949–1964*. Chicago: Contemporary, 2000.

———. *Wild, High and Tight: The Life and Death of Billy Martin*. New York: St. Martin's, 1994.

Hart, Jeffrey. *When the Going Was Good: American Life in the Fifties*. New York: Crown, 1982.

Hines, Rick, Mark Larson, and Dave Platta. *Mickey Mantle Memorabilia*. New York: Krause, 1993.

Leinwand, Gerald. *Heroism in America*. New York: Franklin Watts, 1996.

Linn, Ed. *Hitter: The Life and Turmoils of Ted Williams*. New York: Harcourt Brace, 1993.

Mantle, Merlyn, Mickey Mantle Jr., David Mantle, and Dan Mantle. *A Hero All His Life*. New York: HarperCollins, 1996.

Mantle, Mickey, with Herb Gluck. *The Mick*. New York: Doubleday, 1985.

Mantle, Mickey, and Mickey Herskowitz. *All My Octobers*. New York: HarperCollins, 1994.

Mantle, Mickey, and Phil Pepe. *My Favorite Summer, 1956*. New York: Doubleday, 1991.

Robinson, Ray. *Iron Horse: Lou Gehrig in His Time*. New York: W. W. Norton, 1990.

Schoor, Gene. *The Illustrated History of Mickey Mantle*. New York: Carroll and Graf, 1996.

Smith, Marshall, and John Rohde. *Memories of Mickey Mantle: My Very Best Friend*. Bronxville, N.Y.: Adventure Quest, 1996.

INDEX

Page numbers in *italics* refer to illustrations.

Alexander, Hugh (Cleveland Indian scout), 29–30
All My Octobers (Herskowitz), 248
American League pennant, 104, 178, 208–209
Anna Bea (half-sister), molestation of Mickey, 11–12

Baker, Bentley (high school principal), 29
Ball Four (Bouton), 130, 214, 238–240
Ban Johnson League, 38
Barber, Red, 189
Barnett, Barney, 36–38, *73*
baseball
  golden eras of, 181
  warning tracks, 97
Baseball Assistance Team, 263
batting statistics. *See also* home runs
  regular season, 306–333
World Series, 307
Bennett, LeRoy, 22–23, 37
Berra, Yogi
  as manager, 210, 214
  Most Valuable Player, 158
  recollection of, 78

Betty Ford Center, 256–257, 259–261
Blatner, Buddy, 181
Boulton, Jim, 130
Briggs Stadium (Detroit), 161
Brooke, Holly (Mickey's girlfriend), 83, 101, 112, 150, *151*

Camel cigarettes, endorsement of, 17
Cashman, Terry (balladeer), 246
Catal, Tom, 250, 294
Cerv, Bob, 198–199
Cochrane, Mickey, namesake, 4
Confidential Magazine, 150
Cosell, Howard, 21
Costas, Bob
  eulogy of Mickey, 273, 302–305
  interview of, 261–262
  on Mantle and Maris, 206
Craft, Harry (early manager), 58
Cramer, Richard Ben (DiMaggio biographer), 111, 114–115
Creamer, Robert W. (Stengel biographer), 132–134, 201
Crystal, Billy, 180, 272

Dean, Dizzy, 181
DeMarco, Daniel (gastroenterologist), 264
DiMaggio, Joe (Yankee star)
  career, 21–22, 108
  injuries, 41, 109
  nicknames, 87, 114
  personality, 108, 110
  relationships
    berating of Yogi Berra, 109
    with Kennedys, 218–219
    Marilyn Monroe, 148
    and Mickey Mantle, 55, 107, *153*, 274
    relationship with Stengel, 111
    worshipped by Mickey, 106–107
Dodger Stadium (Los Angeles), 210
Dodgers
  abandoning New York, 178
  "Boys of Summer," 137
  defeat of Yankees, 158
  exhibitions, 79
*Dollar Sign on the Muscle: The World of
  Baseball Scouting* (Kerrane), 32–33,
  40–42, 294
Drysdale, Don, 209
Dynasty (Golenbock), 175

Ebbets Field (New York), 77–78
The Education of a Baseball Player (Mantle), 18
exhibition games, 79, 219

Ferguson, Nick (friend of Mickey), 15, 22–
  23, 37, 58, *73*
Forbes Field (Pittsburgh), 192
Ford, Whitey, 78

Gabby Street League, 18, 23
Gallo, Ray (photographer), *230*
Gaynor, Dr. (Mickey's physician), 122
Gilmore Stadium (Hollywood), 56
Golenbock, Peter (Yankee historian), 161
Greenwade, Tom (Yankee Scout), 30–33
  account of Mickey's signing, 39–42
Griffith Stadium (Washington), 136–137,
  160

Halberstam, David, 42, 136
Hall of Fame (Cooperstown), 240–242
  Mickey's induction (1974), 236, 243–
    244
  Mickey's speech, 298–301
  players developed by Stengel, 90
  tape-measure home run, 137
Halper, Barry, 266, 272
Henrich, Tommy (outfield coach), 85
A Hero All His Life (Mantle), 95, 121, 141,
  236, 259–261
Herskowitz, Mickey (writer), 248, 251
Hodgkin's disease, 20–21, 117, 261, 276
Holland, Gerald, 201
home runs
  career home runs, 307–334
  gift pitch, 222
  tape-measure home run, 136–137, *231*
  World series home runs (1951–1964),
    307
Houk, Ralph (manager), 196
Howard, Elston, 130, 213

Isaacs, Stan, 56

Jacobson, Max (physician), 203
Johnson, Giles (grandfather), 17
Johnson, Greer, 250, 254, 272, *278*, 295
Junior Cardinal League, 22

Kansas City Blues (baseball team), 97
Kennedy, John F. (President of United
  States), 195
Kerrane, Kevin (author), 32–33, 40–42,
  294
Koppett, Leonard, 92

Layton, Eddie (Yankee organist), 225
Life Magazine, 108
Lingo, John (high school coach), 28
Look Magazine, 110

Mantle and Berra batting duo, 160
Mantle, Barbara (sister), 6, 24
Mantle, Billy (son), 248, 261

Mantle, Butch (brother), 23
Mantle, Charles (grandfather),
  death of, 19–20
  switch-hitting, 12–14
Mantle, Danny (son), 250, 256
Mantle, David (son), 147, 237, 271
Mantle, Elvin Clark "Mutt" (Mickey's
  father)
  death of, 123
  dreams for son, 4, 146
  dying wish, 119
  emotional detachment, 8
  failing health, 116
  funeral, 124–125
  meeting Mickey's mother, 3
  with Mickey, 71, 154
  overbearing father, 10
Mantle, Eugene (Mutt's brother), 15
Mantle family
  alcoholism in, 16
  dysfunction in, 16
  Mantle Curse, the, 20–21, 117
Mantle, Larry (brother), 4
Mantle, Lovell Richardson (mother)
  Alzheimer's disease, 264
  former marriage, 3
  love of the game, 15–16
  personality of, 8–11
Mantle, Max (cousin), 26
Mantle, Merlyn (Mickey's wife)
  difficulty communicating, 183
  emotional trauma, 144–145
  engagement to, 83
  first meeting Mickey, 119–120
  with Mickey and Mutt, 73
  Mickey's love for, 112
  Mickey's relationship with his father, 4,
    10
  wedding anniversary, 141
Mantle, Mickey
  alcohol problem
    abstinence, 148, 173, 255
    Betty Ford Center, 256–257, 259–
      261
    "Breakfast of Champions," 248
    drinking as macho, 236

    drinking problems of, 138, 141,
      147–149, 239, 259
    family, 237, 248–249
    hangovers, 208–209
    Mickey Mantle Rule, 258
    personal life, 217–218, 251–253
    suddenly sober, 260–261
  baseball glove, 48–49
  batting
    All-Star Game home runs, 334
    batting slumps, 86, 89, 94, 98, 100
    batting stance changes, 159
    career high average, 174
    career statistics, 307
    first major league at bat, 81
    first regular-season home run, 84
    first World series home run, 135
    fungo-hitting, 4, 44, 214
    home run statistics, 333–334
    Louisville Slugger, 169
    major league batting statistics, 306–
      333
    strikeouts, 90
    switch-hitting, 12–14, 47
    tape-measure home run, 161
    Triple Crown, 232
    World Series home runs, 135, 334.
      See also World Series
  birth of, 4
  business ventures
    bowling alley, 226
    Bowman rookie card, 74
    Canadian Bomb Shelter Survival
      Corp., 226
    endorsements, Camel cigarettes, 17
    Holiday Inn, 242, 277
    Mickey Mantle Enterprises, 176
    "Mr. Twenty percent," 242
    public relations, 246–247
    Roy True, 227–228
    sports memorabilia, 246, 250–252,
      272
    Upper Deck, 263
  career
    baseball imposed separations,
      143–145, 207

Mantle, Mickey, continued
  coaching position, 238
  coming of age, 157, 160
  demotion to Triple A team, 96
  dream of managing, 240–241
  great players (Mickey, Joe, and Ted),
    152
  interview with Costa, 261–262
  in Kansas City uniform, 152
  leader of the team, 196, 213
  Most Valuable Player, 174
  rookie year, 106, 142, 151, 160
  sophomore season, 44, 128
  twilight years, 220, 228
contracts
  1956 contract, 158
  first contract (1949), 32–35
  graduation-night signing of, 29–30,
    33–35
  negotiations, 174
  rookie contract, 59
death of, 271
  crypt inscription, 275
  DiMaggio, 274
  eulogy of Mickey, 273, 302–305
  funeral, 269, 272–273
early years
  childhood diseases. See osteomyelitis
  childhood home, 13
  childhood of, 14, 19, 22–24
  Commerce High, 16, 72
  football, 28
emotional trauma
  bed-wetting, 11, 96
  death threats to, 69–70
  demotion to Triple A, 92–94
  fear, 98, 100
  loss of his father, 126
  nightmares, 255
  panic and anxiety attacks, 98–99,
    249
  quitting baseball, 100
  recalled to the Yankees, 101, 112
  self-destructive behavior, 174–175
  sexual abuse of Mickey, 11–12, 96
  shyness of, 77
  temper of, 88–89, 229

fans
  acceptance by, 205
  Blackburn, Mrs., and Mickey's tem-
    per, 88
  booing of, 110, 179, 188–190
  con men and scam artists, Mickey as
    easy prey, 82
  displeasure of, 186
  "eyeballers," 239
  hero worship of, 183
  national treasure to, 162, 223, 246
  as a role model for, 267
  signing of baseballs, 239
  television's impact on, 180–181,
    182–183
Federal Bureau of Investigation (FBI)
  blackmail investigation, 149–150
  gambling, 175–176
health problems
  anxiety attacks, 98–99, 249
  depression, 254
  final days, 269–270
  Hodgkin's disease, 20–21, 117, 248,
    261, 276
  infected hip, 203–204
  liver cancer, 264–265
  liver transplant, 265–267, 280
  lung cancer, 268
  osteomyelitis, 25–28, 61–63, 70, 101
  panic attacks, 95, 98, 255
  sense of humor toward, 266
  tendency toward, 122
home runs
  gift pitch, 222
  Mickey's called shot, 212
  Mickey's most memorable, 161
  tape-measure home run, 136, 231
honoring Mickey, 216–219
injuries
  bandaging legs, 126–127
  broken foot, 208
  careless accidents, 179–180
  courage enduring, 158
  hamstring injury, 157
  knee injury, 114–115, 122, 135, 138,
    187
  leg, 133

physical rehabilitation, 118, 133, 138, 208
right shoulder, 219
right thigh, 145
tendency toward injury, 122
Mantle Curse, the. *See* Hodgkin's disease
marriage
  dysfunctionality, 144, 248
  extramarital affairs, 172, 245–246, 250, 254
  honeymoon, 121
  marriage to Merlyn, 118, 121, 123, 229
  physical abuse of Merlyn, 147
  separation from Merlyn, 251
  womanizing, 141, 149, 150, 172
military draft, 61–69, 98, 101
Most Valuable Player, (1962), 207
New York City
  Concourse Plaza Hotel, 82
  Copacabana incident, 176–178
  Harwyn Club, 104
  as icon, 172
  Latin Quarter nightclub, 142–143
  nightlife, 104, 142, 150, 172
  Stage Delicatessen, 102
  Toots Shor's, 148–149
nicknames
  The Champ, 56
  Commerce Comet, 16
  Little Mickey, 36
  Mantles, 47
  Mickey Mouse, 101
parents
  loss of his father, 126
  parents, Mutt and Lovell, 7
press and journalists
  Game of the Week, 181
  personal lives of celebrities, 236
  relations with, 159
relationships
  Billy Martin as house guest, 141, *230*
  with Cliff Maples, *72*
  with DiMaggio, 89, 126
  father, 112, 125, 146, *154*, 175, 260– 261

with George Selkirk, *153*
relationship with Stengel, 134
scratch list, 237–238
with sons as drinking buddies, 256
Stengel, friendship with, 190–191, 195–196
with twin brothers, 8, 23
retirement ceremony at White House, 225
spring training, 43–44, 49, 53–54, 122, 135
talent
  defensive playing in the outfield, 57, 85
  hitting ability, 207
  physical prowess, 7, 36, 45–47
  speed of, 25, 81, 84–85, 118, 123
  uniform number, 50, *74*, 101, 182
World Series
  batting statistics, 307
  home run statistics, 334
Mantle, Mickey, Jr. (Mickey's son)
  as ballplayer, 253–254, *277*
  birth of, 143, 183
  health problems, 144
  recollections of, 7
Mantle, Mutt. *See* Mantle, Elvin Clark "Mutt" (Mickey's father)
Mantle, Ray (brother), 8, 23
Mantle, Roy (brother), 8, 23, 276, 295
Mantle-Maris combination
  nicknames for, 186, 198
  as roommates, 199–200
Maris, Roger, 185–186, 198–203, 210, 251, *278*
Martin, Billy, *280*
  Mickey's closest friend, 132
  as Mickey's roommate, 103–104
  unique friendship with DiMaggio, 102
  Yankee hero, 137
Martin, Lois (Billy's wife), 141, *278*
McCarthy, Joe, 52
McGraw, John, 52–53
The Mick (autobiography), 35, 125, 236
Mickey Mantle Day (1965), 279
Mickey Mantle Foundation, 263, 267
Mickey Mantle Museum, 18, 250

Mickey Mantle Restaurant, 272
Monroe, Marilyn (DiMaggio's wife), 148
Murray, James, 224
Musial, Stan, Mickey's first baseball idol, 24
"My Life as an Alcoholic" (*Sports Illustrated*), 262

New York City
    arrival in, 77
    Copacabana incident, 176–177
    effect on Mantle, 148
    Latin Quarter nightclub prank, 142–143
    life in, 82, 104, 150, 172
New York Times, 108
nicknames, for Mickey
    The Champ, 56
    Commerce Comet, 16
    Little Mickey, 36
    Mantles, 47
    Mickey Mouse, 101

osteomyelitis (Mickey's childhood disease), 25–28, 61–63, 70

Patterson, Red (Yankee publicity director), 136
Povich, Shirley, 160
Preston Trail Golf Club, 258

The Quality of Courage (Creamer), 217–218

Reese, Pee Wee, 181
Reynolds, Allie, jinxing Mickey, 85–86
Richardson, Bobby, 269–270
Richardson, Lovell. *See* Mantle, Lovell Richardson (mother)
Robinson, Jackie, breaking of color barrier, 31, 128–131
Rose, Pete, "Charlie Hustle," 208, 294
Rosen, Alan, 252
Ruth, Babe, home run record, 196–197, 201–206

Safe at Home (film), 254
Savitt, Alan, 82–83
Schaap, Dick (journalist), 54
Selkirk, George, 97
Sheehy, Pete (clubhouse attendant)
    first uniform issued by, 50
    Pete Sheehy Clubhouse, 49
    uniform number, 101
Sherrod, Blackie, 241
Shouse, Ivan (childhood friend), 37, 294
Simon, Paul (songwriter), 217
Smith, Marshall (friend), 25, 139, 295
Smith, Red (sportswriter), 79
sports memorabilia, 246, 250–252
Sportsman's Park (St. Louis), 44, 129
spring training camp
    (1951), 43–44, 49, 53–54
    (1952), 122
    (1953), 135
Stengel, Casey (Yankees Manager)
    doghouse, 196
    double talk, 187
    effect of slump on, 91
    expectations and frustrations, 138–139
    first impression of Mickey, 44
    management style, 89, 183, 191–193
    Mickey as successor to DiMaggio, 50
    and Mickey's drinking, 214–215
    molder of young talent, 53
    most remarkable man in baseball, 51
    platoon system, 91
    retirement, 191
    teaching and managing, 52
    temper of, 139
Sturm, Jonny, 38
Sugar, Bert, 197
Summer of '49 (Halberstam), 189
Summerall, Pat (sportscaster), 268
Sweet, Ozzie (photographer), 216–217
switch-hitting, learning to, 12–14, 47

television announcers, 181
Tiger Stadium (Detroit), 222
Toots Shor, 110, 148–149
Topping, Dan, 142–143

uniform numbers, 50, *74*, 101

Vilacky, Andrew, 295

Washington Post, 160
Weiss, George, 193, 213
Whiz Kids, 35–38
Will, George F., 214
Williams, Ted, 21–22, 80, 81
World Series (1951), 113–115, 307, 334
World Series (1951) subway series, 105,
    112–115
World Series (1952), 128, 135, 307, 334
World Series (1953), 137, 307, 334
World Series (1955), 145, 158, 307, 334
World Series (1956), *231,* 307, 334
World Series (1957), 178, 307, 334
World Series (1958), 178, 307, 334
World Series (1960), 190–193, 307, 334

World Series (1961), 203, 307, 334
World Series (1962), 207, 307, 334
World Series (1963), 209, 307, 334
World Series (1964), 210, 213, 307, 334
Wrigley Field (Los Angeles), 56

Yankee Stadium
  center field, 123
  first career appearance, 80
  opening day at, 78
  size of, 179
Yankees, 176–178
  1960 season, 190
  front office personnel, 31
  injuries of, 215–216
  spring training camp, 45, 54–55, 122
  third world championship, 116
  West Coast appearance, 55
Youngman, Harold, 142, 242

ABOUT THE AUTHOR

Tony Castro is the author of the acclaimed civil rights history *Chicano Power: The Emergence of Mexican America*, which *Publishers Weekly* hailed as "brilliant . . . a valuable contribution to the understanding of our time." A former staff writer at *Sports Illustrated* and syndicated political columnist, Tony Castro has published journalism in the *Washington Post*, the *Los Angeles Times*, and the *Dallas Morning News*. He was a Nieman Fellow at Harvard University. With his wife and two sons, he lives in Beverly Hills, California.